ESSEN

C000273671

BRITTANY

Original text by Lindsay Hunt
Updated by Lindsay Hunt

© Automobile Association Developments Limited 2008
First published 2008

ISBN 978-0-7495-5483-5

Published by AA Publishing, a trading name of Automobile Association Developments
Limited, whose registered office is Fanum House, Basing View, Basingstoke,
Hampshire RG21 4EA.
Registered number 1878835.

Colour separation: MRM Graphics Ltd
Printed and bound in Italy by Printer Trento S.r.l.

A03164
Maps in this title produced from mapping © MAIRDUMONT / Falk Verlag 2007
with updates from mapping © ISTITUTO GEOGRAFICO DE AGOSTINI S.p.A.,
NOVARA 2007

About this book

This book is divided into five sections.

The essence of Brittany pages 6–19
Introduction; Features; Food and Drink; Short Break including the 10 Essentials

Planning pages 20–33
Before You Go; Getting There; Getting Around; Being There

Best places to see pages 34–55
The unmissable highlights of any visit to Brittany

Best things to do pages 56–73
Good places to have lunch; top activities; best beaches; places to take the children and more

Exploring pages 74–185
The best places to visit in Brittany, organized by area

Maps
All map references are to the maps on the covers. For example, Dinan has the reference ➕ 13C – indicating the grid square in which it is to be found

Admission prices
Inexpensive (under €4)
Moderate (€4–€7)
Expensive (over €7)

Hotel prices
Prices are per double room per night:
€ budget (under €75); €€ moderate (€75–€120); €€€ expensive (over €120)

Restaurant prices
Prices are for a three-course meal per person without drinks:
€ budget (under €25); €€ moderate (€25–€60); €€€ expensive (over €60)

Contents

The essence of...

As you head westwards, the Celtic ambience of Basse-Bretagne (Finistère) becomes more pronounced. It is here you may still hear the Breton language spoken, and even see a few traditional costumes worn at *pardons* and festivals. Church architecture takes on its idiosyncratic Breton form in the *enclos paroissial* (parish close). In rural areas, the population is still devoutly Catholic. Folk music, however, provides the most active sign of a revival in Breton culture. In the east, Haute-Bretagne slowly merges with the culture of its Norman neighbours and the more Gallic parts of France beyond the Loire.

features

Brittany offers far more than its varied seaside, so visit some of the interior, with its medieval castles and mysterious standing stones. There are also historic churches and those uniquely Breton architectural treasures, the elaborate parish closes and calvaries of central Finistère.

GEOGRAPHY

- 1,800km (1,120 miles) of coastline, parts with a 50m (164ft) tidal range (highest in France).
- 20,000km (12,430 miles) of rivers and streams, including over 600km (370 miles) of navigable waterways.
- 5,000km (3,110 miles) of bridleways and footpaths, including three of France's long-distance *Grandes Randonnées*.
- Two Regional Parks: Armorique – 172,000ha

(425,010 acres) of land and ocean, including the Monts d'Arrée, the dramatic Crozon peninsula and the reef-strewn archipelagos of Ouessant and Sein; La Brière – 40,000ha (98,840 acres) of peat-marsh once submerged below the sea.
- Regions: Haute-Bretagne (Upper Brittany near the eastern Marches) and Basse-Bretagne (Lower Brittany to the west).
- Highest altitude: 384m/1,260ft (Tuchen Gador, Monts d'Arrée).

ADMINISTRATION
● Since 1973, the *département* of Loire-Atlantique has officially formed part of the Pays-de-la-Loire region, but culturally still considers itself to be Breton.
● The other four *départements* are Ille-et-Vilaine, Côtes d'Armor, Finistère and Morbihan.

ECONOMY
● About 60 per cent of Brittany's land is under cultivation, and is one of France's most productive agricultural regions.
● Dairy, poultry and pig-farming are important, but Brittany is especially renowned for market garden produce (artichokes, potatoes, cabbages, cauliflowers, peas, beans, salad crops, apples, strawberries etc).

● Despite dwindling fish stocks and EU quota systems, the fishing industry is a vital mainstay of Breton ports like Le Guilvinec, Douarnenez, Concarneau and Audierne.
● Tourism is one of the biggest earners. Brittany is France's second most popular holiday area.
● Car manufacture and light engineering (electronics, computing, telecommunications) now supersede Brittany's declining shipbuilding and steel industries.

food & drink

Brittany produces an wide range of high-quality foodstuffs. Regional dishes make good use of seafood, pork and vegetables, but Bretons have a sweet tooth too, and love puddings and biscuits. Filled pancakes are a ubiquitous speciality.

SEAFOOD

Brittany is one of France's foremost fishing regions, and its seafood is superb. Visit a *criée* (fish auction) or fish farm for some idea of this marine cornucopoia. If you don't enjoy seafood much, you may be unable to look another assiette de fruits de mer in the eye by the end of your visit. These platefuls of seaweed and crushed ice, piled high with curious sea-creatures, can be a daunting sight. Most include mussels or oysters (prime local products). Crayfish, clams, crabs and scallops also put in an appearance. If you prefer your fish hot, try a traditional Breton *cotriade*, or fish stew, somewhat less spicy than a *bouillabaisse*. Look out for freshwater species, especially in the Brière region. *Brochet beurre blanc* is a classic pike dish in Nantais white butter sauce. Most Breton of all, though, is the lobster, often prepared in a sauce of tomato, garlic, shallots and cognac *(homard à l'armoricaine)*. On many menus it appears as *homard à l'américaine*, often attributed to a spelling mistake in a Parisian restaurant.

MEAT AND POULTRY

Steak Chateaubriand is the most widely known Breton meat dish. But Brittany is more famous for its dairy produce than its beef. More typical meat products include the distinctively flavoured *pré salé* (salt meadow) lambs raised on the saltmarshes of Ouessant and Mont-St-Michel. *Gigot à la bretonne* (roast leg of lamb with haricot beans) is a local speciality. Brittany produces vast quantities of pork, and *charcuterie* takes many forms – especially sausages, black puddings and *andouille*, a sort of pork haggis not to everyone's taste. Hearty peasant soups and casseroles like *Kig-ha-Farz* often contain ham or bacon. Some of France's most succulent chickens come from around Rennes, while the *challan* is a delicious duck from the Nantes region.

PANCAKES

Once, pancakes were a staple diet in Brittany, replacing bread in poor homes. You will find *crêperies* everywhere – a cheap, quick and filling way of satisfying hunger pangs, and a good choice for vegetarians. You can eat pancakes standing up at a market stall cheaply – great for the entertainment value of watching them being made. The variety of fillings offered is imaginative, but the more exotic the filling, the more it will cost.

Two kinds are made: *crêpes* and *galettes*. Generally, crêpes are made with a wheat-flour batter, and have sweet fillings. The more traditional *galettes* are made with heavier buckwheat flour and are generally savoury. You can buy them ready-made in packets or tins, though they are much nicer warm and fresh. *Crêpes dentelles* are paper-thin, lacy pancakes, a speciality of Quimper.

CAKES AND PUDDINGS

Like many Breton dishes, desserts tend to be very rich and heavy. One famous local cake is *far breton*, a solid flan containing prunes or raisins. *Kouign-aman* is a delicious and fattening pastry of sugar, butter and almonds. *Galettes de Pont-Aven* (not to

be confused with pancakes) are buttery biscuits like shortbread.

DRINKS

Brittany produces little wine, apart from Loire-Atlantique's Muscadet (which now officially belongs to the Pays de la Loire region). The local tipples are cider (*cidre*) or barley beer (*cervoise*). Tastings are offered all over the region in cider museums or breweries. Stronger applejack potions are also on sale. *Pommeau* is a local apéritif. *Lambig* is the Breton equivalent of the Norman *calvados*, though quite hard to track down. Another local drink is *chouchen*, a honey-based mead. A sparkling variety is also made.

short break

If you only have a short time to visit Brittany and would like to take home some unforgettable memories, you can do something local and capture the real flavour of the area. The following will give you a wide range of sights and experiences that won't take long, won't cost very much and will make your visit very special.

● **Eat pancakes** A savoury *galette* (made with buckwheat flour) followed by a sweet, lacy *crêpe* makes a quick, inexpensive, filling meal. You'll find *crêperies* of varying standards all over Brittany.

● **Visit some parish closes** These unique sights are mostly clustered around the Armorique Regional Park, and date from the 16th and 17th centuries, when new-found prosperity was lavished on the village churches and cemeteries surrounding them.

● **Order an assiette *de fruits de mer*** Whether oysters, scallops, mussels or langoustines are your favoured seafood, don't leave Brittany without trying one of these awesome platters, often served on beds of seaweed with big chunks of lemon.

● **Head for the coastal extremities** Brittany's westerly capes (Crozon, Sizun and Penmarc'h) and islands are especially dramatic during a gale, but the scenery is always stunning, especially along some of the old coastal watchpaths (*sentiers des douaniers*).

● **Track down some megaliths** Carnac has the best-known concentration of standing stones in Brittany, but dolmens, menhirs and cairns are sprinkled all over the region in quiet fields.

● **Experience a *criée*** Brittany's bustling fish auctions can be visited in a number of ports – but you'll have to get up early to see anything happening. Ask the local tourist office.

● **Take a boat-trip** Brittany is perfect for boating and there's a wonderful choice of river cruises, island hops and trips along the inland waterways. Take your camera and binoculars to watch birds and seals.

● **Look out for festivals** Most communities hold a festival or two during the year. Some are major cultural events attracting visitors from far and wide, but village saints' days and *pardons* can be just as memorable and often more genuinely typical of Breton life.

● **Try a typical Breton cake or pudding** A *kouign aman* (a sugary almond cake) or *far breton* (an eggy flan with prunes or raisins) will stoke up your energy levels. Local *pâtisseries* and specialist shops sell a bewildering variety of Breton biscuits too (packed in attractive tins, they make great presents to take home).

● **Test the beaches** Whatever else you do in Brittany, spend time on its glorious beaches. Scrubbed clean by some of the highest tides in Europe, many have EU Blue Flag status. Some are dangerous – heed flags and warning signs.

Planning

Before you go

WHEN TO GO

JAN	FEB	MAR	APR	MAY	JUN	JUL	AUG	SEP	OCT	NOV	DEC
8°C	9°C	12°C	13°C	16°C	18°C	21°C	21°C	18°C	22°C	11°C	9°C
46°F	48°F	54°F	55°F	61°F	64°F	70°F	70°F	64°F	72°F	52°F	48°F

● High season   ● Low season

Brittany has a mild maritime climate with few extremes of temperature, but the weather is always unpredictable, and can change rapidly. Be prepared for rain at any time of year. The hilly inland areas are often wetter than the low-lying coastal regions, and have wider temperature fluctuations. The wettest months are usually in autumn and winter, but snow and frost are rare and generally short-lived. Average summer daytime temperatures are around 20°C (68°F) and highest in August. The south coast is warmer and quite a bit sunnier than the Channel coast, and some areas are mild enough for vines and subtropical plants to flourish. Coastal regions are usually tempered by sea breezes, which can reach storm force from time to time.

WHAT YOU NEED

● Required ○ Suggested ▲ Not required

Some countries require a passport to remain valid for a minimum period (usually at least six months) beyond the date of entry – contact their consulate or embassy or your travel agency for details.

	UK	Germany	USA	Netherlands	Spain
Passport	●	●	●	●	●
Visa (regulations can change—check before booking your journey)	▲	▲	▲	▲	▲
Onward or Return Ticket	▲	▲	▲	▲	▲
Health Inoculations	▲	▲	▲	▲	▲
Health Documentation (➤ 23, Health Insurance)	▲	▲	▲	▲	▲
Travel Insurance	○	○	○	○	○
Driving Licence (National or International)	●	●	●	●	●
Car Registration Document (if own car)	●	●	●	●	●

WEBSITES

www.bretagne35.com
www.brittanytourism.com
www.cotesdarmor.com
www.finisteretourisme.com

www.loire-atlantique-tourisme-com
www.paysdelaloire.fr
www.morbihan.com
www.tourismebretagne.com

TOURIST OFFICES AT HOME

In the UK

French Tourist Office
178 Piccadilly, London W1V 0AL
☎ 09068 244 123 (60p per minute at all times)

In the USA

French Government Tourist Office
444 Madison Avenue

New York NY 10022
☎ 514/288-1904

French Government Tourist Office
9454 Wilshire Boulevard
Suite 715
Beverly Hills CA 90212
☎ 310/271-6665

HEALTH INSURANCE

Nationals of EU and certain other countries can get medical treatment in France at reduced cost on production of a European Health Insurance Card (EHIC), although private medical insurance is still advised and is essential for all other visitors.

As for general medical treatment (see above), nationals of EU countries can obtain dental treatment at reduced cost. About 70 per cent of a dentist's standard fee can be refunded. Private medical insurance is still advisable for all.

TIME DIFFERENCES

| GMT
12 noon | France
1PM | Germany
1PM | USA (NY)
7AM | Netherlands
1PM | Spain
1PM |

France is on Central European Time, one hour ahead of Greenwich Mean Time (GMT +1), but from late March, when the clocks are put forward one hour, until late October, French summer time (GMT +2) operates.

NATIONAL HOLIDAYS

1 Jan *New Year's Day*	*May Ascension Day*	1 Nov *All Saints' Day*
Mar/Apr *Easter Sunday and Monday*	May/Jun *Whit Sunday and Monday*	11 Nov *Remembrance Day*
1 May *Labour Day*	14 Jul *Bastille Day*	25 Dec *Christmas Day*
8 May *VE Day*	15 Aug *Assumption Day*	

WHAT'S ON WHEN

Most of Brittany's festivals and cultural events take place in the short tourist season between Easter and October. Precise dates may change from year to year. Annually updated events listings are available from regional and local tourist offices.

April

Erquy, Loguivy, St-Quay-Portrieux: *Fête des Coquilles* (scallops)

Nantes: *Carnival*

May

St-Brieuc: *Art Rock Festival*

Tréguier: *Pardon de St Yves*

June

Le Faouët: *Pardon de Ste-Barbe*

Nantes: *Quinzaine Celtique*

St-Jean-du-Doigt: *Pardon de St-Jean-du-Doigt*

July

Binic: *Fête de la Morue* (cod)

Dinan: *Fête des Remparts* (every two years, even-numbered);

Dinan: Celtic Harp *Festival*

Fouesnant: *Fête des Pommiers* (apple trees)

Lamballe: *Fête des Ajoncs d'Or* (golden gorse)

Locquirec: *Pardon de St-Jacques* (sea festival)

Locronan: *Petites/Grandes Troménies* (annual small pilgrimage/large pilgrimage every six years, next one in 2013)

Morlaix: *Les Mercredis de Morlaix* (Wednesday Street Festival)

Nantes: *International Summer Festival*

Paimpol: *Fête des Terre-Neuvas* (celebrating the fishing industry)

Pont l'Abbé: *Fête des Brodeuses* (embroidery)
Quimper: *Festival de Cornouaille*
Rennes: *Tombées de la Nuit* (arts and music festival)
Ste-Anne-d'Auray: *Grand Pardon*
St-Brieuc: *Breton Music Festival*
Vannes: *Jazz Festival*
August
Concarneau: *Fête des Filets Bleus* (blue nets)
Guingamp: *Breton Dance and St-Loup Festival*
Ile de Fedrun: *Fête de la Brière*
Lamballe: *Fête du Cheval* (horses)
Lorient: *Festival InterCeltique*

Moncontour: *Medieval Fair*
Paimpol: *Fête du Chant Marin* (sea-shanties;
odd-numbered years)
Perros-Guirec: *Fête des Hortensias*
(hydrangeas)
Pont-Aven: *Fête des Fleurs d'Ajoncs* (gorse
flowers)
Quimper: *Semaines Musicales*
Roscoff: *Fête de l'Oignon Rosé* (pink onion)
Ste-Anne-la-Palud: *Pardon*
St-Briac-sur-Mer: *Fête des Mouettes* (seagulls)
St-Malo: *La route du Rock Festival*
September
Camaret: *Blessing of the Sea*
Carnac: *Pardon*
Le Folgoët: *Grand Pardon*
Josselin: *Pardon*
October
Dinard: *British Film Festival*
Redon: *La Teillouse Chestnut Festival*
November
Brest: *Festival du Film Court* (short films)
Nantes: *Three Continents Festival* (film and cinema)
December
Rennes: *Transmusicales* (rock festival)

Getting there

BY AIR

Rennes Airport

6km (4 miles) to city centre

🚊 N/A

🚌 10 minutes

🚗 10 minutes

Nantes Airport

12km (7.5 miles) to city centre

🚊 N/A

🚌 20 minutes

🚗 15 minutes

Budget airlines Ryanair (www.ryanair.com) and Flybe (www.flybe.com) operate direct flights to Dinard, Brest, Nantes and Rennes from various UK and Irish airports. British Airways (www.ba.com) and Air France (www.airfrance.com) fly directly to Nantes from London. If you fly to Paris, you can pick up an internal flight with Air France or Brit Air (Air France's Morlaix-based subsidiary) to several Breton towns, including Lannion, Lorient and Quimper, or continue by rail or rental car.

BY RAIL

You can now travel from London's St Pancras International terminal by Eurostar train via the Channel Tunnel in just over two hours. Services are frequent and generally efficient and comfortable. The quickest way to reach Brittany is to leave the train at Lille and board a high-speed TGV Atlantique Ouest connection. This saves the bother and expense of changing stations in Paris (from Gare du Nord to Gare Montparnasse). You can book Eurostar tickets and any connecting services through Rail Europe (www.raileurope.com for the UK; www.eurail.com for the US). The further ahead you can book, the cheaper the fare is likely to be. On-line reservations may be cheaper still, and include no booking fees. Rail passes may be worth considering, but these must be booked in advance. Brittany's rail network is fairly limited and not practical for extensive touring.

BY FERRY

To reach Brittany from the UK, you can take a direct ferry route to a Breton port, or take a short Channel crossing followed by a longish overland haul through northwestern France. The longer sea crossings are obviously more expensive, and possibly uncomfortable in rough weather, but whichever route you choose, overall journey time and costs are unlikely to differ greatly. If you take a short crossing, your choice of operators is between P&O Ferries (www.poferries.com) and Sea France (www.seafrance.com), which operate on the Dover–Calais route, or Eurotunnel, which operates the rapid-transit shuttle service through the Channel Tunnel (www.eurotunnel.com).

The longer routes across the western Channel are run mainly by Brittany Ferries (www.brittanyferries.com), which operates to St-Malo (from Portsmouth) and to Roscoff (from Plymouth). Services from Ireland are run by Irish Ferries (www.irishferries.com), which operates to Roscoff from Rosslare, and Brittany Ferries (from Cork to Roscoff). Condor Ferries (www.condorferries.co.uk) operates fast-craft summer services to St-Malo from Poole and Weymouth via the Channel Islands.

If you're heading for eastern Brittany it is also worth considering the shorter sea crossings to Normandy, though these generally cost much the same as the Breton ones. Brittany Ferries, Condor Ferries and Irish Ferries run crossings to Cherbourg and Caen.

Getting around

PUBLIC TRANSPORT

Internal flights Regular flights from Paris and other French cities with Air France to Nantes, Rennes, Brest, Lannion, Lorient, Quimper (just over 1 hour). BritAir (subsidiary of Air France) operates daily flights between Nantes and Brest. Finis'Air connects Brest and the Île d'Ouessant.

Trains Fast TGV trains connect Paris with Nantes, Rennes, Lorient, Quimper and Brest. Within Brittany, SNCF rail lines run from Rennes along the north and south coasts, but there are few cross-country routes.

Buses All major towns have a bus station *(gare routière)*, but the bus network is fragmented and many different companies operate. The coast has more regular routes than the interior. Some services run in conjunction with the railway (SNCF). Many timetables are designed to serve the needs of commuters and schoolchildren; services are dramatically reduced at weekends.

Boats and ferries A large number of operators serve Brittany's offshore islands, including Belle-Île, Île de Batz, Ouessant, Bréhat and Groix.

Urban transport Major centres have urban bus services. Rennes has a limited metro service, mainly used by commuters. Nantes has an

extensive, well-integrated and very efficient mass transit network, including trams. Tourist passes are available.

TAXIS

Taxis are a costlier option than public transport. They pick up at taxi ranks *(stations de taxi)*, found at railway stations and airports. Hotels and restaurants can usually give a taxi call number. Check the taxi has a meter; there is a pick-up charge plus a rate per minute.

FARES AND TICKETS

Students/youths Students can obtain discounts on transport, admission prices, entertainment and so forth with an International Student Identity Card. If you are under 26 but not a student, an International Youth Travel Card or a European Youth Card (Euro 26 card) can obtain many similar discounts. Both currently cost €12 (www.istc.org).

Senior citizens A Carte Senior gives discounts of up to 50 per cent on rail transport for the over-60s. It costs €50, but is valid for a year (www.senior-sncf.com). If you have your passport, you may get a discount.

DRIVING

- The French drive on the right side of the road.
- Seat-belts must be worn in front seats at all times and in rear seats where fitted.
- Random breath-testing takes place. Never drive under the influence of alcohol.
- Fuel, including unleaded *(sans plomb)*, and diesel *(gasoil)* is widely available. Fuel stations are numerous along main roads but rarer in rural areas. Some on minor roads are closed on Sundays. Maps showing petrol stations are available from main tourist offices.
- Speed limits on toll motorways *(autoroutes)*: 130kph/80mph (110kph/68mph when wet); non-toll motorways and dual carriageways: 110kp/68mphh (100kph/62mph when wet). In fog (visibility less than 50m/55yds): 50kph/31mph all roads
  Country roads: 90kph/56mph (80kph/50mph when wet)
  Urban roads: 50kp/31mph (limit starts at town sign)
- A red warning triangle must be carried if your car has no hazard warning lights. Place the triangle 30m/33yds behind the car in the event of an accident or breakdown. On motorways ring from emergency phones (every 2km/1.2 miles) to contact the breakdown service. Off motorways, police will advise on local breakdown services.

CAR RENTAL

All airports and most major railway stations have car rental offices. Pre-booked car rental packages organized by tour operators, airlines, ferry operators or French Railways (SNCF) may be cheaper than renting locally.

Being there

TOURIST OFFICES
Comité Régional du Tourisme de Bretagne
1 rue Raoul Ponchon 35069 Rennes
☎ 02 99 28 44 30

Departmental Tourist Offices
Comité Départemental de Tourisme de Finistère
11 rue Théodore Le Hars
29104 Quimper
☎ 02 98 76 20 70

Comité Départemental de Tourisme de Côtes d'Amor
7 rue St-Benoît
22046 St-Brieuc
☎ 02 96 62 72 00

Comité Départemental de Tourisme d'Ille-et-Vilaine
4 rue Jean-Jaurès
35060 Rennes
☎ 02 99 78 47 47

Comité Départemental de Tourisme de Loire-Atlantique
2 allée Baco
44005 Nantes
☎ 02 51 72 95 30

Comité Départemental de Tourisme de Morbihan
PIBS allée Nicolas Leblanc
56010 Vannes
☎ 0825 135 656

MONEY
The euro (€) is the official currency of France. Banknotes are in denominations of 5, 10, 20, 50, 100, 200 and 500 euros, and coins in denominations of 1, 2, 5, 10, 20 and 50 cents, and 1 and 2 euros. Travellers' cheques can be changed at most banks, but take some cash. Visa/Barclaycard (Carte Bleue) and MasterCard/Access (Eurocard) are widely accepted in hotels, restaurants and major stores.

TIPS/GRATUITIES
Yes ✓ No ✗

Restaurants/cafés/bars (service included, tip optional)	✗	
Taxis	✓	€1–€1.50
Chambermaids/Porters	✓	€1–€2
Tour guides	✓	€1–€1.50
Toilet attendants	✓	small change

POSTAL SERVICES

Post offices (*bureaux de poste*) are well signed, and generally open Mon–Fri 8–5, Sat 8–noon. In smaller places, opening hours may be shorter and offices may close for lunch. Main post offices sometimes stay open until later in the evenings. Postboxes are yellow.

TELEPHONES

Telephone numbers in France comprise ten digits; the first two numbers for Brittany are 02 (omit 0 if dialling from the UK). Nearly all public phones use pre-paid cards now (*télécartes*). Some cards give cheaper overseas calls than standard *télécartes*, so ask before you buy if you need to phone abroad. Dial the international code if you're phoning abroad with a mobile.

International dialling codes

From France:

UK: 00 44

Germany: 00 49

USA and Canada: 00 1

Netherlands: 00 31

Spain: 00 34

Emergency telephone numbers

Police: 17

Fire: 18

Ambulance: 15

General emergency number: 112

EMBASSIES AND CONSULATES

UK ☎ 01 44 51 31 00

Germany ☎ 01 53 83 45 00

USA ☎ 01 43 12 22 22

Netherlands ☎ 01 40 62 33 00

Spain ☎ 01 44 43 18 00

HEALTH ADVICE

Sun advice The sunniest (and hottest) months are July and August, but the good weather can start in June and continue to October. Generally the weather is relatively mild, though take care on the beach and when walking. Drink plenty of fluids, wear a hat and make sure you apply a good sunscreen.

Drugs Pharmacies – recognized by their green cross sign – have qualified staff able to offer medical advice, provide first aid and prescribe and provide a wide range of drugs, though some are available by prescription (*ordonnance*) only.

Safe water It is safe to drink tap water served in hotels and restaurants, but never drink from a tap marked *eau non potable* (not drinking water). Bottled water is cheap and widely available.

PERSONAL SAFETY

The *Police Municipale* (blue uniforms) carry out police duties in cities and towns. The *Gendarmes* (blue trousers, black jackets, white belts), the national police force, cover the countryside and smaller places. The *CRS* deal with emergencies and riots. To avoid danger or theft:

● Do not use unmanned roadside rest areas at night.
● Cars, especially foreign cars, should be secured.
● In crowded places, beware of pickpockets.
● Police assistance: ☎ 17 from any call box.

ELECTRICITY

The French power supply is: 220 volts. Type of socket: Round two-hole sockets taking two-round-pin (or occasionally three-round-pin) plugs. British visitors should bring an adaptor; US visitors a voltage transformer.

OPENING HOURS

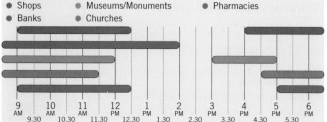

In addition to the times shown above, afternoon times of shops in summer can extend in the most popular centres. Most shops close Sunday and many on Monday. Small food shops open 7am and may open Sunday morning. Large department stores do not close for lunch and hypermarkets open 10am to 9 or 10pm, but may shut Monday morning.

Banks are closed Sunday, as well as Saturday or Monday.

Museums and monuments have extended summer hours. Many close one day a week: either Monday (municipal) or Tuesday (national).

LANGUAGE

French is the native language. English is spoken widely, especially in tourist areas and the larger and most popular centres; in smaller, rural places fewer people speak English. Attempts to speak French, or at least greet others in French, will be much appreciated. Below is a list of helpful words. More coverage can be found in the AA's *Essential French Phrase Book*.

hotel	l'hôtel	reservation	la réservation
guest house	chambre d'hôte	rate	tarif
room	la chambre	breakfast	le petit déjeuner
single room	une personne	toilet	les toilettes
double room	deux personnes	bathroom	la salle de bain
per person	par personne	shower	la douche
per room	par chambre	balcony	le balcon
one/two nights	une/deux nuits	key	la clef/clé
bank	la banque	banknote	le billet
exchange office	le bureau de change	coin	la pièce
post office	la poste	credit card	la carte de crédit
cashier	le caissier	travellers' cheque	le chèque de voyage
foreign exchange	le change extérieur	exchange rate	le taux de change
English pound	la livre sterling		
restaurant/café	la restaurant/le café	starter	le hors d'œuvre
table	la table	main course	le plat principal
menu	le menu	dish of the day	le plat du jour
set menu	le menu du jour	dessert	le dessert
wine list	la carte des vins	drink	la boisson
lunch/dinner	le déjeuner/le dîner	the bill	l'addition
yes/no	oui/non	yesterday	hier
please/thank you	s'il vous plaît/merci	how much?	combien?
hello /goodbye	bonjour/au revoir	expensive	cher
goodnight	bonsoir	open/closed	ouvert/fermé
sorry/excuse me	pardon/excusez-moi	you're welcome	de rien
help!	au secours!	okay	d'accord
today/tomorrow	aujourd'hui/demain	I don't know	je ne sais pas

Best places to see

1 Carnac

www.carnac.fr

An extraordinary array of megaliths continues to baffle and fascinate experts and visitors alike.

It is not so much the town, a pleasant seaside resort, but the astonishing complexes of megaliths on its northern outskirts that attract interest in Carnac. Thousands of visitors head here to see them every year.

A good starting point for learning more about Brittany's megaliths is the **Musée de Préhistoire** on Carnac's main square. This gives a scholarly and rather technical presentation on local antiquities and archaeological theories (ask for the English translation notes). There are three main groups of *alignements* (rows of standing stones or menhirs): Ménec, Kermario and Kerlescan, containing some 2,700 stones altogether. You can see them from the roadside, but raised viewing platforms give a clearer idea of the patterns.

An information centre called **La Maison des Mégalithes** near the Alignements du Menec

shows a video in French explaining the megaliths.

Other types of megalith can be found in and around Carnac, including dolmens (roofed table-like structures), tumuli (cairns) and gallery graves (*allées couvertes*). These are less mysterious in that they were all presumably used as burial places. The megalith complex at nearby Locmariaquer (➤ 172) can be visited on a joint ticket with Carnac.

🚉 20H 🚌 Quiberon, Auray, Vannes; local shuttle TATOOVU and *petit train* (tourist train) serve *alignements* in high season

ℹ️ 7 Avenue des Druides ☎ 02 97 52 13 52

Musée de Préhistoire

✉️ 10 place de la Chapelle ☎ 02 97 52 22 04; www.museedecarnac.com 🕐 Jul–Aug daily 10–6; Apr–Jun, Sep 10–12:30, 2–6 (closed Tue except hols); Oct–Mar Wed–Mon 10–12:30, 2–5 ✋ Moderate 🍴 La Marine, place de la Chapelle

La Maison des Mégalithes

✉️ Route des Alignements ☎ 02 97 52 29 81

🕐 Jul–Aug daily 9–8; May–Jun 9–7; Sep–Apr 10–5.15 ✋ Free; guided visits moderate

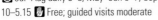

2 Cathédrale St-Pierre, Nantes

Soaring vaults of bright stone give a lasting sense of space and light inside this impressive cathedral in the upper town.

Undaunted by its proximity to the formidable Château des Ducs de Bretagne (► 158, 159), Nantes' cathedral is built of clear, white tufa – quite a contrast to the sombre, weather-worn granite found in most Breton churches. Building works on St-Pierre began in 1434, on the site of an earlier Romanesque building, but it wasn't completed for another four and a half centuries. The towers were added in 1508. For all that, it seems a surprisingly coherent piece of Gothic workmanship, and post-war restoration work has given it a spruce and cared-for look. Its history, however, has been anything but tranquil. In 1800 a massive ammunition explosion in the nearby castle shattered all its precious 15th-century stained glass. During the Revolution, it served as a barn; it was bombed during World War II, and damaged by a fire in 1971, after which its interior had to be completely cleaned yet again. Today, it is light, airy and spacious.

The replacement windows in the choir (containing over 500sq m of modern stained glass) took over 12 years to create, and these alone justify a visit. St-Pierre's other main highlight is the magnificent Renaissance tomb of François II, the last Duke of Brittany, sculpted by the master-craftsman Michel Colombe between 1502 and 1507. The two main effigies depict François and his wife Margaret (parents of the Duchess Anne), and the corner statues are personifications of Justice, Fortitude, Temperance and Prudence. This elaborate tomb was commissioned by Anne in memory of her parents, and she asked that her heart be placed in it after her own death. Her wish was granted, though the heart vanished at some point during the Revolution. Another noteworthy 19th-century tomb commemorates General Lamoricière, famed for his adventures in Algeria.

➕ 26L ✉ Place St-Pierre 🕐 Apr–Oct daily 8–7; Sep–Mar daily 8–6 (except during Mass) 🎫 Free 🍴 Plenty of places near the castle (€–€€€)

3 Château, Fougères

www.ot-fougeres.fr

The dominant feature of this shoe-making town on the Breton borderlands is a magnificent fortress, built to deter French encroachments from the east.

Built piecemeal from around AD1166 until the 15th century, this mighty stronghold of schist and granite is one of the largest and best preserved examples of medieval fortification in France. Its various sections demonstrate the advances in warfare that took place during the Middle Ages. Unusually, it is set *below* the town rather than above it, but on what was believed to be an easily defensible site – a tight loop in the River Nançon flanked by steep cliffs. The castle consists of a series of concentric enclosures protected by massive curtain walls studded with 13 towers, and encircled by a moat of weirs and waterfalls. The structure is in excellent condition, its machicolations and loopholes intact. Despite its impregnable appearance, however, it was repeatedly attacked and captured by Du Guesclin and others, sometimes by stealth rather than force.

The castle made a romantic backdrop to Balzac's novel *Les Chouans* (1829), which describes the anti-Republican uprising in vividly gory detail.

Access for today's visitors leads via a bridge over the Nançon from a picturesque old quarter of tanneries and timbered houses near St-Sulpice church. The castle towers are beautifully reflected in the waters of the moat.

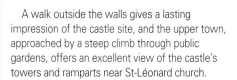

A walk outside the walls gives a lasting impression of the castle site, and the upper town, approached by a steep climb through public gardens, offers an excellent view of the castle's towers and ramparts near St-Léonard church.

✚ 16D ✉ Place Pierre-Simon ☎ 02 99 99 79 59 🕓 Mid-Jun to mid-Sep 9–7; Apr to mid-Jun 9:30–12, 2–6; winter 10–12, 2–5. Closed Jan ✋ Moderate 🍴 Les Voyageurs, 10 place Gambetta 🚌 Lines 9 (Rennes), 14 (Vitré), 17 (St-Malo) ℹ 2 rue Nationale ☎ 02 99 94 12 20

4 Côte de Granit Rose

Bizarrely shaped rocks in improbable colours make the coastline around the popular family holiday resort of Perros-Guirec one of the most memorable scenes in Brittany.

This eye-catching 20km (12.5-mile) stretch of coast takes its name from the vividly coloured rocks mainly between Perros-Guirec and Trébeurden. Dramatic rocks begin at the Ile de Bréhat, particularly noticeable at low tide when many reefs are exposed. But the small resorts of Ploumanac'h and Trégastel-Plage, further west, are the best places to see this russet rockery at its most striking, especially at sunset, when the stones take on an even fierier glow. Not just the colours, but the weird forms they assume are remarkable. The best way to see them is on foot. The *sentier des douaniers* (watchpath) leading around the cliffs from Perros-Guirec through the Parc Municipal to the Pointe de Ploumanac'h is one of the most enjoyable walks in Brittany (➤ 114–115), leading past a grand jumble of rounded boulders weathered into strange organic-looking shapes, given

fanciful names like the Tortoise, the Pancakes and Napoleon's Hat.

The local rock is widely used as a building material, and when cut and polished, it sparkles beautifully and makes a most elegant finish (popular for Parisian shopfronts and luxury bathrooms). Similarly eroded rocks occur on other parts of the Breton coast, but nothing matches the warm rosy tints of the Pink Granite Coast.

The region around Perros-Guirec is one of Brittany's most popular tourist areas, with excellent facilities for family holidays. Inland, just to the west of Ploumanac'h, the Traouïéro valleys (Grand and Petit) offer wonderland walks along wooded creeks fringed by a chaos of huge and precariously balanced granite blocks. One valley contains an ancient tidal flour-mill, in use until the 20th century.

✚ 8A ✋ Free; guided walks inexpensive 🍴 Plenty of cafés and restaurants in the main resorts (€–€€€) 🚌 Line 15 from Lannion 🚢 Excursions to Les Sept Îles (a puffin colony) from Perros-Guirec ℹ️ Maison du Littoral, Sentier des Douaniers ☎ 02 96 91 62 77 (exhibition, guided walks) ❸ Only open during school hols

5 Dinan

www.dinan-tourisme.com

This picturesque medieval town of winding streets and timber-framed buildings overlooking the Rance makes a charming base for a night or two.

Standing high above the Rance estuary at what was for many centuries the lowest bridging point, Dinan was a strategic junction even in Roman times. By the 10th century it had an important Benedictine monastery, and by the 12th it was protected by high ramparts. The warrior knight of the Hundred Years' War, Bertrand Du Guesclin, was born near the town in 1320. The large, tree-lined main square is named after him and has an equestrian statue of the hero. The weekly market is held here on Thursday; at other times the square makes a useful parking area. The Fête des Remparts, a biennial medieval fair, re-creates Dinan's feudal heyday in a colourful pageant.

The château makes a good starting point, with a museum of local history in the machicolated keep.

The 18th-century Gothic-Romanesque basilica of St-Sauveur is the last resting place of Du Guesclin's heart. Dinan's other main church is St-Malo, best seen from the grounds of the Ancien Couvent

des Cordeliers (a former Franciscan monastery). Many quaint buildings with sagging timbers and porticoes can be seen in the old streets. Climb the Tour de l'Horloge (clock tower) for a good town view.

The steep street winding down to the port is lined with picturesque, timbered merchant houses. Some now contain craft studios or shops. Terrace restaurants and cafés overlook the Rance from the quaysides. Discover all about the Rance at **La Maison de la Rance,** through models and displays inside and the flora and fauna of the marshlands reconstructed outside.

➕ 13C 🍴 An excellent choice in the old town and by the port (€–€€€) 🚢 River trips or boat hire from the port; the Rance links with Brittany's major inland waterways 🛈 9 rue du Château ☎ 02 96 87 69 76

La Maison de la Rance
✉ Port de Dinan ☎ 02 96 87 00 40 🕐 Jul–Aug daily 10–12:30, 2–7; Apr–Jun, Sep–Nov Tue–Sun 2–6; Nov–Mar Sun 2–6
✋ Inexpensive

6 Guimiliau

One of the star examples of Finistère's *enclos paroissiaux*, Guimiliau's decorated calvary is a tour-de-force of 16th-century religious art.

Brittany's parish closes are unique to the region, and one of its greatest treasures. Most lie in or near the Parc Naturel Régional d'Armorique, and several of the best, including Guimiliau, are close together in the Élorn Valley near Landerneau.

The phrase *enclos paroissial* refers to the walled plot of hallowed ground around a church. Parish closes are used as graveyards, but their main interest lies in their architectural features. Typically, these consist of a triumphal gateway through

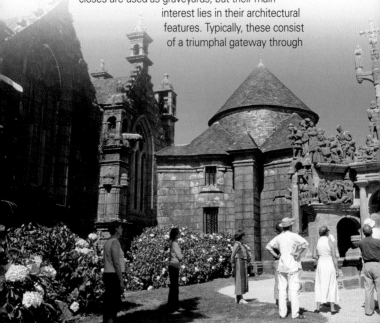

which funeral processions pass, an ossuary or charnel house (used for exhumed bones) and a sculpted granite calvary depicting mostly biblical scenes. The figures are generally portrayed in contemporary Renaissance dress, so they look like something from a Shakespearean play. Today the granite carvings are weather-worn and blotched with lichen, but still remarkable for their energy and detail.

The great era of the parish close was during the 16th and 17th centuries, when communities grew rich on sea trade and linen cloth. Their wealth was used to glorify God in religious art and architecture. Villages vied with each other for the grandest and most elaborate display. Guimiliau has a vast, ornate calvary, one of the largest in the area, with over 200 separate figures over an arched base, including the Virgin, St Peter, St John and St Yves with Christ. Look for a horrific scene showing a young girl being torn apart by demons. This is Catell Gollet, whose downfall came when she stole consecrated wafers for her handsome lover (the Devil in disguise). The church interior is crammed with decoration, including wonderful woodwork and altarpieces, and a finely carved pulpit and 17th-century organ.

✚ 5C 🍴 Ar Chupen (€), a *crêperie* near the church (43 rue du Calvaire) 💷 Free ❓ Guided tours in Jul and Aug

7 Océanopolis, Brest

www.oceanopolis.com

Brest's ambitious aquarium explores many aspects of the sea and the life within it, both off the Breton coast and worldwide.

This huge futuristic complex down by the docks is a major regional attraction in any terms. You could easily spend the best part of a day exploring its many exhibits relating to the seas and marine life of Brittany and other parts of the world. Expansion has resulted in a tripartite exhibition zone of pavilions linked by covered walkways. It has 50 separate aquariums, some containing up to a million litres of water.

The Temperate Pavilion concentrates on the Breton coastal waters and the Finistère fishing industry. Its huge tanks hold a massive number of local marine species, with special emphasis on those of economic importance (seaweeds, edible fish etc). There is also a seal tank, an

oceanography exhibition and a jellyfish collection. The Tropical Pavilion has a shark tank and a colourful array of coral-reef fish, all in beautifully realistic settings. A diver feeds the fish, and a tropical greenhouse simulates a mangrove swamp. The Polar Pavilion has a tank of endearingly comical penguins (strategically placed windows show how they chug through the water). Other species from chillier climes seem happily housed in convincingly authentic pack ice. Special events and temporary exhibitions take place and there are various multimedia presentations.

The aim is to educate as well as amuse. Some visitors detect with regret a recent trend towards mere entertainment. For all that, it's a worthwhile place to go to, easily the best of its kind in Brittany despite much competition and rather steep entrance charges.

✚ 3C ✉ Port de Plaisance du Moulin-Blanc, 2km (1.2 miles) east of city centre ☎ 02 98 34 40 40 🕐 Apr–Sep daily 9–6; winter 10–5 (closed Mon except school hols). Last tickets sold one hour before closing time 🎫 Expensive 🍴 Several on-site eating places: restaurant, self-service café, terrace, takeaway (€–€€) – no entrance charge
🚌 3, 7, 15 from city centre 🚢 Le Fret ferry; harbour trips ✈ Brest-Guipavas Airport; domestic and international flights
ℹ Place de la Liberté ☎ 02 98 44 24 96

8 Presqu'île de Crozon

www.crozon.com

Interesting museums and small, low-key resorts with good fish restaurants add to the natural attractions of one of Finistère's most exhilarating coastal headlands.

This hammerhead peninsula lunges towards the Atlantic in a lather of wave-lashed fury, the foaming tongue of Finistère's mad-dog profile. It forms part of the Parc Naturel Régional d'Armorique, and has some spectacular scenery.

The old town of Le Faou makes a good starting point. Detour though the wooded estuary scenery around Térénez to the romantically set ruins of the **Abbaye de Landévennec** at the mouth of the Aulne. There's a small museum on monastic history and a Benedictine community occupies modern premises near by.

The cider museum and parish close at Argol, and the **Musée de l'École Rurale** at Trégarvan (a typical village schoolroom of the early 20th century), are worth a visit too.

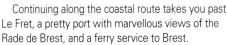

Continuing along the coastal route takes you past Le Fret, a pretty port with marvellous views of the Rade de Brest, and a ferry service to Brest.

Crozon is of no great interest, but the jagged headlands beyond (Pointe des Espagnols, Pointe de Pen-Hir and Pointe de Dinan) vie with each other for coastal charisma. The road to Pen-Hir passes the Alignements de Lagatjar (a group of standing stones). Camaret-sur-Mer is a little lobster port sheltered by a natural shingle bank called the Sillon. Here is a miniature Vauban fortress with a small exhibition, and a clutch of good fish restaurants.

Morgat, a tuna-fishing port turned yachting haven, is another attractive resort with a sandy beach. Boat excursions from here visit caves with vivid mineral colourations. More gorgeous sandy beaches can be found along the southern coast.

✚ 3D 🍴 Restaurants at Le Fret, Camaret and Morgat (€€)
🚌 Brest–Camaret or Quimper–Camaret via Crozon 🚢 Boat trips/ferry services from Le Fret, Camaret and Morgat
🛈 Boulevard de Pralognan, Crozon ☎ 02 98 27 07 92); Camaret ☎ 02 98 27 93 60; and seasonal office at Morgat ☎ 02 98 27 29 49

Musée de l'Ancienne Abbaye de Landévennec
✉ Abbaye de Landévennec ☎ 02 98 27 35 90 🕐 Jul to mid-Sep daily 10–6; Oct–Nov Mon–Fri 2–5; Dec to mid-Feb Mon–Fri 2–5; mid-Feb to Jun Mon–Fri 2–6; May–Jun Sun–Fri 2–6; late Sep daily 10–6; Oct–Apr Sun 2–6
✋ Moderate

Musée de l'École Rurale
✉ Trégarvan ☎ 02 98 26 04 72 🕐 Jul–Aug daily 10:30–7; Sep daily 2–6; Oct to mid-Feb Mon–Fri 2–5; mid-Feb to Jun Mon–Fri 2–6 ✋ Moderate

9 Quimper

www.quimper-tourisme.com

Cornouaille's capital is one of Brittany's most charming historic cities, a pleasure for shopping and strolling.

Good road and rail links, even an international airport, make Quimper easily accessible by public transport. A day-trip gives ample time to enjoy its quintessentially Breton atmosphere, especially on market day. It's a lively place with plenty of cultural activity, most noticeable during its weeklong summer Festival de Cornouaille, when Breton costume is *de rigueur*, and Celtic folk groups converge from far and wide.

The Breton name for the town derives from the word *kemper*, meeting place of rivers. The Steir and Odet run throughout the old quarter lined with pavement cafés and brasseries. Quimper is a good place for gourmet food shopping and dining. On the south bank of the Odet (where you'll find the tourist office) rises Mount Frugy, a wooded hill with panoramic picnic potential.

Crossing the river into the old town, the twin-spired Cathédrale St-Corentin (under restoration) makes an immediate impact. Near by, the **Musée Départemental Breton** displays an extensive collection of pottery,

costumes and furniture. The **Musée des Beaux-Arts,** in the town hall, contains an assortment of Pont-Aven School art. The old quarter stretches mainly west of the cathedral, past flower-decked houses and *hotels particuliers* (mansions).

Quimper dates from Roman times, when a settlement called *Aquilonia* grew up on the site of present-day Locmaria, where Quimper's ceramics industry developed, producing handpainted *paysan* designs of blue and yellow flowers or birds. Oldest of its factories is the Faïenceries HB-Henriot (☎ 02 98 90 09 36; www.hb-henriot.com; tours Mar–Oct). The Musée de la Faïence (☎ 02 98 90 12 72; www.quimper.faiences.com) has a superb display of Quimper ware.

➕ 5E 🍴 Excellent range of eating places (€–€€€) 🚌 A major bus route hub from all parts of Brittany 🚆 Principal SNCF station ⛴ Boat trips on the Odet ✈ Quimper Cornouaille airport; domestic and international flights
🛈 7 rue de la Déesse ☎ 02 98 53 04 05

Musée Départemental Breton
✉ 1 rue du Roi Gradlon ☎ 02 98 95 21 60 🕐 Jun–Sep daily 9–6; Oct–May 9–12, 2–5 (closed Sun am, Mon and public hols) 🎟 Inexpensive

Musée des Beaux-Arts
✉ 40 place St-Corentin ☎ 02 98 95 45 20 🕐 Jul–Aug daily 10–7; May–Jun, Sep–Oct Wed–Mon 10–12, 2–6; reduced hours in winter (closed Tue and Sun am)
🎟 Moderate

10 St-Malo

www.saint-malo-tourisme.com
www.ville-saint-malo.fr

The most appealing of any of the Channel ports, the walled citadel of St-Malo deserves more than a cursory glance en route to the ferry terminal, and there's plenty to see near by.

St-Malo is many visitors' first experience of Brittany. Its attractive setting and architecture, excellent hotels and restaurants, sandy beaches and lively ambience make this no bad landfall. The town developed a strong seafaring tradition and prospered greatly from trade with Spain and the Americas. For a time it was an independent republic. After World War II much of the old town was reconstructed in its original 18th-century style.

The walled city *(intra muros)* is the most interesting part. Park outside the walls and explore on foot. A rampart walk gives a splendid overview of the port's setting. On the seaward side lie sandy beaches and tidal islets. The main points of interest are the Cathédrale St-Vincent and the Château de la Duchesse Anne near the Porte St-Vincent, which contains the **Musée de la Ville** (town museum).

West of the walled town, the St-Servan district is worth a visit for marvellous views of the port and marina from the Aleth headland. The Tour Solidor contains a small museum dedicated to Cape Horn sailors. East of St-Malo are the resorts of Paramé and Rothéneuf, with good beaches. In Rothéneuf visit the Manoir Limoëlou, former home of Jacques Cartier, discoverer of Canada.

✚ 13C 🍴 Good restaurants, cafés and bars throughout the old town (€–€€€) 🚌 Rennes, Mont-St-Michel, Dinard, the Emerald Coast, Fougeres, Dinan 🚆 Rennes, Normandy (TVG link to Paris) ⛴ Brittany Ferries (Portsmouth, UK); shuttle ferry to Dinard; regular services to Channel Isles, Weymouth, Poole; Rance river trips to Dinan ✈ Dinard–St-Malo airport; Aurigny and Ryanair services to UK/Channel Isles

🛈 Esplanade St-Vincent ☎ 02 99 56 64 48

Musée de la Ville

☎ 02 99 40 71 57 🕐 Apr–Sep daily 10–12:30, 2–6; Oct–Mar Tue–Sat 10–12, 2–6 ✋ Moderate

Best things to do

Good places to have lunch

Ar Men Du (€€)

A splendid coastal location overlooking an unspoiled beach and tidal island at this stylish little restaurant-with-rooms.

✉ Raguenez-Plage, Port-Manec'h, Névez ☎ 02 98 06 84 22

Le Bistrot du Marin (€–€€)

Join a throng of sailing folk tucking into huge platters of seafood at this panoramic restaurant overlooking the marina.

✉ 34 cours des Quais, La Trinité-sur-Mer ☎ 02 97 55 73 23

Le Brittany (€€–€€€)

The Yachtman restaurant at this lovely manor-house hotel has splendid harbour views and excellent cooking.

✉ Boulevard Ste-Barbe, Roscoff ☎ 02 98 69 70 78

Café Breton (€–€€)

This charming little bistro is always packed with satsified locals. Friendly, genuine service and excellent cooking.

✉ 14 rue Nantaise, Rennes

Café Terrasses (€–€€)

Overlooking the scenic port, this upbeat bistro is perfect for an informal meal at any time of day.

✉ 2–4 rue du Quai, Dinan ☎ 02 96 39 09 60

La Cigale (€€)

Classic brasserie with superb *fin-de-siècle* décor. Perfect for smart seafood lunches, cakes or after-theatre suppers.

✉ 4 place Graslin, Nantes ☎ 02 51 84 94 94

Continental (€€)

One of the best of the seafood restaurants in this famous oyster port, with views over the oyster beds.

✉ 4 quai Thomas, Cancale ☎ 02 99 89 60 16

Le Décollé (€–€€)

Enjoy a wonderful view at this dramatic bit of Emerald Coast.

✉ Pointe du Décollé, St-Lunaire ☎ 02 99 46 01 70 🕐 Closed Mon, Tue off-season

Mare aux Oiseaux (€€€)

This smart thatched hotel-restaurant in the Grande Brière serves an inventive range of regional dishes using local ingredients.

✉ 162 Île de Fedrun, St-Joachim ☎ 02 40 88 53 01 🕐 Closed Mon

La Sainte-Marine (€€)

One thing you won't forget is the view across the wooded Odet estuary from this place. Book ahead – it's very popular.

✉ 19 rue du Bac, Ste-Marine ☎ 02 98 56 34 79

Top activities

A useful website for information
is www.brittanytourism.com

Canal- and river-boating More
than 600km (370 miles) of
navigable waterways provide an
exceptional network of routes,
and boats can be rented in many
places. Two important waterway
junctions are Redon and Dinan.

Canoeing and kayaking Sea,
lake and river canoeing is
possible in Brittany; several
places offer tuition (such as
Lannion, Rennes, Mur-de-
Bretagne). Choose a millpond
or white-water experience.

Cycling Brittany's gentler
gradients will appeal to non-
masochists, but there's
mountain-biking too for intrepid
off-roaders.

Fishing Besides being one of
Brittany's most important
industries, sea-fishing is a
recreational activity, ranging in
nature from low-tide pêche-à-
pied with bucket and rake for
shellfish to high-tech sport-
fishing off the coast. If you're
not by the sea, Brittany's many

inland waterways provide lots of opportunities for freshwater angling.

Golf Brittany's golf courses range from the exclusive historic links at Dinard to the challengingly designed modern Baden course in Morbihan.

Horse-riding The varied terrain offers a magnificent choice of trekking possibilities You can rent a horse-drawn caravan or *roulotte* in the Armorique regional park.

Sailing Brittany's long and varied littoral with its challenging hazards of reefs and currents make it a mecca for keen sailors. The coast is studded with well-equipped marinas (La Forêt-Fouesnant, La Trinité-sur-Mer etc). The sheltered southern waters around Bénodet, Iles de Glénan and Quiberon are ideal places to learn.

Sand-yachting Also known as sand-karting or landsailing, the landbased windsurfing sport of *char-à-voile* is especially popular on the long, firm strands at Cherreuix on Mont-St-Michel Bay, and other parts of the north coast. It's an exciting spectator sport in a high wind

Walking Nearly 5,000km (3,110 miles) of footpaths make walking Brittany's most popular recreational activity. Coastal walks, canal towpaths and forest trails cater for all fitness levels, but there are three challenging *Grandes Randonnées* (long-distance footpaths) too.

Watersports Surfing, windsurfing and scuba-diving are available in many resorts all around the coast. Most cater for beginners and experts. Underwater photography courses and wreck-diving are specialist activities.

a drive along the Armorique Corniche

This route spans the coastal borderlands of Finistère and Côtes d'Armor, through a landscape of sandy beaches, rocky headlands, fishing ports and estuary scenery.

Take the D786 southwest of Lannion to St-Michel-en-Grève (11km/7 miles), then detour briefly inland on the D30 to Ploumilliau (4km/2.5 miles).

Ploumilliau's 17th-century church contains an unnerving sculpture of Ankou (the Breton representation of Death), ready with scythe and spade to gather in his human crop.

Retrace your route to the D786, and continue westwards along the Lieu de Grève.

St-Michel-en-Grève's beach is a magnificent 4km (2.5-mile) crescent of firm, perfectly golden sand stretching 2km (1.2 miles) out to sea at low tide. Sand-yachting is a popular local sport. At the west end of the bay, St-Efflam's chapel has a domed fountain dedicated to the local hermit saint.

Leave the main D786 at St-Efflam and follow the corniche route to Locquirec (D64).

This attractive resort and fishing port occupies a scenic headland where affluent villas take advantage of the views. Just west of the village, more glorious beaches are visible from roadside viewpoints at Marc'h Sammet (good picnic spots on a clear day).

Continue on minor roads, hugging the coast as closely as possible, to St-Jean-du-Doigt.

St Jean-du-Doigt's parish close has a triumphal arch and a beautiful Renaissance fountain in which St John baptises Christ. John the Baptist's index finger was allegedly brought here in the 15th century and is kept in the church.

Take the D46 northwards to Plougasnou, then trickle round more coastal lanes to the Cairn de Barnenez.

Beyond more pretty fishing ports (Le Diben, Térénez) lies the impressive Cairn de Barnenez. This megalithic site of terraced granite has 11 separate burial chambers overlooking the Baie de Morlaix (excellent guided tours).

Continue down the D76 to Morlaix.

Distance 70km (43 miles)
Time Allow half a day, with time for a walk or picnic, and a visit to the Cairn de Barnenez
Start point Lannion ✚ 8B
End point Morlaix ✚ 6B
Lunch Grand Hôtel des Bains (€€€) ✉ Locquirec ☎ 02 98 67 41 02

Top souvenir ideas

Antiques Bric-a-brac shops and markets abound in Brittany, and while furniture may be difficult to transport, there are plenty of smaller keepsakes to buy, from wooden spoons to butter-moulds.

Cakes, crêpes and biscuits Classic recipes like *kouignamann* or *far Breton* are on sale in all bakeries. Even the famous Breton pancakes *(crêpes* or *galettes)* are packaged ready to take home. Pont-Aven is a leading centre of biscuit manufacture – its buttery cookies are sold in beautifully decorated tins, themselves a collectable item.

Celtic music If you attend any local festivals, you'll probably hear some typical Breton folk music played on mysterious instruments like the *bombarde* and the *biniou*. There's been a great revival of interest in Celtic music, and many shops sell music recordings.

Cider, beer and wine Brittany's main tipple is cider, produced from the lush orchards of the Rance and Odet valleys. Enthusiastic micro-breweries like Coreff and Dremmwell sell interesting

real ales. Other drinks include *chouchen*, a strongly alcoholic mead, and *lambig* a powerful cider brandy, while Nantes is the land of the crisp white wines of Muscadet.

Faïencerie The most famous Breton pottery comes from Quimper, and is hand-decorated with *paysanne* designs of flowers, birds and costumed figures. Local firms like HB-Henriot offer guided tours and discounted stock in their showrooms.

Household linen Brittany has a long tradition of textile manufacture. The hempen rigging of many a galleon once hailed from Locronan, but these days you're more likely to find napkins and tablecloths in its tourist shops. Pont-l'Abbé in Finistère specializes in hand-embroidered linen and lace.

Knitwear Classic marine stripes in red and navy characterize many Breton sweaters and separates. High-quality brands like Saint James and Armor-Lux are widely available.

Seafood If lugging home a sack of live oysters or mussels seems impractical, don't despair. Firms like La Belle-Iloise produce a superb range of gourmet fish products, smoked, cured, marinaded and enticingly packed in tins and jars.

Seaweed products It's amazing what you can do with seaweed. Brest's Océanopolis (➤ 48–49) explains some of its many culinary, cosmetic and pharmaceutical uses, and in places like Roscoff, shops sell locally made soaps, lotions and foodstuffs based on some of Brittany's hundreds of species.

Weatherproof clothing Fishermen's oilskins and yachtsman's jackets besides being strong, warm and comfortable, are very fashionable too. Look for names like Guy Cotten in harbourfront Comptoir de la Mer shops.

Best beaches

The following beaches give a flavour of this coastal wonderland.

La Baule The tourist authorities claim the resort's beach is the most beautiful in Europe. Stretching for 7km (4 miles), it shelves so gently that you can walk 100m (110yds) into the sea within your depth.

Brignogan-Plages The eight linked beaches of this quiet resort make a perfect place to unwind. Strewn with weirdly shaped boulders, this coastline is full of sheltered natural coves and rockpools.

Carantec This smart but relaxing family resort enjoys a lovely stretch of coastal scenery on the west side of Morlaix Bay, and a choice of six different beaches. There's lots for children in summer, and plenty of boat trips and sports. Explore the creeks of Île Callot at low tide, or take a sea canoe around the sheltered waters.

Carnac-Plage While many visitors head for the megaliths, this sheltered beach resort backed by pine trees is ideal for families. With watersports, children's shows, evening markets and a thalassotherapy centre, there's plenty to entertain.

Cherreuix The firm, flat expanses that fringe the Baie de Mont-St-Michel are a great place to watch sand-yachting. Make sure you don't get in the way – these craft can reach incredible speeds in a high wind.

Dinard The best beaches here are perhaps the Plage de l'Écluse, immortalized by Picasso and decked with chic stripy beach-tents in summer, and the dazzling Plage du Prieuré at the rocky mouth of the River Rance.

Plage de la Torche This vast and lonely beach on the wild Penmarc'h coast is a renowned windsurfing venue, but it's definitely not for novices. Nothing stops the Atlantic breakers here, and in a gale it's unforgettable.

Ploumanac'h The tiny beach of St-Guirec is scarcely big enough for all its summer visitors, but the views of this extraordinary bit of Pink Granite coastline are absolute magic. Enjoy them from the Coste Mor restaurant or the coastguard's watchpath round the rocks.

Ste-Anne-la-Palud This tranquil seascape, entirely unspoiled by development, is best enjoyed towards sunset when you can have it to yourself beside the little chapel of St Anne.

Le Val-André Freshly polished by the retreating tide, Le Val-André's fine pale sands gleam mirror-bright against the setting sun. Perfect for beachcombers or watersports enthusiasts.

Places to take the children

Aquarive
A wave-pool, slides and waterfalls at this attractive waterpark on
the banks of the Odet.
✉ Route de Kerogan, Creac'h Gwen, Quimper ☎ 02 98 52 00 15

L'Aquashow
Besides many fishy species from the Breton coast, this aquarium
hosts seabird and falconry shows in summer.
✉ Rue du Goyen, Audierne ☎ 02 98 70 03 03

Château de la Hunaudaye
This ruinous medieval castle presents entertaining 'living history'
events in summer – with lots of family-friendly activities.
✉ Le Chêne au Loup, Plédeliac ☎ 02 96 32 82 10

Domaine de Ménez-Meur
A conservation park with a varied collection of fauna, from wolves
and wild boar to Ouessant's dwarf black sheep. Adventure
playground, nature trails, pony-rides and more.

✉ Near Hanvec in the Monts d'Arrée, off the D18 ☎ 02 98 68 81 71

Jardins de Suscinio
A large botanical garden around a 16th-century turreted manor, divided into zones such as the Corsaire's Garden or the Valley of Lost Worlds. In the children's village there's a ropebridge and a treehouse, and lots of animals and birds.
✉ Chateau de Suscinio, Ploujean ☎ 02 98 72 05 86

Musée de Bretagne/Espace de Sciences
The new museum complex in Rennes is must for any visitor with its engaging exhibits on the region's history. Many toys, games and comic strips. The science sections include a planetarium and an interactive discovery zone with hands-on experiments.
✉ 10 cours des Alliés, Rennes ☎ 02 23 40 66 70 (museum)

Parc de Branféré
Some 1,500 animals are allowed to wander freely through the attractively landscaped park of a stately château. Lots of children's activities, discovery courses and a bird show.
✉ Le Guerno (25km/15 miles southwest of Vannes) ☎ 02 97 42 94 66

Parc des Grands Chênes/Port Miniature
This forest leisure complex has an aerial adventure playground where you can swing through trees on ropes and walkways, and a delightful boating lake with electrically powered scale replicas of ferries, steamers, fishing boats etc. Waymarked trails, pony-rides.
✉ Base de Loisirs Forêt de Villecartier (15km/9 miles southeast of Dol-de-Bretagne) ☎ 06 88 72 73 40 (park); 02 99 98 37 24 (port)

Le Village Gaulois
Over 20 Gallic-themed activities and games in a reconstructed village with thatched huts and wooden boats.
✉ Pleumeur-Bodou (10km/6 miles from Lannion) ☎ 02 96 91 83 95

Best parish closes

Brasparts (► 93) has a fine calvary depicting St Michael slaying a dragon.

Guéhenno This charmingly naïve calvary was damaged in the Revolution, and restored by the local priest. The cock symbolizes Peter's denial of Christ.

Guimiliau (► 46–47) One of Brittany's most striking parish closes – a tour de force of Renaissance sculpture.

La Martyre An ancient parish close with an interesting ossuary and triumphal door. Extensive interior decoration.

Pencran A 16th-century ossuary, carved porch and balconied belfry distinguish this church. The calvary is incorporated into the surrounding wall.

Pleyben Very large calvary with various scenes depicting the life of Jesus from the Nativity to the Passion, and handsome church interior (carved beams and altarpieces).

Plougastel-Daoulas A large, elaborate calvary and plague cross. Carvings of Catell Gollet (► 47).

La Roche-Maurice A classical ossuary with an Ankou figure of death, and twin-galleried belfry. Lovely Renaissance rood screen in the church.

St-Thégonnec A fine calvary and triumphal arch, and splendid church interior too. Notice the local saint with his tame wolf.

Sizun This church has a triumphal arch and a 16th-century ossuary, with rich panelling inside the church (► 92).

Best *pardons* and festivals

PARDONS

Camaret-sur-Mer *1st Sun in Sep* This little lobster-fishing resort on the Crozon peninsula combines its fervent Pardon de Notre-Dame-de-Rocamadour with a Blessing of the Sea ceremony. The focus is a picturesque seaside chapel where sailor pilgrims made landfall in the 11th century.

Le Folgoët *1st or 2nd Sun in Sep* The Grand Pardon here is a huge and splendid affair with lots of Breton coiffes, costumes and banners. Pilgrims gather for Mass with Breton hymns on the village green. It commemorates the legend of Salaün, a local simpleton who could speak only the words Ave Maria. When he died a white lily sprang from his grave bearing the Latin inscription, indicating his sainthood.

Locronan *2nd Sun in Jul* Every year locals celebrate their patron St Ronan by re-enacting his daily penitential climb up the hill near the town. This pilgrimage is called the Petite Troménie. Every sixth year (last in 2007) there's a longer and more elaborate Grande Troménie around the hill, stopping at 12 Stations of the Cross.

Ste-Anne-la-Palud *Last weekend in Aug* The Grand Pardon here celebrates the mother of the Virgin, Brittany's patroness. Pilgrims convene at a chapel by the beach to pay homage in traditional Breton costume. Celebrations last for three days.

Tréguier *3rd Sun in May* St Yves, patron saint of lawyers, championed the poor and oppressed. This pardon commemorates the anniversary of his death. A reliquary is wheeled out of the church and carried through the streets to his birthplace.

FESTIVALS

Festival des Filets Bleus Concarneau *3rd week in Aug* This three-day festival of the 'blue nets' commemorates the harsh times in

the early 20th century when the sardine shoals vanished and the local fishing industry collapsed. It is now one of Finistère's liveliest folk festivals (http://filetsbleus.free.fr)

Festival InterCeltique Lorient *Early to mid-Aug* This massive gathering of all things Celtic attracts visitors from all over Europe for a feast of traditional music, dancing, and folklore. Night parties *(festou-noz)* keep things humming until the small hours (www.festival-interceltique.com).

Fête de Cornouaille Quimper *Mid- to late Jul* One of Brittany's most important cultural events, lasting about nine days. Thousands of artists arrive from all over Europe to put on concerts, exhibitions and entertainments (www.festival-cornouaill.com).

Fête des Remparts Dinan *Late Jul* This biennial festival (held in even-numbered years) turns the fortifications of the old walled town into a blaze of colourful medieval pageantry, with jousting, banquets, fairs and fireworks (www.dinan-tourisme.com)

Tombées de la Nuit Rennes *Early Jul* Breton culture is celebrated in a huge 10-day art-rock festival involving music, dance and theatre all over the city (www.lestdn.com).

Exploring

For the Celtic tribes who first settled here during the Iron Age, Brittany was *Armor* – the Land by the Sea. Generations of Bretons have earned a living from seafaring and today the waves cast up new sources of revenue in the ferry terminals of Roscoff and St-Malo as thousands of British and Irish visitors come to Brittany.

The Emerald Coast around St-Malo, the russet rocks of the Pink Granite Coast further west, and the lush, wooded estuaries of Cornouaille are some of the most charismatic stretches. Finistère's deadly reefs lie half-submerged, waiting for Atlantic storms, treacherous currents or bewildering sea-fogs to serve up their prey. The main feature of Morbihan's coastline is the huge tidal lagoon called the Golfe du Morbihan, scattered with hundreds of islets. Loire-Atlantique's low-lying shores boast the biggest, and some claim, Europe's most beautiful beach at La Baule.

Finistère

Brest

Finistère is the most Breton part of Brittany, a land of priests and pagans, pierced steeples and spectacular parish closes, where fervent piety mingles with ancient superstition. Here, more than anywhere, you may find traditional customs and costumes, and hear Breton spoken. The fertile Ceinture d'Or (Golden Belt) stretches along the north coast, producing early vegetables, but Brittany's age-old maritime economy still figures large in the fishing ports of Douarnenez, Concarneau and Roscoff.

The dramatic extremities of Crozon and Sizun make memorable touring, and the islands of Ouessant and Batz have their own quiet charm. Inland, the wild uplands of the Monts d'Arrée and Montagnes Noires are a chance to escape coastal crowds; a few remnants of Brittany's ancient forests survive at Huelgoat. In the south, the lush wooded estuaries of the rivers Odet and the Aven create the idyllic watercolours immortalized by Pont-Aven's 19th-century artists.

BÉNODET

In the Middle Ages, Bénodet's income sprang from trading salt, fish and wine. Today its economic mainstay is tourism. Apart from its lighthouses and a scrap of fortress, the town has few notable sights or historic buildings. Its popularity is based on the attractions of its natural setting at the mouth of the wooded Odet estuary, and a series of excellent beaches. Families converge to take advantage of Bénodet's resort amenities in summer, which include sailing in Le Letty's tidal lagoon. The **Musée du Bord de Mer** explains the history of yachting and sailing at Bénodet. For more seclusion, take the graceful modern bridge or shuttle ferry across the river to Ste-Marine. Boat trips up the River Odet, or to the Îles de Glénan in the Baie de Concarneau, are highly recommended.

www.benodet.com

✚ 4F 🍴 Good choice throughout resort (€–€€€) 🚍 No 16 (Quimper) 🚢 Trips on the Odet and to Iles de Glénan ℹ️ 29 avenue de la Mer ☎ 02 98 57 00 14

Musée du Bord de Mer

✉️ 29 avenue de la Mer ☎ 02 98 57 00 14 🕐 Jun–Sep daily 10–1, 2–6:30 (6pm Sun) 💰 Moderate

BREST

Brest's strategic location on a magnificent natural harbour (Rade de Brest) at the edge of western Europe has been its fortune, and its undoing. The Romans first spotted its potential and built a camp in the 3rd century. The settlement was fortified by the counts of Léon in the 12th century, and occupied by the English for part of the Hundred Years' War. Louis XIII chose it as his principal naval base in the 17th century. Brest expanded during the seafaring centuries that followed, though its harbour was maintained for defensive rather than trade purposes, and it never accrued the wealth of other Breton seaports.

During German Occupation, Brest became a U-Boat base, plaguing transatlantic convoys and becoming the unwilling target of sustained Allied bombardment towards the end of the war. When Brest fell in 1944, it was utterly devastated. Vast post-war investment has rebuilt, if not entirely revitalised the town in a functional modern style of concrete high-rises. It retains none of its former charm, but is worth a visit for its streamlined docks and roadstead views, and several interesting sights. A university town, it has plenty of cultural activities and events. Harbour cruises are highly recommended.

The castle and the neighbouring Cours Dajot promenade give excellent views of the Rade de Brest. Built between the 12th and 17th centuries, it miraculously withstood the bombs of World War II and now houses both the naval headquarters and the

Musée de la Marine (Maritime Museum). Its eclectic displays include splendid cedar figure-heads, a manned torpedo vessel from World War II and a Vietnamese refugee boat. Near the castle stands the massive Pont de Recouvrance, Europe's highest swing-bridge, and the 15th-century Tour Tanguy, containing a museum of Old Brest, which gives an enlightening view of how the port once looked. In the city centre, the **Musée des Beaux-Arts** (Fine Arts Museum) contains a collection of Pont-Aven paintings (closed Tue). On the north side of town, at Port de Plaisance du Moulin-Blanc, the **Conservatoire Botanique National** preserves endangered species. www.brest-metropole-tourisme.fr

➕ 3C 🍴 Good choice around main sights (€–€€€) 🚌 Major route-hub for public transport; many inner-city buses 🚢 Ferry to Le Fret; harbour cruises

ℹ️ Place de la Liberté ☎ 02 98 44 24 96

Musée de la Marine

➕ *Brest 1f* ✉ Château de Brest ☎ 02 98 22 12 39 🕐 Apr–Sep daily 10–6:30; Oct–Mar 1:30–6:30. Closed Jan ✋ Moderate

Musée des Beaux-Arts

➕ *Brest 2e* ✉ 24 rue Traverse ☎ 02 98 00 87 96 🕐 Daily 10–12, 2–6. Closed Tue, Sun am and public hols ✋ Moderate

Conservatoire Botanique National

✉ 52 allée du Bot ☎ 02 98 02 46 00 🕐 Garden daily 9–6 (until 8 in summer); visitor centre and greenhouses Sun–Thu 2–5:30 (Wed and Sun 2–4:30 off season) ✋ Free to garden; inexpensive to visitor centre and greenhouses

CAP SIZUN

Sizun's jagged finger stretches far into the Atlantic, ending at the Pointe du Raz, where a statue of Notre-Dame-des-Naufragés (Our Lady of the Shipwrecked) is aptly placed. Out to sea, the Île de Sein barely rises

above the waterline, a treacherous obstacle to shipping. If you want to walk around the headland note that the rocks can be very slippery, and take binoculars if you are keen on birdwatching. The **Réserve de Goulien** is a popular destination during the nesting season, and Audierne has another large nature reserve. The **Maison de la Baie** organizes nature walks.

Apart from the fishing ports of Douarnenez and Audierne, there are no large settlements. Inland is quiet farmland. Audierne has a fine setting on the Goyen estuary, large fish farms (visitors welcome), and the impressive **L'Aquashow** (Breton marine species and bird shows).

www.capsizun.com

🛁 2E

Réserve de Goulien
✉ Cap Sizun ☎ 02 98 70 13 53
🕐 Apr–Aug. Guided tours Jul–Aug daily; Apr–Jun Sat–Sun 💶 Moderate

Maison de la Baie
✉ St-Vio, Tréguennec ☎ 02 98 87 65 07
🕐 Feb–Oct call for programme of events
💶 Moderate

L'Aquashow
✉ Rue du Goyen, Audierne ☎ 02 98 70 03 03; www.aquarium.fr 🕐 Apr–Sep daily 10–7; Oct Sun–Thu 2–5; school hols in winter 💶 Expensive

a drive around Cap Sizun

A drive round some of Finistère's most exciting headlands.

From Douarnenez, take the north coast road (D7), ducking northwards at Pointe du Millier.

A few minutes' walk to the point offers a splendid view of the bay. Further west, Pointe de Beuzec (accessible by car) has similar views.

Return to the D7 and head westwards to the Reserve de Goulien at Cap Sizun.

This famous bird sanctuary on a wild granite cape is best visited between April and mid-July when a host of seabirds rear their young on the dark rocky cliffs of Castel-ar-Roc'h.

Return to the D7 again and continue 6km (4 miles) westwards to the Pointe de Brézellec (north off the road).

Park near the lighthouse and enjoy a magnificent vantage point of serrated rocks and cliffs.

Continue west to the Pointe du Van.

A lengthy walk leads to a desolate treeless headland of stone and moss, less spectacular than Pointe du Raz, but less crowded. The cliffs here are dangerous. One lonely hotel guards the headland.

Follow the coast road south past the Baie des Trépassés.

This sweeping crescent of firm sand may look inviting, but the currents are strong. In a gale, it's a terrifying sight.

Join the D784 and head west for 2.5km (1.5 miles) to the Pointe du Raz, the highlight of the journey.

Technically this is not quite France's most westerly point. The point snakes out to sea, ending in razor pinnacles. A path leads round the rocky point with safety ropes, but take care; the rocks are slippery and freak waves may sweep you off.

Return to Douarnenez along the D784 via Audierne, then the D765 via Pont-Croix.

Distance 80km (50 miles) – some walking
Time Allow about half a day – longer with extensive walks or picnics
Start/end point Douarnenez ✚ 4E
Lunch Hotel de la Baie des Trépassés, Pointe du Raz (€€) ☎ 02 98 70 61 34

CHÂTEAU DE KERJEAN

The Château de Kerjean is one of Brittany's finest Renaissance manors. Set in 20ha (50 acres) of sweeping parkland, the château's gabled roofline rises above high ramparts, beyond a drawbridge and a deep moat. It dates from the late 16th century, and suffered much damage during the Revolution, when its last *aristo* was guillotined. In 1911 it passed into State hands. Since then it has been restored and converted into a cultural centre and museum of traditional Breton furniture. As well as a film show, learn about château life in the 18th century through workshops.

www.chateau-de-kerjean.com

✚ 5B ✉ St-Vougay ☎ 02 98 69 93 69 🕐 Jul–Aug daily 10–7; off season Wed–Mon 2–5 ✋ Moderate

CONCARNEAU

Fishing is on the decline in Concarneau (once one of France's most important ports), but it still has a sizeable fleet and lands varied catches in the modern, shed-like fish market by the Arrière-Port. If you arrive early enough, you can see the *criée* (fish auction) in full swing. An organization called **A l'Assault des Remparts** offers guided tours (some in English) of the old town, including visits to the harbour, a working trawler and the quayside fish auction. The evening tours are particularly interesting, when you can see the boats arrive to unload their catches after midnight.

Concarneau's most charming district is the medieval old town, or Ville Close on a rocky island protected by granite ramparts and a fortified bridge. Tourists crowd over the drawbridge to explore quaint old streets and attractive souvenir shops. The Ville Close's best sight is the **Musée de la Pêche,** a well-displayed exhibition on the fishing industry with ancient sardine tins and giant scooping nets. An old trawler moored by the walls reveals the cramped and spartan conditions of life at sea.

Beaches stretch either side of the town, but they are not Brittany's best. Boat trips from Concarneau visit the Îles de Glénan and the Odet estuary. In late August, Concarneau's Fête des Filets Bleus (Blue Nets Festival) attracts many visitors.

www.tourismeconcarneau.fr

🔀 5F 🍽 Snacks and fast food within the Ville Close; the best restaurants are around the port in the main part of town (€–€€) 🚌 No 14 (Quimper–Pont-Aven); No 20 (Rosporden) 🚢 Odet, Îles de Glénan and bay cruises
🛈 Quai d'Aiguillon ☎ 02 98 97 01 44

A l'Assault des Remparts

☎ 02 98 50 55 18 ✋ Moderate ❓ Escorted tours

Musée de la Pêche

✉ 3 rue Vauban, Ville-Close ☎ 02 98 97 10 20 🕓 Jul–Aug daily 9:30–8; Apr–Sep and school hols daily 10–12, 2–6 ✋ Moderate

GUIMILIAU
Best places to see, pages 46–47.

ÎLE D'OUESSANT
Ouessant is the largest of eight islands scattered off the west
coast of Finistère, a treacherous obstacle course for one of the
world's busiest shipping lanes. Despite all the lighthouses and
warning beacons that guard the reefs, disasters still occur, notably
the *Amoco Cadiz*, which foundered in 1978, and the *Erika* in 1999.

Ouessant (anglicised as Ushant) is one of Finistère's remotest
communities, yet it is easily reached on a fast ferry from Le
Conquet or Brest. In fine weather (preferably calm!) a day-trip is
highly recommendable. Ouessant's traditional matriarchal way of
life has all but vanished on the mainland, and although the island
now relies increasingly on tourism for its revenue, the older social
patterns still persist. It is also an important marine conservation
area, and forms part of the Parc Naturel Régional d'Armorique.
Ouessant's maritime climate is surprisingly mild in winter.
Seaweed processing is a local industry.

Ferry passengers alight at the Baie du Stiff, where two
lighthouses (ancient and modern) guard the eastern headlands.
From here the best way to explore the island is by bike (for
hire at the port or the main village of Lampaul). Ouessant (7 by
4km/4 by 2.5 miles) is rather too large to see on foot in a single
day and simple accommodation and restaurants can be found
in Lampaul. The churchyard here contains a monument to the
many islanders lost at sea. The main sights on the island are the
Ecomusée d'Ouessant, housed in two tiny cottages displaying
a typical seafaring home of the 19th century, and numerous
costumes, tools and other exhibits. On the west coast, the Phare
du Creac'h contains a lighthouse museum, the **Musée des Phares
et Balises,** highlighting the elaborate coastal warning system
of western Brittany. The remaining pleasures of Ouessant lie
mostly out of doors, in its dramatic coastal scenery, wildlife and

open heathland where sheep roam freely. Many of the white cottages have blue doors and shutters, the colour of the protecting Virgin's robes.

www.ot-ouessant.fr

🚹 1B 🍴 Several simple eating places in and around Lampaul (€–€€)

ℹ️ Place de l'Église, Lampaul ☎ 02 98 48 85 83

Ecomusée d'Ouessant

✉️ Niou Uhella ☎ 02 98 48 86 37 🕐 May–Sep daily 10:30–6:30; Oct–Dec Tue–Sun 10:30–6:30; Jan–Apr pm only; night visits 9–11pm Wed and Fri in summer ✋ Inexpensive (joint ticket with Musée des Phares et Balises available)

Musée des Phares et Balises

✉️ Phare du Créac'h ☎ 02 98 48 80 70 🕐 Times as Ecomusée d'Ouessant ✋ Moderate (joint ticket with Ecomusée d'Ouessant available)

LOCRONAN

Even when besieged by summer visitors, Locronan's charms are undeniable. Its Renaissance square of gold-grey buildings is as pretty as a film-set, which, indeed, it has been from time to time. Many of the former merchants' houses have been converted into shops, restaurants and hotels. A browse through its craft studios is an ideal way of choosing Breton souvenirs. Locronan's wealth came from the manufacture of sailcloth, and for a period in the 17th century it single-handedly supplied much of Europe's maritime rigging. When Louis XIV abolished its monopoly, Locronan's economy collapsed. The church of St-Ronan is one of the most striking monuments, in 15th-century Ogival Flamboyant style. Stained glass marks scenes of the Passion, while the carved pulpit recounts its patron saint's life. St Ronan was an Irish missionary, and his penitential climb each day up the hill behind the town is re-enacted by annual processions called *Troménies*.

A short distance from Locronan, the seaside chapel of Ste-Anne-la-Palud is the scene of one of the finest *pardon* ceremonies in Brittany (➤ 72) with torchlit processions and Breton costumes. The object of veneration is a painted granite statue of St Anne dating from 1548.
www.locronan.org

✚ 4E 🍴 Plenty of choice in and around the church square, such as Ty Coz (€) place de l'Eglise 🚌 No 10 (Quimper–Plomodiern)
ℹ Place de la Mairie ☎ 02 98 91 70 14

MONTS D'ARRÉE

Aeons ago, these ancient granite hills were once as high as the Alps: now the elements have eroded them to rounded stumps covered with gorse moors. The less accessible stretches provide important wildlife sanctuaries, and you may encounter deer, otters and wild boar. Much of the Monts d'Arrée massif forms part of the Parc Naturel Régional d'Armorique, encompassing hills and woodland, the Aulne estuary, the coast of Crozon and the Ouessant archipelago. A dozen or so little museums sprinkled throughout the park show various aspects of traditional rural life. The park's main information centre is at Ménez-Meur, a wooded estate with a zoo park, and which holds temporary exhibitions on Breton life. Huelgoat is the main community of a last vestige of Brittany's *argoat* or inland forest. Devastated by the hurricane of 1987, there are few venerable trees left, but giant mossy boulders, fern-filled grottoes and a placid lake add interest to local walks.
www.pnr-armorique.fr

✚ 5–6C 🍴 Sporadic. Most options are in Huelgoat (€–€€) 🚌 Nos 52 and 61 serve Huelgoat but no scheduled routes cross the wilder zones
ℹ Ménez-Meur ☎ 02 98 68 81 71

MORLAIX

The town's location at the head of a dramatic estuary gave it a leading role in the maritime trade of the Renaissance, and from embryonic origins as a Gaullish defence camp it burgeoned into a thriving port prospering on fishing, linen, shipbuilding, tobacco-smuggling – and piracy. Like St-Malo, Morlaix was a corsair town, and its daring raids on foreign shipping provoked reprisals. After the English sacked the town in 1522, Morlaix adopted a truculent motto (a pun on its name): 'S'ils te mordent, mords-les' ('If they bite you, bite them back!'), and constructed the Château du Taureau to guard the bay. Today Morlaix is a delightful place.

The old town lies close to the feet of a giant granite viaduct astride the valley. Beyond the viaduct (which you can walk across for excellent views), steep alleys trickle through a maze of churches and timbered buildings, some in an elaborate local style called 'lantern houses'. The **Maison de la Duchesse Anne** is the best of these (see the skylit interior). The **Musée de Morlaix** is well worth a look for its art and history collections.

www.morlaixtourisme.fr

➕ 6B 🍴 Good choice in the old town (€–€€) 🚌 Lannion, Roscoff, Carhaix–Plouguer etc 🚆 Roscoff, Lannion, Brest and St-Brieuc
ℹ️ Place des Otages ☎ 02 98 62 14 94

Maison de la Duchess Anne

✉ 33 rue du Mur ☎ 02 98 88 23 26 🕒 May–Sep Mon–Sat 11–6 (closed Mon and Thu am May and Oct–Apr) ✋ Inexpensive

Musée de Morlaix

✉ Place des Jacobins and 9 Grand'Rue ☎ 02 98 88 68 88; www.musee.ville.morlaix.fr 🕒 Jul–Aug daily 10–12:30, 2–6:30; Apr–May, Sep Mon, Wed–Sat 10–12, 2–6, Sun 2–6. Closed in winter ✋ Moderate

PONT-AVEN

Few of the watermills that once filled the town of Pont-Aven remain, but its picturesque riverside houses would still be recognisable to the painters who flocked here during the 19th century. The most notable member of the Pont-Aven School was Gauguin, though few of his works are on display at the **Musée Municipal**'s art collection.

A wander through the old streets and nearby woods, however, will evoke many of the scenes he painted, notably the charming Chapelle de Trémalo, where a crucifix in the nave was the inspiration for his startling Christ Jaune. Pont-Aven's natural attractions are supplemented by good restaurants, hotels and shops.

www.pontaven.com

✚ 6F 🍴 Good if pricey choices in town (€€–€€€) 🚌 Nos 14, 21 (Concarneau–Quimper) 🚢 Estuary cruises to Port-Manec'h

ℹ 5 place de l'Hôtel de Ville ☎ 02 98 06 04 70

Musée Municipal

✉ Place de l'Hôtel de Ville ☎ 02 98 06 14 43 🕐 Jul–Aug daily 10–7; Sep–Jun 10–12:30, 2–6. Closed Jan 💲 Moderate

a drive in the Monts d'Arrée

The village of Sizun makes a pleasant starting point.

Its church has elaborate panelled vaulting and decorated beams, and a parish close with a magnificent triumphal arch. The Maison de la Rivière and the Maison du Lac deal with aspects of the local waterways and their wildlife.

From Sizun, take the D764 eastwards, pausing at the Moulins de Kerouat after 3km (2 miles).

This restored mill complex of bake-houses and outbuildings is now a museum of country life.

Continue on the same road to Commana.

The landscapes become wilder and the hills higher. Commana has a fine church and an *allée couverte*.

East of Commana on the same road is the Roc'h Trévézel.

At 384m (1,260ft), this is one of the best viewpoints in Brittany, with views as far as Baie de Lannion on a clear day.

Take the D785 southwards, stopping at Montagne St-Michel after 13km (8 miles).

This is a slightly lower summit (380m/1,247ft), and can be reached by car. The surrounding ridge is the highest point in Brittany.

Continue 7km (4 miles) down the D785 to Brasparts.

Brasparts has a fine church and parish close. Inside the church is a lovely baroque altarpiece with blue and gold barleysugar columns decorated with vines and snakes.

Retrace the route for 2.5km (1.5 miles) northwards and take the D30 northwest to St-Rivoal.

This hamlet has an attractive ecomusée, the Maison Cornec. Wind westwards through the lanes to Menez-Meur. This wildlife reserve and information centre are a good place to put the Armorique park in perspective.

Return north up the D342 to return to Sizun.

Distance 60km (37 miles)
Time Allow a day if you want to see most of the sights, and have a walk
Start/end point Sizun ✚ 5C
Lunch Restaurants are scarce, and most museums do not have coffee shops. Take a picnic with you

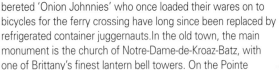

PRESQU'ÎLE DE CROZON
Best places to see, pages 50–51.

QUIMPER
Best places to see, pages 52–53.

ROSCOFF
Roscoff successfully combines the role of ferry port with that of seaside resort and export centre for vegetables and seafood. Thalassotherapy and seaweed research are other sidelines. The pretty, old fishing quarter remains intact despite the demands of modern shipping. But the bereted 'Onion Johnnies' who once loaded their wares on to bicycles for the ferry crossing have long since been replaced by refrigerated container juggernauts.In the old town, the main monument is the church of Notre-Dame-de-Kroaz-Batz, with one of Brittany's finest lantern bell towers. On the Pointe

de Bloscon, subtropical gardens flourish. A good excursion from Roscoff is the 15-minute boat-trip to the Île de Batz, with sandy beaches and another exotic garden.

www.roscoff-tourisme.com

🚌 6B 🍽 Good choice throughout the town (€–€€€) 🚍 Brest, Morlaix, Quimper 🚆 Morlaix 🛥 Brittany Ferries (Plymouth UK); trips to Île de Batz
🛈 46 rue Gambetta ☎ 02 98 61 12 13

ST-POL-DE-LÉON

During the Middle Ages St-Pol was the religious centre of North Finistère. Its most memorable landmark is the magnificent belfry of the Kreisker Chapel, soaring 77m (253ft) high. Near by rise the rival twin spires of the Cathedral. Built of Norman limestone, the interior is full of fascinating details. What looks like an old stone bath-tub (a Roman sarcophagus) serves as a stoup, and a little door below the right tower was used by lepers.

St-Pol is renowned as an agricultural centre of the fertile Golden Belt *(Ceinture d'Orée)* and all around the town early vegetables grow, particularly onions, artichokes, potatoes and cauliflowers. If you catch it on a Tuesday (market day) you will see it at its liveliest.

www.saintpoldeleon.fr

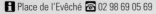 6B 🍴 Auberge Pomme d'Api, 49 rue Verderel (€€) 🚌 🚆 Same services as Roscoff (see opposite)

ℹ️ Place de l'Evêché ☎ 02 98 69 05 69

HOTELS

L'ABER WRAC'H
Baie des Anges (€€–€€€)

This stylish little seaside hotel enjoys an entrancing location overlooking a calm sea inlet on the northwestern Côte des Abers. No restaurant.

✉ 350 route des Anges ☎ 02 98 04 90 04; www.baie-des-anges.com
🕐 Closed Jan

BÉNODET
Armoric (€€–€€€)

A welcoming, smartly refurbished hotel at the approach to the resort, with large gardens and a heated pool.

✉ 3 rue de Penfoul ☎ 02 98 57 04 03; www.armoric-benodet.com

BREST
Citotel de la Gare (€)

A small modern hotel close to the bus and railway stations. Bedrooms are tidy and functional with all the basics for an inexpensive stay. Friendly management. No restaurant.

✉ 4 boulevard Gambetta ☎ 02 98 44 47 01; www.hotelgare.com

BRIGNOGAN-PLAGE
Castel Régis (€€)

A superb beachfront location distinguishes this well-equipped, peaceful resort hotel.

✉ Promenade du Garo ☎ 02 98 83 40 22; www.castelregis.com
🕐 Closed Oct–Mar

CARANTEC
Carantec–Patrick Jeffroy (€€€)

Stunning views over tranquil gardens and coastline make this hotel-restaurant special, along with its ambitious cooking.

✉ 20 rue du Kelenn ☎ 02 98 67 00 47; www.hoteldecarantec.com
🕐 Closed Jan, mid-Nov to mid-Dec, Mon and Tue off-season

CONCARNEAU
Auberge de Jeunesse (€)
Facilities are basic in this friendly youth hostel, but the seafront location couldn't be better and it's just a few minutes' walk to the Ville Close and town centre.

✉ Quai de la Croix ☎ 02 98 97 03 47; www.ajconcarneau.com

DOUARNENEZ
Clos de Vallombreuse (€€–€€€)
Right in the heart of the old town, this secluded mansion has elegant, sophisticated furnishings and a noteworthy restaurant.

✉ 7 rue d'Étienne d'Orves ☎ 02 98 92 63 64; www.closvallombreuse.com

LANDERNEAU
Clos du Pontic (€)
A quiet, well-equipped hotel in an unusual turreted building with modern extensions. Lovely gardens.

✉ Rue du Pontic ☎ 02 98 21 50 91; www.clos-pontic.com

LOCQUIREC
Grand Hôtel des Bains (€€–€€€)
Stylish *belle époque* spa hotel in idyllic coastal setting. Striking, contemporary interior.

✉ 15 rue de l'Eglise ☎ 02 98 67 41 02; www.grand-hotel-des-bains.com

LOCRONAN
Manoir de Moëllien (€€–€€€)
A tranquil 17th-century manor with lots of character and attractive bedrooms in a stable-block annexe.

✉ Plonévez-Porzay ☎ 02 98 92 50 40; www.moellien.com 🕐 Closed Jan

MOËLAN-SUR-MER
Moulins du Duc (€€–€€€)
Luxury hotel-restaurant in a 16th-century watermill. Large grounds, antique furnishings, and a rural setting near the Bélon estuary.

✉ Route des Moulins ☎ 02 98 96 52 52; www.moulins-du-duc.com
🕐 Closed late Nov–Feb

MORGAT
Julia (€–€€)

A welcoming, family-run hotel on the Crozon peninsula, with bright, fresh décor and great home-cooking.

✉ 43 rue du Tréflez ☎ 02 98 27 05 89; www.hoteljulia.fr ⏱ Closed Jan–Feb

NÉVEZ
Ar Men Du (€€–€€€)

This small, smart hotel-restaurant has a wonderful coastal setting overlooking a tidal islet. Bedrooms are well equipped and contemporary. The restaurant is very popular.

✉ Raguenez-Plage, Port Manec'h ☎ 02 98 06 84 22; www.men-du.com
⏱ Closed Nov to mid-Mar except Christmas, New Year

PONT-AVEN
Hôtel des Mimosas (€–€€)

A simple place at the far end of the harbour with seductive waterfront views and a cosy, nautical-looking bistro.

✉ 22 square Théodore Botrel ☎ 02 98 06 00 30; www.hotels-pont-aven.com

ROSCOFF
Le Brittany (€€–€€€)

A tasteful manor-house hotel with good leisure facilities and an excellent restaurant right by the sea. Very popular with UK ferry travellers.

✉ Boulevard Ste-Barbe ☎ 02 98 69 70 78; www.hotel-brittany.com
⏱ Closed mid-Nov to late Mar

Hôtel du Centre (€–€€)

Owned by the same family as Le Brittany, this budget option in the old port has cheerful contemporary rooms and a popular café-bar.

✉ 5 rue Gambetta ☎ 02 98 61 24 25; www.chezjanie.com ⏱ Closed mid-Dec to mid-Feb

QUIMPER
Dupleix (€€)

A useful modern business hotel on the south bank of the Odet,

within easy walking distance of the old town. Pleasant, quiet
atmosphere and private parking.

✉ 34 boulevard Dupleix ☎ 02 98 90 53 35; www.hotel-dupleix.com

STE-ANNE-LA-PALUD
La Plage (€€–€€€)

Tranquil, upmarket hotel-restaurant in isolated beachside location.
Glorious views.

✉ Ste-Anne-la-Palud ☎ 02 98 92 50 12; www.plage.com ⏰ Closed
Nov–Mar

STE-MARINE
Sainte-Marine (€€–€€€)

Just across the peaceful Odet estuary from lively Bénodet, this
chic restaurant-with-rooms has bright, contemporary bedrooms
and wonderful views. Terrace dining. Always very popular.

✉ 19 rue du Bac ☎ 02 98 56 34 79; www.hotelsaintemarine.com
⏰ Closed mid-Nov to mid-Dec

TRÉGUNC
Les Grandes Roches (€–€€)

Just 3km (2 miles) east of Concarneau, this rambling old Breton
house feels surprisingly rural in extensive park-like grounds.

✉ Rue des Grandes Roches ☎ 02 98 97 62 97 ⏰ Closed mid-Dec to Jan

RESTAURANTS

BREST
Maison de l'Océan (€€)

A terrific choice of seafood in this lively restaurant down by the
docks and not far from the castle and central museums. Tables
outside.

✉ 2 quai Douane ☎ 02 98 80 44 84

Ma Petite Folie (€–€€)

This former lobster boat is moored in the pleasure port and serves
delicious fishy fare like grilled lobster and potted crab.

✉ Port de Plaisance ☎ 02 98 42 44 42 ⏰ Closed early Jan

CONCARNEAU
Chez Armande (€€)
Unpretentious, family-run fish restaurant serving excellent menus at good prices.

✉ 15 bis avenue Dr Nicolas ☎ 02 98 97 00 76 🕐 Closed mid- to end Nov, Wed, Tue off-season

L'Amiral (€–€€)
A smart, popular bar-restaurant overlooking the Ville Close, decorated in nautical style. Excellent seafood and good-value lunchtime menu.

✉ 1 avenue Pierre Guéguin ☎ 02 98 60 55 23 🕐 Closed two weeks Jan–Feb and Sep–Oct, Sun eve, Mon off-season

Le Petit Chaperon Rouge (€)
Welcoming *crêperie* in a tiny square near the Ville Close, serving a wide and inventive range of pancakes in a cosy dining room.

✉ 7 place Duguesclin ☎ 02 98 60 53 32 🕐 Closed several weeks in Mar, Jun and Oct

LE CONQUET
Hostellerie de la Pointe St-Mathieu (€€€)
Elaborate seafood dishes are served in the stone dining room of this dramatically set hotel-restaurant facing the Atlantic.

✉ Pointe St-Mathieu ☎ 02 98 89 00 19 🕐 Closed late Jan–late Feb; Sun eve off-season

Relais de Vieux Port (€)
Charming, breezily decorated harbourfront restaurant serving simple snacks, *crêpes*, salads, etc.

✉ 1 quai Drellach ☎ 02 98 89 15 91 🕐 Closed Jan

CROZON
Hostellerie de la Mer (€€)
Book ahead at this family-run hotel-restaurant for a quayside view of the Rade de Brest, along with excellent, mainly fishy menus.

✉ Le Fret ☎ 02 98 27 61 90

Mutin Gourmand (€€)

You'll find whatever's freshest from the market at this hotel-restaurant, renowned for its accomplished seafood dishes.

✉ Place de l'Eglise ☎ 02 98 27 06 51 🕐 Closed Sun eve, Mon–Wed lunch; mid-Nov to mid-Dec and two weeks mid-Feb

GUIMILIAU
Ar Chupen (€)

Lacy *galettes* and *crêpes* with a wide choice of fillings in this old Breton farmhouse a short walk from the famous parish close.

✉ 43 rue du Guimiliau ☎ 02 98 68 73 63 🕐 Closed Sun–Fri eve except in summer

LOCRONAN
Ty Coz (€)

Charming flower-decked *crêperie* and *glacier* in an old stone building on the main square.

✉ Place de l'Eglise ☎ 02 98 81 70 79 🕐 Closed Oct–Easter, Mon (except hols)

MORLAIX
Brasserie de l'Europe (€–€€)

An elegant café-brasserie serving sophisticated snacks and meals, mainly seafood-based. Wine-bar open all day in summer.

✉ Place Emile Souvestre ☎ 02 98 88 81 15 🕐 Closed Sun

L'Hermine (€)

A welcoming *crêperie* with well-crafted pancakes in a picturesque stone building on one of Morlaix's cobbled alleys. Rustic interior; pavement tables and late opening in summer.

✉ 35 rue Ange de Guernisac ☎ 02 98 88 10 91

Marée Bleue (€€)

Traditional menu and interesting wines in an elegant, cosy restaurant in an alley just off Morlaix's main square.

✉ 3 rampe St-Mélaine ☎ 02 98 63 24 21 🕐 Closed Oct, Sun eve, Mon

QUIMPER
La Fleur du Sel (€–€€)
A good place for lunch opposite the *faïenceries* factories in Locmaria, with waterfront views. Light fish dishes.
✉ 1 quai Neuf ☎ 02 98 55 04 71 ⊕ Closed Christmas, New Year, Sat lunch, Sun

RIEC-SUR-BÉLON
Chez Jacky (€€)
Well-known fish-farming enterprise with on-site brasserie on the Bélon waterfront. Sample home-grown oysters, lobsters and other shellfish on sturdy picnic tables.
✉ Port de Bélon ☎ 02 98 06 90 32 ⊕ Closed Oct–Easter, Sun eve and Mon

ROSCOFF
Le Temps de Vivre (€€€)
Top-notch cooking in an old corsaire's house opposite the church. Lobster, onion and artichoke specialities.
✉ Place de l'Eglise ☎ 02 98 61 27 28 ⊕ Closed mid-Mar, early Oct, early Jan, Mon, Tue lunch, Sun eve off-season

ST-POL-DE-LÉON
Auberge la Pomme d'Api (€€–€€€)
Acclaimed fine dining in a 16th-century setting. Features elaborately named dishes using the local produce of the *ceinture d'or* (Golden Belt).
✉ 49 rue Verderel ☎ 02 98 69 04 36 ⊕ Closed Sun eve, Mon off-season

ST-THÉGONNEC
Auberge St-Thégonnec (€€–€€€)
Superb cooking in a smart hotel-restaurant.
✉ 6 place de la Mairie ☎ 02 98 79 61 18 ⊕ Closed late Dec to mid-Jan, Sat lunch, Sun eve, Mon off-season

SHOPPING

CRAFTS AND REGIONAL PRODUCTS

Algoplus

Seaweed is processed into many diverse forms for culinary, cosmetic and pharmaceutical uses by this enterprising firm in the commercial harbour. Free guided tours of the plant in summer.

✉ Port du Bloscon, Roscoff ☎ 02 98 61 14 14; www.algoplus-roscoff.fr

Comptoir des Produits Bretons

This shop has one of the widest selections of Breton crafts and regional products, including seascapes, outdoor gear, jewellery.

✉ 3 quai de Cornouaille, Landerneau ☎ 02 98 21 35 93; www.comptoir-produits-bretons.com

Faïencerie HB-Henriot

The largest and most high-profile local pottery firm, still using traditional hand-decoration methods and personally signed by the artist. Factory tours (some in English) show the process. Large on-site showroom – discounted stock.

✉ Rue Haute, Locmaria, Quimper ☎ 02 98 90 09 36; www.hb-henriot.com

Keltia Musique

A wide selection of Breton and Celtic folk music recordings, books, instrument manuals, and more

✉ 1 place au Beurre, Quimper ☎ 02 98 95 45 82; www.keltiamusique.com

Maison des Artisans

A collection of craft shops and studios selling textiles, ceramics, wood-carvings etc. Linen is a local speciality.

✉ Place de l'Église, Locronan ☎ 02 98 91 70 11

Le Minor

This shop near the castle specializes in the town's local embroidery. Head upstairs for wall-hangings and household linen.

✉ 5 quai St-Laurent, Pont-l'Abbé ☎ 02 98 87 07 22; www.leminorboutique.com

Comptoir de la Mer

This amazing chandlery stocks many items for leisure sailors and holidaymakers, including marine clothing and nauticalia.

✉ Port de Pêche, St-Guénolé ☎ 02 98 58 66 24

FOOD AND DRINK

Biscuiterie

One of many shops selling the town's speciality butter biscuits known as *galettes de Pont-Aven* in attractive tins.

✉ 10 place Gauguin, Pont-Aven ☎ 02 98 06 01 03

Chocolatier Chatillon

This *chocolatier* offers free tours to watch mouthwatering chocolates and biscuits being made, followed by tastings.

✉ 46 place Charles de Gaulle, Pleyben ☎ 02 98 26 63 77; www.chatillon-chocolat.com

Larnicol

An enticing cave-like shop in the Ville Close selling a huge array of sweets and other goodies.

✉ 9 rue Vauban, Concarneau ☎ 02 98 60 46 87

ENTERTAINMENT

NIGHTLIFE

Bar Ecossais

This Scottish-themed pub attracts a lively Celtic fringe.

✉ 241 rue Jean-Jaurès, Brest ☎ 02 98 41 90 05

Stargames Café

Chill out on the scatter cushions with mint tea or even a hookah pipe in this trendy North African-styled cybercafé.

✉ 17 rue des Gentils-Hommes, Quimper ☎ 02 98 95 71 97

Tempo

A cool, popular waterfront bar featuring regular jazz, blues and other music.

✉ Quai de Tréguier, Morlaix ☎ 02 98 63 29 11

Côtes d'Armor

Few visitors would dispute that the coastline of Côtes d'Armor is the most dramatically beautiful in Brittany. Highlights are the Emerald and Pink Granite coasts, where its northerly peninsulas meet the sea in a spectacular series of headlands, cliffs, bizarre rock formations and scattered islands.

Added blessings are its charming old towns (Dinan, Tréguier, Lannion, Paimpol). In summer, its main centres and hotels can become crowded, but nowhere except perhaps St-Brieuc feels overpoweringly urban, and it's never impossible to find a secluded beach.

Some areas have fascinating historic associations: the Côte de Goëlo south of Paimpol was a centre of Resistance operations during World War II. Its less well-known interior, startlingly empty in parts, is worth exploring too. As you travel westwards through Côtes d'Armor towards Basse-Bretagne (Lower Brittany), the Breton character becomes steadily more pronounced and Celtic place-names appear on signposts.

CAP FRÉHEL

This spectacular promontory consists of gnarled grey cliffs of schist and sandstone streaked with red porphyry rising to a height of 70m (230ft) above a sea of jade. Best views are from the sea; summer excursion boats tour the coast from St-Malo and Dinard. The road approach leads through moorland and pine forests, with parking space at the square-towered **lighthouse.** Views extend to Bréhat, St-Malo and the Channel Isles on clear days, and in misty conditions, a foghorn sounds at intervals. Seabirds crowd on the fissured Fauconnière rocks (a nature reserve). Walks around the cape, past aged cannons rusting in a froth of sea-pinks and white campion, are exceptionally beautiful. Take binoculars and a camera.
www.pays-de-frehel.com

🕂 12B 🍴 La Fauconnière (€€) 🚌 02 to Fréhel from St-Brieuc, Lamballe, Erquy, Le Val-André 🛳 Boat trips from several Emerald Coast resorts
ℹ️ Place de Chambly, Fréhel ☎ 02 96 41 53 81

Phare du Cap Fréhel (lighthouse)

☎ 02 96 41 40 03 🕐 Jul–Aug 2–6 or by appointment ✋ Free

CÔTE D'EMERAUDE

The Emerald Coast lies between the Pointe de Grouin (north of Cancale), and Le Val-André – a stretch of rocky headlands, sandy bays, estuaries, capes and islets. West of St-Malo and Dinard

stretches a long string of small resorts, many named after saints and all with lovely sandy beaches – Sables-d'Or-les-Pins and Le Val-André have two of the best. St-Cast-le-Guildo and Le Val-André are the largest and best equipped holiday resorts. East of Cap Fréhel (above) stands Fort la Latte, a romantic coastal fortress (► below). The Baie de la Frenaye is renowned for mussel-farming, while Erquy specializes in scallops.

✚ 12B

CÔTE DE GRANIT ROSE
Best places to see, pages 42–43.

DINAN
Best places to see, pages 44–45.

FORT LA LATTE
This coastal fortress stands on a rocky promontory severed from the mainland by chasms forming a natural tidal moat, and is entered by a drawbridge. The present structure dates back mainly to the 14th century, but was extensively renovated by Louis XIV's military architect Vauban at the end of the 17th century. It is privately owned and still inhabited, but visitors are welcome for guided tours (not obligatory).

www.castlelalatte.com

✚ 12B ✉ Plévenon–Fréhel ☎ 02 96 41 57 11 🕐 Apr–Sep daily 10–12:30, 2:30–6; rest of year Sat–Sun and school hols 2–5:30 ✋ Moderate

ÎLE DE BRÉHAT

Bréhat, about 2km (1.2 miles) north of Paimpol, consists of two main islands linked by a bridge. Beaches of pink granite fringe the indented coastline. The northern island is wilder and less crowded, while the southern island is scattered with elegant villas and subtropical gardens, and contains Bréhat's main community Le Bourg. Here you can visit the Moulin à Marée du Birlot, a restored 17th century windmill (open Jun–Aug weekends, depending on tide). Cars are banned, but Bréhat is criss-crossed by paths, and small enough to walk or cycle across in an hour.

www.ile-de-brehat.com

✛ 9A 🍴 La Potinière, Plage de Guerzido (€€) 🚢 Cruises and ferries from Pointe de l'Arcouest, Erquy, Binic, St-Quay-Portrieux

ℹ La Mairie, Le Bourg ☎ 02 96 20 04 15

LAMBALLE

France's second largest **Haras National** (national stud farm) is in the inland town of Lamballe. An imposing stable-block in extensive grounds just northwest of Lamballe's historic centre provides quarters for around 70 stallions, plus a number of riding horses. The most notable breed is the beefy Breton draught horse, once used for ploughing and cart-pulling, but they share their stalls with fine-boned thoroughbreds, saddle horses and Irish Connemaras.

   Lamballe presides over an agricultural area, and much of its business is related to its role as market centre for the Penthièvre region. Modern suburbs sprawl in all directions, but its most attractive part is the old quarter around the place du Martray, a compact cluster of noteworthy churches and picturesque timbered houses. The tourist office occupies one of the most striking of these, the Maison du Bourreau (the Hangman's House). The Maison du Bourreau also houses the **Musée Mathurin-Méheut** and the **Musée du Pays de Lamballe.** One is a local folk and

history exhibition; the other displays watercolours, drawings and ceramics by the artist Mathurin Méheut, born in Lamballe in 1882.
www.lamballe-tourisme.com

⊕ 11C 🍴 Restaurants and pubs in old town, such as La Tête Noire, rue du Four (€–€€) 🚌 CAT Lines 01 (St-Cast-le-Guildo), 03 (St-Brieuc) HSNCF links to Dinan, St-Brieuc, Rennes ❓ Equestrian events all summer

ℹ️ Place du Martray ☎ 02 96 31 05 38

Haras National

✉️ Place du Champ de Foire ☎ 02 96 50 06 98; www.haraspatrimoine.com
🕐 Mid-Jun to mid-Sep daily 10–5:30; off season Tue–Sun (guided tours; times vary seasonally) 👋 Moderate

Musée Mathurin-Méheut

✉️ Maison du Bourreau ☎ 02 96 31 19 99 🕐 Apr–Sep Mon–Sat 10–12, 2:30–5 (6 in summer); off season Wed, Thu, Sat 2:30–5; closed Jan–Feb
👋 Inexpensive (joint ticket available)

Musée du Pays de Lamballe

✉️ Maison du Bourreau ☎ 02 96 34 77 63 🕐 Jul–Aug daily 9:30–6:30, Sun 10–12; Apr–Jun, Sep Mon–Sat 10–12, 2–6 (off-season 5pm) 👋 Inexpensive (joint ticket available)

LANNION

This attractive port acts is the administrative centre of the Trégor region. A strategic bridging point and route-hub, it gets crowded on market day (Thursday), but is a lively and enjoyable shopping centre. Long wharves and towpaths fringe the waterfront, and fishing boats give the town a seaside air, though it is some distance inland. The lower town is a well-preserved assembly of old gabled houses. Two prominent churches catch the eye on either side of the river: the monastery of Ste-Anne on the west bank and St-Jean-du-Baly in the centre. The most interesting church, Brélévenez, crowns the hill to the north of town and can be reached via a flight of 142 steps, or less arduously by a circuitous road. Founded by 12th-century Templars, it displays a mixture of styles. The Romanesque apse is a maze of pillars and ornately carved capitals, and the crypt below contains a fine Entombment.

Lannion makes a good excursion base. The Léguer estuary and the wooded valleys inland offer excellent touring. Half a dozen châteaux lie within easy reach, including the stately ruins of Tonquédec and Coatfrec, inhabited Kergrist (gardens open) and richly furnished Rosanbo.
www.ot-lannion.fr

✚ 8B 🍴 Cafés and restaurants in old town (€–€€)
🚌 Lines 6 (Guingamp), 7 (Paimpol), 15 (Pink Granite Coast), 30 (Morlaix) 🚆 Morlaix, Guingamp
❓ Canoeing, kayaking, rafting at the white-water stadium Base Nautique de Lannion ☎ 02 96 37 43 90
ℹ 2 quai d'Aiguillon ☎ 02 96 46 41 00

Tricolaine

PAIMPOL

Paimpol's traditional way of life for centuries was cod-fishing in the perilous waters of Newfoundland and Iceland. Today's trawlers stay closer inshore and oyster-farming in the Trieux estuary has brought new wealth, but the **Musée de la Mer** (Maritime Museum) contains many fascinating reminders of the cod industry. The place du Martray is the focal point. Surrounded by charming old houses, it holds a thriving fish and produce market.

Paimpol lacks good sandy beaches, but makes a fine touring base. Pointe de l'Arcouest, to the north, is the ferry terminal for the Île de Bréhat (➤ 108). Southwards lies the Côte de Goëlo, and the impressive ruins of the 13th-century Abbaye de Beauport (www.abbaye-beauport.com). A scenic route near Plouha takes in Plage Bonaparte, scene of several daring escapes from occupied France during World War II. Inland, the church at Kermaria-an-Iskuit contains a *danse macabre* fresco.

www.paimpol-goelo.com

🔁 9B 🍴 Excellent eating places in old town and port (€–€€€) 🚌 Lines 9 (St-Brieuc), 7 (Lannion)

🛈 19 rue du Général Leclerc ☎ 02 96 20 83 16

Musée de la Mer

✉ Rue de Labenne ☎ 02 96 22 02 19 🕐 Jun–Aug daily 10:30–12:30, 2–6:30; Apr–Sep daily 2–6 👐 Moderate

PERROS-GUIREC

The Pink Granite Coast's largest resort has two splendid beaches, a casino, thalassotherapy centre and modern marina, though the town has no special Breton charm or architectural distinction apart from the church of St-Jacques, with a curious spiky belfry and trefoil porch. Boat trips to the bird sanctuary at Les Sept Îles are popular. Don't miss the watchpath walk to Ploumanac'h past the most spectacular section of the Pink Granite Coast (➤ 42–43).

www.perros-guirec.com

🞤 8A 🍴 Wide choice (€–€€€) 🚌 Line 15 (Lannion, Trégastel, Trébeurden, Pleumeur-Bodou)

ℹ 21 place de l'Hôtel de Ville ☎ 02 96 23 21 15

PLEUMEUR-BODOU

From a distance, a huge white golfball seems to have been left on the heathlands northwest of Lannion. This was once the nerve-centre of France's advanced telecommunications research. It now houses the **Cité des Télecoms,** an exhibition on long-distance message-relay from early semaphore to the latest technology. There's also a **Planétarium** and **Le Village Gaulois** (➤ 69).

www.pleumeur-bodou.com

🞤 7A

Cité des Télecoms

✉ Site de Cosmopolis ☎ 02 96 46 63 80; www.leradome.com 🕐 Jul–Aug daily 10–7; Apr, Sep Mon–Fri 10–6 🖐 Moderate 🍴 On-site cafés (€)

🚌 Line 15 (Perros-Guirec, Lannion, and Pink Granite resorts)

Planétarium

✉ Site de Cosmopolis ☎ 02 96 15 80 32; www.planetarium-bretagne.fr
🕐 See website or telephone for show times 🖐 Moderate

Le Village Gaulois

✉ Site de Cosmopolis ☎ 02 96 91 83 95 🕐 Jul–Aug daily 10:30–7;
Apr–Sep Sun–Fri 2–6 🖐 Moderate

LES SEPT ÎLES

The seven scraps of land visible from the coast around Perros-
Guirec are one of Brittany's most important bird sanctuaries, home
to many species, including petrels and puffins. One island, Rouzic,
is noted for a large colony of breeding gannets. Half-day boat trips
from Ploumanac'h and Perros-Guirec sail all round the islands.
Landings are permitted only on Île aux Moines, which has a ruined
fortress and an old gunpowder factory.

➕ 8A 🚢 Gare Maritime de Perros–Guirec ☎ 02 96 91 10 00;
www.armor-decouverte.fr 🕐 Feb–Nov

TRÉGASTEL

This popular family resort has some of the strangest of the Pink
Granite Coast's rock formations. One extraordinary cluster has

been turned into an **aquarium** of local and
Mediterranean species (tel: 02 96 23 48 58). Near
by, a large indoor waterpark called Forum (tel: 02
96 15 30 44) has several pools maintained at a
comfortable 28°C (82°F). Behind is the main
beach of Plage de Coz-Pors. More intriguing
rocks lie stranded at low tide on Grève Blanche.
www.ville-tregastel.fr

➕ 7A 🍴 Cafés and restaurants near the beaches (€–€€)

🚌 Line 15 (Lannion–Perros-Guirec)

ℹ Place Ste-Anne ☎ 02 96 15 38 38

a walk from Perros-Guirec

The coastguard's watchpath by the seashore from Perros-Guirec leads past an astonishing wilderness of rose-tinted boulders weathered into curious shapes. The coppery pink colours are particularly amazing at sunset.

From Perros-Guirec the path begins at Plage de Trestraou, hugging the shore beneath the cliffs.

At first it is pleasant but unspectacular with views of Les Sept Îles and claw-like headlands. At Pors Rolland the rocks suddenly change gear, revealing weird, organic forms strewn chaotically over the seafront like unclaimed suitcases. The most peculiar of all are located in an orderly conservation zone or 'municipal park', where each formation is given some fanciful name (the Tortoise, the Armchair, etc). At the Maison du Littoral on the edge of the municipal park the emphasis is strictly on environmental care: *'La vie est fragile – ne brisez-la!'* A small display on local geology and natural history is housed inside.

Follow the rocks past the lighthouse round to Plage St-Guirec, where an oratory and a statue mark the local patron saint.

This Celtic monk arrived from Welsh shores in the 6th century and obviously appreciated the scenery. His talents ranged from curing abscesses, retarded children and fiery tempers to an occasional spot of marriage guidance counselling.

In Ploumanac'h, notice the eye-catching Château du Diable, an outcrop of granite rocks in the bay. This is where Heinryk Sienkiewicz wrote Quo Vadis? *at the turn of the 20th century. He was awarded the Nobel prize for literature in 1905.*

Distance 6km (4 miles)
Time About 90 mins each way
Start point Perros-Guirec ✚ 8A
End point Ploumanac'h ✚ 7A
Lunch Take a picnic

TRÉGUIER

The historic town of Tréguier occupies a hilly site on the Jaudy estuary. Its most famous resident was Yves, the patron saint of lawyers. The cathedral is its most impressive building, a mainly Gothic construction of pink granite. The great spire at its west end is a masterpiece of the Decorated period, pierced with multi-patterned holes to reduce wind resistance. Inside lies St Yves' tomb, flanked by votive candles. On the anniversary of his death on 19 May, a *pardon* is held. Outside the

cathedral is place du Martray, surrounded by lovely old buildings. Near the tourist office a poignant war memorial shows a woman in Breton dress grieving for lost menfolk.

www.ville-treguier.fr

➕ 8A 🍴 Good choice in old town (€–€€) 🚌 Line 7 (Lannion–Paimpol), 16 (Lannion–Plougrescant)

❓ Mid-May: Pardon de St-Yves

ℹ️ 67 rue Ernest Renan

☎ 02 96 92 22 33

HOTELS

BRÉLIDY

Château de Brélidy (€€–€€€)

A creeper-covered country manor some distance inland in extensive parkland. Elegant, luxurious interior.

✉ Brélidy ☎ 02 96 95 69 38; www.chateau-brelidy.com 🕐 Closed Jan–Easter

DINAN

D'Avaugour (€€–€€€)

A stylish, well-managed hotel on the main square with gardens stretching over the castle ramparts. No restaurant.

✉ 1 place du Champ ☎ 02 96 39 07 49; www.avaugourhotel.com 🕐 Closed mid-Nov to mid-Feb

ERQUY

Beauséjour (€–€€)

This reliable, flower-decked *Logis* has sea views and appetizing regional food. Half-board terms only in high season.

✉ 21 rue de la Corniche ☎ 02 96 72 30 39; www.beausejour-erquy.com 🕐 Closed mid-Nov to mid-Mar; Sun eve and Mon off-season

ÎLE DE BREHAT

Bellevue (€€)

Idyllic little place near the harbour, with simple, fresh bedrooms and a panoramic seafood restaurant.

✉ Port Clos ☎ 02 96 20 00 05; www.hotel-bellevue-brehat.com 🕐 Closed mid-Nov to Christmas and most of Jan to mid-Feb

PAIMPOL

Repaire du Kerroc'h (€€)

A historic corsaire's house on the quayside with stylish rooms and a well-regarded restaurant.

✉ 29 quai Morand ☎ 02 96 20 50 13; www.chateauxhotels.com/kerroch

PERROS-GUIREC
Manoir du Sphinx (€€€)
An elegant turn-of-the-20th-century building in a spectacular cliff-top location.

✉ 67 chemin de la Messe ☎ 02 96 23 25 42; www.lemanoirdusphinx.com
🕐 Closed mid-Jan to late Feb

PLOUËR-SUR-RANCE
Manoir de Rigourdaine (€€)
A rambling country house in a rural setting overlooking the Rance. Elegant bedrooms in converted courtyard buildings. No restaurant.

✉ Route de Langrolay ☎ 02 96 86 89 96; www.hotel-rigourdaine.fr
🕐 Closed mid-Nov to Mar

SABLES-D'OR-LES-PINS
Manoir de la Salle (€€–€€€)
Attractively renovated stone manor on the Emerald Coast.

✉ Rue du Lac ☎ 02 96 72 38 29; www.manoirdelasalle.com
🕐 Closed Oct–Mar

ST-CAST-LE-GUILDO
Port Jacquet (€)
Charming stone-built hotel high above the port with bright bedrooms and good cooking.Sea views and a warm welcome.

✉ 32 rue du Port ☎ 02 96 41 97 18; www.port-jacquet.com

TRÉBEURDEN
Ti al Lannec (€€€)
Long-established luxury hotel in a wonderful Pink Granite Coast location. Welcoming owners, elegant décor and beautiful grounds.

✉ 14 allée de Mezo Guen ☎ 02 96 15 01 01; www.tiallannec.com
🕐 Closed mid-Nov to Feb

TRÉGUIER
Aigue Marine (€€)
A spacious modern hotel by the marina. Light, airy bedrooms, good leisure facilities and an excellent restaurant.

✉ Port de Plaisance ☎ 02 96 92 97 00; www.aiguemarine.fr 🕐 Closed Jan
to mid-Feb

Kastell Dinec'h (€€)
Comfortable converted manor farmhouse in quiet setting just
outside town. Good country cooking.
✉ Route de Lannion ☎ 02 96 92 49 39; www.kastell-dinech.net
🕐 Closed Jan–Apr, mid-Oct

LE VAL-ANDRE
Grand Hôtel du Val-André (€€–€€€)
A glorious seafront location and attractive grounds. Spacious,
comfortable rooms and courteous management.
✉ 80 rue Amiral Charner ☎ 02 96 72 20 56; www.grand-hotel-val-andre.fr
🕐 Closed Jan

RESTAURANTS

DINAN
Café Terrasses (€€)
This bright all-day bistro overlooking the port is a favourite haunt
for a flexible range of well-prepared dishes. Late opening all year.
✉ 2–4 rue du Quai ☎ 02 96 39 09 60

Mère Pourcel (€€–€€€)
A long-established culinary landmark in a handsome timbered
building. Tables outside in summer.
✉ 3 place des Merciers ☎ 02 96 39 03 80 🕐 Closed Mon, Tue in winter,
Sun eve off-season

Le Romarin (€–€€)
A welcoming family-run *salon-de-thé* specializing in home-made
cakes and savoury tarts. Takeaway service.
✉ 11 place des Cordeliers ☎ 02 96 85 20 37 🕐 Closed eves in winter

ERQUY
L'Escurial (€€)
This plain building on the central seafront road disguises one of

the best restaurants in the area. Scallops are a local speciality.

✉ Boulevard de la Mer ☎ 02 96 72 31 56 🕐 Closed Jan, Sun eve off-season, Mon

MÛR-DE-BRETAGNE
Auberge Grand'Maison (€€€)

A gastronomic place of pilgrimage on an inland lake. The chef-patron is one of the best cooks in Brittany. Book ahead.

✉ 1 rue Léon-le-Cerf ☎ 02 96 28 51 10 🕐 Closed mid- to late Feb, most of Oct, Sun eve, Mon, Tue off-season

PAIMPOL
L'Ecluse (€–€€)

Down in the dockyard, this airy shed attracts customers in search of perfectly fresh, simply cooked fare served in an easy-going, nautical atmosphere. Breton music and chalkboard specials.

✉ Quai Armand Dayot ☎ 02 96 55 03 38 🕐 Closed Wed in Jun

PERROS-GUIREC
Les Feux des Iles (€€–€€€)

Upmarket hotel-restaurant with panoramic views towards Les Sept Îles from the modern dining room.

✉ 53 boulevard Clemenceau ☎ 02 96 23 22 94 🕐 Closed early Mar, early Oct, mid-Dec to early Jan, Sun eve, Fri eve off-season

PLANCOËT
Crouzil (€€€)

Formidable cooking and a spectacular wine-list at this celebrated restaurant-with-rooms. Seafood specialities.

✉ 20 les Quais ☎ 02 96 84 10 24 🕐 Closed early Oct, mid-Jan, Mon, Sun eve, Tue lunch off-season

PLOUMANAC'H
Coste Mor (€)

Despite the name, the food is inexpensive and the dining room faces one of Brittany's most dazzling seascapes. Tables outside.

✉ Plage de St-Guirec ☎ 02 96 91 65 55 🕐 Closed mid-Nov to Mar

ST-BRIEUC
Aux Pesked (€€–€€€)
A sophisticated modern restaurant on the hill leading down to the port, using much local produce. Daunting wine list.

✉ 59 rue du Légué ☎ 02 96 33 34 65 🕐 Closed early Jan, one week in May, one week in Sep, Sat lunch, Sun eve, Mon

TRÉGUIER
Le Hangar (€)
No frills at this battered old boatshed down by the marina, but you can eat a hearty plateful of mussels and chips here, served with a local Dremmwell beer.

✉ Port de Plaisance 🕐 02 96 92 47 46 🕐 Closed Mon, Tue off-season

LE VAL-ANDRÉ
Au Biniou (€€)
A well-known local favourite serving interesting seafood dishes in traditional surroundings near the casino.

✉ 121 rue Clemenceau 🕐 02 96 72 24 35 🕐 Closed Feb, Tue eve, Wed off-season

SHOPPING

ANTIQUES
The little port of Dahouët near Le Val-André is a mecca for bargain-hunters. Several of the old sail-lofts on the quayside are now *brocante* or antique stores.

Comptoirs de l'Ouest
An Aladdin's cave of bric-a-brac and second-hand goods crammed into a barn-like junk shop.

✉ Port de Dahouët 🕐 02 96 63 18 84 🕐 Closed Mon–Wed

ARTS AND CRAFTS
Dinan is one of the best places to look for regional products. Many of the ancient buildings on the steep street leading down to the port are now craft studios or galleries.

Angora de France

One of the last angora farms in France. See how the goats are raised and inspect the products made from their silky wool.

✉ Château de Coat-Carric, Pléstin-les-Grèves ☎ 02 96 35 62 49

Tannerie de Callac

Fish skin is an unusual speciality at this leatherware outlet in Callac, southwest of Guingamp. It sells belts, wallets, gloves, handbags and luggage.

✉ ZA de Kerguiniou, Callac ☎ 02 96 45 50 68; www.tannerie-de-callac.com

FOOD
Les Gavottes

This appetizing little shop sells speciality biscuits and sweets including *gavottes* – a crisp, wafer-like version of *crêpes dentelles*.

✉ 9 rue du Château, Locmaria ☎ 02 96 87 06 48; www.locmaria.fr

ENTERTAINMENT

NIGHTLIFE
A la Truye qui File

At the sign of the spinning sow, this atmospheric inn occupies a fine old medieval building in a cobbled alley locally nicknamed 'Thirsty Street' because of all its lively bars.

✉ 14 rue de la Cordonnerie, Dinan ☎ 02 96 39 72 29

Art et Saveur

This arty café in a converted sail-loft overlooking the old port of Daouët morphs into an atmospheric wine-bar and bistro in the evenings, with the odd jazz soirée or art exhibition.

✉ 28 quai des Terre-Neuvas, Port de Dahouët, Le Val-André ☎ 02 96 63 19 17; www.art-et-saveur.com

Le Pub

This piano bar and disco pub near the harbour puts on a varied range of music and appeals to a wide age range. It has a bar on the ground floor and a dance floor upstairs. Bar meals served.

✉ 3 rue des Islandais, Paimpol ☎ 02 96 20 82 31; www.lepub-paimpol.fr

Ille-et-Vilaine

This easterly *département* in Haute-Bretagne has two of Brittany's best-known towns: the popular ferry port of St-Malo, and the stylish resort of Dinard. It has hardly any of Brittany's rugged coastline, yet is by no means devoid of scenery and sightseeing. Don't miss the grand fortresses of Fougères, Combourg and Vitré that once protected the independent Duchy from its jealous French sister. The Breton capital, Rennes, deserves a day or two's exploration. And slip briefly across the Norman border for a look at one of France's greatest sights, the island abbey of Mont-St-Michel.

Rennes

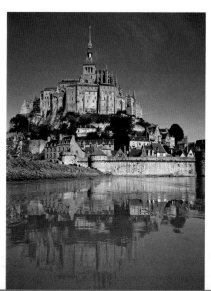

The brief stretch of coast between the Rance and Normandy consists of flat, brackish saltmarshes. Southwards carve the sluggish waterways that give the *département* its name, linking the Channel with the Atlantic and saving fair-weather sailors the anxiety of negotiating Finistère's treacherous coastline.

123

CANCALE

Cancale is renowned for its oysters. The grey shoreline is covered with the shallow concrete beds *(parcs)* where they mature. After harvesting and cleaning, they are piled high on local stalls, or at the seafood restaurants along the waterfront in the La Houle.

Just south of the port lies **La Ferme Marine,** an oyster farm and museum devoted to the life and times of the local mollusc (guided tours). After an introductory film-show, visitors are shown the oyster-beds and the workshops where washing, grading and packing take place. A restored *bisquine* (oyster boat) is now used for pleasure trips.
www.cancale-tourisme.fr

✠ 13B 🍴 Seafood restaurants at the port (€–€€€) 🚌 St-Malo–Mont-St-Michel

ℹ 44 rue du Port ☎ 02 99 89 63 72

La Ferme Marine

✉ Plage de l'Aurore ☎ 02 99 89 69 99; www.ferme-marine.com
🕙 Jun–Sep, tours daily 2 (English); mid-Feb to Oct Mon–Fri 3 (French only)
✋ Moderate

COMBOURG

The massive 11th-century castle by the lakeshore, all crenellations and pepperpot towers, is the main focus of attention in this small town. Literary visitors have an additional interest in the building. The **castle** was the home of René de Chateaubriand, who wrote of his miserable childhood in the haunted bedroom.

www.combourg.org
✠ 14D 🍴 L'Ecrivain, place St-Gilduin (€€) 🚌 11 (Rennes)
🚉 St-Malo–Rennes
ℹ Place Albert Parent
☎ 02 99 73 13 93

Château de Combourg

✉ 23 rue des Princes ☎ 02 99 73 22 95; www.combourg.net 🕐 Apr–Oct 2–5:30 (guided tours). Closed Sat off-peak. Park: Apr–Oct 9–12, 2–6 💶 Moderate

DINARD

This fashionable seaside resort was a mere fishing village until the mid-19th century. The sheltered climate and beautiful setting attracted wealthy visitors who built ornate villas on the wooded cliffs above three sandy beaches (best admired from the Promenade du Clair-de-Lune). Holiday homes, smart yachts and striped beach-huts jostle along the seafront. Dinard's excellent facilities include an Olympic-sized swimming pool, a casino, the modern Palais des Arts et Festivals and boat trips up the Rance and along the Emerald Coast. Regattas, tennis tournaments, bridge and afternoon tea punctuate the social calendar. On the Rance estuary just south of Dinard is the world's first tidal power station (➤ 139).
www.ot-dinard.com

➕ 13C 🍴 Wide choice (€–€€€) 🚌 16 (St-Malo–Emerald Coast), 7a (Rennes) ⛴ Ferry to St-Malo; Rance cruises to Dinan; coastal trips
ℹ 2 boulevard Féart ☎ 02 99 46 94 12

DOL-DE-BRETAGNE

Dol stands on the remains of a cliff amid low-lying pastureland reclaimed from the sea. The surrounding fields are famous for the prized *pré-salé* lamb raised here. Dol was founded in the 6th century by St Samson, one of Brittany's 'founding saints'. Its gaunt granite cathedral still dominates the town. A former school beside the cathedral houses an ambitious exhibition on medieval cathedrals, and the construction methods used during the period, called **Cathédraloscope.** The explanatory labels to the models, diagrams and photographs have been translated into English but are rather technical. Several streets of picturesque timbered houses dating from the Middle Ages lie nearby.

Just north of the town, the Mont-Dol, a granite mound topped by an ancient chapel, erupts suddenly from the saltmarsh plains, offering extensive views of the surrounding countryside. A legend declares this is the site of St Michael's apocalyptic struggle with Satan, and if you let your imagination run away with you, it is just about possible to spot St Michael's footprint in a clifftop rock by the chapel.

www.pays-de-dol.com

➕ 14C 🍴 Le Moulin du Mont, Mont-Dol (€–€€) 🚌 Line 17 (Mont-St-Michel, St-Malo, Fougéres) 🚆 Caen, Dinan, St-Malo, Rennes
ℹ️ Place de la Cathédrale ☎ 02 99 48 15 37

Cathédraloscope

✉️ Place de la Cathédrale ☎ 02 99 48 35 30 🕐 Apr–Oct daily 10–7
✋ Moderate

FOUGÈRES

Fougères is a frontier town, former capital of the swampy Marches dividing France and Brittany. For Victor-Hugo it was 'the Carcassonne of the North'. Its dominant feature is its castle (➤ 40–41), set in a tight loop of the River Nançon. The rocky spurs

above the castle walls cradle the upper town of mostly 18th-century buildings – a stiff climb from the riverbank. Precipitous steps and alleys lead from the back of St-Léonard's church down to a much older sector around the place du Marchix, where tanneries and mills can be seen among a cluster of stone and half-timbered 16th-century houses, dominated by the slender spire of St-Sulpice.

Fougères grew wealthy, like many Breton towns, on the textile trades of wool and hemp. Later it turned to shoe manufacture, supplemented by post-war ventures into electronics and robotics. Northeast of Fougères, beyond uninspiring modern suburbs, extends a state forest of beech, spruce and chestnut.

www.ot-fougeres.fr

➕ 16D 🍴 Restaurants and cafés in upper town, such as Les Voyageurs, 10 place Gambetta, or in old quarter around castle (€–€€) 🚌 Line 9 Rennes, 17 St-Malo, 14 Vitré
ℹ️ 2 rue Nationale ☎ 02 99 94 12 20

a walk around old Fougères

Head for the upper town and park in one of the squares near the tourist office. From here, walk along the pedestrianised rue Nationale.

Notice the elegant 14th-century belfry behind the covered market. Further along, a picturesque jettied and porticoed 16th-century house contains a museum dedicated to the Impressionist painter Emmanuel de la Villéon (1858–1944), a native of Fougères. About 60 of his drawings and watercolours (mostly local scenes) are displayed inside. Near the end of the street stands the church of St-Léonard by the Renaissance town hall. Behind the church, which dates from the 16th century, neatly kept municipal gardens give a splendid terrace vantage point over plunging wooded chasms, the mellow, brown-beamed houses of the Marchix quarter and the tremendous fortress below.

Using these as your target, thread your way down the stepped alleys and across the river via rue des Tanneurs.

The streets around the place du Marchix contain many ancient buildings. Gothic St-Sulpice church, built in Flamboyant style, contains fine 18th-century woodwork, 15th-century granite altarpieces and a charming 12th-century statue of the Virgin Mary (Notre-Dame-des-Marais) suckling a Child who looks well past weaning age.

Visit the castle (➤ 40–41) next, but take a walk outside the walls for an impressive overview before going inside. Walk the ramparts.

Notice the foundations of the keep (destroyed in 1166), and the waterwheels by the gatehouse.

Return to the upper town via rue de la Pinterie, a steep climb. More gardens halfway up the hill offer a chance to catch your breath, and a final panorama of the castle and river.

Distance 3km/2 miles (very hilly! – a petit train will spare your legs if you can't face the final climb)
Time Allow half a day with time to look round the sights
Start/end point The tourist office in the upper town (2 rue Nationale)
Lunch Les Voyageurs (€–€€) ✉ 10 place Gambetta (100m/110yds east of tourist office) ☎ 02 99 99 14 17

HÉDÉ

Woods and water are the lasting impressions of this hill village. Streams, cascades and ponds gleam all around, and lush, terraced gardens almost hide the crumbling stone houses and castle ruins perched on an outcrop of rock. In the churchyard, bronze memorials commemorate fallen war heroes.

Just north of the village at La Madeleine, the Ille-et-Rance canal passes through a magnificent staircase of 11 locks. The towpath walk is pleasant, though overgrown in places. A small exhibition about the Ille-et-Rance canal stands near the locks.

🛏 13D 🍴 Charming restaurants in quaint buildings, such as La Vieille Auberge, Hostellerie du Vieux Moulin, Le Genty Home (all on Tinténiac road, €€) 🚌 Line 8 (Rennes–St-Malo)
ℹ️ La Mairie ☎ 02 99 45 46 18

MENHIR DE CHAMP-DOLENT

Just southeast of Dol-de-Bretagne, off the D795, is a large, single standing stone about 9m (30ft) high, stuck incongruously in a maize field. The menhir is alleged to have fallen from heaven to divide the armies of two warring brothers (Champ Dolent means 'Field of Sorrow'). It is said to be gradually sinking into the ground a couple of centimetres every century, and when it vanishes the world will end. The stone is freely accessible near the road, and can even be admired from a picnic table, though it has no markings or particular features of interest.
🛏 14C

REDON

This attractive flower-filled town is an important junction: roads,
railways, waterways and regional boundaries converge here.
The Nantes–Brest Canal crosses the Vilaine at this point, joining
the Oust to the north of the town. Ille-et-Vilaine,
Morbihan and Loire-Atlantique meet on Redon's
doorstep, and six major roads intersect. When the
River Vilaine was fully navigable, Redon was a
significant inland port. The elegant homes of former
shipowners line the waterfront and parts of the old
town. Today, river access to the south coast is
blocked by the Arzal dam near La Roche-Bernard,
but pleasure craft ply the local waterways in great
numbers, negotiating Redon via a complicated
series of locks.

The Grande Rue is one of its finest streets, full of
splendid stone and half-timbered buildings decked
with bright window-boxes.

Redon's main landmark is the church of St-Sauveur, a curious mixture of styles. A Romanesque lantern tower sits unexpectedly on Gothic buttressing, with a separate bell tower nearby. The **Musée de la Batellerie** charts the history of the port and its waterborne trade. Redon makes an enjoyable excursion base for a day or two, with useful hotels and some excellent restaurants. You can hire bikes, canoes or canal boats from numerous outlets in the town and port. In late autumn, the chestnut forests on the outskirts of town take centre stage in a festival called the Fête de Teillouse. During the October harvest, local restaurants compete to produce chestnut-based dishes – its terrines are justly renowned.

The quiet moorland around St-Just, about 18km (11 miles) northeast of Redon, is sprinkled with neolithic monuments. The standing stones and dolmens at Landes de Cojoux and Croix St-Pierre can be freely explored (summer weekend guided tours in French only from St-Just).

www.redon.fr

🕐 24H 🍴 Good choice in town centre and port, such as La Bogue, 3 rue des États 🚌 10 (La Gacilly–Rochefort-en-Terre), 10B (Rennes) 🚆 Rennes, Vannes, Quimper and Nantes 🚢 River and canal cruises along the Oust and down the Vilaine to the Arzal dam; boat hire ❓ Fête de Teillouse (a chestnut festival and gastronomic fair, late Oct) 🛈 Place de la République ☎ 02 99 71 06 04

Musée de la Batellerie

✉ Quai Jean-Bart ☎ 02 99 72 30 95 🕐 Jun to mid-Sep daily 10–12, 3–6; Mon, Wed and weekends 2–6 off-peak 💶 Inexpensive

RENNES

Rennes is a burgeoning industrial and academic centre with a cosmopolitan air. Its inland location entices few holidaymakers from the coastal areas, but it's worth a day's excursion. Driving and parking in the city centre can be difficult, but Rennes is well served by public transport from most Breton cities. The central sights are compact and easily explored on foot. Nightlife is lively, especially in the old quarter. During July, Rennes hosts a major arts festival called Les Tombées de la Nuit (www.ville-rennes.fr), where rock and jazz fans congregate.

The city developed in Roman times from a

Gaulish settlement. It became a strategic route-hub, the Breton capital in 1562, and played a leading role in Brittany's struggle to retain an independent voice after unification with France. In 1720 a fire in the old town burned for nearly a week. The charred centre was rebuilt in neoclassical style. Today, examples of this grand civic architecture stand alongside the medieval buildings that survived the fire. In 1994 the **Palais du Parlement** (Breton Parliament) was badly damaged during fish-price riots. It has now been restored to its former glory. The Hôtel de Ville (town hall) dominates the place de la Marie. St-Pierre, Rennes' cathedral, is a relatively undistinguished 19th-century building containing a fine Flemish altarpiece. East of the old town, the peaceful Jardin

du Thabor was once the garden of the Benedictine abbey of St-Melaine.

Rennes has several excellent museums. The **Musée des Beaux-Arts** has an important collection. The **Musée de Bretagne** has been relocated at Les Champs Libres, a dynamic cultural centre with an interactive science museum, planetarium and exhibition galleries. Southeast, at Ferme de la Bintinais, the **Ecomusée du Pays de Rennes** traces the evolution of agricultural life in Brittany from the 16th century.

www.tourisme-rennes.com

✚ 14E 🍴 Excellent choice in central areas (€–€€€) 🚇 The Métro is mainly geared to commuter travel (www.star.fr) 🚌 Major route-hub for inter-urban and local services throughout Brittany; many local buses 🚆 National TGV and regional services throughout Brittany ✈ International and domestic flights (Air France/Brit'Air/Flybe)

🛈 11 rue St-Yves ☎ 02 99 67 11 11

Musée des Beaux-Arts

✚ Rennes 3c ✉ 20 quai Émile Zola ☎ 02 23 62 17 45; www.mbar.org 🕐 Wed–Sun 10–12, 2–6, Tue 10–6. Closed Mon and public hols 🖐 Moderate 🚇 République

Musée de Bretagne

✚ Rennes 4e ✉ 10 cours des Allies ☎ 02 23 40 66 00; www.leschampslibres.fr 🕐 Tue 12–9, Wed–Fri 12–7, Sat and Sun 2–7 🖐 Moderate

Ecomusée du Pays de Rennes

✚ Rennes 3f (off map) ✉ South of centre on Noyal–Chatillon road ☎ 02 99 51 38 15; www.ecomusee-rennes-metropole.fr 🕐 Apr–Sep Tue–Sun 9–6; Oct–Mar Tue–Fri 9–12, 2–6, Sat 2–6, Sun 2–7. Closed Mon and public hols 🖐 Moderate 🚌 Line 15 🚆 Triangle

a walk around old Rennes

Start in place de la Mairie by the imposing Hôtel de Ville.

This building with its huge clocktower is one of Jacques Gabriel's most confident municipal statements after the great fire of 1720 (free guided tours). Opposite stands a charmingly ornate theatre.

Head west along rue du Guesclin then north along rue Clisson and west again along rue de la Monnaie.

Notice the rococo-style church of St-Sauveur. Our Lady of Miracles saved Rennes from the English in 1357. Marble plaques thank her for latterday favours, including success in exams. The cathedral of St-Pierre, a 19th-century building in Roman style, contains a Flemish altarpiece in a side chapel. Find the light-switch to enjoy its amazing 3-D effects.

Thread through a quaint maze of streets lined with picturesque houses south of the cathedral, then north via rue des Dames.

The Porte-Mordelaise is the last remnant of the 15th-century ramparts, through which the dukes of Brittany passed for their coronations.

Head northeast through the place des Lices.

Medieval jousts were held in this fine old square. The art nouveau halles (covered market) dates from 1622.

Pass through place St-Michel and place Ste-Anne, head south via place du Champ Jacquet, then east along rue la Fayette and rue Nationale to the place du Parlement de Bretagne.

The tall, stripy buildings in place du Champ Jacquet are 17th-century, predating the Great Fire. Brittany's restored Parliament building makes an impressive statement on a spacious square of orderly gardens.

Head east along rue Victor Hugo, north up rue du Général M Guillaudot and through the Jardin du Thabor via place St-Mélaine. Finish the walk on the south bank of the river, at the Musée des Beaux-Arts (quai Émile Zola).

Distance 3.5km (2 miles)
Time Half a day, including visiting the main sights
Start point Hôtel de Ville 🚉 Rennes 2C
End point Musée des Beaux-Arts 🚉 Rennes 3C
Lunch Lots of choice en route. Try Crêperie Ste-Anne (€)
✉ 5 place Ste-Anne ☎ 02 99 79 22 72

LA ROCHE AUX FÉES
Stranded way inland some 15km (9 miles) west of La Guerche-de-Bretagne, La Roche aux Fées attracts far fewer visitors than Carnac or Locmariaquer. It is, however, a most impressive megalithic monument, consisting of 42 slabs of mauve schist carefully balanced into what looks like

an *allée couverte* or gallery grave high enough to walk upright inside (freely accessible). There is much speculation about its age and origins. Traditionally, engaged couples come here and separately count the stones. If they agree on the number, a happy future is presaged.

✚ 27G

ST-MALO
Best places to see, pages 54–55.

USINE MARÉMOTRICE DE LA RANCE
A huge concrete barrage blocks the mouth of the Rance, creating a large reservoir upstream, and used as a bridge by the St-Malo–Dinard road. From parking places at either end, walkways lead across the dam, from which you can watch sinewy torrents racing through the sluice gates with colossal force to the generators beneath. A visitor centre on the Dinard side explains its internal workings.

The dam was first opened in 1967, and spans 750m (820yds), curbing a reservoir of 22sq km (8.5sq miles). A lock surmounted by a swing-bridge enables sizeable boats to pass through. The 24 generators housed in a vast tunnel within the barrage generate over 600 million kWh a year, using both ebb and flow tides. However, this massively imaginative and costly project generates only about 3 per cent of Brittany's total electricity needs, and although it sounds environmentally friendly, its effects on local wildlife are significant.

www.edf.fr

✚ 13C ✉ La Richardais ☎ 02 99 16 37 14 🕐 Fri 1–7 (daily during school hols) ♿ Free 🚌 Lines 14 (St-Malo–Dinard), 11 (Dinan–Dinard) ⛴ Rance cruises; ferry (St-Malo–Dinard)

AN EXCURSION TO LE MONT-ST-MICHEL

The fickle course of the River Couesnant (the Norman boundary) now deprives Brittany by a hair's breadth of one of France's most evocative sights. The abbey-crowned island of Le Mont-St-Michel tapers mirage-like above the swirling mudflats of the bay. A golden statue of the Archangel Michael is poised on its topmost spire. It attracts more visitors than anywhere else in provincial France. Once in a lifetime, at least, everyone should see it.

Arrive early to beat the crowds (preferably before 9am when the abbey opens). Drive across the causeway, and park beside it, taking careful note of the tide tables (parts of the car-park flood at high tide). Enter the island near the tourist office, and collect a plan of the site. Make your way up the steep, narrow Grande Rue, lined with souvenir shops and cafés.

The touristy village at the base of the Mount may be off-putting, but the medieval buildings are undeniably quaint. Soon the crowds thin out and the atmosphere becomes much more peaceful. Flights of steps lead everywhere, and it's a steep climb. Several little museums can be visited on the way to the abbey. The Musée Maritime is an exhibition about the bay and its exceptional tides, which race across the flat sands faster than a horse can gallop (or so it is claimed). Next is the Archéoscope, an archangelic multimedia presentation about the abbey (St Michael is your guide). Still further up near the parish church is Tiphaine's House, built by the medieval warrior Bertrand Du Guesclin (then commander of the Mount) for his scholarly wife in 1365.

Continue up the hill and enter the abbey.

The abbey is a masterpiece of Romanesque and Gothic architecture. Founded in 708 by the Bishop of Avranches, it has been a place of pilgrimage for over a thousand years. Known as La

Merveille (The Marvel), it seems as delicately balanced as a house of cards, some sections cantilevered over thin air, others tightly buttressed to the living granite. Beyond the church, a signed route leads through the refectory, cloisters and Knights' Hall to the crypt.

After visiting the interior, take a walk around the ramparts and gardens for a breathtaking overview of the abbey and the bay.

✚ 15C ☎ Abbey 02 33 89 80 00; www.ot-montsaintmichel.com or www.monum.fr 🕐 May–Aug daily 9–7; Sep–Apr 9:30–6 (abbey church service at 12:15) 🎫 No charge to visit the Mount but parking and sights expensive. Abbey ticket price includes a choice of self-guided, escorted or audio-tour; individual or combined tickets available for the museums 🍴 Cafés and restaurants in the village; such as La Mère Poulard (€–€€€) ✉ Grande Rue ☎ 02 33 89 68 68 or Les Terrasses Poulard (€€) ☎ 02 33 89 02 02 🚌 Line 17 (St-Malo–Pontorson), then Line 15, or some direct services from St-Malo (Les Courriers Breton)

VITRÉ

After Dinan, Vitré is perhaps Brittany's best-preserved medieval town. Close to the town, a hilly belvedere by the Vilaine, called the Tertres Noires, gives a splendid view of its bristling turrets, drum towers and ramparts. This **château** dates mainly from the 13th century, but was enlarged and modified during the 16th and restored after years of neglect in the late 19th century. Vitré's location on the borders between France and Brittany made it a constant target during struggles in the Middle Ages. The castle houses several interesting **museums.**

The old town stretches through cobbled hilly streets below the castle. Some if its half-timbered houses are now converted into shops and restaurants. Best are those along rue de la Baudrairie. Much of the town's revenue comes from tourism; in former centuries its prosperity came mostly from the textile trade. Wealthy merchants settled here and built fine mansions.

Southeast of Vitré stands Madame de Sevigné's former home, the Château des Rochers-Sevigné.

www.ot-vitre.fr

🕂 15E 🍴 La Taverne de l'Eau (€€), 12 rue de la Baudrairie 🚌 Line 14 (Fougères), 20 (La Guerche-de-Bretagne) 🚆 Rennes and Normandy
ℹ️ Place du Général-de-Gaulle ☎ 02 99 75 04 46

Château/museums

✉ Place du Château ☎ 02 99 75 04 54 🕐 Apr–Jun daily 10–12, 2–5:30; Jul–Sep daily 10–6; Oct–Mar Wed–Fri 10–12, 2–5:30 💷 Moderate (museum pass gives entrance to all museums and the Château des Rochers-Sevigné)

HOTELS

CANCALE

Continental (€€–€€€)

Attractive waterfront hotel with panoramic sea views. Excellent restaurant.

✉ 4 quai Thomas ☎ 02 99 89 60 16; www.hotel-cancale.com

🕐 Closed mid-Nov and Jan

Pointe de Grouin (€€)

Solid stone-built hotel on spectacular promontory overlooking the Île des Landes. Often crowded with day-trippers, but peaceful at night. Traditional cooking.

✉ Pointe de Grouin ☎ 02 99 89 60 55; www.pointedugrouin.com

🕐 Closed mid-Nov to Mar

CHÂTEAUBOURG

Ar Milin (€€–€€€)

Large, well-equipped hotel-restaurant in converted mill with wooded grounds. Good leisure facilities.

✉ 30 rue de Paris ☎ 02 99 00 30 91; www.armilin.com 🕐 Closed early Dec–early Jan

Pen-Roc (€€)

A bright, luxurious hotel in a modernized farmhouse with rural surroundings and lovely grounds. Excellent facilities and ambitious cooking.

✉ La Peinière, St-Didier ☎ 02 99 00 33 02; www.penroc.fr

🕐 Closed Christmas, New Year and late Feb

COMBOURG

Du Château (€–€€€)

A comfortable superior *Logis* with a wide selection of rooms, some with castle views. Fine restaurant and a generous buffet breakfast.

✉ 1 place Chateaubriand ☎ 02 99 73 00 38; www.hotelduchateau.com

🕐 Closed mid-Dec to mid-Jan

DINARD
Grand Hôtel Barrière de Dinard (€€€)
A grand seafront institution occupying a prime location at the mouth of the Rance. Formal, impressive interior and luxurious facilities.

✉ 46 avenue George V ☎ 02 99 88 26 26; www.lucienbarriere.com
🕐 Closed mid-Nov to Feb

Reine Hortense (€€€)
Refined *fin-de-siècle* residence with lovely views of the main beach from peaceful gardens. Breakfast terrace. No restaurant.

✉ 19 rue Malouine ☎ 02 99 46 54 31; www.villa-reine-hortense.com
🕐 Closed Oct–Mar

FOUGÈRES
Balzac (€)
A simple but charming old granite house on the main street of the upper town. Attractively refurbished bedrooms.

✉ 15 rue Nationale ☎ 02 99 99 42 46; www.balzachotel.com

LA GOUESNIÈRE
Tirel-Guérin (€€–€€€)
Acclaimed restaurant-with-rooms beside a quaint old railway station near Cancale. Excellent facilities include an indoor swimming pool. Superb cooking.

✉ Gare de la Gouesnière, St-Méloir-des-Ondes ☎ 02 99 89 10 46; www.tirel-guerin.com 🕐 Mid-Dec to Jan

RENNES
Le Coq-Gadby (€€–€€€)
In a quiet residential district, this period mansion in spacious grounds has the air of an elegant private home, with antiques and *objets d'arts*. Acclaimed restaurant.

✉ 156 rue d'Antrain ☎ 02 99 38 05 55; www.lecoq-gadby.com

ST-MALO
L'Ascott (€€–€€€)
An elegant 19th-century house in quiet gardens, with dashingly designed bedrooms and high-quality fittings. No restaurant.

✉ 35 rue du Chapitre, St-Servan ☎ 02 99 81 89 93; www.ascotthotel.com
🕐 Closed Jan

Le Beaufort (€€–€€€)
Chic décor in cool muted tones gives this seafront hotel a classy feel. Direct access to the beach. Piano bar. No restaurant.

✉ 25 chausée de Sillon ☎ 02 99 40 99 99; www.hotel-beaufort.com

Manoir du Cunningham (€€–€€€)
Stylishly renovated 17th-century building near the ferry terminal. Spacious, exotic bedrooms and marina views.

✉ 9 place Monseigneur Duchesne, St-Servan ☎ 02 99 21 33 33; www.st-malo-hotel-cunningham.com 🕐 Closed mid-Nov to mid-Mar

La Rance (€€)
This friendly and civilized little place at Port Solidor has lovely estuary views and well-equipped bedrooms. No restaurant.

✉ 15 quai Sébastopol, St-Servan ☎ 02 99 81 78 63; www.larancehotel.com

Le Valmarin (€€–€€€)
A charming old *malouinière* (corsair's home), elegantly furnished and in tranquil grounds. No restaurant.

✉ 7 rue Jean XXIII, St-Servan ☎ 02 99 81 94 76; www.levalmarin.com
🕐 Closed Jan

VITRÉ
Petit-Billot (€)
This simple place on the edge of the old town offers a warm welcome and neat, modern rooms. Excellent value. No restaurant – but special terms at Le Potager next door.

✉ 5 bis place Général Leclerc ☎ 02 99 75 02 10; www.hotel-vitre.com
🕐 Closed Christmas–New Year

RESTAURANTS

CANCALE

Maisons de Bricourt (€€€)

Olivier Roellinger's acclaimed cooking can be sampled in several locations near Cancale, but the grand stone house in the town centre is his family home. Superb seafood.

✉ 1 rue Duguesclin ☎ 02 99 89 64 76; www.maisons-de-bricourt.com
🕐 Closed mid-Dec to mid-Mar, Mon lunch, Tue, Wed, Fri lunch off-season

Le Surcouf (€€)

One of the best waterfront restaurants in La Houle. Splendid seafood and home-baked buckwheat bread.

✉ 7 quai Gambetta ☎ 02 99 89 61 75 🕐 Closed Dec, Jan, Wed, Tue off-season

COMBOURG

L'Ecrivain (€–€€)

This well-regarded place opposite the church serves a limited but inventive choice of dishes. Good-value set menus.

✉ 1 place St-Gilduin ☎ 02 99 73 01 61 🕐 Closed early Oct, Feb hols, Thu, Wed and Sun eves off-season

DINARD

Didier Méril (€€)

Polished, affable service and accomplished cooking in sleek, modern premises near the beach and casino. Regularly changing menus.

✉ 1 place Général de Gaulle ☎ 02 99 46 95 74 🕐 Closed late Nov–early Dec, Wed off-season

FOUGÈRES

Les Voyageurs (€€–€€€)

Reliable, classic cooking in the upper town. Lots of regional produce and tasty desserts.

✉ 10 place Gambetta ☎ 02 99 99 14 17 🕐 Closed Easter–Sep, Fri, Sat lunch off-season

LA GUERCHE-DE-BRETAGNE
La Calèche (€–€€)
Good-value lunch menus in a bright dining room near La Roche-aux-Fées.

✉ 16 avenue Général Leclerc ☎ 02 99 96 21 63 🕐 Closed early Aug, Fri eve, Sun, Mon

HÉDÉ
La Vieille Auberge (€–€€)
A pretty, terraced restaurant in a 17th-century granite house beside a lake.

✉ Route de Tinténiac ☎ 02 99 45 46 25 🕐 Closed late Aug–early Sep, mid-Feb to early Mar, Sun eve, Mon

REDON
La Bogue (€€)
Enterprising regional cooking in a quaint setting near the town hall. Seasonal chestnut specialities.

✉ 3 rue des Etats ☎ 02 99 71 12 95 🕐 Closed Sun eve, Mon

RENNES
Au Marché des Lices (€)
A fine *crêperie* in the marketplace, with a cosy, rustic interior. No formal menus, but tasty *plats du jour* as well as pancakes.

✉ 3 place du Bas des Lices ☎ 02 99 30 42 95 🕐 Closed early Jan, three weeks Aug

Four à Ban (€€)
An 18th-century setting for above-average cooking using the freshest seasonal produce.

✉ 4 rue St-Mélaine ☎ 02 99 38 72 85 🕐 Closed end Jul, Sun, Mon eve

Le Khalifa (€)
A welcoming Moroccan restaurant serving huge platefuls of couscous, tagines, brochettes etc.

✉ 20 place des Lices ☎ 02 99 30 87 30 🕐 Closed three weeks Aug, Mon

ST-MALO
À la Duchesse Anne (€€€)
A long-established restaurant by the ramparts. Specialities include lobster and *tarte tatin*. Book ahead.

✉ 5 place Guy La Chambre ☎ 02 99 40 85 33 ⏰ Closed Dec–Jan, Mon lunch, Wed, Sun eve off-season

Le Brigantine (€)
This popular old-town *crêperie* in a stone building has a keen following for omelettes, pancakes and inexpensive light meals.

✉ 13 rue de Dinan ☎ 02 99 56 82 82 ⏰ Closed late Nov, most of Jan, Tue, Wed off-season

VITRÉ
Taverne de l'Ecu (€€)
Reputable restaurant in a lovely Renaissance building with large fireplaces and exposed timbers. Seasonal menus.

✉ 12 rue Beaudrairie ☎ 02 99 75 11 09 ⏰ Closed Tue eve, Wed, Sun eve off-season

SHOPPING

CRAFTS
St-Méloir-des-Ondes, between Cancale and Dol-de-Bretagne, is a well-known crafts centre. In summer a number of artisans' workshops and studios can be visited.

L'Atelier du Verre
Watch skilled craftsmen blow glass into a kaleidoscopic range of bright decorative objects. On-site showrooms.

✉ 4 rue de Radegonde, St-Méloir-des-Ondes ☎ 02 99 89 18 10; www.idverre.net/durand-gasselin

Ateliers Helmbold
A specialist glassworks southeast of Rennes, producing decorative housewares and imaginative contemporary works (mirrors, vases, stained-glass panels etc).

✉ Le Choizel, Corps-Nuds ☎ 02 99 44 12 37; www.ateliers-helmbold.com

La Droguerie de Marine
A marine chandler selling ship's models, compasses and regional products. Some English-language books.

✉ 66 rue Georges Clemenceau, St-Servan ☎ 02 99 81 60 39; www.droguerie-de-marin.fr

FOOD
Le Chèvrerie du Désert
A goat farm selling home-made cheese and other regional foods.

✉ Le Désert, Plergeur ☎ 02 99 58 92 14

Chocolaterie Durand
A lovely 19th-century building selling chocolate in unusual flavours (basil, wormwood etc).

✉ 5 quai Chateaubriand, Rennes ☎ 02 99 78 10 00

Grain de Vanille
Top chef Olivier Roellinger's tiny, unobtrusive master-bakery selling biscuits, cakes, speciality bread, home-made ice cream, buckwheat flakes and more. On-site *salon de thé*.

✉ 12 place de la Victoire, Cancale ☎ 02 23 15 12 70; www.maisons-de-bricourt.com

ENTERTAINMENT

CINEMA
Les 2 Alizés
This cinema just behind the main beach sometimes puts on undubbed or *version originale* films (VO).

✉ 2 boulevard Albert 1er, Dinard ☎ 02 99 88 17 93; www.emeraude-cinema.fr

Cine Manivel
This avant-garde cinema next to the maritime museum puts on independent art-house films, some in *version originale*. There's a foyer café, open half an hour before the first screening, with modern art and occasional live music.

✉ 12 quai Jean Bart, Redon ☎ 02 99 72 28 20; www.cinemanivel.fr

NIGHTLIFE

Casino Barrière de Dinard

This excusive casino overlooks Dinard's superb main beach. Dinner shows; live music; cocktail bar. Food served all day. Smart dress.

✉ 4 boulevard Wilson, Dinard ☎ 02 99 16 30 30; www.lucienbarriere.com

Le Coquelicot

On a hilly street near the old town, this popular bar is a well-known pub-concert offering live music (jazz, folk, rock, blues etc) and café-theatre. Some 70 different beers are on sale.

✉ 18 rue de Vitré, Fougères ☎ 02 99 99 82 11; www.barcoquelicot.free.fr

Le Cunningham

A lively bar down by the yacht harbour in St-Servan, beautifully panelled in chestnut wood by a ship's carpenter. Live music all year – jazz soirées, Latin, soul.

✉ 2 rue des Hauts-Sablons, St-Servan, St-Malo ☎ 02 99 81 48 08;
www.st-malo-hotel-cunningham.com

THEATRE

Péniche Spectacle

Two barges make unusual venues for world music, jazz, cabaret, workshops, readings and exhibitions. Performances for children.

✉ 30 quai St-Cyr, Rennes ☎ 02 99 59 35 38; www.guideinfo.com/Prog-Cultu/peniche.htm

Théâtre National de Bretagne (TNB)

A leading arts venue with three separate performance halls for drama, dance, jazz and classical music. Also cinema screenings of independent films in their original language. Restaurant and bar.

✉ 1 rue St-Hélier, Rennes ☎ 02 99 31 12 31; www.t-n-b.fr

Théâtre St-Malo

This leading theatre hosts major touring productions, concerts, opera, big band, plays, musicals and children's performances.

✉ 6 place Bouvet, St-Malo ☎ 02 99 81 62 61 (box office);
www.theatresaintmalo.com

Loire-Atlantique

In 1973, Brittany's southeastern wing was torn away to form part of a neighbouring region, Pays-de-la-Loire. But for many Bretons, the natural boundary of Brittany is still the final reach of the River Loire. In this book, Loire-Atlantique is treated as part of Brittany, at least as far as that great southern moat.

The beaches are among Brittany's best. Besides the magnificent crescent of sand at La Baule, or Monsieur Hulot's holiday beach at St-Marc, there are many unspoilt hideaways. Nature-lovers will enjoy the fascinating boglands of La Grande Brière, now a regional park, and the strange saltmarshes of Guérande.

Inland, Loire-Atlantique has fine border castles at Ancenis, Châteaubriant and Grand-Fougeray. The waterways around Nantes and the canals of La Grande Brière suggest interesting boat trips. Highlight of this *département*, though, is Nantes, Brittany's former capital and one of France's liveliest provincial centres.

BATZ-SUR-MER

At Batz, the low-lying saltmarshes are interrupted by the 60m (197ft) pepperpot tower of St-Guénolé, a prominent land- and seamark (climbable – excellent views). The chancel is draped with fishing nets, a reminder of its seafaring patronage. The ruined chapel behind St-Guénolé is Notre-Dame-du-Mûrier (Our Lady of the Mulberry Tree), legendarily built by a 15th-century nobleman saved from shipwreck by the light of a miraculous burning tree. In rue Pasteur is the **Musée des Marais Salants** (Saltmarsh Museum), a fascinating exhibition about the local salt industry. On the coast road to Le Pouliguen, **Le Grand Blockhaus** re-creates life in a World War II German command post in one of the biggest concrete bunkers of the Atlantic Wall.

www.marie-batzsurmer.fr

✚ 22K 🍴 Simple crêperies and cafés in resort. Good seafood at L'Ecume de Mer (€€, La Govelle) ✉ Route de la Grande Côte ☎ 02 40 23 91 40
🚌 Lines E or L (Le Croisic–La Baule)
ℹ 25 rue de la Plage ☎ 02 40 23 92 36

Musée des Marais Salants
✉ 29 bis rue Pasteur ☎ 02 40 23 82 79; www.maraissalants.com
🕐 Jul–Sep daily 10–12, 2:30–7; Jun daily 10–12, 2–6:30; Oct–May daily 10–12, 2–6 🖐 Moderate

Le Grand Blockhaus
✉ Côte Sauvage ☎ 02 40 23 88 29; www.grand-blockhaus.com
🕐 Apr to mid-Nov and Feb hols daily 10–7 🖐 Moderate

LA BAULE

La Baule-Escoublac is one of the smartest and largest resorts in northern France, packed at weekends with affluent sophisticates from Paris and other cities. The low-lying seafront, periodically engulfed in Loire silt and shifting sands, supported a single fishing village, Escoublac, until 1840, when pine trees were planted to stabilize the dunes and act as a windbreak. In 1879, after the arrival of the railway, the first holiday developments began to appear.

A 5km (3-mile) beach of gleaming golden sand is its main attraction, shelving so gently that you can safely wade far out to sea. Apartment blocks and hotels line the seafront road, some awesomely grand, most charmlessly modern and boxlike. Behind lie tree-lined avenues of villas dating from a more gracious *belle époque* age. The marina at Le Pouliguen is full of elegant craft.

La Baule offers every kind of seaside diversion, from genteel pursuits like bridge and golf to a casino and the latest high-tech watersports and thalassotherapy. The streets near place de la Victoire bristle with up-market shops and restaurants, and during the season the social diary is never empty.

🚌 23K 🍴 Wide choice throughout the resort (€–€€€) 🚍 Lines A, D, E, G, H, J, N (Guérande, Pénestin, St-Nazaire. *Petit train* (tourist train) along seafront to Pornichet 🚆 Regular TGV connections with Paris
ℹ 8 place de la Victoire ☎ 02 40 24 34 44; www.labaule.fr

CHÂTEAUBRIANT

Set well inland amid lake-strewn woodland, Châteaubriant stands guard on the Anjou border, part of the line of fortified bastions protecting Brittany from invasion. Its red sandstone church, St-Jean-de-Béré, dates back to the 11th century; its altarpieces are mostly 17th century. The main landmark is the **castle,** a piecemeal structure, partly feudal, partly Renaissance. The keep is the oldest section; the Seigneurial Palace was built by Jean de Laval, Count of Châteaubriant. A balcony at the top of the central staircase overlooks the Court of Honour gardens and the rest of the castle.
www.tourisme-chateaubriant.fr

✚ 27H 🍴 Restaurants on outskirts; simple eating places near castle, such as Le Bilig (€) ✉ Place St-Nicolas ☎ 02 40 81 48 49 🚌 Lines 40, 41, 42, 44 (Angers, Nantes, St-Nazaire) 🚉 Rennes and Nantes
ℹ 22 rue de Couéré ☎ 02 40 28 20 90

Château de Châteaubriant
✉ Rue du Château ☎ 02 40 28 20 90 🕐 Mid-Jun to mid-Sep. Guided tours Wed–Mon (Sat–Sun only off season) 🖐 Inexpensive

LE CROISIC

Le Croisic occupies a bulbous headland on the shores of the Grand Traict lagoon. Three islets linked by bridges form separate basins in the port, a picturesque scene when the fishing fleets arrive with catches of prawn. A modern *criée* (fish market) occupies one of these islands. You can watch the early-morning proceedings from a gallery (5am). The pleasantly shabby old town nearby contains 17th-century houses with wrought-iron balconies. Port-Lin, on the bracing ocean side of Le Croisic, is the main resort area, where several hotels overlook the waves crashing on dark rocks. Le Croisic's main attraction is its splendid **Océarium,** a star-shaped aquarium with well-organized displays of local and exotic species. The fish-farming exhibits are particularly interesting: baby eels and fingernail-sized turbot gulp gently at their spectators, and mussels cluster like maritime grapes on wooden posts *(bouchots)*. The shark tank has a slightly alarming 'walk-through' tunnel.

www.ot-lecroisic.com

🚑 22K 🍴 Good choice throughout resort (€–€€€) 🚌 Lines E, K (La Baule, St-Nazaire) 🚆 La Baule, Nantes, Paris (TGV), St-Nazaire

🛈 Place du 18 Juin 1940 ☎ 02 40 23 00 70

Océarium

✉ Avenue de St-Goustan ☎ 02 40 23 02 44; www.ocearium-croisic.fr

🕐 Daily 10–12, 2–6 (Jul until 7). Closed Jan 🖐 Expensive 🍴 On-site snack-bar (€) ❓ Fish fed by hand by a scuba diver

LA GRANDE BRIÈRE

Before the last Ice Age, the low-lying basin north of La Baule was covered with woodland. When the ice melted and sea levels rose, the area flooded and a thick layer of peat was formed. Gradually the sea retreated, and the marshes were drained and settled. The native Brierons developed an insular lifestyle based on hunting, fishing and turf cutting. Using local reeds to thatch their cottages and make wicker fish-traps, they negotiated the marshes in flat-bottomed punts.

In 1970, the Grande Brière was designated a 20,000ha (49,420-acre) regional nature park. It is now a popular holiday area offering fishing, riding, birdwatching and boating. The main villages of Kerhinet, St-Lyphard and St-Joachim are clusters of tidily restored thatched cottages; several house restaurants, craft-shops or little

ecomusées. Le Musée du Chaume (Thatch Museum), La Maison de l'Eclusier (Lock-Keeper's House) and La Maison de la Mariée (the Bride's House) are examples. La Réserve Ornithologique is a nature reserve with walks and hides (binocular hire).

www.parc-naturel-briere.fr

🚺 23K 🍴 Several auberges serve regional specialities, such as Le Nézil, St-Lyphard (€€; ➤ 165) 🚌 Lines C, D, G (Guérande–St-Lyphard) 🚤 Barge or punt *(chaland* or *blain)* hire or trips through the marshes

🛈 38 rue de la Brière, La Chapelle-des-Marais ☎ 02 40 66 85 01

GUÉRANDE

The medieval ramparts encircling Guérande are visible for miles across the flat *marais salants* (saltmarshes). Inside these tower-studded walls, the old town is a maze of quaint streets with overhanging timber-framed houses. The Porte St-Michel (the former governor's residence) contains an idiosyncratic local history museum.

South of Guérande, heaps of salt fringe a mosaic of glittering pools linked by sluice gates and drainage channels. Egrets and herons patrol the pans for fish. Seawater floods into the larger lagoons at high tide, trickling gradually into ever-smaller and shallower clay-lined pits *(oeillets)* to evaporate in the sun and wind. Purified salt is on sale by the roadside. Visit the nearby Maison des Paludiers (www.maisondespaludiers.fr) or the Terre de Sel (www.terredesel.fr), a lively interactive discovery centre on the salt industry.

www.ot-guerande.fr

🚺 23K 🍴 Good choice in old town, such as Roc-Maria (€; ➤ 165)

🚌 Lines A, B, D, G, H, J (St-Nazaire, La Baule, St-Lyphard/Grande Brière)

🛈 1 place du Marché au Bois ☎ 02 40 24 96 71

NANTES

Nantes' historic centre is full of good shops, restaurants and museums, most of it compact enough to explore on foot. It's a good base for visiting the vineyards and châteaux of the Loire Valley.

During the 16th to 18th centuries the town prospered on the notorious 'ebony' (slave) trade with Africa and the Caribbean. As the Loire silted up, the port became inaccessible to large cargo vessels and Nantes diversified into other industries. Much of its attractive 18th- and 19th-century architecture remains intact despite war damage.

The **Château des Ducs de Bretagne** was built by François II (Duchess Anne's father) in 1466. It has been greatly altered throughout the centuries and now houses a museum devoted to the history of Nantes. Only the courtyard and ramparts can be visited free of charge. The **Musée Jules-Verne** has the largest collection of manuscripts, portraits and objects once belonging to the writer, born here in 1828. Near by in the upper town are the Cathédrale St-Pierre (► 38–39), and the **Musée des Beaux-Arts** (Fine Arts Museum), strong on 19th- and 20th-century art. The Jardin des Plantes contains an extensive collection of ancient magnolias and a huge Palmarium with a miniature jungle of exotic plants.

Towards the lower town are the 15th- and 16th-century houses of Ste-Croix and the shipowners' mansions in the Ancienne Ile Feydeau. The **Palais Dobrée** has an excellent archaeological collection and many *objets d'art*, including a casket which once held the heart of Brittany's beloved Duchess Anne. The **Muséum d'Histoire Naturelle** is a fascinating 19th-century collection. Its most bizarre exhibit is the skin of a soldier whose dying wish was to be made into a drum.
www.nantes-tourisme.com

✚ 26L 🍴 Excellent range (€–€€€) 🚌 Good network of inner-city buses and trams (day-pass available) 🚆 Major regional rail terminal; TGV connections with Paris 🚢 River cruises on Erdres, Loire and Sèvre

ℹ️ 3 cours Olivier de Clisson ☎ 08 92 46 40 44

Château des Ducs de Bretagne
✉️ 4 place Marc Elder ☎ 02 51 17 49 48; www.chateau-nantes.fr
🕐 Museum: mid-May to mid-Sep daily 9:30–7, closed Tue off season. Couryard/ramparts: daily 9–8 (until 11pm Fri in summer for concerts, *son-et-lumière* shows etc) ✋ Moderate–expensive

Musée Jules Verne
✉️ 3 rue de l'Hermitage ☎ 02 40 69 72 52 🕐 Daily 10–12, 2–6. Closed Tue and Sun am ✋ Inexpensive

Musée des Beaux-Arts
✉️ 10 rue Clémenceau ☎ 02 51 17 45 00 🕐 Wed–Mon 10–6, Thu 10–8 ✋ Inexpensive

Palais Dobrée
✉️ 18 rue Voltaire ☎ 02 40 71 03 50; www.culturecg44.fr
🕐 Tue–Fri 1:30–5:30, Sat–Sun 2:30–5:30 ✋ Inexpensive

Muséum d'Histoire Naturelle
✉️ 12 rue Voltaire ☎ 02 40 99 26 20; www.museum.nantes.fr
🕐 Wed–Sun 10–6 ✋ Inexpensive

a walk around old Nantes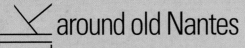

Start in the place St-Pierre (by the cathedral).

After visiting the main sights (castle, cathedral and fine arts museum), relax for a while in the Jardin des Plantes.

Head back along rue de Richebourg, deviating briefly to the late Gothic Chapelle de l'Immaculée. Skirting the château, make for the Ste-Croix district via rue du Chât.

This is one of the oldest and most delightful parts of Nantes. Here 15th- and 16th-century houses line the streets (see rue de la Boucherie, rue de la Juiverie and rue Bossuet near the church of Ste-Croix).

Walk down rue d'Orléans to place Royale.

Here the architecture leaps ahead a couple of hundred years to the 18th century. The central fountain represents the Loire and its tributaries. A block southwest, passage Pommeraye is an elegant fin-de-siècle shopping centre.

Take rue de la Pérouse from place Royale, then turn west into place du Commerce (the tourist office is here).

The Ancienne Ile Feydeau to the southeast, once embraced by arms of the Loire, is no longer an island. It has many wealthy shipowners' houses decorated with quaint carvings and ornate wrought-ironwork.

Head up rue J J Rousseau into place Graslin.

This fine square has a mix of 18th- and 19th-century buildings, best appreciated from the tables outside the Brasserie La Cigale (➤ 58). The art nouveau interior is

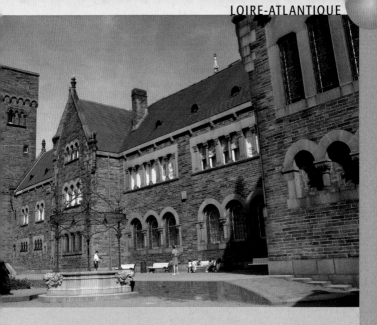

a riot of mirrors, mosaic tiles and swirling plasterwork.

*Take Cours Cambronne southwest of place Graslin,
another fine collection of 18th- and 19th-century
houses. Head for the waterfront (quai de la Fosse).*

The Musée de l'Imprimerie (No 24) is an interesting little
museum of printing, with working machinery.

*Finish the walk at the Dobrée museum complex
(➤ 159) on rue Voltaire.*

Distance 4km (2.5 miles)
Time Allow most of the day if you want to see museums or do
some shopping.
Start point Place St-Pierre
End point Palais Dobrée
Lunch La Cigale (€€; ➤ 58)

ST-NAZAIRE

St-Nazaire was all but obliterated during World War II and most of the city was later rebuilt in rather brutal, functional concrete. Today, several of its high-profile visitor attractions reveal St-Nazaire's key role in France's maritime history.

The **Ecomusée** at the heart of the port traces the story of the town, with special emphasis on the wartime era. The best section is the submarine exit, a covered lock from which U-boats could slip out of the harbour in secret. It now contains the French nuclear-powered submarine *Espadon*, which once sailed the polar ice-caps (the museum ticket includes a tour of the vessel – living quarters, engines and torpedo room).

St-Nazaire's shipbuilding industry has declined sharply, but some vessels are still built here, including the huge cruise-liner *Queen Mary 2* in recent times. **Escal'Atlantic** is an impressive discovery centre re-creating the world of the ocean liner, with multimedia special effects and historic movie footage. Other attractions in the port complex include the **Aker shipyards.** Out of town at Gron is the **French Airbus factory** (tours of both available; book ahead and take your passport).

South of the town a suspension bridge arcs across the Loire, providing a fast link from Brittany to the Atlantic seaboard.
www.saint-nazaire-tourisme.com

🚩 23K 🍴 Le Grand Café (€) ✉ Place des 4 Z'Horloges ☎ 02 40 22 37 66
🚌 Lines to Guérande, La Baule, Pornichet, St-Marc 🚤 Speedboat river cruises to Nantes ☎ 02 40 69 40 40
ℹ Base Sous-Marine, boulevard de la Légion d'Honneur ☎ 02 40 22 40 65
Port museums and dockland attractions
✉ Ville-Port ☎ 0 810 888 444 or 02 28 54 06 40 🎟 Escal'Atlantic and *Espadon*: Jul–Aug daily 10–7; Apr–Sep daily 10–12:30, 2–6; Feb–Mar, Nov–Dec Wed–Sat 2–6, Sun 10–12:30, 2–6; closed Jan
💰 Moderate–expensive (combined tickets available)

HOTELS

BATZ-SUR-MER
Le Lichen de la Mer (€€–€€€)
Traditional waterfront hotel with panoramic Côte Sauvage views from some rooms.
✉ Baie du Manérick ☎ 02 40 23 91 92; www.le-lichen.com

LA BAULE
Castel Marie-Louise (€€€)
The resort's most exclusive hotel occupies an imposing belle époque mansion in immaculate grounds. Acclaimed restaurant.
✉ 1 avenue Andrieu ☎ 02 40 11 48 38; www.castel-marie-louise.com
🕒 Closed Jan

St-Christophe (€€)
This elegant period villa stands in a quiet part of the resort. Traditional family atmosphere.
✉ Place Notre-Dame ☎ 02 40 62 40 00; www.st-christophe.com

St-Pierre (€)
A charming, friendly B&B with prettily decorated rooms. Excellent breakfast. No restaurant.
✉ 124 avenue de Lattre de Tassigny ☎ 02 40 24 05 41; www.hotel-saint-pierre.com

BRIÈRE
La Mare aux Oiseaux (€€–€€€)
A typical Brière thatched cottage with charming, stylish bedrooms. Pretty gardens; interesting regional cooking (pike, eel, duck etc). Children's menus.
✉ 162 Île de Fedrun ☎ 02 40 88 53 01 🕒 Closed Jan–Mar

LE CROISIC
Fort de l'Océan (€€€)
A sophisticated hideaway attracting many celebrities for its designer interior and fashionable restaurant.
✉ Pointe du Croisic ☎ 02 40 15 77 77; www.hotelfortocean.com

NANTES
L'Hôtel (€€)
A chic place opposite the Château. No restaurant.

✉ 6 rue Henri IV ☎ 02 40 29 30 31; www.nanteshotel.com

🕐 Closed Christmas, New Year

PORNICHET
Sud-Bretagne (€€–€€€)
A gorgeously individual hotel, full of quirky charm and character, but relaxing and comfortable too.

✉ 42 boulevard de la République ☎ 02 40 11 65 00; www.hotelsudbretagne.com

Villa Flornoy (€€)
This refined villa has elegant bedrooms and pleasant staff.

✉ 7 avenue Flornoy ☎ 02 40 11 60 00; www.villa-flornoy.com
Closed mid-Nov to Jan

RESTAURANTS

LA BAULE
La Ferme du Grand Clos (€–€€)
This smart farmhouse *crêperie* offers dishes like *cassoulet* and duck *confit* as well as delicious pancakes.

✉ 52 avenue de Lattre-de-Tassigny ☎ 02 40 60 03 30 🕐 Closed mid-Nov to mid-Dec, Mon, Tue, Wed off-season

Rossini (€€–€€€)
Classic 1930s décor adds to the atmosphere of this hotel-restaurant. Exceptional seafood and fillet of beef.

✉ Hotel Lutétia, 13 avenue Olivier Guichard ☎ 02 40 60 25 81

🕐 Closed Jan, Sue eve, Tue lunch, Mon off-season

LE CROISIC
L'Océan (€€€)
A magnificent waterfront setting adds to the enjoyment of the excellent seafood at this well-managed hotel-restaurant.

✉ Port-Lin ☎ 02 40 62 90 03 🕐 Lunch, dinner

GUÉRANDE
Les Remparts (€€)
Regional cuisine and good seafood in a modern setting at this
place near the tourist office.

✉ 14–15 boulevard du Nord ☎ 02 40 24 90 69 🕐 Closed Dec to mid-Jan,
one week Feb, Sun eve, Mon off-season

Roc-Maria (€)
Charming *crêperie* in a 15th-century building within the town walls.
✉ 1 rue Vieux Marché aux Grains ☎ 02 40 24 90 51 🕐 Closed mid-Nov to
mid-Dec, Wed and Thu off-season

NANTES
L'Atlantide (€€–€€€)
A smart fourth-floor restaurant in a modern block. Innovative
contemporary cuisine served with a panoramic view of the city.

✉ 16 quai Ernest-Renaud ☎ 02 40 73 23 23 🕐 Closed three weeks Aug,
Sat lunch, Sun

La Cigale (€€)
See page 58.

KERBOURG
Auberge de Kerbourg (€€)
A memorable thatched restaurant in the Grande Brière. Splendid
inventive cooking using local ingredients.

✉ Route de Guérande, Kerbourg ☎ 02 40 61 95 15 🕐 Closed mid-Dec to
mid-Feb, Sun eve, Mon, Tue lunch

ST-LYPHARD
Le Nézil (€€)
Another typical thatched restaurant in local style offering a fine
range of local dishes.

✉ St-Lyphard ☎ 02 40 91 41 41 🕐 Closed early Oct, mid-Nov to mid-Dec,
late Jan–early Feb, Sun eve, Mon, Wed eve off-season

SHOPPING

REGIONAL PRODUCTS
Brasserie de la Brière
Classic real ales from a local micro-brewery in a pretty Brière village. Tours and tastings.
✉ Le Nézyl, St-Lyphard ☎ 02 40 91 33 62

Chaumière des Saveurs et de l'Artisanat
Specialities from the Brière region (salt, samphire and local crafts) are on sale at this thatched cottage in the heart of the park.
✉ Kerhinet, St-Lyphard ☎ 02 40 61 95 53

Manuel
Best place in town for ice cream: also chocolates and other sweets.
✉ 2 avenue du Général de Gaulle, La Baule ☎ 02 40 60 20 66

Mignon
This sells the famous 'Niniches' lollypops along the seafront.
✉ Promenade du Port, Le Pouliguen ☎ 02 40 42 35 24

ENTERTAINMENT

NIGHTLIFE
Casino
Sharing premises with the exclusive Marie-Louise hotel, this smart casino offers the usual range of slot machines and gaming tables.
✉ 24 esplanade Lucien Barrière, La Baule ☎ 02 40 11 48 28

Théâtre Graslin
The region's leading concert hall and opera venue.
✉ 1 rue Molière, Nantes ☎ 02 40 69 77 18

L'Univers
Live jazz in a cosy pub every other Thursday.
✉ 16 rue J J Rousseau, Nantes ☎ 02 40 73 49 55

Morbihan

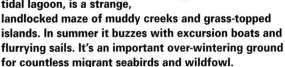

Vannes

The name Morbihan means 'Little Sea' in Breton, a reference to the *département's* most striking geographical feature. The Golfe du Morbihan, a huge tidal lagoon, is a strange, landlocked maze of muddy creeks and grass-topped islands. In summer it buzzes with excursion boats and flurrying sails. It's an important over-wintering ground for countless migrant seabirds and wildfowl.

Morbihan's megaliths are world-famous. Carnac's *alignements* (mysterious lines of standing stones) is one of the region's prime visitor attractions, rivalled by Locmariaquer and the island of Gavrinis, which boasts Brittany's most ornate prehistoric tomb.

The low-lying coastline lacks the drama of the Pink Granite or Emerald coasts, but sheltered sandy beaches and offshore islands, especially Belle-Ile, compensate. Exploring the area via the Nantes–Brest Canal offers a new dimension.

AURAY

This ancient place has played a significant role in Breton history. It is now a bustling and sizeable town, and its principal activities include tourism and oyster-raising. Auray is believed to be the last place reached by Julius Caesar in his conquest of Gaul. The Romans established their camp in the river port known today as St-

Goustan, the most picturesque part of the town. Flower-decked, timbered houses and inns surround the quayside place St-Sauveur and the hilly streets near by. The eye-catching schooner moored by the quayside is an old tuna-fishing vessel. Across a quaint 17th-century stone bridge, the church of St-Gildas in the town centre has a fine Renaissance porch. On Auray's northwestern outskirts, shrines and chapels commemorate the martyred members of the Chouan movement led by Georges Cadoudal, who staged an unsuccessful Royalist uprising against Revolutionary forces in 1795.

To the northeast, Ste-Anne-d'Auray is one of Brittany's most important religious sites. A colourful *pardon* on 25 and 26 July attracts thousands of pilgrims to its gloomy basilica, built in honour of a 17th-century ploughman's miraculous vision. Of more general interest is the vast war memorial alongside, dedicated to the 250,000 Bretons who perished in the Great War.

www.auray-tourisme.com; **www.**auray.fr

🕇 21H 🍴 Good choice (€–€€) 🚌 Lines 1 (Quiberon–Carnac–Vannes), 6 (Golfe du Morbihan–Vannes) 🚆 Vannes, Quiberon and Lorient (TVG connections to Paris and Quimper) 🚢 Pleasure cruises on the River Auray or to the Golfe du Morbihan

🛈 20 rue du Lait ☎ 02 97 24 09 75 (Auray) ✉ 9 rue de Vannes ☎ 02 97 57 69 16 (Ste-Anne-d'Auray)

BELLE-ÎLE-EN-MER

Brittany's largest island is a popular excursion from Quiberon, near Carnac. Attractive beaches, historic sights and good holiday facilities are the main reasons to venture here. Most people go just for a day-trip and explore the island on a guided coach tour, but Belle-Île's hotels make longer stays feasible (book well ahead).

Ferry passengers land at Le Palais. Above the harbour looms the 16th-century, star-shaped **citadelle.** A former prison and garrison, it now houses a museum of local history.

Belle-Île's interior consists of a plateau of moorland schist cut by fertile sheltered valleys that protect the white houses from the prevailing wind. The east coast has good safe beaches with watersports facilities; Grandes Sables is the largest and best. The west coast is ruggedly

beautiful but dangerous, with a fiordlike inlet at Port-Goulphar. Sauzon, on the northeast side, is a charming lobster-fishing port. A fort on the nearby Pointe des Poulains was once the holiday home of the actress Sarah Bernhardt. It was destroyed by the Germans in World War II.

www.belle-ile.com

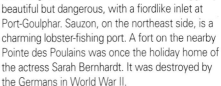

🚢 20K 🍴 Good choice (€–€€) 🚌 Taol Mor (Le Palais–Sauzon); excursion buses tour the island 🚤 Boat trips to and from Morbihan's main ports (mainly Quiberon)

ℹ️ Quai Bonelle, Le Palais ☎ 02 97 31 81 93

CARNAC
Best places to see, pages 36–37.

GOLFE DU MORBIHAN
The 'Little Sea' (a huge, almost landlocked lagoon over 20km/12 miles wide and 15km/9 miles from north to south) that forms such a prominent feature of the Morbihan coastline resulted from a fall in land levels several thousand years ago. Vast numbers of migrant seabirds and wildfowl colonise its varied habitats of dunes, mudflats, oyster beds, saltmarshes, creeks, reedbeds, heath and pine wood.

The muddy shores do not boast good beaches, and swimming can be dangerous – tides tear in and out of the narrow straits near Locmariaquer with great force – but it is a popular holiday area, with hotels, restaurants and campsites. The small resorts along its wooded northern shores (such as Arradon and Baden) are particularly attractive. The main attraction is boating; in summer a mass of pleasure craft weaves among its grassy islets.

The lushly vegetated Île aux Moines has pretty villas (sailings from Port-Blanc). The wilder, bleaker Île d'Arz is linked by ferry from Conleau (the port of Vannes). If you have time to see only one, make it the Île de Gavrinis, site of an elaborately carved burial chamber, **Cairn de Gavrinis,** beneath a stone cairn.

The Presqu'île de Rhuys (Rhuys peninsula), enclosing the gulf on the southern side, has a very mild climate where camellias and figs flourish. The **Château de Suscinio** is the main sight, a lonely marshland fortress, now restored as a museum.

www.golfe-du-morbihan.com
✚ 21J

Cairn de Gavrinis

✉ Cale de Pen-Lannic ☎ 02 97 57 19 38 ⏰ Apr–Oct daily for guided tours
(numbers limited, so book ahead) 💷 Expensive (includes ferry fare) ⛴ Boat
trips and entrance tickets from Larmor Baden ☎ 02 97 57 19 38

Château de Suscinio

✉ Kermoizan, Sarzeau ☎ 02 97 41 91 91; www.suscinio.info ⏰ Apr–Sep
daily 10–7; reduced hours off season; closed Wed 💷 Expensive

JOSSELIN

The most memorable feature of this medieval town is its mighty
fortress, mirrored in the waters
of the Oust. The turreted
Château dates mainly from the
14th century. Its Renaissance
façade was added around the
turn of the 16th century. The
Musée des Poupées (doll
museum) in the stable-block
contains exhibits several
centuries old.

In the town centre, the 12th-century church of Notre-Dame-
du-Roncier (Our Lady of the Brambles), contains the tomb of
Josselin's erstwhile master, Olivier de Clisson, Constable of
France. A *pardon* reveres the patron Virgin. Northeast of Josselin,
the Forêt de Paimpont is a popular touring and walking area,
mainly for its Arthurian legends. Ploërmel, en route, was the site of
a chivalric tournament in 1351, known as the Battle of the Thirty.

www.paysdejosselin-tourisme.com
✚ 10F 🍴 Choice in old town (€–€€) 🚌 Line 2 (Pontivy–Ploërmel)
ℹ Place de la Congrégation ☎ 02 97 22 36 43

Château de Josselin/Musée des Poupées

☎ 02 97 22 36 45 ⏰ Apr–Sep daily 2–6; Oct Sat–Sun 💷 Moderate–expensive

LOCMARIAQUER

This pretty oyster port guarding the neck of the Golfe du Morbihan rivals Carnac in archaeological importance. Its main sights lie in a fenced compound north of the village. They include a huge recumbent menhir, broken into four sections, which would have measured over 20m (65ft) high. Near by is a large decorated dolmen, the **Table des Marchands,** one of several good examples to be seen in the area. In Roman times the town of *Dariorigum* stood on this site, and the Gaullish *Veneti* used it as their naval base. Today, Locmariaquer is a peaceful place with attractive south-facing beaches, a pleasant old harbour quarter and lots of boat trips. Seafront walks from the Pointe de Kerpenhir are excellent.
www.ot-locmariaquer.com

✚ 21H 🍴 Good choice by the port (€–€€) ⛴ Boat trips round Golfe du Morbihan; crossings to Belle-Île and Port-Navalo

ℹ Rue de la Victoire ☎ 02 97 57 33 05

Site Mégalithique de la Table des Marchands

✉ Route de Kerlogonan ☎ 02 97 57 37 59 🕐 Jul–Aug daily 10–7; May–Jun 10–6; Sep–Apr 10–12:30, 2–5:15 💰 Moderate (combined ticket available for Carnac)

PORT-LOUIS

Port-Louis was named after Louis XIV, under whose reign the town flourished. It avoided the devastating air-raids of World War II

that destroyed much of Lorient, and
retains the air of a modest fishing port.
The fortified citadel at the harbour
entrance was founded in 1591, and later used as a prison, barracks
and arsenal. It now houses a museum complex which includes the
Musée de la Marine (maritime museum) and the **Musée de la
Compagnie des Indes,** dedicated to the history of the East India
Company during the 17th and 18th centuries. Rampart walks give
excellent views of the Lorient roadsteads.

www.ville-portlouis.fr

➕ 19H 🍴 A few modest options in town centre (€–€€) 🚌 Line 18 (Carnac)
🚢 Batobus (Lorient)

ℹ️ 1 rue Citadelle ☎ 02 97 82 52 93

Musée de la Marine/Musée de la Compagnie des Indes

✉️ Citadelle de Port-Louis ☎ 02 97 82 56 72 🕐 Mid-May to Aug daily
10–6:30, Apr to mid-May Wed–Mon 10–1, 2–6:30; Feb–Mar Wed–Mon 2–6;
Sep to mid-Dec Wed–Mon 1:30–6; closed mid-Dec to Jan 💰 Moderate

PRESQU'ÎLE DE QUIBERON

A narrow neck of tidal sediment links this feather-shaped peninsula
with the mainland, in places barely wider than the access road
which runs past windswept conifers and dunes of blown sand. The
resort of Quiberon is one of Morbihan's liveliest. As well as its good

sandy beaches and thalassotherapy centre, it is the
main ferry terminal for Belle-Île and always crowded
in summer. A sailing school is based in its sheltered
eastern waters. On the west coast, the Côte
Sauvage, the Atlantic beats furiously on cliffs, crags
and caves. The Pointe de Percho offers good views.

www.quiberon.com

➕ 20J 🍴 Good choice by the port (€–€€) 🚌 Line 1
(Auray–Plouharnel) 🚆 Auray–Vannes 🚢 Frequent ferries
to Belle-Île; also to Houat and Hoëdic islands

ℹ️ 14 rue de Verdun ☎ 02 97 50 07 84

LA ROCHE-BERNARD

Since the building of the Arzal dam, the Vilaine no longer provides an outlet to the open sea, and pleasure craft are the only boats to reach the town. In past years, however, La Roche-Bernard was a great riverine trading centre, handling cargoes of grain, wine, salt and timber. The **Musée de la Vilaine Maritime,** housed in the Château des Basses-Fosses on the west bank of the river, recounts these prosperous times. Today, the town's revenue comes mainly from tourism. Classed as a *petite cité de charactère*, it makes a most attractive touring base, with an excellent range of restaurants and hotels. The old quarter is packed with charming, flower-decked houses. A graceful suspension bridge spans the river, replacing an earlier version accidentally destroyed when lightning struck a German ammunition base.

www.cc-pays-la-roche-bernard.fr

✚ 23J 🍴 Auberge Bretonne, Place Duguesclin (€€€)
☎ 02 99 90 60 28 🚌 Lines 8 (Vannes–Nantes), 10 (Redon–Rochefort-en-Terre)
🚢 Boat trips on the Vilaine to Redon and the Arzal dam
ℹ 14 rue Dr-Cornudet ☎ 02 99 90 67 98

Musée de la Vilaine Maritime
☎ 02 99 90 83 47 ⏰ Mid-Jun to mid-Sep daily 10:30–12:30, 2:30–6:30; late Sep 2:30–6:30 💰 Inexpensive

ROCHEFORT-EN-TERRE

The attractions of this village are very obvious. The setting on a schist spur surrounded by plunging wooded slopes and rushing

water is a postcard scene. Mansions decorated with carvings and window-boxes line a cobbled street restored to tastefully pristine condition. Rochefort's main source of revenue is tourism, yet it retains its dignity and a sense of life with classy shops and restaurants. The 12th-century church of Notre-Dame-de-la-Tronchaye was granted collegiate status in 1498. Points of interest include a 16th-century calvary, a fine gallery and Renaissance altarpieces. The **castle** at the top of the town was restored at the beginning of the 20th century, and has a small museum.

www.rochefort-en-terre.com

✚ 23H ◼ Attractive choices in old town ◼ Lines 9 (Vannes), 10 (Redon)
◼ Place des Puits ☎ 02 97 43 33 57

Château

☎ 02 97 43 31 56 ◉ Jul–Aug daily 10–7; Jun–Sep 2–7; Apr–May Sat–Sun only ◼ Moderate

VANNES

This busy commercial centre is one of Brittany's best-looking towns, and more cosmopolitan than most. Its well-preserved old quarter lies behind imposing ramparts, best observed from the promenade de la Garenne, a raised walkway beside colourful public gardens.

Vannes' most picturesque sight, the old *lavoir (washhouse)*, stands near the Porte Poterne. The main monument within the walls is the Cathédrale St-Pierre, a hotchpotch of styles from Romanesque to baroque. It houses the tomb of Vannes' patron saint, St Vincent Ferrier. Opposite the cathedral, **La Cohue** is a medieval covered market that once housed the law courts. This building now provides display space for temporary exhibitions and the **Musée des Beaux-Arts,** containing an assortment of Breton paintings. Its star exhibit is Eugène Delacroix's *Crucifixion*.

A wander through Old Vannes reveals many other handsome buildings and squares. The place des Lices, once used for medieval tournaments, holds a produce market every Wednesday and Saturday. Near by are the Maison de Vannes, adorned with quaint carvings of a rustic couple popularly known as Vannes and his Wife, and the Maison de St-Vincent Ferrier.

Vannes is one of southern Brittany's main excursion centres, principally offering boat trips on the Golfe du Morbihan. Pleasure craft moor outside the walled old town, at the *gare maritime* on the Conleau peninsula. The Parc du Golfe here is a leisure park with attractions such as a **butterfly garden** and an **aquarium.**
www.tourisme-vannes.com

✚ 18H 🍽 Good choice of bars, cafés and restaurants in the old town (€–€€€) 🚍 TPV local urban services; others run to all main centres in Morbihan 🚆 Redon/Nantes, Auray/Quiberon and Lorient (TGV Paris–Quimper) ⛴ Wide range around Golfe du Morbihan, and to Belle-Île
❓ A *petit train* provides tours of the old town (with commentary)
ℹ 1 rue Thiers ☎ 02 97 47 24 34

La Cohue/Musée des Beaux-Arts

✉ 9 and 15 place St-Pierre ☎ 02 97 01 63 00 🕙 Mid-Jun to Sep daily 10–6; off-peak 1:30–6 (closed Sun and public hols) ✋ Moderate (charges vary for temporary exhibitions)

Le Jardin aux Papillons (butterfly garden)

✉ Parc du Golfe, rue Daniel Gilard ☎ 08 10 40 69 01 🕙 Jul–Aug daily 10–7, Apr–Jun, Sep daily 10–12, 2–6 ✋ Moderate

Aquarium de Vannes

✉ Parc du Golfe ☎ 02 97 40 67 40; www.aquarium-du-golfe.com 🕙 Jul–Aug daily 9–7:30; Apr–Jun and school hols daily 10–12, 2–6; Sep daily 10–12; Oct–Dec daily 2–6; closed Jan–Mar ✋ Expensive

a walk around old Vannes

Start from the tourist office in rue Thiers and head northeast to place Gambetta, just north of the canalized port.

Place Gambetta consists of a terraced crescent of 19th-century buildings, especially lively with cafés and bars in the early evening.

Enter the ramparts via the Porte St-Vincent, and proceed up rue St-Vincent to the place des Lices.

The largely pedestrianised streets inside the walls are a relief after the noisy traffic outside. Place des Lices, once a medieval tiltyard, is now the marketplace. Just north of the square, on the corner of rue Noë, stands the quaint Maison de Vannes. Near by is Vannes' history and archaeology museum, in an elegant urban manor called the Château Gaillard. It contains a fine collection of prehistoric objects.

Head northeast to the place Valencia.

At No 17 stands the home of St Vincent Ferrier, the town's patron saint, marked by a niched statue.

Head up rue des Orfevres, and visit the Cathédrale St-Pierre and La Cohue. Then stroll west from place Henri IV along rue St-Salomon to rue Thiers.

Here are the imposing Hôtel de Limur (a 17th-century town house), and (on place M Marchais) the 19th-century Hôtel de Ville with its fine equestrian statue.

Walk back past the cathedral via rue Burgault and rue des Chanoines. Pass through the machicolated Porte-Prison, then head south past the ramparts along the promenade de la Garenne.

Bright waterside gardens cheer up the stern rampart towers. Notice the picturesque 18th-century *lavoir* (washhouse) by the bridge near Porte Poterne.

Return to place Gambetta and the port, near the starting point.

Distance 3km (2 miles)
Time Allow half a day with time for sightseeing
Start point Tourist office (rue Thiers)
End point Place Gambetta
Lunch Roscanvec (€€) ✉ 17 rue des Halles ☎ 02 97 47 15 96

HOTELS

ARRADON
Les Vénêtes (€€–€€€)
A superb waterfront location and stylish décor give this place its special appeal. Smart restaurant with splendid views.

✉ La Pointe ☎ 02 97 44 85 85; www.lesvenetes.com 🕐 Closed two weeks in Jan

AURAY
Le Marin (€)
A charming little B&B hotel quietly tucked behind the historic quayside of St-Goustan. The décor is modern, but the building has quaint old beams.

✉ 1 place du Rolland ☎ 02 97 24 14 58; www.hotel-lemarin.com 🕐 Closed Jan to mid-Feb

BELLE-ÎLE-EN-MER
La Desirade (€€–€€€)
A delightful village-like hotel of low-rise, shuttered buildings set around a swimming pool. Relaxing atmosphere.

✉ Le Petit Cosquet, Bangor ☎ 02 97 31 70 70; www.hotel-la-desirade.com 🕐 Closed mid-Nov to Mar

BILLIERS
Domaine de Rochevilaine (€€€)
Romantic luxury hideaway in converted coastguard buildings. Spectacular coastal views and relaxing atmosphere. Fine restaurant and on-site spa.

✉ Pointe de Pen Lan ☎ 02 97 41 61 61; www.domainerochevilaine.com

CARNAC
Hostellerie des Ajoncs d'Or (€–€€)
Stone farmhouse in pretty gardens just outside the town. Cosy, rustic interior. Regional cooking.

✉ Route de Plouharnel, Kerbachique ☎ 02 97 52 32 02; www.lesajoncsdor.com 🕐 Closed mid-Oct to Mar

LARMOR-BADEN
Auberge du Parc Fétan (€–€€)
Welcoming hotel on the port road with glimpses of the sea from some rooms. Some apartments with kitchenettes.

✉ 17 rue de Berder ☎ 02 97 57 04 38; www.hotel-parcfetan.com

LOCMARIAQUER
Les Trois Fontaines (€€)
Close to the megaliths, this well-designed, spacious hotel has light, elegant bedrooms, some with sea views.

✉ Route d'Auray ☎ 02 97 57 42 70; www.hotel-troisfontaines.com

🕐 Closed mid-Nov to Jan

PÉNESTIN
Loscolo (€–€€)
A headland charmer on a quiet, scenic beach near the mouth of the Vilaine. Friendly and well-kept.

✉ Pointe de Loscolo ☎ 02 99 90 31 90; www.hotelloscolo.com

🕐 Closed mid-Nov to Jan

QUIBERON
Le Neptune (€–€€)
A well-priced, family-run Logis on the seafront near the *gare maritime*. Friendly staff and spacious, well-decorated bedrooms.

✉ 4 quai de Houat, Port-Maria ☎ 02 97 60 09 62 🕐 Closed Jan

LA ROCHE-BERNARD
Auberge des Deux Magots (€)
A pretty, stone-built restaurant-with-rooms on a picturesque old-town square. Good regional cooking.

✉ 1 place du Bouffray ☎ 02 99 90 60 75; www.auberge-les2magots.com

🕐 Closed Christmas, New Year

Manoir du Rodoir (€€)
Country house hotel set back from the main road in large gardens.

✉ Route de Nantes ☎ 02 99 90 82 68; www.lemanoirdurodoir.com

🕐 Closed Christmas to mid-Feb

VANNES
Le Roof (€€€)
A modern hotel in a waterfront setting by the port. Good facilities and spacious, comfortable rooms.

✉ Presqu'île de Conleau ☎ 02 97 63 47 47; www.bestwestern.com

RESTAURANTS

BELLE-ÎLE-EN-MER
Roz Avel (€€)
Behind the church, this is a safe bet. Tables outside in summer.

✉ Sauzon ☎ 02 97 31 61 48 🕐 Closed mid-Nov to mid-Dec, Jan–late Mar

CARNAC
La Côte (€–€€)
Family-friendly restaurant offering wide-ranging, flexible menus near the megaliths. Lots of regional produce.

✉ Alignments de Kermario ☎ 02 97 52 02 80 🕐 Closed Tue lunch Jul–Aug, Mon, Sat lunch, Sun eve off-season

HENNEBONT
Château de Locguénolé (€€€)
Elegant, extremely grand, riverside hotel with elaborate menus.

✉ Route de Port-Louis ☎ 02 97 76 76 76 🕐 Closed Jan to mid-Feb, lunch Mon–Sat, Mon off-season

ÎLE AUX MOINES
Les Embruns (€–€€)
A reliable choice on one of the islands in the Golfe du Morbihan, regularly visited by boat trips in summer.

✉ Rue du Commerce ☎ 02 97 26 30 86 🕐 Closed early Oct, Jan–Feb, Wed

JOSSELIN
La Table d'O (€–€€)
A smart but friendly choice with lovely views over the town and river. Accomplished cooking and good-value lunch menus.

✉ 9 rue Glatinier ☎ 02 97 70 61 39; www.latabledo.com 🕐 Closed Tue eve, Wed eve off-season

LORIENT
Le Jardin Gourmand (€€€)
This place by the railway station has a fine reputation and an
elegant setting with tables outside.
✉ 46 rue Jules-Simon ☎ 02 97 64 17 24 🕐 Closed Feb hols, late Aug to
mid-Sep, Sun, Mon

MALESTROIT
Le Canotier (€–€€)
This unpretentious place on the main square serves a flexible
and varied menu. Terrace dining in summer.
✉ Place du Dr-Queinnec ☎ 02 97 75 08 69 🕐 Closed Sun eve, Mon

PORT-NAVALO
Le Grand Largue (€€–€€€)
Acclaimed fish dishes are served in this nautically styled
restaurant. Cheaper fare in the brasserie oyster-bar downstairs.
✉ 1 rue du Phare ☎ 02 97 53 71 58 🕐 Closed Mon, Tue eve, Sun eve

QUESTEMBERT
Le Bretagne (€€€)
Award-winning restaurant-with-rooms serving exotic gourmet fare.
✉ 13 rue St-Michel ☎ 02 97 26 11 12

QUIBERON
La Criée (€–€€)
If you're tired of elaborate set menus, try Michel Lucas's freshly
cooked catch of the day straight from the fish market.
✉ 11 quai de l'Océan, Port-Maria ☎ 02 97 30 53 09 🕐 Closed early Dec,
Jan, Sun eve, Mon

LA ROCHE-BERNARD
Auberge Bretonne (€€€)
Another leading chef running a celebrated restaurant-with-rooms.
Refined service and elegant surroundings.
✉ 2 place du Guesclin ☎ 02 99 90 60 28 🕐 Closed mid-Nov to mid-Jan,
Thu and Mon, Tue and Fri lunch

LA TRINITÉ-SUR-MER
Le Bistrot du Marin (€€)
See page 58.

VANNES
Roscanvec (€€)
Inventive menus based on whatever's best at the market in an old timbered house in the walled town.
✉ 17 rue des Halles ☎ 02 97 47 15 96 🕐 Closed Sun eve

SHOPPING

FOOD
La Huche à Pains
A wonderful bakery on the marketplace, selling lots of Breton specialities and a fine range of prepared snacks – ideal for picnics.
✉ 23 place des Lices, Vannes ☎ 02 97 47 23 76

Le Rucher Fleuri
Traditional bakery near the main square. Its speciality is *pain d'epices* (spiced bread) in various flavours (nut, raisin, orange etc).
✉ Rue du Porche, Rochefort-en-Terre ☎ 02 97 43 35 78

La Trinitaine
Many outlets of this large biscuit producer are scattered around Morbihan, but this is one of the largest. Honey, sweets, liqueurs.
✉ Route de Crac'h, St-Philibert, Locmariaquer ☎ 02 97 55 02 04
www.latrinitaine.com

Maison Lucas
Top-quality fish products. On-site shop. Tours and tastings.
✉ ZA Plein Oues, Quiberon ☎ 02 97 50 59 50

REGIONAL SPECIALITIES
Le Comptoir Celte
A good place to look for classic Breton products such as woodcarvings, ceramics, boat models and music recordings.
✉ 8 rue St-Vincent, Vannes ☎ 02 97 47 34 03

Galerie Plisson

Philip Plisson is a renowned photographer of seascapes, and his gallery includes many memorable Breton scenes.

✉ Cours des Quais, La Trinité-sur-Mer ☎ 02 97 30 15 15; www.plisson.com

Vannerie Ty Ar Man

A quaint little shop crammed with rustic caneware – mainly baskets of all shapes and sizes, also mats, furnishings, ornaments.

✉ Rue des Douves, Rochefort-en-Terre ☎ 02 97 43 41 64

Yves Rocher

The beauty magnate has turned his home town and production HQ into a tourist attraction with botanical gardens showing plants used for cosmetic and pharmaceutical purposes. Naturally, the products are on sale.

✉ La Croix des Archers, La Gacilly ☎ 02 99 08 35 84; www.yves-rocher.fr

ENTERTAINMENT

NIGHTLIFE

Casino de Carnac

The usual range of slot machines and gaming tables, plus a lively programme of dinner-dancing, disco evenings and other events.

✉ 41 avenue des Salines, Carnac ☎ 02 97 52 64 64

Palais des Arts

This large theatre with varied productions has something to please everyone: plays, circus acts, ballet, dance, jazz, chansons, classical music and opera.

✉ Place de Bretagne, Vannes ☎ 02 97 01 62 00; www.mairie-vannes.fr/palaisdesarts

Rhumerie Le Nelson

This lively rum pub down near the port serves about 50 different types of rum, with live music about twice a week. Internet access.

✉ 20 place Hoche, Quiberon ☎ 02 97 50 31 37; www.lenelson.com

Index

Acknowledgements

The Automobile Association would like to thank the following photographers, companies and picture libraries for their assistance in the preparation of this book.

Abbreviations for the picture credits are as follows – (t) top; (b) bottom; (c) centre; (l) left; (r) right; (AA) AA World Travel Library.

4l Pontrieux, AA/A Kouprianoff; **4c** Redon, AA/A Kouprianoff; **4r** Quimper, AA/R Strange; **5l** Josselin, AA/A Kouprianoff; **5c** Morlaix, AA/R Strange; **6/7** Pontrieux, AA/A Kouprianoff; **8/9** Carving, St-Thégonnec, AA/A Kouprianoff; **10t** Restaurant, Dinan, AA/A Kouprianoff; **10c** Dinan, AA/A Kouprianoff; **10b** Church, Lampaul, AA/J A Tims; **10/11** Lacronquaiquer, AA/J A Tims; **11cl** Traditional lace, Quimper, AA/A Kouprianoff; **11cr** Festival dancers, Landerneau, AA/A Kouprianoff; **11b** Domaine de Rochevilaine, Billiers, AA/J A Tims; **12/13** Fresh crabs, AA/A Kouprianoff; **13** Crêpe, AA/B Smith; **14t** La Brasserie des Halles, Vannes, AA/J A Tims; **14b** French bread, AA/A Kouprianoff; **14/15** La Belle Meuniere, St-Cast-le-Guildo, AA/J A Tims; **15tl** Artichokes, AA/R Strange; **15tr** Breton cider, AA/R Strange; **15c** Beers, AA/A Kouprianoff; **16/17t** Crêperie sign, AA/J A Tims; **16c** Brasparts parish close, AA/A Kouprianoff; **16b** Seafood, AA/R Victor; **17t** Pointe de Dinan, AA/R Strange; **17c** Carnac, AA/J A Tims; **17b** Seafood, AA/A Kouprianoff; **18t** Île de Bréhat, AA/P Bennett; **18/19t** Medieval festival, Moncontour, AA/P Kenward; **19l** Beach, Bénodet, AA/R Strange; **19r** Café Breton restaurant, Rennes, AA/J A Tims; **20/21** Redon, AA/A Kouprianoff; **24/25** Medieval festival, Moncontour, AA/P Kenward; **27** Toll point, outside Calais, AA/J A Tims; **28c** Brest, public transport, AA/J A Tims; **28b** Taxi sign, AA/M Jourdan; **31** Pharmacy sign, AA/J A Tims; **34/35** Quimper, AA/R Strange; **36/37t** Carnac, AA/J A Tims; **36/37b** Carnac, AA/J A Tims; **38/39** Catédrale St-Pierre, Nantes, AA/R Strange; **40/41t** Castle, Fougères, AA/S Day; **40/41b** Castle, Fougères, AA/S Day; **42** Côte de Granit Rose, Penmarc'h, AA/A Kouprianoff; **42/43** Pink granite rocks, near Ploumanac'h, AA/P Bennett; **44t** Castle, Dinan, AA/A Kouprianoff; **44b** Port, Dinan, AA/A Kouprianoff; **44/45** Timber framed shops, Dinan, AA/A Kouprianoff; **46/47** Parish close, Guimiliau, AA/A Kouprianoff; **47t** Gargoyle, Guimiliau, AA/A Kouprianoff; **47b** Carvings, Guimiliau, AA/R Strange; **48/49t & 48/49b** Océanopolis, Brest, AA/A Kouprianoff; **50** Morgat, AA/R Strange; **50/51 & 51** Pointe de Dinan, AA/A Kouprianoff; **52/53** Bridge, Quimper, AA/A Kouprianoff; **53** Café, Quimper, AA/J A Tims; **54/55t** St Malo, AA/S Day; **54/55b** View from St Malo Castle, AA/S Day; **55** Port St Vincent, St-Malo, AA/S Day; **56/57** Josselin, AA/A Kouprianoff; **58/59** Restaurant, Cancale, AA/J A Tims; **60/61** Cyclists, Josselin, AA/P Bennett; **62/63t** Lieue de Grève beach, AA/R Strange; **62/63b** Locquirec Bay, AA/A Baker; **64** Traditional lace, Quimper, AA/A Kouprianoff; **66/67** La Baule, AA/R Strange; **68** Children playing, River Blavet, AA/S Day; **71** Guéhenno, parish close, AA/R Strange; **73** Le Folgoët, AA/R Victor; **74/75** Morlaix, AA/A Kouprianoff; **77** Concarneau, AA/A Kouprianoff; **78t** Bénodet, AA/R Strange; **78b** Château and gardens, Brest, AA/A Kouprianoff; **79** Port, Brest, AA/J A Tims; **80/81** Cap Sizun, AA/A Kouprianoff; **82** Pointe du Raz, AA/A Kouprianoff; **83** Cap Sizun, AA/A Kouprianoff; **84/85 & 84** Château de Kerjean, AA/A Kouprianoff; **85** Concarneau, AA/A Kouprianoff; **86/87** Île d'Ouessant, coastline, AA/J A Tims; **88** La Place de L'Église, Locronan, AA/P Kenward; **89t** Locronan, Church of St Ronan, AA/R Strange; **89c** Forest of Huelgoat, Monts d'Arrée, AA/R Victor; **90** Morlaix, AA/A Kouprianoff; **90/91** Moulin du Grand Poulguin, Pont-Aven, AA/A Kouprianoff; **91** Gauguin statue, Pont-Aven, AA/A Kouprianoff; **92/93** Parish close, Sizun, AA/R Strange; **93** Kérouat Mills, AA/R Strange; **94t & 94b** Roscoff, AA/A Kouprianoff; **94/95** St-Pol-de-Léon, AA/R Strange; **105** Abbaye de Beauport, AA/P Bennett; **106** Lighthouse, Cap Fréhel, AA/A Kouprianoff; **106/107** Pointe de la Latte, AA/S Day; **107** St-Briac-sur-Mer, AA/S Day; **108** Île de Bréhat, AA/A Kouprianoff; **109** Lamballe, AA/A Kouprianoff; **110/111** Place du Général Leclerc, Lannion, AA/R Strange; **111** Port Plaisance, Paimpol, AA/P Bennett; **112/113** Lighthouse, Perros-Guirec, AA/A Kouprianoff; **113** Trégastel beach, AA/P Bennett; **114 & 114/115** Perros-Guirec, AA/A Kouprianoff; **116t** Tréguier, AA/A Kouprianoff; **116b** Tréguier Cathedral, AA/A Kouprianoff; **123** Mont-St-Michel, AA/J Dawson; **124t** Oysters, Cancale, AA/J A Tims; **124b** Château de Combourg, AA/S Day; **124/125** Dinard, AA/S Day; **126t** Mont-Dol, AA/S Day; **126/127** Dol-de-Bretagne, AA/S Day; **127** Castle, Fougères, AA/S Day; **128 & 128/129** Fougères, AA/S Day; **130t & 130c** Hédé, AA/A Baker; **131** Menhir de Champ-Dolent AA/S Day; **132/133** River and boats, Redon, AA/A Kouprianoff; **132** Redon, AA/R Victor; **133** Grand Rue, Redon, AA/A Kouprianoff; **134** St-Pierre church, Rennes, AA/A Kouprianoff; **134/135** Port Mordelaise arch, Rennes, AA/A Kouprianoff; **135** Jardin du Thabor, Rennes, AA/A Kouprianoff; **136/137** Place de Mairie, Rennes, AA/A Kouprianoff; **138 & 138/139** La Roche aux Fées, AA/A Baker; **140/141** Mont-St-Michel, AA/C Sawyer; **142** Tertres Noirs, Vitré, AA/A Kouprianoff; **151** Guérande, AA/R Strange; **152** Batz-sur-Mer, AA/R Strange; **153** La Baule, AA/R Strange; **154** Châteaubriant, AA/R Strange; **154/155** Le Croisic, AA/J Edmanson; **156t** Brière Regional Nature Park, AA/R Strange; **156b** Brière Regional Nature Park, AA/N Setchfield; **157** Brière Regional Nature Park, AA/A Baker; **158/159** Place Royal, Nantes, AA/R Strange; **159** Castle, Nantes, AA/R Victor; **160/161** Palais Dobrée, Nantes, AA/R Strange; **162** Memorial Park, St-Nazaire, AA/J Edmanson; **167** Port-Coton, looking towards Aiguilles, AA/A Kouprianoff; **168** Ste-Anne d'Auray, AA/R Strange; **168/169** Pointe des Poulains, Belle-Île, AA/A Kouprianoff; **169** Suazon, Belle-Île, AA/A Kouprianoff; **170/171t** Locmariaquer, AA/J A Tims; **170/171b** Locmariaquer, AA/J A Tims; **172t** Château, Josselin, AA/P Bennett; **172b** Dolmen des Pierres Plates, Locmariaquer, AA/R Victor; **172/173** Point du Percho beach, Presqu'île de Quiberon, AA/A Kouprianoff; **173** Port-Louis, AA/R Strange; **174** La Roche-Bernard, AA/R Strange; **174/175** Rochefort-en-Terre, AA/A Kouprianoff; **176** Garden, Vannes, AA/J A Tims; **176/177** Hôtel de Ville, Vannes, AA/A Kouprianoff; **178/179** Cathedral, Vannes, AA/A Kouprianoff

Every effort has been made to trace the copyright holders, and we apologise in advance for any accidental errors. We would be happy to apply the corrections in the following edition of this publication.

Sight Locator Index

This index relates to the maps on the cover. We have given map references to the main sights in the book. Some sights within towns may not be plotted on the maps.

Dear Reader

Your comments, opinions and recommendations are very important to us. Please help us to improve our travel guides by taking a few minutes to complete this simple questionnaire.

You do not need a stamp (unless posted outside the UK). If you do not want to cut this page from your guide, then photocopy it or write your answers on a plain sheet of paper.

Send to: **The Editor, AA World Travel Guides,
FREEPOST SCE 4598, Basingstoke RG21 4GY.**

Your recommendations...

We always encourage readers' recommendations for restaurants, nightlife or shopping – if your recommendation is used in the next edition of the guide, we will send you a **FREE AA Guide** of your choice from this series. Please state below the establishment name, location and your reasons for recommending it.

_____
_____
_____
_____
_____
_____

Please send me **AA Guide** _____

About this guide...

Which title did you buy?
    AA _____
Where did you buy it?_____
When? m m / y y
Why did you choose this guide? _____
_____
_____
_____
_____

Did this guide meet your expectations?

Exceeded ☐   Met all ☐   Met most ☐   Fell below ☐

Were there any aspects of this guide that you particularly liked? _____
_____
_____
_____

continued on next page...

Is there anything we could have done better? _____
_____
_____
_____

About you...

Name (*Mr/Mrs/Ms*) _____

Address _____

_____

_____ Postcode _____

Daytime tel nos _____

Email _____

Please only give us your mobile phone number or email if you wish to hear from us about other products and services from the AA and partners by text or mms, or email.

Which age group are you in?
Under 25 ☐ 25–34 ☐ 35–44 ☐ 45–54 ☐ 55–64 ☐ 65+ ☐

How many trips do you make a year?
Less than one ☐ One ☐ Two ☐ Three or more ☐

Are you an AA member? Yes ☐ No ☐

About your trip...

When did you book? m m / y y   When did you travel? m m / y y

How long did you stay? _____

Was it for business or leisure? _____

Did you buy any other travel guides for your trip? _____

If yes, which ones? _____
_____
_____

Thank you for taking the time to complete this questionnaire. Please send it to us as soon as possible, and remember, you do not need a stamp (*unless posted outside the UK*).

> **AA** Travel Insurance call 0800 072 4168 or visit www.theAA.com

THE DIGITAL
PHOTOGRAPHER'S A-Z

Peter Cope

THE DIGITAL
PHOTOGRAPHER'S A-Z

With 410 colour illustrations

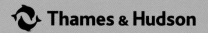

Thames & Hudson

First published in the United Kingdom in 2002 by
Thames & Hudson Ltd
181A High Holborn, London WC1V 7QX

www.thamesandhudson.com

Copyright © 2002 **The Ilex Press Limited**

This book was conceived, designed and produced by
The Ilex Press Limited
Cambridge CB2 4LX
England

Art Director: Alastair Campbell
Technical Editor: Allen Zuk
Production Editor: Jannie Brightman
Project Editor: Mandy Greenfield
DTP Designer: Ginny Zeal
Illustrations: Alastair Campbell, Peter Cope

The author and publisher are grateful to Adobe Systems, Apple, Compaq,
Corbis, Fujifilm, Hasselblad, Iomega, Kingston, Microtech and Nikon for
the use of images originated by them.

British Library Cataloguing-in-Publication Data
A catalogue record for this book is available from the British Library

For up-to-date information on digital photography,
please visit www.digitalphotographya-z.com

ISBN 0-500-54247-3

Printed and bound in China

CONTENTS

1

PHOTOGRAPHIC TERMS

2

COMPUTER SECTION

FILE MANAGEMENT

IMAGE **MAN**IPULATION

5

PRINT TERMS

6

WEB TERMS

7

GENERAL TERMS

HOW TO USE THIS BOOK

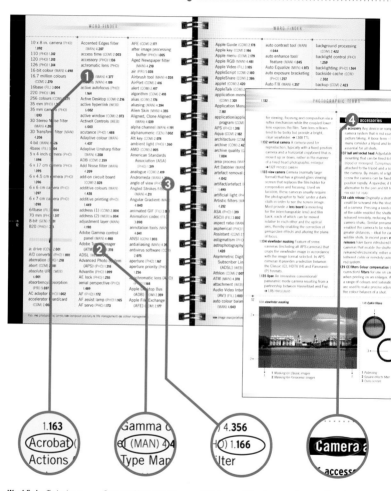

Word finder To look up the meaning of a term, first refer to the Word Finder, where all 3,000 terms in the A–Z are listed in alphabetical order.

Category Next to each term in the Word Finder is a category abbreviation. Category names are listed in full on the contents page of the A–Z.

Entry number This gives the location of the explanation of the term. Each number features the chapter number first, then the specific entry number.

Category heading Terms are listed alphabetically within each category, where terms that are related are grouped together.

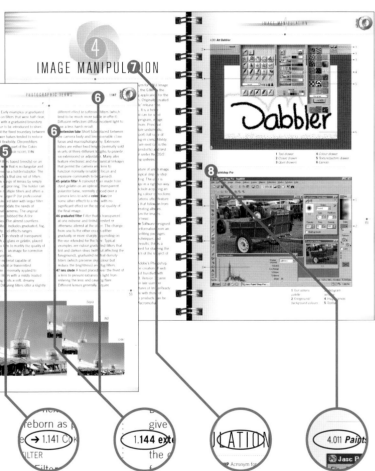

IMAGE MANIPULATION

4

7

IMAGE MANIPULATION

4.030 *Art Dabbler*

1 *Tool drawer*
2 *Closed drawer*
3 *Open drawers*
4 *Colour drawer*
5 *Texture/picture drawer*
6 *Canvas*

PHOTOGRAPHIC TERMS

6

5

1147

6

8

Paintshop Pro

1 *Tool options palette*
2 *Foreground/background colours*
3 *Histogram*
4 *Image window*
5 *Toolbar*

9

reborn as
→ 1.141 C
ILTER

1.144 ext
the

ICATION

MP Acronym for

4.011 *Paint*

Jasc P

Cross-references Similar
or relevant terms are
cross-referred to the
appropriate location in
the A–Z.

Entry numbers run
consecutively within
each category. Much
like a thesaurus, the
span of entry numbers
is indicated at the
head of each page.

Chapter Each chapter
is subdivided into
categories that group
together associated
terms – listed in
alphabetical order.

Illustration captions
These are linked by
entry numbers to their
explanations in the A–Z.
Some illustration
captions may refer to
more than one term.

Part 1
WORD FINDER

10 x 8 inch camera (PHO) 1.**092**
10-on camera (PHO) 1.**098**
110 (PHO) 1.**312**
120 (PHO) 1.**313**
126 (PHO) 1.**314**
16-bit colour (MAN) 4.**498**
16.7 million colours (COM) 2.**270**
16base (FIL) 3.**004**
220 (PHO) 1.**315**
256 colours (COM) 2.**271**
35 mm (PHO) 1.**316**
35 mm camera (PHO) 1.**093**
3D Stereo Noise filter (MAN) 4.**205**
3D Transform filter (MAN) 4.**206**
3M (PRI) 5.**108**
4-bit (MAN) 4.**526**
4base (FIL) 3.**004**
5 x 4 inch camera (PHO) 1.**094**
6 x 17 cm camera (PHO) 1.**095**
6 x 4.5 cm camera (PHO) 1.**096**
6 x 6 cm camera (PHO) 1.**097**
6 x 7 cm camera (PHO) 1.**098**
64base (FIL) 3.**004**
645 camera (PHO) 1.**096**
70 mm (PHO) 1.**317**
8-bit (GEN) 7.**001**
81A (PHO) 1.**162**
81B (PHO) 1.**162**
81C (PHO) 1.**162**
820 (PHO) 1.**313**

A

AA (PHO) 1.**058**
AAA (PHO) 1.**058**
a: drive (COM) 2.**001**
A/D converter (PHO) 1.**001**
aberration (PHO) 1.**218**
abort (COM) 2.**081**
absolute URL (WEB) 6.**001**
absorbency/absorption (PRI) 5.**037**
AC adaptor (PHO) 1.**002**
accelerator board/card (COM) 2.**002**
Accented Edges filter (MAN) 4.**207**
access time (COM) 2.**003**
accessory (PHO) 1.**136**
acetic acid (PHO) 1.**484**

achromatic lens (PHO) 1.**163**
Acrobat (MAN) 4.**377**
action mode (PHO) 1.**304**
Actions (MAN) 4.**189**
active autofocus (PHO) 1.**164**
Active Desktop (COM) 2.**216**
active hyperlink (WEB) 6.**002**
active window (COM) 2.**073**
ActiveX Controls (WEB) 6.**003**
acutance (PHO) 1.**488**
Adams, Ansel (PHO) 1.**311**
Adaptive colour (MAN) 4.**437**
Adaptive Unsharp filter (MAN) 4.**208**
ADB (COM) 2.**359**
Add/Delete Point tools (MAN) 4.**134**
Add Noise filter (MAN) 4.**209**
add-on circuit board (COM) 2.**028**
additive colours (MAN) 4.**438**
additive printing (PHO) 1.**449**
address (1) (COM) 2.**004**
address (2) (WEB) 6.**004**
adjustment layer (MAN) 4.**190**
Adobe Gamma control panel (MAN) 4.**480**
Adobe Type Manager (ATM) (MAN) 4.**378**
ADSL (WEB) 6.**005**
Adanced Micro Devices, Inc. (COM) 2.**04**
Advanced Photo System (APS) (PHO) 1.**318**
Advantix (PHO) 1.**099**
AE lock (PHO) 1.**255**
aerial perspective (PHO) 1.**489**
AF (PHO) 1.**172**
AF assist lamp (PHO) 1.**165**
AF servo (PHO) 1.**173**
AFE (COM) 2.**177**
Affine (MAN) 4.**114**
after image processing buffer (PHO) 1.**005**
against the light (PHO) 1.**374**
Aged Newspaper filter (MAN) 4.**210**
AIM Alliance (COM) 2.**059**
air (PRI) 5.**038**

Airbrush tool (MAN) 4.**038**
AirPort (COM) 2.**416**
Aladdin Systems (COM) 2.**214**
Aldus (MAN) 4.**386**
alert (COM) 2.**417**
algorithm (COM) 2.**418**
alias (COM) 2.**176**
aliasing (MAN) 4.**394**
Alien Skin (MAN) 4.**355**
Aligned, Clone Aligned (MAN) 4.**039**
alkaline cell (PHO) 1.**003**
alpha channel (MAN) 4.**191**
alphanumeric (GEN) 7.**002**
Alt key (COM) 2.**074**
Altavista (WEB) 6.**068**
Alternate (COM) 2.**074**
Alt-Prt Scn (COM) 2.**074**
ambient light (PHO) 1.**360**
AMD (COM) 2.**005**
American National Standards Institute (GEN) 7.**003**
American Standard Code for Information Interchange (FIL) 3.**002**
American Standards Association (ASA) (PHO) 1.**319**
Amount (Unsharp Mask) (MAN) 4.**346**
Amplitwist (MAN) 4.**114**
analogue (COM) 2.**419**
analogue to digital converter (PHO) 1.**001**
anchor point (MAN) 4.**134**
Andromeda (MAN) 4.**356**
angle of view (PHO) 1.**166**
Angled Strokes filter (MAN) 4.**211**
Angular Gradient (MAN) 4.**040**
animated GIF (FIL) 3.**001**
Animation codec (FIL) 3.**090**
annotation tools (MAN) 4.**041**
Ansel Adams (PHO) 1.**311**
ANSI (GEN) 7.**003**
antialiasing (MAN) 4.**395**
Antimatter (effect) (MAN) 4.**359**
antivirus software (COM) 2.**075**
anti-blooming gate (PHO) 1.**004**
A-PEN (PHO) 1.**334**
aperture (PHO) 1.**167**

MAN *image manipulation;* **PRI** *print terms;* **WEB** *web terms;* **GEN** *general terms*

Behind (merge mode)
(MAN) 4.**473**
bellows (PHO) 1.**101**
Benbo (PHO) 1.**160**
Bent-bolt (PHO) 1.**160**
BeOS (COM) 2.**078**
Bernoulli drive (COM)
2.**324**
best point of focus (PHO)
1.**218**
beta test copy (COM) 2.**079**
beta version (COM) 2.**079**
between the lens shutter
(PHO) 1.**260**
Bézier control point (MAN)
4.**192**
Bézier curve (MAN) 4.**192**
Bézier outline (MAN) 4.**195**
Bicubic (MAN) 4.**413**
bicubic interpolation (MAN)
4.**398**
bilevel, bilevelled (MAN)
4.**499**
Bilinear (MAN) 4.**413**
binary (GEN) 7.**005**
binary file (FIL) 3.**005**
binding (PRI) 5.**029**
BinHex (FIL) 3.**006**
BIOS (COM) 2.**077**
bit (COM) 2.**429**
bit depth (COM) 2.**272**
Bit Planes filter (MAN)
4.**215**
bit rate (WEB) 6.**009**
bitmap (MAN) 4.**399**
bitmap mode (MAN) 4.**439**
bitstream (COM) 2.**430**
Black Box (MAN) 4.**359**
black light (PHO) 1.**418**
black, rich (PRI) 5.**090**
blad (PRI) 5.**020**
bleed (GEN) 7.**006**
Bleed control (MAN) 4.**051**
bleeding (GEN) 7.**007**
blending mode (MAN)
4.**460**
Bloat (MAN) 4.**114**
bloomed lens (PHO) 1.**179**
blooming (1) (PHO) 1.**004**
blooming (2) (PHO) 1.**174**
blowup (PHO) 1.**451**
Bluetooth (COM) 2.**431**
Blur filter (MAN) 4.**216**
blur filters (MAN) 4.**217**
Blur More filter (MAN)
4.**218**
BMP (FIL) 3.**007**
Bookmark (WEB) 6.**010**
boom (PHO) 1.**367**
boot disk (COM) 2.**066**

boot/boot up/booting up
(COM) 2.**432**
bootstrapping (COM) 2.**432**
bounce lighting/bounce
flash (PHO) 1.**368**
bracketing (PHO) 1.**422**
brick (MAN) 4.**230**
briefcase (COM) 2.**217**
brightfield illumination
(PHO) 1.**369**
brightness (MAN) 4.**500**
brightness range (PHO)
1.**492**
brolly (PHO) 1.**370**
browser (WEB) 6.**011**
brush (MAN) 4.**128**
Brush Options (MAN)
4.**052**
Brush Size cursor (MAN)
4.**139**
Brush Strokes filters (MAN)
4.**219**
Bryce (MAN) 4.**002**
bubblejet printer (COM)
2.**255**
Bucket tool (MAN) 4.**127**
buffer (COM) 2.**303**
buffer memory (PHO) 1.**005**
bug (COM) 2.**433**
built-in flash (PHO) 1.**371**
bulb (setting) (PHO) 1.**261**
bulletin board service
(BBS) (WEB) 6.**012**
Bump Map (MAN) 4.**276**
bureau (PRI) 5.**096**
burlap (MAN) 4.**230**
burn (1) (PHO) 1.**423**
burn (2) (COM) 2.**325**
Burn tool (MAN) 4.**053**
burning-in tool (PHO) 1.**423**
burst mode (PHO) 1.**006**
bus (COM) 2.**016**
byte (COM) 2.**434**

C

c (1) (MAN) 4.**502**
C (2) (MAN) 4.**521**
c: drive (COM) 2.**008**
C format (PHO) 1.**320**
C-22 (PHO) 1.**452**
C-41 (PHO) 1.**453**
C/C++ (COM) 2.**080**
cable, coaxial (COM) 2.**390**
cable, crossover (COM)
2.**360**
cable, null modem (COM)
2.**367**
cable, peripheral (COM)
2.**370**

cable release (PHO) 1.**138**
cable, twisted-pair (COM)
2.**413**
cache (COM) 2.**304**
Cadmium Sulphide sensor
(PHO) 1.**303**
cameo coated paper (PRI)
5.**032**
camera (PHO) 1.**102**
camera angle (PHO) 1.**424**
camera, digital (PHO)
1.**020**
camera, disposable (PHO)
1.**130**
camera, electronic (PHO)
1.**028**
camera, field (PHO) 1.**111**
camera, half-frame (PHO)
1.**093**
Camera Image File Format
(FIL) 3.**009**
camera movements (PHO)
1.**103**
camera, moving chip
(PHO) 1.**055**
camera, panoramic (PHO)
1.**121**
camera, pinhole (PHO)
1.**125**
camera, process (PHO)
1.**127**
camera resolution (PHO)
1.**007**
camera, roll film (PHO)
1.**128**
camera shake (PHO) 1.**425**
camera, single-use (PHO)
1.**130**
camera, three chip (PHO)
1.**085**
camera, vertical (PHO)
1.**132**
camera, view (PHO) 1.**133**
cancel/abort (COM) 2.**081**
candids (PHO) 1.**426**
Canoma (MAN) 4.**379**
Canon iON (PHO) 1.**028**
Canto Cumulus (MAN)
4.**380**
canvas (MAN) 4.**054**
Canvas filter (MAN) 4.**220**
Canvas/Deneba Canvas
(MAN) 4.**003**
caption (PHO) 1.**493**
capture (PHO) 1.**494**
Carbon (COM) 2.**189**
Card F (MAN) 4.**507**
card formatting (PHO)
1.**008**
card reader (COM) 2.**240**

H

H format (PHO) 1.**341**
HAD CCD (PHO) 1.**038**
halation (PHO) 1.**503**
half-frame camera (PHO) 1.**093**
halftone (1) (PRI) 5.**004**
halftone (2) (PRI) 5.**005**
halftone dot (PRI) 5.**066**
Halftone filter (MAN) 4.**268**
Halftone Pattern filter (MAN) 4.**269**
halftone screen (PRI) 5.**116**
Hand tool (MAN) 4.**096**
hard (disk) drive (COM) 2.**023**
Hard Light (MAN) 4.**469**
hardware (COM) 2.**449**
Hasselblad (PHO) 1.**115**
HDTV (PHO) 1.**341**
heat sealing (PRI) 5.**031**
Help (COM) 2.**117**
Help menu (MAN) 4.**097**
Hertz (Hz) (GEN) 7.**032**
Hewlett Packard (COM) 2.**256**
hexachrome (PRI) 5.**067**
Hexadecimal (hex) (FIL) 3.**030**
HFS (FIL) 3.**123**
Hide Balloons (COM) 2.**184**
hierarchical file system (HFS) (FIL) 3.**123**
hierarchical menu (FIL) 3.**124**
hierarchical structure (FIL) 3.**125**
high key (PHO) 1.**433**
High Pass filter (MAN) 4.**270**
High resolution (PHO) 1.**039**
High Sierra standard (FIL) 3.**031**
high-level language (COM) 2.**118**
highlight (GEN) 7.**033**
highlight reading (PHO) 1.**277**
histogram (MAN) 4.**098**
History (MAN) 4.**099**
History Brush (MAN) 4.**100**
History Brush tool (MAN) 4.**101**
history (list) (WEB) 6.**029**
HLV (MAN) 4.**451**
Hockney (MAN) 4.**341**
Hole Accumulation Diode CCD (PHO) 1.**038**

home page (WEB) 6.**030**
honeycomb metering (PHO) 1.**278**
Horizon (PHO) 1.**121**
horizontal format (GEN) 7.**034**
host (WEB) 6.**031**
hostname (WEB) 6.**032**
hot shoe (PHO) 1.**116**
Hot Wax Coating filter (MAN) 4.**271**
HotBot (WEB) 6.**068**
hotlist, hot list (WEB) 6.**033**
HSB (MAN) 4.**451**
HSL (MAN) 4.**451**
HTML (WEB) 6.**036**
http (WEB) 6.**037**
hue (MAN) 4.**530**
Hue (MAN) 4.**470**
hue, lightness, value (HLV) (MAN) 4.**451**
hue, saturation, brightness (HSB) (MAN) 4.**451**
hue, saturation, lightness (HSL) (MAN) 4.**451**
HueSlider (MAN) 4.**372**
Huffmann coding (FIL) 3.**098**
Hybrid format (FIL) 3.**032**
hybrid photography, imaging (PHO) 1.**504**
hyperfocal distance (PHO) 1.**213**
hyperfocal mode (PHO) 1.**279**
hyperlink (WEB) 6.**034**
hypersonic motor (HSM) (PHO) 1.**251**
hypertext (WEB) 6.**035**
hypertext link (WEB) 6.**034**
Hypertext Markup Language (HTML) (WEB) 6.**036**
Hypertext Transfer Protocol (http) (WEB) 6.**037**
hypo (PHO) 1.**467**
Hz (GEN) 7.**032**

I

IBM PC (COM) 2.**038**
iBook (COM) 2.**039**
ICC (MAN) 4.**532**
ICC profile (MAN) 4.**492**
icon (COM) 2.**119**
ideal tone reproduction curve (MAN) 4.**531**

IEEE 1394 (COM) 2.**365**
If Darker (merge mode) (MAN) 4.**473**
If Lighter (merge mode) (MAN) 4.**473**
IFF (FIL) 3.**036**
Ilfochrome (PHO) 1.**469**
iLink (COM) 2.**364**
illumination, brightfield (PHO) 1.**369**
illumination, darkfield (PHO) 1.**375**
Illustrator (MAN) 4.**384**
iMac (COM) 2.**040**
image analysis software (MAN) 4.**007**
image area (MAN) 4.**102**
image colour reduction (FIL) 3.**099**
image editor (COM) 2.**120**
image file (FIL) 3.**033**
image library (GEN) 7.**035**
Image Magic (GEN) 7.**036**
image map (WEB) 6.**038**
Image menu (MAN) 4.**103**
image Online Network (PHO) 1.**046**
Image Pac (FIL) 3.**034**
Image Pac Extension (FIL) 3.**038**
image quality setting (PHO) 1.**039**
image resolution (MAN) 4.**411**
image resource (MAN) 4.**412**
image size (GEN) 7.**037**
image stabilization (PHO) 1.**214**
image stack (MAN) 4.**190**
image-editing application (COM) 2.**120**
Image-editing application interface (MAN) 4.**104**
image-manipulation program (COM) 2.**120**
ImagePort (MAN) 4.**362**
ImageReady (MAN) 4.**008**
imagesetter (PRI) 5.**117**
ImageWorks/PDF ImageWorks (MAN) 4.**363**
imaging device (PHO) 1.**505**
IMG (FIL) 3.**035**
import (FIL) 3.**126**
import/export filter (FIL) 3.**127**
imposition (PRI) 5.**119**

MAN *image manipulation;* PRI *print terms;* WEB *web terms;* GEN *general terms*

Key: **PHO** *photographic terms;* **COM** *computer section;* **FIL** *file management;*

29

MAN *image manipulation*; **PRI** *print terms*; **WEB** *web terms*; **GEN** *general terms*

Part 2

DIGITAL
PHOTOGRAPHY TERMS

1

PHOTOGRAPHIC TERMS

Digital cameras

1.001 A/D converter (Analogue to digital converter) Strictly speaking any circuitry designed to convert an input analogue signal (which may be sound, temperature or an image) to a digital one. In a digital camera the A/D converter transforms the incoming image into a digital signal that can then be stored in an appropriate format using the memory storage in the camera, or fed directly to a computer.

1.002 AC adaptor Power adaptor permitting a digital camera to be connected to mains electricity when the camera's location permits. Digital cameras tend to drain batteries very quickly and mains power can be used either to drive the camera directly or to recharge the batteries in situ (or both). AC adaptors often include an external battery charging facility to enable spare batteries to be charged while another is in use. **DC adaptors** have the same functionality but are supplied with direct current from, say, a car battery.

1.003 battery Except for studio locations, digital cameras rely on batteries for their power. The nature of a digital camera is such that its power demands are high (**memory effect**) and this puts heavy demands on the batteries. There are a number of options available. Many digital cameras use AA-sized (sometimes called penlight) batteries. Though in most cases it is possible to use ordinary or high performance **Alkaline cells**, these give out rapidly and are expensive to replace (depending on usage of flash and LCD panels, a fresh set may last for only a dozen or two shots). Rechargeable **Nickel Metal Hydride batteries** (NiMH) are more expensive to buy but have a greater yield (and, of course, can be recharged). It is always advisable to have a second or third

set for a long day's shooting. Many cameras are now supplied with specialized (and unique) NiMH or Lithium-ion (Lion) batteries that can be recharged in camera or externally. → 1.051 LITHIUM-ION BATTERY; 1.058 NiCd BATTERY; 1.059 NiMH BATTERY

1.004 blooming (1) A defect in early charge-coupled device (CCD) imaging chips that caused charge from a pixel to 'leak' to neighbouring pixels when imaging an object that produced charge levels larger than its nominal maximum. The defect is controlled in CCDs today by providing **anti-blooming gates** that allow the excess charge to be drained away before it has the chance to influence any of the surrounding pixels. → 1.011 CHARGE-COUPLED DEVICE (CCD)

1.005 buffer memory A region of **intermediate memory** in some digital cameras reserved for temporary storage of image data. This temporary storage can enable the camera to take shots more rapidly than would otherwise be the case, but only as long as there is sufficient capacity in the buffer memory. Early (and some very basic) cameras do not include buffer memory – in such cases you have to wait for a shot to be written to a storage card before a second shot can be taken. Larger buffers permit digital motordrive functions so that several shots can be taken in very close succession. Often this is called burst mode. There are two main buffer types: **before image processing (IP) buffers** and **after IP buffers**. The former stores the raw data from the CCD in the buffer and later performs the image processing. After IP buffers are processed (say, into a JPEG format) before being stored in the buffer. → 1.006 BURST MODE

1.006 burst mode Sometimes called **continuous mode**, burst mode permits the taking of several shots in close succession, far more rapidly than several individual shots. The speed at which successive shots can be recorded will depend on several variables, principal of which is the capacity of the buffer memory. This stores the image data prior to writing to the memory card (it is the writing to the memory card that takes the most time in between conventional non-burst shots). This also gives the maximum number of frames that can be exposed in a single burst – typically between 12 and 25 frames. → 1.005 BUFFER MEMORY

1.007 camera resolution Specific resolution of the imaging chip of a digital camera, measured in pixels. Many different resolutions are possible but the most popular are QVGA (320 x 240), VGA (640 x 480), SVGA (800 x 600), XGA (1024 x 768) and UXGA (1600 x 1200), based on monitor resolutions. → 1.515 OPTICAL RESOLUTION; 4.106 INPUT RESOLUTION

1.008 card formatting The formatting of a new or existing memory card in the camera, prior to being used to take more images. Like disc formatting, the process deletes all data on the disc. → 2.447 FORMATTING

1.009 card slot Aperture in a digital camera in which a memory card is inserted. Analogous to the film chamber in a conventional camera, the slot is normally concealed behind a flap or door for protection. Some cameras can accept two or three different types of memory card, either using adaptors or via twin slots.

1.010 CCD raw format Data received directly from a camera's CCD before interpolation, image formatting or compressions are applied.

1.011 charge-coupled device (CCD) A tiny light sensor ('photosite') – sensitized by giving it an electrical charge prior to exposure – used in flat-bed scanners and digital cameras for converting light into data. A CCD imaging sensor comprises a two-dimensional array of CCDs. → 1.102 CAMERA

1.012 CMOS Complementary Metal Oxide Semiconductor. Alternative imaging sensor chip to the more widespread CCD. It is cheaper to produce (and leads to cheaper cameras) but is less efficient, as less of the surface of the chip is available for use as a light gatherer. In practice, however, differing sizes and scales between the chips can make differences greater or less than the fill factor (the percentage of the surface that acts as a sensitized area) might suggest. → 1.032 FILL FACTOR

1.013 colour filter array (CFA) The individual 'pixels' or, more correctly, the photodiodes that comprise a digital camera's CCD and measure the amount of light received, are panchromatic. A **color 1 shot** camera was a single two-dimensional photodiode array, suitable for web design. To make each responsible for the detection and measurement of a particular colour, a colour filter array is placed over the CCD. This is composed of red, green and blue sensors. The colour filter array then filters the light so that only the correct wavelength for the appropriate photodiode passes through. A full-colour image results from combining the photodiode outputs from the neighbouring red, green and blue

1.011 *charge-coupled device (CCD)*

1.013 *colour filter array (CFA)*

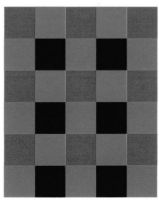

39

pixels. The most common form of colour filter array is the Bayer or GRGB **Bayer Pattern** array. This features twice as many green filters due to the eye's greater sensitivity to this colour. More green filters lead to a higher degree of colour accuracy.

1.**014 colour fringing** Effect that manifests itself as a coloured rim or halo around an object. Can be due to lens aberrations, **CCD artefacts** or (on computer monitors) poor convergence in the tube. → 1.218 LENS ABERRATION

1.**015 CoolPix** Proprietary name for digital cameras produced by Nikon. CoolPix cameras tend to be of compact-sized design and are principally aimed at the enthusiast, business and consumer markets. Nikon's professional cameras are based on their 35mm SLR models.

1.**016 custom settings** Camera settings based on user preferences or pre-programmed for specific purposes.

1.**017 date and time mode** Records date and time of exposure (and sometimes additional information such as exposure details and sequential numbers) along with the image. Unlike databacks (which imprint the information indelibly with the image), digital cameras encode this information as digital data. Depending on the software available this information can be displayed either overlaying the print or separately (for example along with any notes appended to the image).

1.**018 daylight balance** An adjustment of the white balance of a camera so that it gives 'correct' results (i.e., minimal colour casts) under daylight conditions. This setting may represent full or partial sunlight or overcast conditions or there might be multiple settings, one for each. → 1.091 WHITE BALANCE

1.**019 digital back** A digital image recording unit that replaces a conventional camera's back and film mechanism, in a similar manner to Polaroid film backs. Usually, but not exclusively, designed for medium-format cameras such as Hasselblads.

1.**020 digital camera** A photographic camera that uses a digital imaging chip to capture and record image data in digital form on an onboard memory block, removable memory card (subsequently uploaded to a computer) or directly connected computer. → 1.028 ELECTRONIC CAMERA

1.**021 digital film** A colloquial term for memory cards used for image storage in digital cameras. Although such cards can be reused, this relies on the card's images being downloaded to a computer. For long shoots it is often advantageous to have several cards available. → 1.054 MEMORY CARD

1.**022 digital photography** General term describing the process of capturing an image with digital equipment and/or of manipulating photographic images on a computer. Also used to describe the technique of recording and manipulating images as data rather than on film. → 1.020 DIGITAL CAMERA; 2.429 BIT

1.**023 Digital Print Order Format (DPOF)** A feature on some cameras that enables the photographer to specify how many copies

40

1.019 *digital back (attached to Hasselblad 6 x 6 body)*

1 *Lens*
2 *Hasselblad 6 x 6 cm body*
3 *Digital back*
4 *Direct vision viewfinder*

1.020 *digital camera*

1 *Mode selection dial*
2 *Shutter release button*
3 *Flash unit (pop-up)*
4 *Optical viewfinder*
5 *Metering system window*

Nikon Coolpix 950
(mid-range)

1 *Interchangeable lens*
2 *Viewing assembly*
3 *Digital back*

Hasselblad nfinity
(professional)

1 *Mode select dial*
2 *Standard hotshoe*
3 *Flash unit (pop-up)*
4 *Viewfinder lens*

Fuji MX 2900
(entry level)

41

1 *Mode/release control*
2 *Hotshoe*
3 *SLR pentaprism*
4 *Lens (standard Nikon mount)*

Nikon D1
(professional)

of an image are to be printed. Useful if multiple copies of an individual print are required, but only one (say) of all the remaining. Requires that the printer used is compatible with DPOF data and that the feature is enabled. Additional functionality also permits the printing of data on the image and even the non-printing of certain images. DPOF settings are normally made via the camera's **menu system**.

1.024 digital zoom Zoom feature offered on many digital cameras and most digital video cameras. Rather than using optical methods, digital zooms enlarge central areas of an image by recording the central area of the image only. Some cameras will even interpolate the resulting image up to higher resolution, resulting in blurring rather than pixelation. Zooming of this type can be achieved in software later; it is therefore more appropriate not to use digital zooms and to record the whole scene. Better crops can also be achieved in this way. Some cameras offer both conventional and digital zooms. → 1.228 OPTICAL ZOOM; 1.254 ZOOM LENS

1.025 direct viewing A camera viewing system that permits the direct view of a subject, such as a conventional viewfinder, as opposed to **indirect viewing**, e.g., via an LCD screen.

1.026 download (1) To transfer images (image data) from a digital camera (or storage device) to a computer. Transfer may be achieved by direct connection, via a storage device or Internet connection.

The transfer of data in the opposite direction is known as 'uploading'.

1.027 effective pixels The number of pixels on a CCD that contribute to the actual image. This is always less than the total number of pixels on a CCD as some are covered with a black dye (to establish a true black level – usually called **video signal shading**) and others are cropped from the edges. Sometimes there are engineering difficulties that also limit the number of effective pixels – such as a lens that does not cover the whole CCD surface. Most camera manufacturers will quote the effective pixels, but this is often overshadowed by the total number!

1.028 electronic camera Camera that uses electronic techniques to deliver an image. The term was coined in the 1980s and applied to cameras that used contemporary analogue video technology to produce still images. The **Sony Mavica** and **Canon iON** cameras are examples of electronic cameras. Though digital cameras are electronic, the term is not usually used to describe cameras that store image data in digital form. → 1.046 iON; 1.052 MAVICA

1.029 electronic photography, electronic still photography Photography using electronic cameras (as distinct from digital cameras). → 1.028 ELECTRONIC CAMERA

1.030 erase mode Camera mode that permits selected or all digital images stored in the camera (whether using internal memory or memory card) to be erased, freeing space for additional images.

1.028 *electronic camera (Canon iON)*

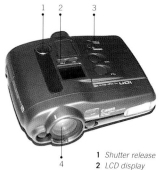

1 *Shutter release*
2 *LCD display*
3 *Exposure/Mode controls*
4 *Lens*

1.048 *LCD panel*

1 *Optical viewfinder* 3 *Four-way controller*
2 *Zoom control* 4 *Mode dial*

1.**031 file size setting** Camera control (usually provided as a menu option) to enable the selection of different file sizes for the stored images. The number of images that can be stored on a memory card will depend upon the file size. Selecting an alternate file size will alter the pixel resolution at which images are stored. Two alternate settings might be, for example, 1800 x 1200 pixels and 640 x 480 pixels.
→ 1.039 IMAGE QUALITY SETTING

1.**032 fill factor** The percentage of the surface of a photodiode in a CCD or CMOS imaging sensor that is 'active' as a light gathering sensor. CCDs typically have fill factors of 90 to 95% (highly efficient) whereas CMOS chips are around 30%, making them somewhat less efficient. → 1.011 CHARGE-COUPLED DEVICE (CCD); 1.012 CMOS

1.**033 FinePix** Proprietary name for digital cameras produced by **Fujifilm**, mainly for the consumer market. Innovative for the inclusion (in later models) of the advanced interpolative SuperCCD imaging chip.
→ 1.084 SUPER CCD SENSOR

1.**034 flash memory** Chip-based memory that retains data when power is switched off and forms the basis of virtually all image storage in cameras and on memory cards.

1.**035 fluorescent balance** An adjustment of the white balance of a camera so that it gives 'correct' results (i.e., minimal colour casts) under fluorescent lighting. Many cameras offer two fluorescent balance settings: one compensating for the green cast of certain tubes, the other for a magenta cast. Under 'auto white balance' settings the adjustment is normally achieved automatically. → 1.091 WHITE BALANCE

1.**036 frame lines** Feature of digital camera LCD preview screens. Some cameras provide grids and line overlays to aid in composition of shots. Typical patterns include portrait frames (provides multiple frames which a subject's head should fill), group frames and rule-of-thirds frames (particularly useful for landscape compositions). → 1.445 RULE OF THIRDS

1.**037 frame protection** Camera feature that enables single or multiple frames on a memory card to be protected from erasure (until an **'unprotect' command** is issued). Useful for protecting important shots.

1.**038 HAD CCD Hole Accumulation Diode CCD**. Proprietary imaging chip developed by Sony using a modified diode structure.
→ 1.011 CHARGE-COUPLED DEVICE (CCD)

1.**039 image quality setting** A digital camera control (either provided as a directly adjustable switch or as a menu option) that permits the selection of image quality to be recorded on the memory card. Most cameras offer several resolutions (with names such as **Basic**, **Normal**, **Fine** and **High**, in increasing resolution). Other than the highest, all other resolutions offer the capacity to store a greater number of images but at reduced quality, either because they are compressed or a lower pixel resolution is used. For all discerning applications the highest resolution should always be selected. → 1.031 FILE SIZE SETTING

1.**040 in-camera effects** Digital effects that are applied to an image within the camera either at the time of taking or subsequently. Such effects include black and white (turns the picture black and white), sepia (applies a sepia tone to the black and white image), starburst (gives highlights a star-like appearance) and **mosaic** – a heavily pixelated effect. As there is little or no control over these effects, most digital photographers prefer not to use them and to apply equivalent effects, if needed later, on the computer.

1.**041 incandescent balance** An adjustment of the white balance of a camera so that it gives 'correct' results (i.e., minimal colour casts) under incandescent lighting. Sometimes this is combined with tungsten lighting as an 'indoor balance'. Under 'auto white balance' settings the adjustment for incandescent sources is normally achieved automatically.

1.**042 integration time** The exposure time given to picture elements in a CCD array.

1.**043 internal storage** Memory included within a camera (and normally distinct from the on-board buffer memory) used to store image data. Early digital cameras had only internal storage (the camera had to be connected to the computer to download once 'full') whereas many newer models only have external storage capabilities.

1.**044 interval shooting** Recording images (usually of a fixed view) with exposures taken at set intervals for time-lapse effects.

A feature found on some digital and conventional cameras.

1.**045 interval timer** Feature (also available on some conventional cameras) that permits a shot to be taken at pre-set intervals to record changes, such as plants growing or traffic flowing.

1.**046 iON** Contraction of '**image Online Network**' [sic]. An early electronic camera developed by Canon and first released around 1989. Used an electronic imaging element but stored images on small floppy disks recorded in analogue technology.

1.**047 ISO equivalent** A term for relating the sensitivity of a digital camera to that of conventional film stock. Giving an ISO equivalent rating (which, in a digital camera, may be switchable over a considerable range) enables users to use familiar aperture and exposure values.

1.**048 LCD panel** Display panel on some cameras (conventional and digital) that uses liquid crystal display technology to relay information regarding camera settings, remaining exposures and battery condition to the user. Digital cameras often feature a second or more comprehensive display that can show (and replay) images and allow users to make custom settings of camera parameters.

1.**049 linear array CCD** A CCD imaging system that comprises a single row of CCD imaging elements at the focus plane. The array passes over the focus plane rather in the manner of a CCD array on a flatbed scanner, building up an image line by line. As this takes time it is suitable only for studio-based photography of inanimate objects. → 1.011 CHARGE-COUPLED DEVICE (CCD)

1.**050 Lion battery** Contraction of Lithium-ion battery → 1.051 LITHIUM-ION BATTERY

1.**051 Lithium-ion battery** Battery used for cameras and camcorders that uses Lithium-ion technology (as opposed to Nickel Cadmium – NiCad – or alkaline technology). Though more expensive than other options, Lithium-ion (sometimes contracted to Lion) batteries are not prone to the memory effect that ultimately limits charge capacity and longevity.

1.**052 Mavica** Contraction of **MAgnetic VIdeo CAmera** used by Sony to denote their first electronic stills camera. The name

returned in the late 1990s as the company's name for their latest digital cameras. These included models that used floppy disks and even recordable 8 cm CDs for image storage. Using these media means that no dedicated equipment (such as a card reader or connecting cable) is required to download the images from the camera.

1.**053 megapixel** Term for 'million pixels'. Hence a three-megapixel camera has a CCD imaging chip with at least 3 million pixels (photodiodes). As photodiodes are monochromatic devices the number does not correspond with resolution. Three photodiodes (sensitive to red, green and blue) are required to define each point in the image. → 1.013 COLOUR FILTER ARRAY (CFA); 1.061 PHOTODIODE

1.**054 memory card** Removable storage medium used in digital cameras. Several formats and card types exist, with image data capacities ranging from 2 megabytes through to 1 gigabyte. Popular formats include SmartMedia and CompactFlash, but other cameras accept PC (PCMCIA) cards and even Iomega's Clik! drive. Certain Sony cameras use that company's Memory Stick. → 2.333 COMPACTFLASH; 2.348 PERSONAL COMPUTER MEMORY CARD INTERNATIONAL ASSOCIATION (PCMCIA); 2.351 SMARTMEDIA

1.**055 moving chip camera** Variation on the scanning camera that uses a conventional imaging chip but moves it across and down the image. Gives high resolution at modest cost but suffers from very long exposure times. → 1.074 SCANNING CAMERA

1.**056 multi-frame playback** Playback mode that enables several images (usually 9 or 16) to be viewed as thumbnails on the camera's LCD screen.

1.**057 multi-zone focusing** Feature of high-end Nikon digital cameras that can automatically select a viewfinder zone to focus on. In practice this means there is no need to ensure a subject is centrally placed in order for the autofocus to function correctly.

1.**058 NiCd battery** Nickel Cadmium batteries. A common form of rechargeable battery normally found in **AA** and **AAA** size for digital cameras. Can typically be recharged between 500 and 1000 times but suffer from the memory effect wherein recharging before fully discharging results in a reduced level of charge subsequently. Hence they should always be fully discharged before recharging. Dedicated charging units for NiCds often feature a discharge button that ensures that the batteries are fully discharged prior to charging. → 1.003 BATTERY

1.059 NiMH battery Nickel Metal Hydride battery. Offering up to 40% more capacity than NiCd batteries, these are extensively used with digital cameras. They do not suffer from the memory effect, meaning they can be recharged without first discharging. They are, however, more expensive than NiCds and can only be recharged a maximum of around 500 times.

1.060 orientation sensor A sensor mounted in some digital cameras that can sense whether the camera is being held horizontally or vertically. When images are downloaded they are then displayed in either portrait (vertical) or landscape (horizontal) format, according to the information supplied by the sensor.

1.061 photodiode A light-sensitive diode that produces an electrical voltage in proportion to the amount of light falling upon it. A CCD image sensor is comprised of a grid of such photodiodes. A photodiode is a monochromatic device; to produce a colour image a layer of coloured filters is placed over the image sensor so that individual photodiodes output a voltage corresponding to red, green or blue light. → 1.013 COLOUR FILTER ARRAY (CFA)

1.062 photosite The small area on the surface of a photodiode in a CCD or CMOS image sensor that captures a light level for a pixel in the image. → 1.061 PHOTODIODE

1.063 picture shuttle A software application supplied with many digital cameras (and with varying specifications and names) that enables the images from a camera to be downloaded to the computer. In most cases the edited images can also be returned to the camera (or, rather, the camera's memory card) to enable the new images, for example, to be taken to a photofinisher to be printed.

1.064 playback mode Mode of a digital camera that permits the images stored in the camera to be viewed (either using internal memory storage or memory cards) often using the in-built LCD panel.

1.065 playback zoom Feature that enables the zooming in on images that are being played back through the camera's LCD screen. A useful feature for checking on sharpness and focus.

1.066 power down The switching off of power to a camera either manually or automatically, usually after a fixed period of inactivity, to conserve battery power.

1.067 power grip Part of a camera, or accessory item, that provides a handgrip and supplementary electrical power.

1.068 power up Turning on of a camera and the applying of power to all internal elements.

1.069 power up time The time taken between turning on a camera and the camera being available for the first exposure.

1.052 *Mavica*

1 *CD-R housing*
2 *Zoom lens*

1.084 *Super CCD sensor*

Conventional CCD arrangement

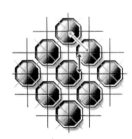

Closer-packed Super CCD arrangement

1.070 preview screen Alternative name for the LCD panel on the back (usually) of a digital camera that enables shots to be previewed for composition and reviewed after recording.

1.071 recovery time Time between making an exposure and the camera being available for the next.

1.072 reset Camera feature that permits all camera settings to be returned to their factory, 'out of the box' or default setting. Often an easy way to reset all features to ensure that settings like exposure compensation and white balance are all reset.

1.073 resize Camera command that enables an image already stored in the camera to be resized, generally to a smaller image size.
➔ 1.031 FILE SIZE SETTING

1.074 scanning camera Digital camera (or digital camera back for a conventional camera with interchangeable backs) that uses a linear array CCD to scan the subject. This takes time, so is usually restricted to studio and still-life subjects. The advantage is that it can create a very high resolution image – on a 5 x 4 inch film plane 360 megabyte files can be created (compared with the typical 3 megabytes of a consumer digital camera). ➔ 1.049 LINEAR ARRAY CCD

1.075 self-timer Feature of digital and conventional cameras that delays the shutter release for a predetermined period, typically to enable the photographer to be photographed.

1.076 sepia mode In-camera effect offered by some digital cameras. Selected images can be recorded in monochrome with a sepia cast (or images in the camera can be re-recorded) to give an 'antique' feel to the image. ➔ 1.040 IN-CAMERA EFFECTS; 1.482 SEPIA TONING; 4.556 SEPIA

1.077 serial download Downloading of images from a digital camera using a serial cable link to the computer.

1.078 sharpness setting Setting available on some cameras that varies the sharpness of an image being recorded. This feature uses **edge-sharpening software** to improve the perceived sharpness of an image, much in the same manner as sharpening filters provided in image-editing software.

1.079 signal to noise ratio (S/N, SNR) The ratio between the recorded image signal data and the inherent noise of the electronics (and, possibly, any interference). This ratio should be as high as possible. Noise is more noticeable in darker scenes where the image signal levels are lower. The signal to noise ratio is measured in **decibels (db)**.

1.080 sound recording Facility offered with some digital cameras to record a short memo note or ambient sounds along with the image. These sounds can be replayed when the image is viewed with the appropriate software.

1.081 still image mode Mode offered by certain digital video cameras that enables the capture of a still image (also known as **snapshot mode**). In early models, this comprised a still image recorded on the digital video tape for several seconds, but more recent models (particularly Sony models) feature memory cards upon which images can be recorded. Note that pixels used in many video cameras are not square like those of a digital still camera. As a result there may be linearity problems when still images from a video camera are manipulated in imaging software.

1.082 still video Description of early electronic stills camera. The image is formed by a focal plane CCD but recorded as an analogue signal (rather than digital) on disk, tape or card. Occasionally used now to describe the video camera feature enabling a 'snapshot' to be taken and recorded on video tape.

1.083 stitch mode Feature offered by a limited number of digital cameras. Enables consecutive shots of a broad scene to be assembled into a seamless panorama. Stitching in-camera is usually fairly effective but dedicated software such as MGI's PhotoVista can create more precise panoramas.

1.084 Super CCD sensor A derivation of the CCD created by Fujifilm in Japan and first announced in 1999. By using a new pixel shape (octagonal) and arrangement **(close packing honeycomb)** the photodiodes are packed at a much higher density than with conventional CCDs. Resolution is improved without increasing the pixel count. Hence a Super CCD sensor with 3 million pixels will offer a similar resolution to a conventional sensor of 4 million pixels.

There is also a larger surface area for the photodiodes resulting in better signal to noise ratio and sensitivity. → 1.011 CHARGE-COUPLED DEVICE (CCD); 1.027 EFFECTIVE PIXELS; 1.079 SIGNAL TO NOISE RATIO (S/N, SNR)

1.**085 three chip camera** Digital camera that uses a **beam splitter** to split the incoming image into three, with one beam each directed to a red, green and blue image sensor. The beam splitter is an optically pure prism with semi-mirrored faces. The more complex three chip cameras use dichroic coatings on the prism to split the beam into its three colours, meaning there is no need for image sensor filters.

1.**086 three-pass system** A design of digital camera that scans an image three times, each time with a different colour filter in the light path. The three images are then combined to create a single full-colour image. These three passes are often preceded by a **'no filter' exposure** used for focusing, exposure and compositional needs. Normally the need for multiple exposures precludes the recording of moving objects.

1.**087 video output** Some digital cameras offer an additional output of a video signal that enables the images to be directly viewed on a television. A simple video cable connects the camera and the TV, which must be set to an appropriate A/V mode (typically using a video-in SCART lead or – in the US – an RCA connector). Most cameras allow the video output to be selected as PAL or NTSC depending on the local television standard. When images are viewed using the video output they remain in the camera and can be downloaded to a computer at a later time. Also, by connecting to a video tape recorder the images can be recorded on tape as a slide show. Because such recordings are of lower quality than the original, it is not recommended as the principal storage medium.

1.**088 viewfinder** Part of the camera used to frame and view the scene to be photographed. Can be direct vision (has own optical system) or TTL (provides a view through the taking lens). Also called a finder.

1.**089 viewfinder frame coverage** Expressed as a percentage, the amount of the image area that is covered by the viewfinder. In almost all cases this is less than 100%. **Print frame coverage** describes the area covered by the print frames (that indicate each of the three picture formats) in APS cameras. → 1.318 ADVANCED PHOTO SYSTEM (APS)

1.**090 viewfinder screen** Screen, normally of ground glass or synthetic equivalent, upon which the image is formed in an SLR camera. Often features **framing aids** and focusing aids.

1.**091 white balance** 'White' light is rarely pure white and tends to have unequal levels of red, green or blue, resulting in a colour cast. This colour cast may not be visible to the human eye but can become very pronounced when a scene is recorded digitally. Almost all video cameras and many digital cameras feature a 'white balance' setting that enables these to be neutralized, either by reference to a neutral white surface or against presets (precalibrated settings for tungsten lighting, **overcast sky**, fluorescent lighting, etc.). An **auto white balance (AWB)** setting ensures that the white balance is neutral by continuous or periodic monitoring (for example, prior to exposure) of environmental lighting conditions.

Conventional cameras

1.**092 10 x 8 inch camera** Camera using 10 x 8 inch **cut film sheets**.

1.**093 35 mm camera** Any camera that uses the 35 mm film format. **Half-frame cameras** use 35 mm film but expose only half the frame area and thus expose a portrait format image when held conventionally.

1.**094 5 x 4 inch camera** Camera that uses 5 x 4 inch **cut film sheets**.

1.**095 6 x 17 cm camera** Camera that employs 120 or 220 roll film to take wide panoramic shots. The extreme width allows only four shots on 120 film or eight on 220. Fujifilm is the only current producer of these cameras.

1.**096 6 x 4.5 cm camera** Sometimes called **645 camera**, it uses 120 format roll film, exposing 15 or 16 images of 6 x 4.5 cm nominal size. Some cameras (such as Hasselblads) that normally expose 6 x 6 cm images can be fitted with film backs dedicated to the 6 x 4.5 cm format. Other

Conventional (film-based) cameras

1.096 *6 x 4.5 cm camera*

1.104 *(35 mm) compact*

1 Shutter release
2 Flash
3 Lens

1 Pop-up flash
2 Mode dial
3 Shutter release
4 Passive and active IR
   focusing mechanism

1.098 *6 x 7 cm camera*

1 Pentaprism
2 Camera body
3 Lens
4 Power pack
5 Film back

48

1 Manual film advance
2 Viewfinder (matched
   to lens)
3 Lens guard
4 Interchangeable lens

1.095 *6 x 17 cm camera*

6 x 6 cm cameras feature focal plane masks that enable exposures of this size when used in conjunction with a modified wind-on. The chief benefit of 6 x 4.5 cm cameras is the more economic use of filmstock and the more compact nature of the cameras.

1.097 6 x 6 cm camera Camera that exposes 6 x 6 cm shots on 120 or 220 roll film, giving 12 and 24 exposures respectively. The square format is appreciated by many as it can be cropped to either landscape or portrait formats. The archetype of this camera type is the Hasselblad.

1.098 6 x 7 cm camera Camera designed to take 6 x 7 cm shots on 120 or 220 roll film formats. These yield 10 or 20 exposures respectively. Sometimes called a **10-on camera**, these cameras, despite offering image sizes only slightly larger than 6 x 6 cm cameras, are often much larger and feature rotating backs. The back containing the film can be rotated through 90° to take landscape or portrait format shots without the need to remove the camera from its (essential) tripod. Though most 6 x 7 cm cameras are large SLRs there are some smaller, 'compact' format cameras that make excellent 'field' cameras.

1.099 Advantix Brand name for Advanced Photo System cameras produced by Kodak. → 1.318 ADVANCED PHOTO SYSTEM (APS)

1.100 automatic camera Camera with built-in coupled exposure meter that automatically adjusts the aperture and/or the shutter speed to achieve correct exposure. → 1.167 APERTURE

1.101 bellows The accordion-like folding fabric section of some cameras (or lenses) that provides a light-tight link between the lens and the camera body. Typically found with monorail cameras, close-up lens systems and in Hasselblad's **ArcBody**. → 1.120 MONORAIL

1.102 camera A device in which light passes through a lens to record an image. The image can be recorded onto pre-sensitized film or paper, or by means of electronic sensors (CCDs) which digitally 'write' the image to a storage device such as a memory card or hard disk. → 1.011 CHARGE-COUPLED DEVICE (CCD); 1.127 PROCESS CAMERA; 1.132 VERTICAL CAMERA

1.103 camera movements Feature of large format view cameras and specialized medium format cameras. Lens plane and film plane can be moved relatively to correct image defects such as incorrect perspectives and to alter the plane of focus.

1.104 compact Strictly any camera that is compact for its format, but more usually applied to non-SLR 35 mm cameras and rangefinder medium format cameras.

1.105 darkslide An opaque sheet of metal (usually) that can slide over the film plane of a medium format (or larger) camera to prevent light reaching the surface. Usually used when changing film backs of medium format cameras; also used to denote the film holders and slides of 5 x 4 inch and larger cameras.

1.106 data exchange (DX) A method of passing data from a 35 mm film cassette to a camera. A pattern of black and metallic squares on the cassette makes contact with contacts in the film chamber that pass information to the camera with regard to film speed, film type and film length. Not all cameras so equipped (usually denoted as '**DX compatible**') make use of all the data available with the DX coding regime: more basic cameras default to ISO 100 settings for films that are not recognized as either ISO 100 or ISO 400. → 1.343 INFORMATION EXCHANGE (IX)

1.107 databack Feature of some 35 mm cameras and all APS cameras. Enables data, usually, but not exclusively, time and date, to be imprinted directly on the film. Such data usually appears in the corner of the shot, on the rebate between frames or (in the case of APS cameras) is encoded on the magnetic coating on the film.

1.108 Dynax Name of **Minolta** 35 mm SLR cameras in most world markets.

1.109 EOS The name for most Canon 35 mm and APS SLR cameras.

1.110 eyepiece blind/viewfinder blind A cover for the viewfinder eyepiece that prevents light entering through the eyepiece when the camera is being used remotely (i.e., there is no photographer looking through at the time of exposure) and preventing stray light from influencing the exposure meter reading. Some cameras feature an eyepiece or **viewfinder cap** that is clipped

49

over a flange on the eyepiece to achieve the same effect.

1.111 field camera Strictly any camera used on location rather than in the studio. The term is often more precisely ascribed to a large format camera used on location.

1.112 film advance The winding of an exposed film frame to the next, which is usually accomplished by a motor on many contemporary cameras. Also the name for the manual mechanism for achieving the wind-on in non-motor-driven cameras.

1.113 film plane The position of the film emulsion surface within a camera from which distances (such as focal lengths and subject distances) are referenced. Some cameras feature a bisected circle symbol to indicate this point for precise measurements (for example, macrophotography). → 1.206 FOCAL PLANE

1.114 finder Part of a camera that illustrates to the photographer the view that will be recorded on film. Can be a direct vision viewfinder, frames (often used, e.g., for underwater photography where it is difficult to use a conventional viewfinder) or a separate viewer.

1.115 Hasselblad Archetype of the medium format reflex camera. With a reputation for the highest build quality, Hasselblads are renowned for their longevity and the interchangeability of their components. More recently (and in association with Fujifilm) Hasselblad has introduced the Xpan, a 35 mm rangefinder camera that offers full frame panoramic or conventional shots at the flick of a switch. → 1.135 XPAN

1.116 hot shoe Electrically connected mounting point on the top of a camera that supports a small flashgun (or an appropriate cable to a separately mounted gun). The connection provides a direct connection to trigger the flash when an exposure is made. Additional contacts on the mount enable dedicated flashguns to communicate with the camera to give information regarding the lens, focal length, etc. → 1.376 DEDICATED FLASH; 1.386 FLASH SYNCHRONIZATION

1.117 large format In contemporary usage, term to describe any film format (and associated cameras and accessories) larger than 120 roll film format.

1.118 medium format Any film or camera equipment based around 120 or 220 roll film. Typical formats for this film include 6 x 6 cm, 6 x 4.5 cm and 6 x 7 cm. More unusually formats of 6 x 9 cm and the panoramic 6 x 17 cm are used.

1.119 mid roll change (MRC) Feature of Advanced Photo System cameras that allows the user to change films before reaching the end of the roll and to replace partially exposed films to continue exposing. The camera will automatically wind to the next available shot when a film is replaced. Although part of the specification of the APS format, mid roll change is not a feature on all APS cameras. → 1.318 ADVANCED PHOTO SYSTEM (APS)

1.120 monorail A type of studio support for standard-view cameras to which the

1.106 *data exchange (DX) (shown on 35 mm canister)*

1 *DX contacts*
2 *Film bar code*

1.115 *Hasselblad*

1 *Viewfinder and hood*
2 *Film back*
3 *Camera body*
4 *Lens*

lens plate and the film holder are attached and aligned. Also the name given to such cameras.

1.121 panoramic camera Camera designed to take panoramic images using the maximum width of the filmstock. Typical cameras include the 35 mm-based **Horizon** (based on the Russian **Zenith** camera body), the **Noblex** (also available in medium format) and the Fujifilm 6 x 17 that takes large 6 x 17 cm shots. There are currently no commercial digital panoramic cameras, but digital techniques can be used to 'stitch' separate images into a single panorama. → 1.095 6 x 17 CM CAMERA; 1.440 PANORAMA; 4.028 PHOTOVISTA

1.122 panoramic mode A mode in some 35 mm cameras and all APS cameras for taking panoramic shots. In APS cameras the whole frame is exposed but the information exchange (IX) system advises the printing system to only print the central band (but to enlarge the image correspondingly). In 35 mm cameras, the top and bottom of the frame is masked so only the central band is exposed. Also a mode on the Hasselblad Xpan camera that offers conventional 35 mm exposures and super-wide ones on the same film. This is a genuine wide panorama, with the full frame height retained. → 1.351 P FORMAT

1.123 PC cord Connecting cable used to link a flashgun with a PC terminal on a camera. Enables synchronization between camera and gun in the same manner as a hot shoe. → 1.116 HOT SHOE

1.124 PC terminal Socket on a camera body used to connect a flash system or flashgun PC cord. In this case PC stands for **Prontor Compur** (a shutter type), not personal computer! → 1.123 PC CORD

1.125 pinhole camera Camera that uses a pinhole as an imaging device rather than a lens. Used today mostly for creative purposes.

1.126 point and shoot A colloquial description for cameras that are totally automatic.

1.127 process camera A specialist graphics art camera used in photomechanical reproduction. Sometimes called a '**repro camera**' or '**reproduction camera**'. → 1.132 VERTICAL CAMERA

1.128 roll film camera Any camera that uses roll film (as opposed to film supplied in a cartridge or cassette, such as 35 mm). Only 120 and 220 roll films are widely available today; a narrower film, 127 has limited availability and 820 cameras can (in general) use 120 format film.

1.129 single lens reflex (SLR) A camera in which the lens used for the photograph also transmits, via a mirror, the same image to the viewfinder. Most SLR cameras use 35 mm format film.

1.130 single-use camera A **disposable camera** designed for use only with the enclosed roll of film and subsequently broken open for processing. Designed to be cheap, they offer photographic opportunities where conventional camera usage would be dangerous or risky.

1.131 twin lens reflex (TLR) Camera featuring a dual lens system. The upper lens is used

1.121 *panoramic camera*

1 *Panoramic viewfinder*
2 *Film wind-on*
3 *Rotating lens mechanism*

1.129 *single lens reflex (SLR)*

1 *Viewfinder*
2 *Pentaprism*
3 *Mirror (for viewfinder)*
4 *Lens*

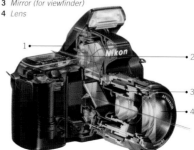

for viewing, focusing and composition via a reflex mechanism while the coupled lower lens exposes the film. Twin lens reflexes tend to be bulky but provide a bright, clear viewfinder. → 1.308 TTL

1.132 vertical camera A camera used for reproduction, typically with a fixed position camera and a horizontal copyboard that is moved up or down, rather in the manner of a fixed head photographic enlarger.
→ 1.127 PROCESS CAMERA

1.133 view camera Camera (normally large format) that has a ground-glass viewing screen that replaces the film holder for composition and focusing. Used on location, these cameras usually require the photographer to 'hide' under a dark cloth in order to see the screen image. Most provide a **lens board** (a mounting for the interchangeable lens) and film back, each of which can be moved relative to each other and the optical axis, thereby enabling the correction of perspective effects and altering the plane of focus.

1.134 viewfinder masking Feature of some cameras (including all APS cameras) that crops the viewfinder image in accordance with the image format selected. In APS cameras it provides a selection between the Classic (C), HDTV (H) and Panoramic (P) formats.

1.135 Xpan An innovative conventional/panoramic mode camera resulting from a partnership between Hasselblad and Fuji.
→ 1.115 HASSELBLAD

Camera accessories

1.136 accessory Any device or component of a camera system that is not essential to picture taking. A loose term – for example, many consider a tripod and lens hood essential for all shots.

1.137 ball and socket head Adjustable camera mounting that can be fixed to the top of a tripod or monopod. Comprises a ball attached to the tripod and a socket fixed to the camera. By means of a tightening screw the camera can be fixed at any position rapidly. A speedier, if less precise, alternative to the pan and tilt head. → 1.150 PAN AND TILT HEAD

1.138 cable release Originally a short cable that could be screwed into the shutter release of a camera. Pressing a knob on the end of the cable enabled the shutter to be released remotely, reducing the risk of camera shake. Similar pneumatic devices enabled the camera to be released at greater distances – ideal for candid or wildlife shots. In recent years **electronic releases** have been introduced for most cameras that enable the shutter to be released electronically, either using a tethered cable or remotely using an infra-red system.

1.139 CC filters Colour compensation (or colour correction) **filters** for use on camera or when printing on an enlarger. Available in a range of colours and saturations, they are used to make precise adjustments to the colour balance of a shot.

1.134 *viewfinder masking*

2
2
1   1

1 Masking for Classic images
2 Masking for Panoramic images

1.141 *Cokin filters*

1
2
3

1 Polarizing
2 Square effects filter
3 Cross screen

1.140 Chromofilter Early examples of graduated filters. Screw-on filters that were half clear, half coloured with a graduated boundary. Enabled colour to be introduced to skies, seas, etc., but the fixed boundary between upper and lower halves tended to reduce compositional flexibility. Chromofilters were later reborn as part of the Cokin filter range. → 1.141 COKIN FILTERS; 1.146 GRADUATED FILTER

1.141 Cokin filters Filters based (mostly) on an **optically clear resin** that is rectangular and fixed to the lens via a holder/adaptor. The principal benefit is that one set of filters can fit a whole range of lenses by simply changing the adaptor ring. The holder can accommodate multiple filters and offers a lens hood. The larger P (for professional range) was released later with larger filter sizes to accommodate the needs of medium-format cameras. The original filters were then dubbed the A (for amateur) series. The almost countless selection of filters includes graduated, fog, neutral density and effects ranges.

1.142 colour filters Thin sheets of transparent material, such as glass or gelatin, placed over a camera lens to modify the quality of light or colours in an image for corrective or creative purposes.

1.143 diffuser Any material capable of scattering incident or transmitted light. The term is normally applied to photographic filters with a mildly frosted surface, giving shots a soft, dreamy appearance. Diffusing filters offer a slightly different effect to softening filters (which tend to be much more subtle in effect). Diffusion reflectors diffuse incident light to give a less harsh result.

1.144 extension tube Short tube placed between the camera body and lens to enable close focus and macrophotography. Extension tubes are either fixed length (normally sold in sets of three different lengths to provide six extensions) or adjustable. Many also feature electronic and mechanical linkages that permit the camera and lens to function normally (enabling focus and exposure commands to be passed).

1.145 gelatin filter A coloured filter made from dyed gelatin on an optically transparent polyester base, normally placed over a camera lens to add a **colour bias** (or some other effect) to a shot with no significant effect on the optical quality of the final image.

1.146 graduated filter Filter that is transparent at one extreme and tinted, frosted or otherwise altered at the other. The change from one to the other occurs either gradually or more sharply depending on the use intended for the filter. Typical examples are colour graduated filters that tint and darken skies (without affecting the foreground), graduated neutral density filters (which preserve sky colour but reduce the brightness) and fog filters.

1.147 lens shade A hood placed over the front of a lens to prevent extraneous light from entering the lens and causing flare. Different lenses generally require

1.146 *graduated filter*

Sepia

ND

Lilac

individual lens shades to ensure not only that unwanted light does not enter, but also that the shade never appears in shot.

1.148 monopod Camera support comprising a single pole often adjustable in height and with a camera mount at the top. Less bulky than a tripod, monopods can offer effective support for all but the longest of exposures.

1.149 neutral density filter (ND) Filter that reduces the amount of light passing through, but not altering the values of any colours. Usually supplied in densities corresponding to f-stops (equivalent to closing down a lens one, two or three f-numbers, for example). Neutral density filters enable the light reaching the film to be reduced in the same way as closing down the lens but enable the lens aperture to remain wide and, consequently, retain a shallow depth of field. They may also be used to allow more flexible use of fast films in bright conditions.

1.150 pan and tilt head Camera mounting that can be fixed to the top of a tripod or monopod. Designed to let the camera move horizontally and up and down. Though used by many still photographers, this is more useful to the movie photographer, as changing between portrait and landscape formats is more cumbersome than with the alternate ball and socket head. → 1.137 BALL AND SOCKET HEAD

1.151 polarizing filter Filter comprising Polaroid material designed to remove polarized light from an image. Polarized light tends to include reflected light, and use of a polarizing filter can remove reflections, resulting in brighter colours and richer skies. A single layer polarizer is known as a **linear polarizer**. Most autofocus and digital cameras need a **circular polarizer**: this is a two-stage filter which polarizes the light at the first stage then 'rescatters' it. This prevents the focusing and other electronic monitoring elements from receiving an incorrect exposure reading.

1.152 Polaroid back A camera back that can be substituted for the original to enable Polaroid film stock to be exposed in the camera. Polaroid backs are common for medium and large format cameras, but can be obtained for certain 35 mm SLR cameras. Polaroid images can be taken to preview compositions and settings prior to the final shot on conventional film. The immediacy of Polaroid film is to some degree now being replaced by digital backs that can often be used for preview and final shots.

1.153 power pack Accessory unit that contains batteries to supplement or replace that of the camera. Power packs are often connected to, but not part of, the camera body enabling the pack to be placed somewhere warm (such as in the photographer's pocket) when conditions are cold and might compromise the performance of batteries in the camera.

1.154 Quantum pack Proprietary name for a popular range of power packs for cameras and flashguns that typically provide

1.149 *neutral density filter*

No filter

ND filter (equivalent to two stops underexposure)

substantially more power than could be accommodated on board any device.
→ 1.153 POWER PACK

1.155 reflector Any device designed to reflect light into a scene. Reflectors such as the Lastolite models can be used to cast neutral, warm or daylight balanced light into a scene, yet fold away to a convenient size – useful for location photography. Flash reflectors reflect light from a flashgun onto a scene, avoiding the harshness of direct flash.

1.156 right angle finder Unit attached to the eyepiece of a camera viewfinder that reflects the light through 90°. Useful for when the camera is on the ground or when direct vision through the eyepiece is difficult. Some models also include a magnifier that enlarges the central portion of the viewfinder image as an aid to focusing.

1.157 slide copy attachment Unit attached to a camera lens, or in some cases replacing the camera lens, that permits copies to be made of slides or negatives. Useful for in-camera creative effects such as combining slides or photographing 'sandwiches' of slides and filters.

1.158 Softar An image softening lens used (mostly) for flattering portraiture. It features a plane glass filter with a pattern of clear 'drops' that produce diffusion without compromising the overall resolution. Extensively used with Hasselblad cameras.

1.159 starburst (filter) A photographic filter inscribed with one or more series of fine, parallel lines. This creates the effect of 'streaks' from any highlights in a direction perpendicular to the rulings. By inscribing multiple sets of lines, starbursts with 2, 4, 8 or more points are possible.

1.160 tripod Three-legged camera support. Typical tripods feature legs that can be individually adjusted for height and reach. Many designs also offer a central column which gives extra height and quick variations to camera height. **Bent-bolt** tripods (offered by **Benbo** and **Uniloc**) are based on the mounting of wartime Bren guns and feature a bent bolt that, when secured, locks the tripod legs and independent central column in almost any position. Cameras can be mounted directly on the top of a tripod but are more usually attached via a ball and socket or pan and tilt head. → 1.137 BALL AND SOCKET HEAD; 1.150 PAN AND TILT HEAD

1.161 UV filter Filter designed to cut down the amount of UV light that passes through to the lens.

1.162 warm-up filter Filter designed to introduce a warm colour balance to an image. Typically pale salmon in colour, filters are available in different strengths to give various degrees of warming. Most filters still carry the 'traditional' numbering of the **Kodak Wratten** series: **81A**, **81B** or **81C** (increasing in strength). Warm-up filters are also available in image-editing software, sometimes introducing a warming effect that can be directly correlated with the Wratten values.

1.151 *polarizing filter*

Before

After

Lenses and focusing

1.163 achromatic lens Compound lens in which multiple elements are used to reduce the degree of chromatic aberration present in the resultant image. Usually comprises a double convex lens used for focusing the incident light, supplemented by a double concave (or plano-concave) lens of different refractive index. Achromatic lenses tend to focus blue and red light at the same point, but not intermediate frequencies (for example, green). Where light of all colours is focused at the same point, the lens is known as an apochromatic or APO lens. → 1.168 APOCHROMATIC LENS (APO)

1.164 active autofocus An autofocus system that sends out a signal (which may be infra-red light, or, in the case of some Polaroid cameras, sound) to determine subject range. The time taken for a reflection is interpreted by the camera to find the distance. → 1.231 PASSIVE AUTOFOCUS

1.165 AF assist lamp Small lamp provided on some cameras (digital or conventional) to illuminate a subject under low lighting conditions to assist in making an accurate autofocus setting. **Autofocus illuminators** function in the range of 5 m or less and can offer infra-red light (barely visible as a red glow) or white light. Some cameras combine this with a red-eye reducing lamp to help reduce the effect of red-eye.

1.166 angle of view The area of a scene that a lens 'sees', determined by a combination of the focal length of the lens and the film format. It is conventionally measured in degrees across the diagonal of the film format. → 1.205 FOCAL LENGTH; 1.335 FILM FORMAT

1.167 aperture The opening behind the camera lens through which the imaging light passes en route to the film plane. Usually described using f-numbers: the larger the f-number, the smaller the opening. → 1.199 F-NUMBER

1.168 apochromatic lens (APO) A lens (almost always a telephoto) that is optically corrected for red, green and blue wavelengths of light. → 1.163 ACHROMATIC LENS

1.169 aspherical A lens element, where the radius of curvature changes very slightly

with the distance from the optical axis. This can enable powerful correction of aberrations, especially in wide-angle lenses.

1.170 astigmatism Aberration where off-axis points are smeared in either the radial or tangential directions. It is only possible to focus one – focusing tangential elements will cause greater smearing of the radial. This aberration is not identical to astigmatism in the human eye.

1.171 auto-servo AF Modification of autofocus servo offered by Nikon in some camera models. Provides an automatic selection between single-servo AF (focus is locked after subject is focused upon) and continuous AF (where the focus continues to alter to a moving object remains in focus). → 1.173 AUTOFOCUS SERVO (AF SERVO)

1.172 autofocus (AF) Lens or camera that can focus automatically on a subject or point in the field of view.

1.173 autofocus servo (AF servo) A focusing option (normally reserved for high end professional and semi-pro cameras) that enables the camera's focusing system to 'lock on' to the subject and retain focus when that subject moves from the original plane of focus. This mode is described as **Continuous AF** by Nikon and **AF servo** by Canon, when implemented on their cameras. → 1.171 AUTO-SERVO AF

1.174 blooming (2) Optical term for the process of applying an anti-reflective coating to camera lenses (and other optical equipment). Such lenses are then said to be bloomed.

1.175 catadioptric lens A lens in which reflective elements and lens elements feature. Typical designs feature mirror lens design along with a supplementary lens (usually at the aperture) that corrects aberrations in the prime mirror. The **Schmidt** design, for example, uses a simple (and cheap) spherical mirror coupled with a lens of complex form to remove spherical aberrations from the mirror. **Maksutov lenses** use a concave lens for similar effect. The optical alignment and construction tends to make for a more delicate lens system; such lenses may not be so resilient to rough handling. The use of catadioptric lenses, like mirror lenses, is often betrayed on an image by the presence of a doughnut-shaped highlight, an artefact of the annular mirror. Though obvious, this can be used to creative effect. → 1.226 MIRROR LENS

1.176 circle of confusion Illuminated area when a lens images a point source of light. Parts of the image can be incorrectly focused leading to overlapping circles of confusion and a blurred result.

1.177 close-up lens A subsidiary lens fitted to the filter ring of a conventional lens to enable close-up shots to be taken at a distance less than that which the lens alone would allow. Available in a range of 'strengths' denoted by dioptres. → 1.192 DIOPTRE/DIOPTER

1.178 closest focusing Distance from the film plane at which the lens can focus when set to the minimum focus position.

1.179 coated lens A lens coated with a thin film of mineral-based material which reduces 'flare' (undesirable scattered light); sometimes referred to as a **bloomed lens**. A multicoated lens has multiple coatings applied to further reduce reflection and internal reflection. Coatings are very thin (of the order of the wavelength of light) and work by causing reflections from their upper and lower surfaces to cancel out. → 1.382 FLARE

1.180 coma A photographic lens aberration which causes blurring at the edge of a picture. Off-axis highlights tend to grow radial tails (rather like comets, hence the name) and are due to differential magnification at the centre and edge of the image.

1.181 compound lens A camera lens comprising more than one lens (elements). The use of compound lenses enables the lens to be optically adjusted for aberrations and distortion.

1.182 condenser (lens) A photographic lens which concentrates light into a beam. Used in enlargers and process cameras (a camera used for preparing film and plates for printing). → 1.127 PROCESS CAMERA

1.183 contrast detection Technique employed by passive autofocus systems to achieve correct focus.

1.184 CPU lens Lens featuring a central processing unit or one that links to a camera's CPU to aid in the setting of lens functions. Cameras designed to operate with CPU lenses generally offer limited functionality with other lenses with the appropriate lens mount. → 2.010 CENTRAL PROCESSING UNIT (CPU)

1.185 definition The overall quality – or clarity – of an image, determined by the combined subjective effect of sharpness and graininess (or resolution in a digital image). → 1.340 GRAININESS; 1.525 RESOLUTION

1.186 depth of field The distance in front of, and behind, the point of focus in a photograph in which the subject remains acceptably sharp or focused. By altering the lens aperture, the depth of field can be altered: the smaller the aperture, the greater the depth of field or sharpness and vice versa. → 1.167 APERTURE

1.187 depth of field preview Camera or lens control that closes the aperture to the user

1.186 *depth of field*

With limited depth of field, only a small region is in sharp focus

Varying the aperture alters the depth of field

1 Small aperture
2 Wide aperture

Depth-of-field scale on lens

or an automatically selected setting to enable the photographer to gauge the depth of field in the image.

1.188 depth of field scale Scale engraved on the barrel of some lenses, or provided as a separate diagrammatic table that indicates the depth of field for a particular aperture.

1.189 depth of focus The distance through which the film plane can be moved from the point of focus and still record an acceptably sharp image. Normally relates to cameras that have adjustable film holder backs. → 1.186 DEPTH OF FIELD; 1.205 FOCAL LENGTH; 1.208 FOCUS

1.190 diaphragm The opening, or 'aperture', behind or within a camera lens which can be adjusted to control the amount of light that reaches the film. The aperture opening is calibrated on the camera lens by f-stop numbers. Also called an '**iris diaphragm**'. → 1.199 F-NUMBER

1.191 diffraction When a beam of light passes through a lens or aperture it spreads out; the degree of spreading depends on the size of the aperture. Diffraction will ultimately determine how sharp an image can be formed by a lens.

1.192 dioptre/diopter The measurement of the refractive properties of a lens. Normally used to describe the 'power' of close-up lenses. A concave lens is measured in negative dioptres, a convex lens in positive dioptres. → 1.198 EYESIGHT CORRECTION LENS; 1.217 LENS

1.193 diverging/divergent lens A camera lens which causes light rays to bend outwards from the optical axis. Also called a '**negative element**'. Teleconverters act as a negative element with the result that an effective increase in focal length is introduced.

1.194 E-TTL Evaluative through-the-lens (TTL) exposure system using a brief preflash before the main flash to assist in calculating exposure. → 1.306 THROUGH-THE-LENS (TTL) METER; 1.308 TTL

1.195 element A single lens within a compound lens system. A camera lens might contain eight elements assembled in three groups. → 1.212 GROUP

1.196 extra low dispersion glass (ED) An extreme version of low dispersion glass often denoted by the letters ED in the lens specification. → 1.222 LOW DISPERSION GLASS

1.197 eye-control focusing Refinement of auto-focus technology employed (principally) in Canon SLRs. After calibration to the user's eyesight the camera will focus on subjects at different points in the viewfinder.

1.198 eyesight correction lens A supplementary lens usually mounted on the eyepiece of a camera viewfinder to enable users who normally wear glasses to use the viewfinder without glasses. Some cameras feature adjustable eyesight correction to accommodate a wide range of sight adjustment. **Dioptre correction lenses** can also assist in close-ups.

1.199 f-number/f-value/f-stop The calibration of the aperture size of a photographic lens. This is the ratio of the focal length ('f' = focal) to the diameter of the aperture. The numbers are marked on the equipment. For example, a camera lens normally calibrated in a standard series would include the following numbers: f1, f1.4, f2, f2.8, f4, f5.6, f8, f11, f16, f22, f32 and so on, and these set the aperture size. The maximum amount of light that can be transmitted through a lens determines the 'speed' of a lens – a lens with a minimum aperture of, e.g., f1 is a 'fast lens' (it lets in more light), whereas a lens with a minimum aperture of f3.5 is described as a 'slow lens'. → 1.167 APERTURE; 1.190 DIAPHRAGM

1.200 field curvature A lens aberration in which the plane of sharpest focus is curved rather than the flat surface needed at the film plane.

1.201 fish-eye lens A camera lens with an extremely wide angle of view, producing a distorted image with an exaggerated apparent curve. In the 35 mm format lenses of focal length 8 mm provide a full, circular fish-eye, 16 mm give a full frame fish-eye. → 1.253 WIDE-ANGLE LENS

1.202 fixed focus Description of a lens (or camera) which has a fixed, predetermined focus set for a particular subject distance (normally around 3 metres), in order to have group shots and middle-distance objects in best focus. The use of small apertures on such cameras generally means there is reasonable depth of field.

1.203 fixed-focus lens A photographic lens offering no focus adjustment. Usually found on basic cameras or those for specialist applications.

1.204 flare A bright streak, disc or other bright artefact seen through the viewfinder, or on an image, due to extraneous light entering the camera lens. Usually the use of a lens hood can reduce the extent of flare. → 1.179 COATED LENS; 2.120 IMAGE-EDITING APPLICATION; 4.275 LENS FLARE FILTER

1.205 focal length The distance between the optical centre of a lens and its point of focus (usually the film plane) when the lens is focused on infinity. It is normally measured in millimetres. → 1.166 ANGLE OF VIEW; 1.199 F-NUMBER

1.206 focal plane The plane at which a camera lens forms a sharp image; also the 'film plane', the point at which the image is recorded.

1.207 focal range The range over which a camera or lens is able to focus (or be manually focused) on a subject. On interchangeable lenses the range is usually marked on the lens barrel and might be, for example, 0.5 m to infinity.

1.208 focus The adjustment of the distance setting (either manually or automatically) in an autofocus camera to produce the sharpest definition across an image plane. Also the point at which light rays converge to produce the sharpest image. → 1.186 DEPTH OF FIELD; 1.205 FOCAL LENGTH

1.209 focus lock A method of fixing the focus of an autofocus camera at a particular point. Usually achieved by light pressure on the shutter release or by pressing a separate button. Useful for focusing on a non-central subject.

1.210 focus priority Setting which prevents the shutter being released unless the subject is in focus. Used when correct focus is critical. → 1.173 AUTOFOCUS SERVO (AF SERVO)

1.211 follow focus Focus option to enable the following of a moving object that may be approaching or receding from the camera. The camera constantly monitors and adjusts the focus to ensure the intended subject remains sharp, ready for an exposure (or exposures) to be made at any time.

1.212 group An assembly of lens elements fixed together (either through being cemented together, or held rigidly together as a sub-assembly) within a camera lens. → 1.195 ELEMENT

1.213 hyperfocal distance The closest distance at which a lens records a subject sharply when focused at infinity. Will vary with aperture. If the camera is set to the hyperfocal distance, the region from half that distance to infinity will be in focus.

1.214 image stabilization Technique for reducing camera shake. **Optical image stabilizers** use **fluid-filled prism** assemblies to counteract camera shake by altering the field of view slightly to compensate. **Electronic image stabilizers**, found in digital video cameras, counteract movement by locking on to image elements even when those elements move slightly in the field of view. All stabilizing techniques will degrade image quality slightly.

1.215 infinity In photographic terms, the notional point of the most extreme distant focus.

59

1.201 *fish-eye lens*

1 Wide-angle lens hood
2 Focusing ring
3 Aperture

1.223 *macro lens*

Macro lenses enable extreme close-ups, normally up to and greater than 1:1 (when using conventional filmstock)

1.**216 interchangeable lenses** Lenses with bayonet or screw threads that enable them to be attached to or removed from the camera body. Most SLR cameras, and some compact, digital, digital video and large format cameras, feature interchangeable lenses.

1.**217 lens** The name describing a cylindrical tube containing one or more glass 'elements' which collect and focus light rays to create an image. Also the name given to an individual element within a lens assembly.

1.**218 lens aberration** A deficiency in a photographic lens wherein light rays do not pass 'correctly' through the lens, causing degraded images. This can be due to faults or shortcomings in the optical construction. With **chromatic aberration**, light of different colours comes to different focal planes, resulting in coloured haloes around objects. In spherical **aberration**, imprecise (or incorrect) curvature of the lens surface prevents light from coming to a single focal point; instead there is a focal patch from which the '**best point of focus**' must be selected. Certain **lens distortions** are also classed with aberrations. **Barrel distortion** causes objects to 'bulge', with rectangles appearing barrel-like. Pincushion distortion is the converse, with rectangles appearing 'pinched' along their sides. → 2.287 PINCUSHION DISTORTION

1.**219 lens hood** Integral or accessory unit that shades the front of the lens from extraneous light. The most effective are rectangular or square in section (depending on the film format), and allow only that part of the scene which will comprise the recorded image on the film to pass through. A good lens hood will minimize flare, even when bright light sources are forward of the camera.

1.**220 lens speed** The widest setting to which a lens can be set. Corresponds to the smallest f-number.

1.**221 long-focus lens** A camera lens with a focal length longer than the diagonal measurement of the film format. Thus, for 35 mm film, a lens longer than about 50 mm is considered long-focus, but in common usage the term tends to denote longer telephoto lenses. → 1.242 SHORT-FOCUS LENS; 1.250 TELEPHOTO LENS

1.**222 low dispersion glass** A specialist glass used for lens making, whose refractive index varies slightly according to the wavelength of light. Chromatic aberration, especially, is easier to correct using low dispersion glass.

1.**223 macro lens** Lens with a focusing range from infinity to extreme close-up. Normally macro lenses are capable of reproducing objects at a 1:1 scale on film (i.e., life size). Some macro lenses use supplementary close-up lenses to achieve even greater magnifications.

1.**224 macro mode** A mode offered by some lenses (and some cameras) that enables focusing in the macro range. Selecting the macro mode results in changes to the internal configuration of the lens elements and groups to make close focusing possible. Where indication is possible (such as on a camera's LCD display) macro mode is often denoted by a **tulip icon**.

1.**225 minimum aperture** The smallest aperture that can be set on a lens. In a 35 mm format lens this is typically f22 or f16. → 1.199 F-NUMBER

1.**226 mirror lens** A camera lens that forms an image by reflecting it from curved mirrors rather than by refraction through a series of lenses. A mirror lens is more compact than a traditional lens of the same focal length (a telephoto lens, for example) but may not be capable of the same optical performance. → 1.250 TELEPHOTO LENS

1.**227 optical axis** An imaginary line through the centre of lens elements through which a light passes from a central subject. Light passing through other parts of the lens is described as off-axis.

1.**228 optical zoom** Term used mainly with digital cameras and digital video cameras to denote a conventional zoom lens where the position of lens elements is altered to achieve different focal lengths. 'Optical' is used to distinguish this from the 'digital' zoom also found on many of these cameras. → 1.024 DIGITAL ZOOM

1.**229 optimum aperture** Lens designs tend to offer the best performance (in terms of achieving a good focus and suppressing aberrations) at an optimum aperture. This is usually two or three f-stops down from the maximum aperture. When the highest quality is sought this aperture should be used, although being stopped down will mean that exposure times are substantially longer than at full aperture.

1.**230 parallax error** A **subject-framing error** found with non-SLR cameras (such as compacts, rangefinders and twin lens reflex cameras). As the viewfinder and the taking lens are slightly offset, their view is also slightly different. This becomes a problem at close subject distances where a degree of compensation needs to be introduced. Many camera viewfinders either adjust their view at this range or feature '**parallax marks**'.

1.**231 passive autofocus** An autofocus system that analyses subject parameters (usually contrast) to establish distance. This is used in most SLR autofocus cameras.
→ 1.164 ACTIVE AUTOFOCUS

1.**232 perspective control (PC) lens** A camera lens used mainly to correct converging verticals in architectural photography. Also called a '**shift lens**'. The lens can be moved laterally with respect to the film plane and also tilted to achieve corrective results.

1.**233 perspective correction** Adjusting an image geometry so that converging verticals (for example, when photographing buildings from a low viewpoint) are compensated for to give 'straight' verticals. Can also be used to correct other perspective effects and usually achieved on 35 mm and medium format cameras with a perspective control (PC) lens. Large format cameras usually feature a camera back that can be tilted or moved relative to the

lens to achieve a similar result. → 1.232 PERSPECTIVE CONTROL (PC) LENS

1.**234 portrait lens** Generally a term applied to lenses of between 90 mm and 110 mm focal length (in the 35 mm format) used for portraiture work. Lenses of this length give a face or head and shoulder view in correct perspective (anything shorter tends to over-emphasize the nose) and give a shallow depth of field useful for isolating the subject from the background. Specialist portrait lenses feature integral soft focus filtration that can be dialled in or out from the lens barrel when required.

1.**235 predictive autofocus** An autofocus technique that uses 'fuzzy logic' to predict the movement of the subject so that focus is retained on that subject.

1.**236 prime lens** Fixed focal length lens. Though a zoom lens may replace several prime lenses, these lenses are usually capable of better optical performance and are to be preferred for exacting work.
→ 1.254 ZOOM LENS

1.**237 rangefinder** A focusing aid in many non-autofocus cameras that aids precise focusing. Some autofocus cameras (typically compact cameras) feature electronic rangefinders to provide the autofocus function.

1.**238 release priority** Shutter can be released at any time, irrespective of whether that subject is in focus. Usually the release priority condition applies when continuous AF is set on the camera. → 1.173 AUTOFOCUS SERVO (AF SERVO)

1.241 *sharpness*

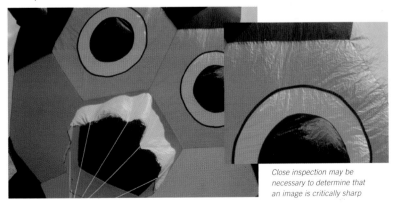

Close inspection may be necessary to determine that an image is critically sharp

1.**239 resolving power** The ability of a lens (or, sometimes, photographic emulsion) to record fineness of detail.

1.**240 rotating lens** Term usually applied to a lens whose front element rotates when the focus is adjusted or, where appropriate, the zoom mechanism is adjusted. Although this does not affect the optical performance, the rotating front will cause any mounted filters to rotate similarly. The action of certain filters (polarizers and graduated) will be adversely affected by such movement.

1.**241 sharpness** A measure of the clarity of focus present in a photographic image. → 1.185 DEFINITION

1.**242 short-focus lens** A camera lens with a focal length shorter than the diagonal measurement of the film format. Thus for 35 mm film, a lens shorter than 35 mm is short-focus. → 1.221 LONG-FOCUS LENS

1.**243 soft focus** An effect which 'softens' or slightly diffuses the lines and edges of an image without altering the actual focus. Slightly opaque 'softening' filters are employed to confer a 'romantic' feel to portraits and landscapes, but are also useful for hiding minor skin blemishes. Filters with stronger effects are termed diffusers. → 1.143 DIFFUSER

1.**244 spherical aberration** The failure of a lens to exactly focus light rays at its centre and at its edges. → 1.218 LENS ABERRATION

1.**245 standard lens** The fixed focus lens normally sold with SLR cameras and boasting a focal length of between 45 mm and 55 mm. This gives a view that most closely echoes the proportions and perspective of the original scene, although it often has too narrow a field of view for use with interiors and is not selective enough for longer range views. Also known as a '**normal lens**'.

1.**246 standard zoom** A zoom lens including the range of a standard lens (around 50 mm) in its focal range. Although this might apply to some of the '**superzooms**' (with focal ranges from 28 mm to 300 mm) it normally applies to more modest ranges (typically 28–80 mm, for example). → 1.254 ZOOM LENS

1.**247 stop** The aperture size of a camera lens. → 1.199 F-NUMBER; 1.248 STOP DOWN

1.**248 stop down** The action of closing down the aperture of a lens, e.g., from f4 to f5.6.

1.**249 teleconverter** A negative lens placed between a camera body and lens to increase the effective focal length of that lens. Typical teleconverters multiply the focal length of the lens by 1.4, 2 or 3 times. Teleconverters tend to degrade image quality to a degree: this degree tends to increase with the value of the multiplier. The highest quality teleconverters are matched to a specific lens. Sometimes (historically) described as a '**Barlow lens**' or, for a dedicated lens, a '**matched multiplier**'.

1.**250 telephoto lens** A photographic lens with a long focal length that enables distant objects to be enlarged. Telephoto lenses have a limited angle of view and offer

1.253 *wide-angle lens*

1 *Lens hood*
2 *Distance indicator*
3 *Aperture*

1.250 *telephoto lens*

1 *Locking ring*
2 *Tripod mount*
3 *Focusing control*

limited depth of field for a given f-number.
→ 1.221 LONG-FOCUS LENS; 1.226 MIRROR LENS;
1.254 ZOOM LENS

1.251 ultrasonic motor (USM) A special **ring motor** that acts almost silently to adjust the focus in many Canon autofocus lenses. A similar system is employed with some Nikon lenses where it is termed a **Hypersonic Motor (HSM)**. Other manufacturers (notably Sigma) offer, or will offer, these lenses in the future.

1.252 vignetting A reduction in the light levels at the edge of an image or print due to deficiencies in the lens used for taking or enlarging the print. The use of an incorrect lens hood or too many filters can also cause vignetting. → 4.348 VIGNETTE FILTER

1.253 wide-angle lens A photographic lens with wider field of view than a standard lens, so that more of the subject can be included. For 35 mm cameras the term wide angle usually applies to focal lengths of 35 mm or less. The widest wide angles have focal lengths of around 14 mm. Normally the term wide angle denotes lenses that do not introduce obvious distortion. Those that are wider and make no attempt at correcting distortions are described as fish-eye lenses. Wide-angle lenses are ideal for including sweeping landscapes and capturing small interiors. → 1.201 FISH-EYE LENS; 1.221 LONG-FOCUS LENS; 1.242 SHORT-FOCUS LENS

1.254 zoom lens A camera lens with a focal length that can be adjusted over a range of focal lengths giving, in effect, a set of lenses of different focal length in one body. Useful for framing a subject, but generally a zoom lens is likely to have a smaller maximum aperture, suffer more aberrations and distortion. Wide-angle zooms provide a range of focal lengths that cover several equivalent wide-angle lenses (such as 24 mm to 35 mm in 35 mm format). Standard zooms give a range that includes the 'standard' 50 mm focal length. → 1.250 TELEPHOTO LENS

Metering and exposure settings

1.255 AE lock A facility to lock the camera's calculated (and set) exposure settings so they can be applied to a number of exposures, or enabling the exposure to be set for one situation and applied to another. This is useful where shots will be of adjacent areas and will later be co-joined (for example, using panoramic software). Convincing stitching of images is dependent on consistent exposure. The term is short for Auto Exposure lock.

1.256 aperture priority Camera exposure mode which allows the user to set the aperture while a corresponding shutter speed is set automatically by the camera. The shutter speed will change if light levels change or the selected aperture is altered. → 1.295 PROGRAM EXPOSURE; 1.301 SHUTTER PRIORITY

1.257 auto exposure bracketing Bracketing is important for conventional film stock (particularly transparency film) to enable a perfect shot. Multiple exposures are made with different exposure settings – typically differing by 0.5 EV. Although digital cameras tend to be more forgiving of exposure shortcomings, bracketed exposures are still useful, especially if a scene has a high dynamic range. With such scenes, images (or elements) can be combined from separate exposures to produce a well-exposed final image. Auto exposure bracketing will produce sequences of three, five, seven or more shots centred on the automatically assessed 'correct' exposure. → 1.422 BRACKETING

1.258 average reading The average light meter reading for a scene, normally not biased in favour of any particular region or scene. Hand-held meters will usually give average readings.

1.259 backlight control Control that enables a longer exposure (or a wider aperture) to be used when a subject is strongly lit from behind. Normally around 1.5 stops, this increase in exposure will prevent the subject becoming a silhouette (since the meter reading takes backlighting into account). In some cameras this is activated by pressing a backlight button; in others an adjustable control is provided.

1.260 between the lens shutter A shutter usually comprising interlocking blades or leaves, also known as a **leaf shutter**, that open for a specified time to perform the exposure. The actual exposure time might vary from the camera setting to account for the opening and closing of the blades. As the name suggests, this shutter is built into the **lens shutter** and normally sits between lens groups or elements.

1.261 bulb (setting) Shutter speed setting that allows the shutter to remain open as long as the shutter release is pressed. Compare with the time (T) exposure setting, which opens the shutter on the first press of the shutter release and closes it on the second press. → 1.307 TIME EXPOSURE

1.262 centre-weighted exposure In automatic TTL-metered cameras, the method of measuring exposure where the calculation is biased towards the centre of the scene. The extent of this bias and the contribution from the surroundings does vary from camera to camera. → 1.306 THROUGH-THE-LENS (TTL) METER

1.263 close-up mode A mode that can be selected to enable close-up shots. This mode is often provided when the camera does not offer a true macro mode. → 1.427 CLOSE-UP

1.264 direct reading The common term for taking a meter reading directly from light reflected from a subject.

1.265 evaluative metering A complex but ultimately very effective metering system, that breaks a scene down into a large number of metering areas (sometimes called **matrix metering** or **multi-pattern metering**). An exposure is evaluated for each and then an overall exposure assessed by combining the results in a very precise way. Implementation differs according to the camera.

1.266 exposure The amount of light allowed to reach a photosensitive material, such as photographic film or CCD imaging sensor, to enable the recording of an image. This is usually determined by a combination of the length of time and the intensity at which the light shines upon the material.

1.267 exposure compensation A facility provided on many digital and conventional cameras that permits the overriding of the camera's metered exposure settings by amounts usually of 1/3 stops (or 1/3 EV) up to a maximum, typically, of + or -3 stops. This can be used, for example, to introduce manual backlight compensation. → 1.259 BACKLIGHT CONTROL

1.268 exposure latitude A range (**latitude**) of exposure settings appropriate to a given photographic film or imaging sensor that will still provide an acceptable result.

1.269 exposure lock A method of locking the exposure setting of the camera so that, for example, the scene can be reframed but retain the original camera settings. This is often an easy way to set an exposure compensation without altering the camera settings. → 1.255 AE LOCK; 1.267 EXPOSURE COMPENSATION

1.270 exposure meter Device used to measure the amount of light falling on a subject in order that the correct exposure can be set. Can work either by recording the light reflected from a subject or by measuring the light incident upon that subject. Also called a 'light meter'. It can be a hand-held or camera-mounted device, or an integral unit.

64

1.243 *soft focus*

Soft focus applied

Original

1.270 *exposure meter*

1 Light level read-out
2 Film speed setting
3 Aperture/exposure combinations

1.271 exposure setting The combination of shutter speed and amount of aperture (lens opening). Because different combinations result in the same amount of light reaching the film (for example, 1/30s at f/8 is the same as 1/60s at f/5.6), exposure settings are sometimes calibrated in exposure values (EV).
→ 1.272 EXPOSURE VALUE (EV)

1.272 exposure value (EV) A method of quantifying the brightness value of a scene. It is based on the sensitivity of the imaging sensor (which is usually equated to an ISO film speed equivalent), the aperture, and shutter speed. This gives a single number which quantifies the amount of light for a particular exposure and can then be used to calculate the correct combination of shutter speeds and apertures.

1.273 filter factor The amount of compensation that is required (lengthening) of a photographic exposure if a filter is used.
→ 1.142 COLOR FILTERS

1.274 flash meter An exposure meter designed to measure the transient output of electronic flash and provide details of the exposure required. These tend to be used in studio situations where multiple fully adjustable flash heads are used and conventional calculations of exposure are too problematic. Flash meters can work off incident or reflected light and usually feature a PC cord socket to activate the flash units.

1.275 focal plane shutter A camera shutter located close to the focal plane, in which two blinds form an adjustable gap which moves across the film, determining the exposure. This lateral or vertical motion can be problematic when shooting certain subjects, such as computer or TV displays, as banding (a shadow of the shutter slit) can compromise the image. → 1.260
BETWEEN THE LENS SHUTTER

1.276 gray card A card with a mat surface and colored neutral gray that reflects 18% of the incident light. This is the average reflectance for a subject and the one for which most exposure meters are calibrated. Thus by taking a meter reading from the gray card only, the meter will evaluate a correct exposure based on the incident light. That exposure setting can

then be locked, the card removed, and the exposure made.

1.277 highlight reading A light meter reading that is taken from a subject highlight in the scene.

1.278 honeycomb metering A metering system introduced by Minolta that divides the image area into a pattern of close packed honeycomb cells that individually meter the subject. The results can then be combined in different ways to provide optimum metering and exposure for specific subjects.

1.279 hyperfocal mode Exposure mode that selects a maximum depth of field to ensure a close subject and a distant background are in focus. → 1.213
HYPERFOCAL DISTANCE

1.280 incident light reading Light meter reading of the light falling on an object rather than that reflected from it. Incident light meters (which are typically hand-held devices) need a degree of skill to use and interpret effectively; the efficacy of modern TTL meters is such that these devices have been rendered redundant.

1.281 landscape mode An exposure mode (sometimes a programmed exposure mode) optimized for landscape photography. Sets a moderate to small aperture to keep close and distant parts of the scene in sharp focus. This will result in comparatively long exposure times— it is presumed the camera will be used on a tripod.

1.282 light meter A light meter that measures light levels, but more specifically applied to a photographic exposure meter.
→ 1.270 EXPOSURE METER

1.283 manual mode A mode found on automatic cameras that permits the user to set both the shutter speed and the aperture. Normally an indication of the "correct" exposure setting is shown and the results of the user settings can often be previewed on a digital camera by using the LCD preview screen.

1.284 manual override An option that permits the automatic settings of a camera to be overridden. The term also applies to the focusing settings.

1.285 metering range The range of brightness within which the camera's metering system can function. Usually expressed in the form **EV(min)** to **EV(max)** at ISO(x), where EV(min) and EV(max) are the minimum and maximum EV recordable and x is the typical film speed rating or its digital equivalent to which these EVs refer (usually 100 or 200). → 1.272 EXPOSURE VALUE (EV)

1.286 mode A set of camera function settings (including, but not limited to, **exposure mode** and measurement, aperture, shutter speed, and focusing method). Many cameras, both digital and conventional, offer a range of modes from fully automatic program modes through to manual.

1.287 multispot metering Metering system that calculates an average or weighted exposure value based on multiple spot metering results. A variation on this (used by Olympus in the OM3 and OM4 cameras) allows up to eight spot readings to be combined and also enables highlight or shadow spot readings to be incorporated. A very accurate system but slow to use.

1.288 multimode Description of a camera that offers multiple operation modes. → 1.286 MODE

1.289 multipattern metering An exposure metering system in which areas of the image are measured separately, and assessed according to a predetermined program. Different camera manufacturers have different patterns which each believes to be optimum.

1.290 night mode Exposure mode designed to capture subject and background when taken at night. Also called **night-scene mode**. Can include a flash (or fill-in flash) to illuminate the subject, and a time exposure to record the background.

1.291 off-the-film (OTF) metering Technique pioneered and exploited by **Olympus** with its **OM** camera range. Light readings are taken from the light that is reflected from the film emulsion during the actual exposure. As such, it is very responsive and can actually alter exposure time if changes in light levels are detected. It also functions for flash photography. The drawback is the need for a second meter system in order to preadvise the photographer of the approximate exposure time.

1.292 open up To increase the aperture of a lens by decreasing the f-number. A

lens would be opened up when going from f/8 to f/2.8.

1.293 overexpose/overexposure A condition wherein too much light reaches the film, due to too large an aperture being set and/or too long an exposure. The result is a very dense negative or light slide (or print).

1.294 portrait mode Exposure mode that automatically selects a wide aperture to make the subject stand out against a defocused background.

1.295 program exposure An exposure mode whereby the camera determines both the aperture and shutter speed. Programs are usually biased toward the hand-holding of cameras so, light levels permitting, they tend to keep shutter speeds high at the expense of the aperture size. Many cameras have multiple **program modes** that offer special shutter speed/aperture combinations suited for, say, sport photography, portraits, or landscapes. Shift Program (or **Program Shift**) modes allow the same exposure to be made but by altering exposure time and aperture in tandem. This can be useful if the original program did not give a sufficiently short exposure time, or sets an incorrect depth of field for the chosen subject.

1.296 reciprocity failure An exception to the mathematical reciprocity law in photographic processing. A short exposure under a bright light does not produce the same result as a long exposure in a dim light, although mathematically it should. In other words, at very short and very long exposures, the reciprocity law ceases to hold true, and an extra exposure is needed. The effect produced varies with film types, but on color film the three dye layers suffer differently and a color cast may occur, so only the exposure range that the film was designed for should be used. → 1.297 RECIPROCITY LAW

1.297 reciprocity law A law that states that photographic exposure is the result of both the intensity of light and the time taken to make the exposure. If you double one, you need to halve the other to achieve the same exposure. This law works linearly to a point, but does break down under extreme conditions, e.g., exposures longer than 1 second and low light levels. → 1.296 RECIPROCITY FAILURE

1.298 reflected light reading A light meter reading of the light reflected from a subject. TTL light meters and those mounted on cameras take readings of this type.

1.299 shutter The mechanical device in a camera which controls the length of time a film is exposed to the light. → 1.260 BETWEEN THE LENS SHUTTER; 1.275 FOCAL PLANE SHUTTER

1.300 shutter lag The time delay between pressing the shutter release on a digital camera and the exposure being made. Longer than for conventional cameras, as exposure, white balance analysis, and focusing need to be performed.

1.301 shutter priority An automatic camera exposure mode that allows the user to select the shutter speed. The corresponding aperture is then set automatically according to the camera's metering system. If the user subsequently changes the shutter speed, or the ambient light levels change, the camera compensates automatically. An alternative to aperture priority. → 1.256 APERTURE PRIORITY; 1.302 SHUTTER SPEED

1.302 shutter speed The time a shutter remains open during an exposure. Most cameras with manual control of shutter speed offer options of 1/1000s, 1/500s, 1/250s, 1/125s, 1/60s, etc., where each shutter speed is approximately twice the previous. → 1.301 SHUTTER PRIORITY

1.303 Silicon Photodiode (SPD) Light sensor used in exposure meters, both hand-held and in-camera devices. **Cadmium Sulphide sensors (CdS)** were used in earlier meters.

1.304 sport/action mode Exposure mode that is offered on some cameras (digital and conventional) which give a bias toward shorter exposure times in order to "freeze" action. Provides a fully automatic alternative to the shutter priority mode that is usually preferred by sports photographers.

1.305 spot meter A specialized light meter, or a function of a camera light meter, that enables an exposure reading to be taken from a precise area of a scene. Typically, this would be an area about 1° across or representing 1% of the viewfinder scene. In SLR cameras, spot meter readings are usually made by placing the central circle over the subject and then taking a reading. Particularly useful for ensuring that a specific element in the scene is correctly exposed.

1.306 through-the-lens (TTL) meter An exposure meter built into a camera which calculates an exposure based on the amount of light that is passing through the camera lens. In most cases this is a coupled system that gives a direct readout in the viewfinder.

1.307 time exposure An exposure typically of more than one second's duration, or longer than the longest exposure that can be set on the camera. A "time" setting on some cameras makes time exposures easier: pressing once on the shutter release opens the shutter, and it remains open until the shutter release is pressed again.

*1.309 **underexposure***   *1.293 **overexposure***

Normal exposure

1.**308 TTL** Abbreviation for through-the-lens, usually used to describe metering systems that use the light passing through the taking lens to evaluate exposure details.
→ 1.306 THROUGH-THE-LENS (TTL) METER

1.**309 underexpose, underexposure** The provision of insufficient light to effect the correct exposure of a photosensitive material. The result is a print or transparency that is too dark and a negative that is too "thin" (resulting in a dark print). In a digital image the signal to noise ratio becomes smaller, resulting in a "noisier" image.
→ 1.079 SIGNAL TO NOISE RATIO (S/N, SNR)

1.**310 vari-program modes** A programmed exposure mode that features aperture and exposure settings optimized for the specific subject matter. Typical vari-program modes, include **sport program** mode, landscape mode, and portrait mode.

1.**311 zone system** An exposure regime popularized by American landscape photographer **Ansel Adams**. Divides scenes into nine zones, each one stop apart in brightness, ranging from **zone I** (the darkest black it is possible to print) through to **zone IX**, the purest paper-based white.

Film

1.**312 110** A cassette-loading film format derived from the larger 126 format. 110 cameras were mostly small, flat devices, capitalizing on the low profile of the film cassette. More comprehensive designs were produced by Minolta and Pentax, including interchangeable lens SLRs.

1.**313 120** One of the roll film formats. Comprises a length of film approximately 64 mm wide backed with opaque paper and wound on a slim spool. Backing paper prevents light penetrating and fogging the film. This backing paper is marked with frame numbers corresponding to the medium format frame sizes of 6 x 7-cm, 6 x 9-cm, and 6 x 6-cm. These numbers are designed to be viewed through small windows in the backs of cameras without automatic wind-on to ensure frames are correctly advanced. An older version of 120, **820**, had similar dimensions but was wound on a spool with a smaller spindle. Many 820 format cameras can use 120 film

either directly or when re-wound on an 820 spool.

1.**314 126** A cassette-loaded film that yielded square negatives on 35-mm width unperforated film. Launched to counter consumer resistance to 35-mm cameras. Market reseach had shown that loading 35-mm cameras proved problematic for many. The format fell into decline with the rise of alternatives and particularly by the launch of easy loading 35-mm cameras.

1.**315 220** Variation on the 120 medium-format roll film. Features a double length film but with no backing paper. Opaque paper is attached to each end of the roll to enable film to be loaded and unloaded without fogging. As there is no backing paper, these films cannot be used in cameras with film-back windows. Many medium-format cameras can use 120 or 220 format films, either using different camera backs or by adjusting the pressure plate at the back of the camera to allow for the different thicknesses of film (or film and paper in the case of 120 film). → 1.313 120

1.**316 35 mm** Common term for the 135 film format. Based on 35-mm-wide movie film (originally), it features double edge perforations that provide precise in-camera framing. Full frame 35-mm uses 24-mm by 35-mm frames. Half frame cameras squeeze two images into this area, while some specialized cameras such as panoramic cameras use a 58 mm x 24-mm frame size.

1.**317 70 mm** Film format based on 70-mm movie film, and twice the width of 35-mm film. As the image area is the same as 120 and 220 format film, this can be used (with special backs) in many cameras designed for these formats. Has the advantage of allowing much longer film lengths but suffers from limited availability in a restricted number of emulsions.

1.**318 Advanced Photo System (APS)** A film format using 24-mm-wide cartridge-loaded film. A magnetic coating allows the transfer of photographic data to viewing and processing devices using information exchange (IX) circuitry. Such information advises the photofinishing lab of the film format used (classic, wide HDTV, or ultrawide panoramic) and exposure information. Uses a unique **polyester film** that enables the film to be "fired" out from the cartridge into the host camera but to remain flat.

1.319 American Standards Association (ASA) The US association that defined the scale used for rating the speed (light-sensitivity) of photographic film. → 1.047 ISO EQUIVALENT; 1.327 DEUTSCHE INDUSTRIE-NORM (DIN); 1.344 INTERNATIONAL STANDARDS ORGANIZATION (ISO)

1.320 C format One of the three print formats for the APS. Short for Classic format, it trims the shorter edges of the image to give a conventional 4:3 aspect ratio. → 1.318 ADVANCED PHOTO SYSTEM (APS); 1.341 H FORMAT; 1.351 P FORMAT

1.321 cartridge Sealed film container used (principally) for 126 and 110 format films. Unexposed film passes from one spool, across an aperture window to a second, take-up spool. → 1.312 110; 1.314 126; 1.322 CASSETTE

1.322 cassette Light-tight film container from which film is withdrawn during exposure; typical examples are 35-mm film and APS. An APS cassette also contains indicators to advise whether the film inside is exposed, partially exposed, unexposed, or processed. → 1.316 35 MM; 1.318 ADVANCED PHOTO SYSTEM (APS); 1.321 CARTRIDGE

1.323 chromogenic Black and white films that use color negative technology in image formation. Instead of the conversion of silver halide grains to black in the image, the halide crystals are replaced with a dye. **Dye image film** gives very fine grain characteristics and the film has very high exposure latitude. Typical films of this type include Ilford's XP2. → 1.268 EXPOSURE LATITUDE

1.324 color negative film Photographic film in which an image is formed in negative colors after processing. Positive prints can then be made on negative paper. Compare with color transparency film, which is positive and is not generally used for making prints. → 1.325 COLOR TRANSPARENCY FILM

1.325 color transparency film A photographic image on transparent film generated, after processing, as a positive image. Color **transparencies** are ideal as originals for color separations for process color printing, as they provide a greater range of colors than do reflective prints. Color

transparency film is supplied for a variety of camera formats, from APS through to 35-mm, 2¼-inch square, and 4 x 5-inch. Color transparencies are also known variously as "**slides**" (which generally refers to 35-mm film only), and "**color reversal film**." → 1.324 COLOR NEGATIVE FILM

1.326 daguerrotype The first practical method of creating and fixing a photographic image. Invented by **Louis J. M. Daguerre** in 1833, the process involved exposing a silvered copper plate to iodine or bromine vapor, which made it light-sensitive.

1.327 Deutsche Industrie-Norm (DIN) A code of standards established in Germany and used widely throughout the world to standardize such things as size, weight, and other properties of particular materials and manufactured items—for example, computer connectors and photographic film speed—so that they are universally compatible. → 1.319 AMERICAN STANDARDS ASSOCIATION (ASA); 1.344 INTERNATIONAL STANDARDS ORGANIZATION (ISO)

1.328 diapositive A photographic transparency in which the image is positive.

1.329 disk (film) Now redundant film format that used a disk of film mounted in a small floppy-disk-like cartridge. The tiny size of each negative prevented acceptable enlargements beyond 4 x 5 inches. Principal benefit came with processing— multiple disks could be threaded on a spindle for mass processing. The disk format did, however, pioneer on-film information systems that evolved into the DX and IX information exchange systems.

1.330 edge numbers Numbers imprinted on the edge of films before exposure in the camera to enable identification of the frame later. Often now featuring additional information relating to the film emulsion and speed.

1.331 emulsion The light-sensitive coating of a photographic material which, when exposed and processed, reveals the image. Colloquially (but incorrectly) called "the film."

1.332 fast film Term normally applied to film with an ISO rating of 400 or greater. Sometimes referred to as general purpose or "universal" film. The growing acceptance of ISO 400 film and the appearance of credible ISO 800 film has caused many to regard the latter as the starting point for "fast" film.

1.333 film A **cellulose acetate** or **polyester-base** material which is coated with light-sensitive emulsion so that images can be recorded photographically. **Photographic film** may be color or black and white, line or tone, negative or positive.

1.334 film base A transparent substrate used as a carrier for light-sensitive photographic emulsions. Most are acetate-based, though APS film uses the more rigid **A-PEN** (annealed polyethylene naphthalate), a type of polyester, to enable a thinner flatter film that can be expelled from the APS film cartridge without damage.

1.335 film format Standard measurements (and presentation) for sheet and roll photographic film, corresponding to usual film widths and standard camera sizes. Typical formats include 35-mm, APS, 12 on 120, 4 x 5-inch, and 8 x 10-inch. Less common (or defunct) formats include 110, 126, 127, and Disc.

1.336 film speed A quantitative measure of the sensitivity of a film or emulsion to light. Measured in ISO. Films with ratings of less than ISO 100/21 are considered "slow" (less light-sensitive), while those rated ISO 400/27 and over are "fast." Some **emulsion speeds** are still denoted by ASA (such as 50 ASA). The ASA and the first number of the ISO rating are equivalent. Though filmstock should meet the nominal speed printed, manufacturing tolerances and the effect of aging can affect the speed by one

stop or more. It is always advisable, in critical applications, to shoot a test film or perform a clip test to establish the effective film speed. → 1.327 DEUTSCHE INDUSTRIE-NORM (DIN); 1.344 INTERNATIONAL STANDARDS ORGANIZATION (ISO); 1.456 CLIP TEST

1.337 fog A clouding of the film emulsion, varying from mild to complete obliteration of an image due to light hitting the emulsion other than through the imaging process. Typically, fog affects the whole of the film, not just the frame area, and can be due either to light leaks in the camera or exposure to light during processing.

1.338 frame (1) Individual image on a film strip.

1.339 grain The density of tiny light-sensitive silver bromide crystals—or the overlapping clusters of crystals—in a photographic emulsion; the finer the grain, the better the detail but the slower (less light-sensitive) the film. Noticeably coarse grain can be used for graphic effect. → 1.340 GRAININESS

1.340 graininess The granulated effect present in a negative, print, or slide. The degree to which it is visible depends on such things as film speed (it increases with faster films), enlargement, and processing. Graininess can be introduced into images for creative effect using image-editing grain or noise filters. → 4.266 GRAIN FILTER; 4.421 NOISE

1.341 H format One of the three APS print formats. Short for **HDTV** (because its aspect ratio of 16:9 echoes that of wide-screen high-definition television screens), the

1.340 *graininess*

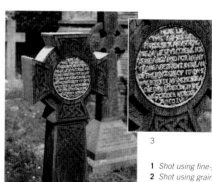

3

1 *Shot using fine-grain film*
2 *Shot using grainy film*
3 *Detail of grain*

1

2

H format uses the entire area of an APS frame. → 1.318 ADVANCED PHOTO SYSTEM (APS); 1.320 C FORMAT; 1.351 P FORMAT

1.342 **index print** An "**electronic contact sheet**" comprising small thumbnails of a set of images. Index prints generally accompany processed 35-mm films, APS films, PictureCDs and PhotoCDs, or image memory cards submitted to photofinishers. Some software packages will also produce index prints of digital images stored.

1.343 **information exchange (IX)** A feature of the APS that enables the film to communicate information with the camera (prior to, during, and after exposure) and subsequently to the photofinishing equipment. A thin magnetic coating on the film is used to store relevant digital data. Scene, exposure, and focusing information are currently recorded, but the system has the facility to store considerably more information, possibly forming the basis of increased functionality in future models. → 1.318 ADVANCED PHOTO SYSTEM (APS)

1.344 **International Standards Organization (ISO)** The International Standards Organization (ISO) is the name of the body responsible for the defining and implementation of international standards. ISO has defined the standard for film speeds, nominally based on the existing ASA proportional system (a doubling of the film speed corresponds to a doubling of the ASA number) and the German DIN logarithmic system (where a doubling of the film speed corresponds to an increase of three in the DIN rating). An ISO film rating is quoted thus: ISO 100/21. → 1.319 AMERICAN STANDARDS ASSOCIATION (ASA); 1.327 DEUTSCHE INDUSTRIE-NORM (DIN)

1.345 **internegative/interneg** A photographic negative used as the intermediate step when making a copy (usually a print) from a transparency or flat original. Internegatives were more common when photographic papers suitable for printing direct from transparencies tended to be very high contrast; prints could be produced using conventional lower contrast negative materials instead.

1.346 **IX 240** "Formal" name for the APS film format. → 1.318 ADVANCED PHOTO SYSTEM (APS)

1.347 **line film** Negative or positive photographic film in which the image consists of solid elements, such as lines or text matter, with no continuous tones or halftones. → 1.349 ORTHOCHROMATIC

1.348 **negative/neg** Photographic film or paper in which all the dark areas appear light and vice versa. Negative film is used extensively in the reproduction process and is either made directly from originals, or produced by an imagesetter.

1.349 **orthochromatic** A photographic emulsion which is sensitive to all colors except red, and used extensively in conventional reproduction. Also called "**lith film**" or "**ortho film**." → 1.350 ORTHOGRAPHIC

1.350 **orthographic** Photographic emulsion which is sensitive only to green, blue, and ultraviolet light. Tends to be used only for specialized applications and is not readily available. → 1.349 ORTHOCHROMATIC

1.351 **P format** One of the three APS formats. The **Panoramic setting** uses only the central band of the APS frame to create a wide print with an aspect ratio of 5:2. The small image area used can sometimes lead to grainy or ill-defined images. → 1.318 ADVANCED PHOTO SYSTEM (APS); 1.320 C FORMAT; 1.341 H FORMAT

1.352 **panchromatic** Photographic emulsion that is sensitive to all colors in the visible spectrum in broadly the same way as the human eye. Most readily available "consumer" and standard professional emulsions are panchromatic. → 1.350 ORTHOGRAPHIC

1.353 **reversal film** Film emulsion that produces a positive image, as in color transparencies ("slides"). → 1.325 COLOR TRANSPARENCY FILM

1.354 **roll film** A general term for film supplied rolled on a spool. Specifically, this applies to the current film formats of 120 and 220 and older formats such as 127 and 820.

1.355 **sheet film** Film supplied as individual sheets, each providing one exposure. 4 x 5-inch and 8 x 10-inch are the most common formats using sheet film.

1.356 **silver halide** Crystals, suspended in gelatin, that comprise the active part of film emulsions. When struck by light (or light of a sufficient intensity) they are exposed, changing them to silver. These silver points are too small to be visible but through the development process the "latent image" is made visible.

1.357 slow film Film with a low sensitivity to light. In common usage this applies to film of ISO 50 sensitivity or less. → 1.332 FAST FILM; 1.359 UNIVERSAL FILM

1.358 tungsten film A photographic film that delivers "neutral" or normally color-balanced results when exposed under tungsten lighting (conventional filament bulbs), instead of daylight (or daylight equivalent lighting). → 1.417 TUNGSTEN LIGHTING

1.359 universal film A general term for a consumer film that is suitable for all occasions. Usually denotes fast film (ISO 400). The term tends to be used as a marketing device to prevent baffling lay users with ASA or ISO film speeds.

Lighting

1.360 ambient light An alternate name for available light. This is the light (natural, artificial, or both) that lights the photographic subject. It is specifically that illumination not provided by the photographer.

1.361 artificial light Strictly, any light source not naturally occurring in the environment, but usually a term to describe incandescent, tungsten, or fluorescent lighting.

1.362 axial lighting The lighting of a photographic subject by shining a light along the lens axis, as this gives little or no shadow, the resulting "flat" lighting tends to be used more for creative than for practical purposes.

1.363 back projection The technique of projecting an image behind a photographic subject from an appropriate projector mounted behind the screen. Used to create in-camera montage. This technique has often been exploited in the commercial world (for catalog clothes shopping, for example) but digital image manipulation can now produce more flexible images of this type more cheaply (and more convincingly).

1.364 backlighting The principal light sources shine from behind the subject and are directed (broadly) toward the camera lens. This tends to produce results that have a lot of contrast, with silhouettes. A specific form of backlighting is called contre jour. Many cameras feature

backlight controls that increase aperture (or exposure time) to compensate for backlighting and to prevent the silhouetting of foreground objects. → 1.374 CONTRE JOUR/CONTREJOUR

1.365 barn doors Reflectors that usually surround a studio flash unit. By adjusting the barn doors (which may have reflective or black, light-absorbing surfaces), the direction and intensity of the flash light can be altered. Such **studio flash systems** usually include modeling lamps that help with the positioning of the doors.

1.366 base lighting Sometimes known as "**ground lighting**," this is the technique of lighting a subject from below with an upward-pointing light source. Often used for still-life photography of glassware and metallic objects to provide full lighting but without the flash highlights that would occur with front or side lighting. Causes a reversal of normal shadow profiles. Synonymous with ground light, although the latter term is sometimes reserved for ground-mounted lighting designed to up-light a background, instead of the subject.

1.367 boom Long arm to which a flash unit or a microphone can be attached to enable it to be positioned to appropriately light or record the subject.

1.368 bounce lighting/bounce flash Lighting (flash or otherwise) that indirectly lights a subject or background, having first been reflected from a dedicated reflector, or the walls or ceiling, to give a more natural effect. Sometimes used to describe the use of a large "fill-in" reflector to direct ambient light to fill shadows. → 1.381 FILL-IN LIGHT

1.369 brightfield illumination Lighting technique employed for photomicrography. A form of backlighting where the light is directed through a section of the subject being viewed. → 1.443 PHOTOMICROGRAPHY

1.370 brolly An umbrella coated on the inside with reflective material (silver, gold, or a mix, depending on the "warmth" required) to which a flashgun is fixed. The flash fires into the brolly and the diffused reflected light is used to illuminate the subject.

1.371 built-in flash A flash unit built into a camera. Common on APS and 35-mm compact cameras, these are also included in some 35-mm SLRs and medium-format cameras. Being necessarily small, they are often insufficient, so many cameras also feature a hot shoe for attaching a separate flash unit. → 1.116 HOT SHOE

1.**372 catchlight** Reflection of the flash light or other discrete light source in the eyes of the subject being photographed.

1.**373 color temperature** A measure, in degrees Kelvin, of the composition of light. This is defined as the temperature to which a black object would need to be heated to produce a particular color of light. The color temperature is based on a scale that sets zero as absolute darkness and increases with an object's brightness, for example, a light bulb filament. A tungsten lamp, for example, has a color temperature of 2,900°K, whereas the temperature of direct sunlight is around 5,000°K and is considered the ideal viewing standard in the graphic arts.

1.**374 contre jour/contrejour** From the French "**against the light**," this is a specific (and usually deliberate) form of backlighting in which the picture is taken with the camera lens pointing toward the light source.
→ 1.364 BACKLIGHTING

1.**375 darkfield illumination** Lighting technique employed for photomicrography. A form of backlighting where the subject is lit from multiple directions forming a cone of light. This gives a lit subject in the foreground with a dark background. → 1.369 BRIGHTFIELD ILLUMINATION; 1.443 PHOTOMICROGRAPHY

1.**376 dedicated flash** General term for any flashgun or flash system designed to work with specific makes or models of camera. Such systems often incorporate special circuitry to communicate with the camera, enabling camera settings to be detected by the flash and vice versa. In certain cases the camera's light sensors can be used to control flashgun output. Dedicated flash units are available from the camera manufacturer and third party companies.

1.**377 diffuse lighting** Light that has low contrast and no obvious highlights or "hotspots." Bounce lighting can be diffuse if well spread. Overcast skies also represent a natural diffuse light source.

1.**378 effects light** Photographic light designed to produce an effect rather than illuminate the subject or scene. A studio light equipped with a gobo is an example; a

light positioned to provide rim lighting is another. → 1.391 GOBO; 1.408 RIM LIGHTING

1.**379 existing light** Alternative name for available light, the term describes all natural and environmental light sources (i.e., those not specifically employed for the purpose of photography).

1.**380 fill-in flash** Sometimes called fill flash or flash fill, a technique that uses a flashgun in combination with ambient lighting to reduce shadows. As the converse of flash key, the flash light output is secondary to the ambient light. → 1.381 FILL-IN LIGHT; 1.384 FLASH KEY

1.**381 fill-in light** Additional lighting deliberately added to a scene to soften, lighten, or remove shadows or dark regions due to the main light source. Fill-in flash performs the same role by using flash light. Many cameras feature a fill-in flash mode that fires the flash even though the ambient lighting is sufficient.

1.**382 flare** Scattered light which degrades the quality of a photographic image, usually caused by too much light being reflected. In some situations flare can be used for beneficial effect. Image-editing software applications often provide the **Lens Flare** filters that emulate the effect but in a controllable and adjustable way. → 1.179 COATED LENS; 2.120 IMAGE-EDITING APPLICATION; 4.275 LENS FLARE FILTER

1.**383 flash** A split-second, intense burst of artificially generated light used in photography to light a subject. Called **electronic flash** if it originates from an electronic flashgun.

1.**384 flash key** A lighting situation where the flash is the main (but not necessarily only) lighting source. As the predominant light source, the flash creates the light pattern for the photograph.

1.**385 flash output compensation** Conceptually similar to exposure compensation in enabling a preset adjustment for the flash output. On most digital cameras where this option is available, this is calibrated in EV (normally over a range of + or −2 EV).
→ 1.272 EXPOSURE VALUE (EV)

1.**386 flash synchronization** A camera control in which the shutter opening and the peak output from the flash unit are timed to occur simultaneously. With focal plane shutters there is a limited number of shutter speeds at which flash synchronization can occur. At high speeds the narrow slit of the shutter uncovers only a small piece of the film during the time of the flash. → 1.275 FOCAL PLANE SHUTTER

1.387 flat lighting Lighting that is usually low in contrast and shadows. → 1.377 DIFFUSE LIGHTING

1.388 forced flash Technique where a flashgun (or multiple flashes) are fired when the camera system would not normally activate them. Fill-in flash is one example. → 1.380 FILL-IN FLASH

1.389 front projection The process of projecting an image (usually a transparency) onto a background screen from the front. It offers better image quality and brightness compared with back projection. → 1.363 BACK PROJECTION

1.390 front-curtain flash Sometimes called **normal synchronization**, this is a flash exposure triggered by the opening of a focal plane shutter. The result is a sharp, correctly exposed image of the subject taken at the start of the exposure with a blurred trail of the same subject if it moves subsequently. Fast-moving objects leave ambient light trails *preceding* the subject. This is counterintuitive to the way we normally perceive motion and can look very unnatural. For time exposures coupled with flash, there is therefore often an alternate rear-curtain flash option that gives more natural results. → 1.405 REAR-CURTAIN FLASH

1.391 gobo Short for GO Before Optics, a template that is inserted in the optical path of a lighting system (usually at a focal point) to produce brightly lit patterns on the background. Gobos come in hundreds of options but window, flame, and hearts are typical of the options available.

1.392 guide number (GN) The result of multiplying flash exposure aperture by the subject distance normally referenced to ISO 100 film. The number is a measure of the light output power of the lens.

1.393 inverse square law Law that states that if the distance from a photographic light source is doubled, the light falling on the subject is reduced to one quarter.

1.394 joule A unit of electronic flash output, used to provide an easy and useful comparison of flash outputs. 1 joule is equivalent to 1 watt per second. → 1.392 GUIDE NUMBER (GN)

1.395 light hose A fiber-optic **light pipe** connected to a light source (which can provide either continuous or multiple flash lighting). The photographer can set this device in a darkened studio, room, or outdoor location and walk around the subject illuminating highlights and "painting the subject with light," using bulb or time exposure settings.

1.396 lighting ratio The ratio between any two lighting sources illuminating a scene.

1.397 macro flash Flash unit designed for close-up macrophotography. Provides automatic compensation for the small subject distances and any macro lens extension. Note that the sensors of conventional flash units are not calibrated

1.393 *inverse square law*

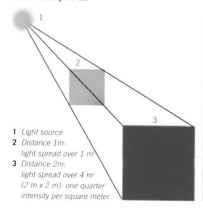

1 *Light source*
2 *Distance 1m:*
   light spread over 1 m²
3 *Distance 2m:*
   light spread over 4 m²
   (2 m x 2 m): one quarter
   intensity per square meter

1.382 *flare*

Image with lens flare

Corrected image

or accurate enough for use at extreme close-up distances.

1.398 MIRED/Mired/Mired value Short for **Micro Reciprocal Degrees**, this is a measure of color temperature. A standard for comparing different light sources to aid in the setting of color compensations. Any light source can be evaluated if the color temperature of the source is known, by dividing 1,000,000 by the color temperature expressed in degrees Kelvin.

1.399 mixed lighting Lighting comprising several different sources—such as tungsten and fluorescent artificial sources mixed with daylight. Such mixes are difficult to compensate for, but can be used to creative effect.

1.400 modelling lamp Small lamp included in some flashguns (such as ring flash units and studio flashes) that provides a similar illumination pattern to the flash. As they can be illuminated continuously, they can be used to aid in the composition of a flash-lit scene.

1.401 monobloc Smaller studio-based flash unit that resembles large portable flashguns. Described as "monobloc" since all of the components are integrated into a single enclosure—flash tube, modeling light, reflector, electronics, and controls, benefiting from the concise construction and relative economy of the unit.

1.402 multiple flash Lighting situation where more than one flash is used. These multiple flashes can be concurrent (when more than one flashgun is used simultaneously) or sequential, when one flash is used from one or more locations to "paint" a scene with light.

1.403 painting with light Technique where a flashgun or light pipe is used to light different parts of a subject or scene using multiple flashes. Typically done at night, or in a darkened enclosure, painting with light enables a subject to be lit comprehensively in a manner that would not be possible with a single flash.

→ 1.395 LIGHT HOSE

1.404 preflash Flashes emitted prior to the main flash to reduce red-eye in the subjects or, in certain camera and flashgun combinations, to gather information about the subject (e.g., spatial information and reflectance), with the monitor preflash. Normally the red-eye reducing flash is a bright visible light whereas the monitor preflash is invisible.

1.405 rear-curtain flash Flash technique where the flash is synchronized to fire immediately prior to the closing of the rear blind of a focal plane shutter. On a time exposure of a moving object, this freezes the motion at the end of its journey across the scene. This is the natural way we perceive motion. Another effect can be achieved by using **slow-sync flash** in order to give ambient exposure to shadow areas.

1.406 recycle time The time taken for the batteries (or electric current, if available) to recharge the capacitors and prime the associated circuitry of a flashgun after a flash exposure.

1.407 red-eye Artifact visible in some photographic portraits taken with flash due to the flash light reflecting off the subject's retina. This normally occurs when camera flash units are used. Alternatively, the subject distance can be reduced (in effect increasing the axial distance of the flash) to diminish the effect. Can be relieved in-camera by moving the flash away from the subject–camera axis or using bounce flash. Red-eye in existing images can be removed digitally.

1.408 rim lighting A variation on backlighting where a strong light source is placed behind (and completely concealed by) the subject. In portraiture situations, this light is diffused through the hair to create a rim of bright light—the rim light. Careful metering is often required to balance the rim light with that directed at the subject from the front.

1.409 ring flash/ringflash Specialized ring-shaped flashgun that can be screwed directly to the front of a lens. It normally features six to eight flash tubes with a diffusive window that give the impression of a single circular flash tube. Many designs also include modeling lights that can be turned on continuously prior to the exposure to gauge the effect. Used in medical and specialized applications, though the intriguing circular catchlights that can be seen in a portrait sitter's eyes mean ringflashes are often used in creative and advertising photography too.

1.410 Scandles Specialist lighting designed to provide high output and consistent lighting for scanning digital cameras and digital camera backs. Because these cameras scan the scene (taking between several seconds and several minutes) for each of the three primary colors, the color and intensity stability in any image source is essential.

1.411 sidelighting Lighting that hits the subject from the side, causing sharp, and often very profound, shadows.

1.412 slave unit/slave flash Flashgun triggered by another flash. Using a photosensor that detects the original flash burst, the attached or connected flashgun is then triggered. Useful for providing additional lighting without the need to physically connect additional flash units.

1.413 snoot A cone or reducing cylinder placed over a flashgun head to concentrate and limit the light to one small area.

1.414 softbox A large diffusing enclosure fitted over a flashgun to provide a large area of diffuse light.

1.415 specular highlight (1) An intense highlight usually resulting from reflection of a light source from a convex section reflector. Specular highlights are plentiful on photographs of cars, for example, where curved brightwork produces such highlights. → 1.527 SPECULAR HIGHLIGHT (2)

1.416 strobe Multiple flashes of constant or near constant output, often of high frequency. Some flashguns offer this facility and can capture details of a moving subject—such as a tennis player serving a ball.

1.417 tungsten lighting Conventional filament bulb domestic lighting is technically tungsten lighting, but in photography the term is usually applied to Photoflood bulbs which are brighter and more consistent.

1.418 ultraviolet (UV) light (1) Sometimes called "**black light**," UV lighting can be used to cause fluorescence in certain materials. By covering the light source (specialized bulbs or fluorescent tubes) with material that is transparent to UV, but opaque to the visible spectrum, photographs can be taken purely by the light of the fluorescence.

1.419 x-sync Camera flash synchronization often describing the fastest shutter speed permissible.

Technique

1.420 astrophotography Photography of any astronomical body with or without additional optics.

1.421 balance The creation of a balanced scene by placing shape, form, and color in a harmonious way throughout the scene. Sometimes aided by the rule of thirds. → 1.445 RULE OF THIRDS

1.422 bracketing A series of exposures made of the same subject from the same viewpoint differing only in exposure. By varying progressively to either side of the estimated exposure, uncertainties in exposure and processing can be

1.407 *red-eye*

1.417 *tungsten lighting (compared with daylight balanced lighting)*

accommodated and an accurately exposed shot assured. Bracketed shots usually involve altering exposure times (so that depth of field is maintained) but can also be made by altering the f-number. → 1.199 F-NUMBER; 1.257 AUTO EXPOSURE BRACKETING; 1.266 EXPOSURE; 1.268 EXPOSURE LATITUDE

1.**423 burn (1)** Giving additional exposure to regions of an enlarged print to make those regions darker on the finished print. Masks with apertures are usually employed to control the position and extent of any such actions. Duplicated in image editing by the burn or **burning-in tools**. → 4.053 BURN TOOL

1.**424 camera angle** A general term describing the viewpoint of the camera, but also specifically used with reference to its angle from the horizontal. Converging verticals can occur if camera angles relative to the horizontal are used (particularly) for architectural subjects, causing obvious image distortion.

1.**425 camera shake** A description of the (usually undesirable and unintentional) movement of a camera at the moment a photograph is taken. This can result in obvious movement artifacts in the image but can also result in an image that is not critically sharp. The use of a rigid support such as a tripod can contain the problem.

1.**426 candids** Photographs of people taken without their knowledge and designed to capture them in natural, unposed activities.

1.**427 close-up** Photograph taken with the camera lens close to the closest focusing distance. Normally applies to shots taken at distances of between several centimeters and a meter. Shorter distances are regarded as macro.

1.**428 composition** The effective arrangement of elements within a scene. This can be achieved in-camera or subsequently by cropping the original scene, or even by digital manipulation. Various rules exist with regard to composition, but many of the most powerful photographs are those that break the rules. → 1.506 IN-CAMERA

1.**429 decisive moment** The precise moment when a scene is at its photographic best. Although somewhat subjective, it could occur when the lighting is right or the position of moving objects in the scene is "just right" in compositional terms.

1.**430 differencing** A process of subtracting the pixel information of one image from another, usually of the same subject from the same position. The difference image that results shows only the changes (in position, color, or other parameters) that have occurred between the shots. Used in forensic and medical applications.

1.**431 electrophotography** Creation of digital or conventional images using an electrical charge rather than light photons. A typical example is **Kirlian Photography**.

1.**432 foreground interest** The provision in a scene—usually of a broad landscape—of nearby objects to help the composition.

1.**433 high key** An image comprising predominantly light tones and often

1.439 *panning*

1.445 *rule of thirds*

1.422 *bracketing*

Bracket (–1)

Bracket (+1)

Bracket (–2)

Bracket (0)

Bracket (+2)

1.444 *posterize*

Posterize (original image)

Posterize (2 levels)

Posterize (4 levels)

Posterize (6 levels)

imparting an ethereal or romantic appearance. → 1.436 LOW KEY

1.**434 lead-in lines** The inclusion in an image of some natural or contrived objects that lead the eye to the principal feature of the image. Lead-in lines may be provided by a road or a fence, for example, leading to a building.

1.**435 location photography** Photography undertaken at a particular venue or location, e.g., landscape and architectural photography, rather than in a studio.

1.**436 low key** A photographic image comprising predominantly dark tones either as a result of lighting, processing or image editing.

1.**437 macrophotography** The photography of large-scale objects, often used erroneously to describe "photomacrography," which is close-up photography. → 1.442 PHOTOMACROGRAPHY; 1.443 PHOTOMICROGRAPHY

1.**438 multiple exposure** The taking of two (**double exposure**) or more photographic images of the same or different objects on the same frame to produce a single image.

1.**439 panning** Technique of moving the camera so that a moving object maintains the same position relative to the viewfinder while the picture is taken. The net result is a sharp image of the moving subject against a blurred background.

1.**440 panorama** In photographic terms, a description of images with an aspect ratio of at least 2:1 but not necessarily a picture of a landscape. Can be created using dedicated panoramic cameras or by joining ("stitching") adjacent shots of the same scene with software tools.

1.**441 photogram** A photographic image normally made without using a camera by placing an opaque, translucent, or transparent object on a sheet of emulsion and briefly exposing it to light. The result depends on the object but is usually a shadow or silhouette of that object.

1.**442 photomacrography** Close-up photography usually defined to be in the range of 1x to 10x life-size when recorded on film or an equivalent scaled image sensor. → 1.437 MACROPHOTOGRAPHY

1.**443 photomicrography** Photography at great magnifications using a microscope equipped for mounting a camera. → 1.437 MACROPHOTOGRAPHY

1.**444 posterize** Originally a conventional photographic technique where the number of shades of gray (or colors) in an image is reduced to a specified number. The result is more effective if this number is low. Most image-editing applications produce the same effect instantly.

1.**445 rule of thirds** Compositional regime that divides the frame symmetrically into thirds vertically and horizontally. The image will be stronger if horizontal or vertical elements (such as the sky, or edge of a building) are placed against one of these guides. A very strong composition will result from placing important subjects at one of the four intersection points.

1.**446 selective focus** The process of focusing selectively on one element in the scene for emphasis and in order to improve the overall composition.

1.423 *burn*

1 Burning tool darkens area of sky

1.461 *dodge/dodging*

2 Dodge tool lightens area of sky

1.447 stereography A type of photograph in which two simultaneous exposures are made in such a way as to give the impression of three-dimensional depth. **Digital stereo cameras** have been produced that enable two digital images to be taken simultaneously and combined electronically.

1.448 time-lapse photography Photographs of a fixed scene taken at predetermined intervals to monitor changes in that scene.

Processing

1.449 additive printing Photographic printing process using additive color; colors were mixed during the printing to produce all spectral colors. Used in early color printing but also used for some specialist applications and for particular special effects.

1.450 back printing Data printed on the reverse of a print by automated printing equipment. This can be specific to the photofinishing laboratory and can include date of processing, frame number, and, in the case of APS film, any compensations applied or read from the film itself. APS cameras also provide more detailed information, such as actual time and date of exposure and even selected text titles that can be printed by suitably equipped printing equipment. → 1.318 ADVANCED PHOTO SYSTEM (APS)

1.451 blow-up Colloquial term for an enlargement made from a small negative or slide.

1.452 C-22 Processing chemistry for negative films, superseded in the 1970s by the C-41.

1.453 C-41 Principal processing chemistry for negative films.

1.454 chemical reversal Chemical treatment of a photographic image to convert it from negative to positive, or vice versa. In reversal films and original monochrome images, the color layers are reversed by chemical reversal to give the final positive image. "Chemical reversal" is distinct from "light reversal," where the film is flooded with light to effect the reversal process.

1.455 Cibachrome A proprietary process for producing photographic color prints directly from transparencies. The system was developed by Ilford when under the ownership of the **Ciba-Geigy Corporation**. Cibachrome prints are characterized

by powerful colors, due to embedded dyes, a high-gloss finish (the original Cibachrome "paper" was a plastic film), and impressive light fastness. Cibachrome also featured a processing chemistry that—for its day—was easy for amateurs to exploit. Due to a change of ownership Cibachrome is now marketed as "Ilfochrome."

1.456 clip test A small piece cut from the end of an exposed roll of film which is processed in advance to determine whether any adjustment may be necessary in processing to account for any difference in actual film sensitivity compared with the nominal speed (that printed on the film carton).

1.457 contact print/contact Photographic print made by placing an original negative or positive film in direct contact with the photographic paper. A contact sheet usually comprises an entire film contact-printed onto a single sheet of paper. Contact prints made from large format negatives are sufficient to stand alone as "finished" prints.

1.458 darkroom Any light-tight room used for the processing and handling of light-sensitive materials. The term "**digital darkroom**" has been applied to a computer system that includes image input and output devices and is equipped with image-editing software.

1.459 developer The chemical solution used to convert an invisible latent image (on a film emulsion or photographic paper) into a visible image.

1.460 developing tank A light-tight tank used for processing rolls of film. Allows the processor to work with economical amounts of chemicals and in daylight. There are also tanks that are capable of fully automatic operation and for paper processing.

1.461 dodge/dodging A method of obtaining lighter areas in a photographic print by the selective use of masking (hiding relevant areas from light). The opposite effect—darkening areas of an image—is called burning. Both these effects can be created in image-editing software. → 1.423 BURN (1); 4.053 BURN TOOL; 4.119 MASK

1.462 E-4 Superseded processing chemistry for color reversal films.

1.463 E-6 Principal processing chemistry for color reversal films.

1.464 easel Baseboard of an enlarger that holds photographic paper flat during exposure. Usually incorporates a masking frame for setting the print borders and for cropping.

1.465 enlargement A reproduction that is greater than 100% of its original size. Usually applied to prints (or copy transparencies/negatives) made from a medium-format (or smaller) original. As digital images do not have a nominal physical size, the term tends not to be used for digitally produced photographs.
→ 1.451 BLOWUP

1.466 enlarger Conventional device for enlarging photographic negatives or transparencies for printing. Comprises a light source, negative/slide holder, lens assembly and easel. Adjustments for focus, image size and (where appropriate) colour are also provided.

1.467 fixer/fixing bath Usually the penultimate processing solution (prior to washing) for a film emulsion. Removes any light-sensitive material not affected by the developer. Sometimes called '**hypo**' in black and white photography.

1.468 grade The classification of photographic printing paper by the degree to which it affects the contrast of an image. Although not all makes are the same, the most common **paper grades** range from 0 (the lowest contrast, for use with high-contrast negatives) to 5 (the highest contrast, for use with low-contrast negatives). Image editors provide contrast controls that can emulate much of the effect of using paper of different grades. → 1.487 VARIABLE CONTRAST (VC) PAPER

1.469 Ilfochrome New name for reversal printing paper from Ilford, formerly marketed as Cibachrome. → 1.455 CIBACHROME

1.470 intensification A technique for chemically adjusting the density of developed photographic emulsion. The chemicals are known as '**intensifiers**'.

1.471 latent image In photography, this is used to describe an image recorded on film at the point of exposure that only becomes apparent after it is processed. → 1.323 CHROMOGENIC; 1.356 SILVER HALIDE

1.472 minilab An automated machine capable of processing and printing unexposed film. Normally operated by photofinishers in retail outlets, the latest systems can produce prints direct from digital media such as Picture/Photo CD, SmartMedia or CompactFlash memory cards.

1.473 negative carrier, holder Support for negative, or negative strip, when placed in enlarger or digital scanner. Smaller formats are normally supported by their edges, though carriers for larger formats often have glass plates in order to prevent negative curvature and the resulting image distortion.

1.474 positive An image emulating an original scene, made photographically on paper or film, usually from a negative. Negatives scanned digitally can be converted into positive images either as part of the scanning procedure or later, using an appropriate command (such as Invert).
→ 1.348 NEGATIVE/NEG

1.475 print A photographic image, traditionally made from a negative but now equally likely to come from a transparency or be a computer output.

1.476 printing-in Alternate term for the darkroom technique of burning-in areas of a print. → 1.423 BURN (1)

1.477 processing The developing, fixing and washing of photographic media to produce prints, negatives or transparencies.

1.478 pull-processing Giving film a shorter development time than recommended to compensate for overexposure in the camera (due to the setting of incorrect film speed). Pull-processing can also be used to reduce image contrast. → 1.479 PUSH-PROCESSING

1.479 push-processing or forced processing Giving film a longer or **forced development** time than normal to compensate for underexposure, resulting in increased contrast. → 1.478 PULL-PROCESSING

1.480 reticulation From the Greek meaning 'net-like', reticulation can be viewed as either a processing special effect or processing fault depending on when it occurs. A reticulated film features a 'crazed' surface and is normally due to subjecting the emulsion to abrupt temperature changes or incorrect chemical formulations.

1.481 Sabattier effect The partial reversal of tone or colour in a photographic emulsion due to brief exposure to light during development. → 1.454 CHEMICAL REVERSAL

81

1.**482 sepia toning** A process of making sepia prints from standard black and white prints. Various bleaches and dyes are employed in the process. → 4.556 SEPIA

1.**483 spotting** Physical retouching of a photographic print with dyes or watercolour stains to remove blemishes due to dust or scratches on the original negative. Either a clone/rubber stamp tool or an effects filter (such as Dust & Scratches) can perform the same retouching action on a digital image. Dust & Scratches filters can remove large numbers of blemishes, but can compromise some detail in the image. → 1.526 RETOUCHING; 4.056 CLONE TOOL; 4.248 DUST & SCRATCHES FILTER

1.**484 stop bath** A dilution of **acetic acid** used between the developer and the fixer to arrest development and extend the life of the fixer.

1.**485 toning** Adding a brown or blue tone to a photographic print, supplanting the usual black silver halide component. The end result is easy to duplicate digitally.

1.**486 unsharp masking (USM)** A traditional film composition technique used for 'sharpening' an image. An image is combined with a slightly defocused positive of the same image. In this image pair the extremes of brightness are reduced allowing fine detail in the original (sharp) image to be discerned. This can also be achieved digitally, with image-editing applications which use filters to enhance the details in a scanned image by increasing the contrast of pixels, the exact amount depending on various criteria such as the 'threshold' specified and the radius of the area around each pixel. → 1.241 SHARPNESS; 4.413 INTERPOLATION

1.**487 variable contrast (VC) paper** Specialized printing paper whose contrast grade can be altered using coloured filters. → 1.468 GRADE

Miscellaneous terms

1.**488 acutance** An objective measurement of the quality of an edge in a photographic image.

1.**489 aerial perspective** The recording (or, with digital image manipulation, the creation) of depth in a scene through increasing haze with distance.

1.**490 artifact/artefact** A visible flaw in an electronically prepared image usually occurring as a result of the imaging technique employed. JPEG compression, for example, reduces image data in square blocks of pixels that can become clearly visible, particularly when high contrast or colour effects are applied.

1.**491 background (2)** Description of those elements visible in a scene that are behind the subject of the scene.

1.**492 brightness range** The range of tones in a photographic subject, from darkest to lightest.

1.**493 caption** The 'title' of an image that will advise not only of the principal subject but also other relevant data such as photographic data, time and date of

1.481 *Sabattier effect*

Same view with film exposed briefly to light

Conventionally processed

1.486 *unsharp masking (USM)*

Defocused

Sharp

Image is sandwiched with slightly defocused negative

exposure and any other significant details. Some also include keywords for searches by image databases. Captions can be provided on the mount of a slide, rear of a print or as a separately filed sheet; for digital images the caption data (and more text information) can be embedded in the file.

1.494 capture The action of 'getting' an image, whether by taking a photograph, scanning an image into a computer or 'grabbing' an image using a frame grabber. → 1.502 FRAME GRAB(BING); 2.292 SCREEN CAPTURE

1.495 converging verticals Effect resulting from not pointing a camera squarely at a subject. Most obviously manifested when pointing a camera upwards – even slightly – while photographing buildings. Can be corrected by either adopting a higher viewpoint or using a perspective control (PC) lens. → 1.232 PERSPECTIVE CONTROL (PC) LENS

1.496 dense Term used to describe an image that is too dark.

1.497 diffuse A softened effect in a photographic image, created by scattered light giving an object the appearance of being viewed through translucent glass. → 1.243 SOFT FOCUS

1.498 digital video (DV) Video photography based on digital imaging and image storage. Normally the term DV is applied to the domestic digital format based on mini DV tapes. DV uses intraframe image compression (compression of image data within each frame, similar to a digital (still) camera), rather than interframe compression (compression of data in multiple frames) used for DVD video.

1.499 dupe A duplicate copy of an original image, usually a transparency. Dupes are normally equivalent-sized copies but 35 mm transparencies are often 'duped' as larger 6 x 9 cm or even 5 x 4 inch transparencies.

1.500 flat Descriptive term for an image which lacks sufficient colour or contrast and perceived 'depth'. A subjective rather than quantitative term.

1.501 foreground The region of a scene between the camera and the main subject. → 1.432 FOREGROUND INTEREST

1.502 frame grab(bing) The capture of a single still frame usually from an analogue video sequence. Normally external devices are required that digitize the video signal making frame grabbing easier.

1.503 halation An unwanted spread of light beyond its natural boundary in the highlight areas of a photographic image, caused by overexposure or deliberately in digital images.

1.504 hybrid photography, imaging Photography that uses elements of both conventional and digital technologies. Although not a digital imaging system, the APS, which uses digital data to provide information about photographs and camera configurations, can be considered a hybrid technology. → 1.318 ADVANCED PHOTO SYSTEM (APS); 3.058 PHOTOCD

1.498 *digital video (DV) camera*

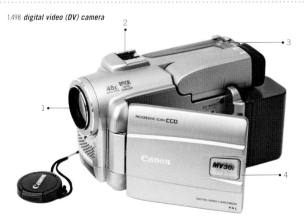

1 *Lens*
2 *Hot shoe (for light or auxiliary microphone)*
3 *Zoom control*
4 *Fold-out LCD display screen*

1.**505 imaging device** A general term describing any dedicated piece of equipment that either captures an image from an original such as a scanner or camera, or generates an image from a previously captured original such as a contact printing frame or imagesetter.

1.**506 in-camera** The creation of effects within the camera, rather than at postproduction, processing or otherwise. Filter effects and multiple exposures are typical examples of in-camera effects. Photographic processing that takes place inside the camera, such as with Polaroid products, is also referred to as in-camera.

1.**507 interpolated resolution** The use of a complex algorithm to add extra pixels to an image to make it appear sharper. As no new image information is added the results are purely subjective and the absolute result is only a larger image. This is more common with scanners than digital cameras.

1.**508 jaggies** Colloquial term for the jagged and 'stepped' appearance of curves and angled lines on a digital image (and on bitmapped screen graphics). The extent of the effect is proportional to the number of pixels. It is more prominent if the pixels are large relative to the image size.

1.**509 key tone** The principal or most important tone in a photographic scene that must be recorded accurately.

1.**510 LED** Light Emitting Diode. Small diode that emits light when a current is applied. Usually used as indicator lights in cameras.

1.**511 mAh milliAmperehour**: Rating unit used to describe the consumption of power in a camera (or other electronic equipment). The storage capacity of batteries is also expressed in mAh, making it possible to calculate the maximum possible usage time of such batteries in a camera.

1.**512 marque** The manufacturer's brand name for a camera or imaging system. Examples include Fujifilm, Nikon, Canon and **Microtek**.

1.**513 model release** A form signed by a photographer and model employed (whether for payment or not) for a photographic session that gives the photographer (or their agents) specified permission to use the photographs. Though model releases are normally used for sessions where the model is the principal subject (such as portraiture or glamour), strictly any photography where a person is deliberately used or positioned to augment a scene (rather than just relying on passersby to do so) requires the use of a model release. This will indemnify the photographer in the event that the model takes exception to the final use of the photograph (though where such use grossly misrepresents the model or his/her actions, the model can still bring an action against the photographer).

1.**514 movie clip** Short sequence of motion video captured on a digital camera in AVI, MOV or MPEG formats. Digital camera movie sequences tend to be of low quality (sub-VHS) and limited in duration.

1.**515 optical resolution** Actual resolution achievable by a digital camera (also other digital imaging devices, such as scanners). A measure of the absolute number of pixels that can be recorded. The greater the optical resolution, the better the image quality. Though lower than interpolated resolution, optical resolution captures the greatest amount of image data.
→ 4.413 INTERPOLATION

1.**516 pentaprism** Five-sided prism used in SLR optical systems to deliver an upright laterally correct image to the viewfinder.

1.**517 photo library** Also called **stock library** or **stock picture library**, this is a collection of photographic images, traditionally stored as prints or transparencies but now increasingly held digitally. Libraries may hold photos taken or commissioned by the library owner or submitted on a speculative basis by contributors. Many libraries issue '**want lists**' of particular images or image types that they have a particular need for, or specialize in. Virtually all libraries have their own regimes and rules regarding the promotion of their images, but most now have online catalogues where thumbnails can be browsed. On payment of the agreed fee the full-size image can be downloaded or received on a CD. Typical fees for images that are held by a library are split 50:50 between the library and the author.
→ 1.519 PICTURE AGENCY; 1.520 PICTURE PORTAL

1.**518 photo researcher/picture researcher** The usual intermediary between a publisher who is seeking images and a picture library or agency. They may be employed by a publishing house or work freelance. A typical assignment will see a researcher tasked to find specific images meeting a tight brief from a publisher. They then scan the catalogues of libraries, either conventionally or digitally, or (particularly in the case of specialized subjects) they may work with the library in procuring images. → 1.517 PHOTO LIBRARY; 1.519 PICTURE AGENCY

1.519 picture agency/photo agency An agency that represents photographers in both obtaining and negotiating assignments or for handling their images. In the latter respect the agency works much like a photo library. → 1.517 PHOTO LIBRARY

1.520 picture portal Internet sites where picture researchers (or others with an interest in finding specific images) can visit to seek images. Also where photographers can store their images (or low resolution surrogates) and put them up for sale or licensing. → 6.063 PORTAL

1.521 reflection copy Any flat item which is to be reproduced photographically by light reflected from its surface, as distinct from a 'transparency' or 'slide' original in which the light passes through.

1.522 reflex viewing Camera viewing system where the light is bent through 90°. In most SLR designs the light is bent through 90° twice; first due to the 45° mirror behind the lens and then through the pentaprism. → 1.516 PENTAPRISM

1.523 refraction The bending of light due to its passage between media of different refractive indices. Such bending occurs when light enters a lens and passes between the different elements of the lens. → 1.524 REFRACTIVE INDEX

1.524 refractive index The measurement of the degree to which light is bent by passing through one medium to another, expressed as a ratio of the speed of light. The use and manipulation of refractive indices is a fundamental part of lens design. → 1.523 REFRACTION

1.525 resolution The degree of quality, definition, or clarity with which an image is reproduced or displayed in a photograph, or via a scanner, monitor screen, printer or other output device. The more pixels in an image, the sharper that image will be and the greater the detail. The likelihood of jaggies is also reduced the higher the image resolution. → 1.007 CAMERA RESOLUTION; 1.508 JAGGIES; 4.106 INPUT RESOLUTION; 5.079 OUTPUT RESOLUTION

1.526 retouching Altering an image, artwork or film to make modifications or remove imperfections. Retouching was originally a mechanical task, where imperfections were scraped or cut from the surface or painted over using suitable dyes. Image editors can perform all traditional retouching tasks – and more – without compromising the original image. → 1.483 SPOTTING

1.527 specular highlight (2) The lightest highlighted area in a photograph, usually reproduced as unprinted white paper.

1.520 *picture portal*

This portal provides options for uploading, printing and creating web galleries from your images.

2
COMPUTER SECTION

Hardware CPU

2.001 a: drive Conventional name for the floppy-disk drive of a PC. Sometimes there is also a b: drive, usually reserved for a second disk drive. Before the universal adoption of the 3.5 inch floppy disk computers featured a: and **b: drives**, one for the old, 5.25 inch floppy disk, the other for the 3.5 inch disk.

2.002 accelerator board/card A circuit board added to a computer (as an optional extra or as part of an enhanced specification) to speed up certain computer operations. Mathematical and onscreen graphics-rendering functions can be improved by the addition of such boards. Boards with the latter purpose are known as graphics accelerators. → 2.010 CENTRAL PROCESSING UNIT (CPU); 2.028 EXPANSION BOARD/CARD

2.003 access time The time taken by a disk drive to access data. Access time is a combination of the seek time – the time taken for the head to move to the position of the data – and the latency time, that time taken for the data to pass under the read head. Sometimes referred to as average access time. → 2.481 SECTOR

2.004 address (1) A number specifying the location of data stored on a computer. Less likely to be encountered day to day, the address information is more likely to be important if there is a system problem.

2.005 AMD (Advanced Micro Devices, Inc.) Company producing the Athlon processor, an alternative to Intel's Pentium.

2.006 architecture The physical design and structure of a computer and its components. Can be a general term or applied specifically to a computer design. → 2.055 OPEN ARCHITECTURE

2.007 Athlon CPU chip produced by AMD and equivalent to Intel's Pentium. Used for running Unix, Linux, and OS2/Warp operating systems as well as the Windows family.

2.008 c: drive Conventional name for the hard disk (or principal partition on a hard disk) of a PC.

2.009 Celeron CPU chip produced by Intel, also responsible for the Pentium CPU. Designed as a complementary product to the Pentium for less intensive applications.

2.010 central processing unit (CPU) The 'brain' of the computer, the main computational and management centre. In most desktop computers the CPU is a single-chip microprocessor; it performs the principal computational calculations and governs the operation of other components. Some older machines feature coprocessors, processors that have specific tasks. → 2.015 COPROCESSOR; 2.060 PROCESSOR (CHIP)

2.011 circuit board An insulating baseboard (usually epoxy or **phenolic resin**) upon which electronic circuits are built. Basic designs use simple interconnecting cables between the electronic components mounted on the board; more sophisticated ones use printed or etched tracks. Also known as **printed circuit board**, **PC board** and **logic board**.

2.012 closed architecture The opposite of 'open architecture', a computer or computer system that cannot be freely modified as the specifications are not public and cannot normally be changed, on legal grounds. The ROM chip, which forms the basis of the Macintosh operating system, is an example of a closed architecture as it can only be used in Apple computers.

2.013 complex instruction set computing (CISC) A type of microprocessor used in most Windows-based computers → 2.062 REDUCED INSTRUCTION SET COMPUTING (RISC)

2.014 computer An electronic device which can process structured input (usually binary data) according to a predetermined set of variable instructions – a 'program' – and produce an output. → 7.005 BINARY

2.015 coprocessor A secondary microprocessor chip designed to sit alongside a

2.014 *computer (Macintosh G4)*

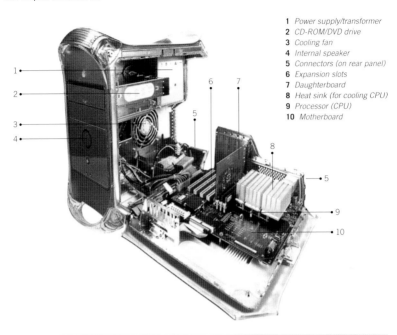

1 Power supply/transformer
2 CD-ROM/DVD drive
3 Cooling fan
4 Internal speaker
5 Connectors (on rear panel)
6 Expansion slots
7 Daughterboard
8 Heat sink (for cooling CPU)
9 Processor (CPU)
10 Motherboard

2.058 *personal computer (PC)*

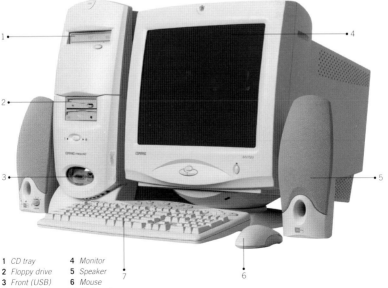

87

1 CD tray
2 Floppy drive
3 Front (USB) connections
4 Monitor
5 Speaker
6 Mouse
7 Keyboard

computer's principal processor (the CPU) and given the task of performing certain specialized functions. The architecture of such chips is such that they are better able, and more efficient, at these tasks than the CPU. Typical coprocessors are often known by their functional name (for example, '**floating-point unit**' (FPU), or '**math coprocessor**' ('**numeric coprocessor**'), both of which carry out math calculations). Most contemporary CPUs incorporate coprocessor functions into their own architecture. ➔ 2.010 CENTRAL PROCESSING UNIT (CPU)

2.016 data bus The path, or circuitry, along which data is transmitted around a computer. The data bus (or more simply, '**bus**') is a shared route connecting the elements of the computer including the CPU, disk drive controller input/output ports and memory. ➔ 2.308 MEMORY

2.017 daughterboard A circuit board which plugs into another board, such as the 'motherboard' (the board with the main circuitry and processors of a computer) to add extra capabilities to the computer. ➔ 2.011 CIRCUIT BOARD; 2.050 MOTHERBOARD

2.018 desktop computer Personal computers which not only perform all the necessary functions of desktop publishing, but will also fit on a real desktop. Originally named to distinguish them from the more substantial (room-sized) mainframe machines and smaller portable computers. ➔ 2.058 PERSONAL COMPUTER (PC); 5.051 DESKTOP PUBLISHING (DTP)

2.019 device A generic term for any computer system or subsystem. A disk drive, printer and card reader are all devices and often require their own software routine. This is known as the 'device driver'. ➔ 2.104 DRIVER/DEVICE DRIVER; 2.444 EXTERNAL DEVICE; 2.471 PERIPHERAL DEVICE

2.020 digital signal processor (DSP) A specialized integrated circuit optimized for high-speed data manipulations, especially image manipulation and data acquisition.

2.021 DIP (dual inline package) switch Small two-way switches on some hardware devices which are used to select an operating mode, e.g., giving the device a unique identity number when connected to others. ➔ 2.377 SCSI ID (NUMBER)

2.022 disk/disc A circular platter with a magnetic surface on which computer data

is stored. Data is written to, and read from, the disk by a mechanism called a disk drive. Disks may be rigid ('hard disk') or flexible ('floppy disk'), and may reside on a disk drive installed inside your computer ('**internal disk drive**'), in a device connected to your computer ('**external disk drive**'), or in a cartridge which can be transported between disk drives ('removable disk'). A disk drive may contain several 'platters', but is referred to in the singular – 'disk'. Often the alternate 'UK' spelling 'disc' is used to describe discs that use optical rather than magnetic techniques to store data. There is also a third type of disc which combines both techniques and is called a 'magneto-optical disc' (MO). ➔ 2.343 MAGNETO-OPTICAL DISC (MO/MOD)

2.023 disk/disc drive Often contracted ambiguously to 'drive', this is a hardware device which writes data to, or reads it from, a disk (or **disc**). A disk drive may contain several 'platters' housed in a sealed unit (sometimes called a **hard [disk] drive** to distinguish it from other kinds), or it may be a device which reads disks (or discs) which are inserted into it. Disk drives that are installed inside a computer are described as 'internal disk drives' while those connected to the computer are described as 'external disk drives'. ➔ 2.019 DEVICE; 2.022 DISK/DISC

2.024 dock The action of connecting one device – usually a computer – to another; used to describe the connection of a laptop computer to a base unit to provide the functionality of a desktop system, or a camera (usually a digital video model) to a 'docking station'.

2.025 dongle A hardware access 'key' which plugs into a computer port to enable its associated software to run. Dongles are used as security devices to ensure that only one copy of a purchased software application can be run at one time. Serial, parallel and USB versions exist although there is considerable user resistance to them as they can compromise the normal operation of the respective ports.

2.026 dual inline package (DIP) The particular way in which some chips are mounted – with two parallel rows of pins – so that they can be plugged into a computer circuit board. ➔ 2.011 CIRCUIT BOARD

2.**027 dumb terminal** A system comprising monitor, video adaptor and keyboard/mouse which does not possess any computing power on its own, but which is networked to a server on which it relies for intelligent processing. → 2.068 TERMINAL

2.**028 expansion board/card** An **add-on circuit board** designed to extend the computer's capabilities → 2.002 ACCELERATOR BOARD/CARD; 2.011 CIRCUIT BOARD

2.**029 expansion slot** A **slot** in a computer where additional circuit boards can be plugged in. → 2.011 CIRCUIT BOARD; 2.028 EXPANSION BOARD/CARD

2.**030 firmware** Any permanent software incorporated into a hardware chip (usually a 'ROM' chip). All computers and computer-based equipment (such as digital cameras and associated peripherals) feature firmware of some kind. The term describes its nature as intermediate between software and hardware. On Macintosh computers part of the operating system is built into a hardware ROM chip.

2.**031 floppy (disk) drive** A hardware device for reading and writing data to and from floppy disks. → 2.023 DISK/DISC DRIVE; 2.338 FLOPPY DISK

2.**032 FPU** Abbreviation for **Floating Point Processor**, a form of coprocessor dedicated to mathematical functions. → 2.015 COPROCESSOR

2.**033 G3** PowerPC RISC processor produced by the Apple/IBM/Motorola consortium and used in Apple computers. Runs at

speeds of up to 600 MHz (PowerPC RISC speeds do not relate directly to Pentium – or equivalent processor – speeds).

2.**034 G4** More powerful version of the G3 PowerPC processor. → 2.033 G3

2.**035 GeForce3** Graphics card featuring a graphics processing unit (GPU) from graphics specialist **NVIDIA**. Launched in 2001, its 57 million transistors can perform nearly one million million operations per second.

2.**036 graphics accelerator** An additional computer circuit board used to provide additional functionality and performance in the execution of graphics commands. → 2.002 ACCELERATOR BOARD/CARD

2.**037 graphics processing unit (GPU)** Chip dedicated to enhancing graphics handling. Normally mounted as part of a graphics card. → 2.035 GEFORCE3

2.**038 IBM PC** IBM personal computer. Strictly a PC made by IBM but also generally used as a generic term for any PC which is 'IBM compatible' and, in general, one that runs either Microsoft's 'DOS' or 'Windows' operating systems. → 2.047 MACINTOSH; 2.058 PERSONAL COMPUTER (PC); 2.135 MS-DOS; 2.235 WINDOWS

2.**039 iBook** Compact, consumer portable from Apple, promoted for educational use. Hence it is light in weight, but has only a 12 inch/31 cm screen. Features and connectivity are similar to those of the iMac.

2.**040 iMac** Computer produced by Apple Computers and first launched in the

2.039 *iBook*

2.040 *iMac*

summer of 1998. Distinguished –
like the original Macintosh – by a single-
unit design housing all the principal
components – monitor, processor and
CD drive (latterly a DVD drive). It also
lost the traditional floppy drive and
conventional 'Mac' connectors (ADB and
SCSI) in favour of the emergent USB and
FireWire connections.

2.**041 integrated circuit (IC)** The electronic
circuit comprising a number of transistors
and resistors embedded in a microchip.

2.**042 Intel** Company responsible for the
Pentium and Celeron families of central
processing chips that provide the bulk of
the CPUs used in Windows computing.

2.**043 internal modem** A modem installed
inside, or integrated with, a computer.
→ 2.400 MODEM

2.**044 interrupt button** A button unique to
Macintosh computers that is designed to
be used by programmers to 'interrupt'
applications to help with debugging.

2.**045 keyboard** The principal data entry device
for a computer capable of entering
alphanumeric and functional data.
Although all keyboards are broadly similar,
there are special keys specific to the
computer or operating system used on
that computer.

2.**046 laptop (computer)** A small, portable
computer, as distinct from the larger
'desktop' variety, designed to be used on
the move and provided with battery power
options. The smallest examples are often
called notebooks and sub-notebooks.

2.**047 Macintosh** The brand name of the
computer range produced by Apple
Computers. The Macintosh was the first
commercially available computer to
successfully utilize the 'graphical user
interface' (GUI) pioneered by **Xerox
Corporation's Palo Alto Research Center
(PARC)**, although the concept was first seen
in Apple's unsuccessful '**Lisa**' computer.
The Macintosh introduced 'plug and play'
computing, where peripheral devices
could be plugged in and used immediately
(requiring only the installation of a
software driver, rather than the more
complex reconfigurations required for
other computer installations). The use of a
GUI gave rise to desktop publishing and
later digital imaging, bringing about a

revolution in the art and design business.
Original Macintoshes used the **Motorola
68000** series processor but these were
replaced in the mid-1990s by the
PowerPC RISC processors, which are
faster and more powerful. The iMac
introduced legacy-free technology
(dumping 'traditional' SCSI and serial
connectors for USB, and abandoning the
increasingly feeble floppy disk altogether).
In 2001 Apple introduced its latest
operating system, OS X, which
incorporates a UNIX core for improved
performance and stability. → 2.197 MAC OS

2.**048 mainframe** A large computer system
used mainly to manage vast databases
where simultaneous processing of
transactions is required, such as in
banks or insurance companies. A typical
mainframe comprises a central computer
to which a number of terminals are
connected. → 2.068 TERMINAL

2.**049 MMX** Appellation given to some early
Pentium PC chips used to denote those
processors with enhanced multimedia
capabilities. Later versions incorporated
the MMX technology as part of the
specification and the suffix was dropped.

2.**050 motherboard** The principal circuit board
in a computer, holding the CPU, the
memory chips, support circuitry, bus
controller, connectors for subsidiary
'daughterboards' and other components.
→ 2.011 CIRCUIT BOARD

2.**051 multimedia personal computer (MPC)**
A 'standard' set by the manufacturers
and resellers of multimedia-capable PCs
in the mid-1990s to define minimum
performance capabilities.

2.**052 multiprocessor** A computer architecture
that uses more than one central
processing unit. Actions are divided
among two or more chips. Usually found
only on the most powerful computers.
→ 2.006 ARCHITECTURE

2.**053 NuBus** The 'bus architecture' found
mostly in older Macintosh computers
which provide 'slots' for adding circuit
boards such as video cards and
accelerator cards. → 2.011 CIRCUIT BOARD

2.**054 numeric keypad** A **keypad** of number
keys (normally) situated to the right on
most keyboards and designed for the
rapid input of numerical data. Sometimes

this is available as a separate keyboard that can be particularly useful for left-handed users.

2.055 open architecture The facility, in the design of a computer system, for unrestricted modification and improvement of the computer and/or its system.

2.056 Pentium Name of the processor series produced by Intel for use in personal computers and following on from the 80486 series. The name was coined when Intel discovered that the logical name – 586 – was already used elsewhere.

2.057 peripheral component interconnect (PCI) A high-performance, 32-bit or 64-bit 'bus' for connecting external devices to a computer.

2.058 personal computer (PC) The name originally used to describe computers designed to be used by one person but normally used as the acronym for IBM PCs. The term is now loosely applied to any personal computer that conforms to the original IBM specifications or agreed subsequent modifications – 'IBM-compatible'. All such machines usually run the 'Windows' operating systems, but more recently the open system 'Linux' has been made widely available for use on PC computers. Computers that run the Mac OS are also personal computers in the strictest sense of the term, but the term is normally reserved for IBM compatibles.

2.059 PPC Abbreviation for Power PC, the chip produced by the **AIM Alliance** – a grouping of Apple Computers, IBM and Motorola – and used in Power Macintosh computers and elsewhere. The PPC is a RISC chip, and the latest variants used by Apple are the G3 and G4 models, though other versions are used by IBM in mainframe applications. → 2.062 REDUCED INSTRUCTION SET COMPUTING (RISC)

2.060 processor (chip) The silicon **chip** that contains millions of micro-transistorized 'switches' that respond to binary electrical pulses and perform specific functions in a computer. The main processor of a computer, the 'central processor' (CPU), is the most obvious example. Also known as a '**microprocessor**' or '**microchip**'. → 2.015 COPROCESSOR

2.061 processor direct slot (PDS) An expansion slot that connects to the CPU directly rather than indirectly through a bus.

2.062 reduced instruction set computing (RISC) A microprocessor designed to provide fast processing while requiring only a limited number of instructions. Unlike the traditional 'complex instruction set computing' (CISC) processor (which requires more instructions and is thus slower), RISC processors of a given clock speed are nominally faster than CISC processors of equivalent nominal speed. Apple's PowerPC processors feature the RISC design.

2.063 rescue disc Removable disc (normally a CD, but often a floppy disk on PC computers accepting this medium) used as a startup disc on a computer that is

2.075 *antivirus software*

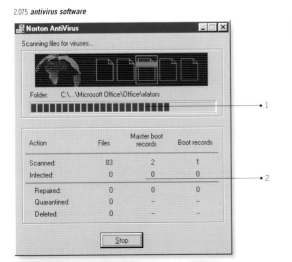

1 Progress bar
2 Scan results to date

unable to start using its standard startup disc. Such a disc usually comprises a minimal installation sufficient for debugging and 'fixing' any problems with the main disc.

2.**064 scalar processor architecture (SPARC)** A microprocessor developed by Sun Microsystems; it forms the basis of SPARC workstations, powerful UNIX-based computers. → 2.166 UNIX

2.**065 seek time** The time it takes for a disk head of a disk drive to move from the current track to what it has been requested to read next. → 2.003 ACCESS TIME

2.**066 startup disc** Any computer drive or disc (floppy disk, Zip disk or CD) containing an operating system which is used to start up a computer. Also called a '**boot disk**'. In most computers this is normally the hard disk.

2.**067 surge suppressor** A device installed in the mains supply chain of a computer and its peripherals to protect the CPU from power surges and voltage fluctuations. Sometimes called a '**spike suppressor**' or '**power filter**'.

2.**068 terminal** Any device used to communicate with another computer via a network. Though terminals can sometimes be computers themselves, they are more often 'dumb', comprising video adaptors, keyboard and monitor. Keystrokes and actions are merely passed directly to the main, host computer. → 2.402 NETWORK

2.**069 twin processor** The use of two principal processing (CPU) chips in a single computer. Employed by Apple with their twin processor G4 computers and by some Sun and Silicon Graphics workstations, they require software applications which are enabled for twin processors to exploit the full power of the architecture. → 2.010 CENTRAL PROCESSING UNIT (CPU); 2.034 G4

2.**070 video card** A plug-in board that provides dedicated control for an external monitor. The board contains the components that generate the video signal, which is then passed to the monitor. Also known as a **video adaptor**. It can sometimes form part of the motherboard. → 2.050 MOTHERBOARD

2.**071 workstation** A single computer dedicated to one person's use. It can be part of a network or 'stand-alone'. Also used specifically for a powerful computer –

often UNIX-based – which is typically used for applications such as advanced-image editing, CAD/CAM and 3D applications. High processor speeds and large RAM memory allocations often characterize these computer systems. → 2.166 UNIX

2.**072 write/writing head** The part of a disk drive that reads data from, and writes data to, a disk. One read/write head is positioned above each side of every disk platter in a hard disk drive, which moves on rails across the surface of the platter while the platter rotates at speed. A pair of heads move in a similar way across the surface of a disc in removable-disk drives. → 2.023 DISK/DISC DRIVE

Software/OS/commands

2.**073 active window** The currently selected desktop or document window. Usually the active window is the only one in which the content can be modified, although with some types of window (such as floating palettes) editing of one window simultaneously updates others. The active window is usually indicated by a bold title bar and active scroll bars. → 2.171 WINDOW

2.**074 Alt key** Modifier key used to access secondary characters assigned to a keyboard key and for menu shortcuts. In Windows menus, you can select an item by holding down the Alt (**Alternate**) key and pressing the key corresponding to an underlined letter in the menu item. This feature relates back to very early Windows versions which were designed to be used with or without a mouse. The Alt key also has additional functions when used with other keys. For example, **Alt-Prt Scn** (print screen) copies the active window to the clipboard. Macintosh computers have an Option key that performs some equivalent actions to the Alt key. → 2.199 OPTION KEY

2.**075 antivirus software** Software applications designed to detect, disable and remove viruses from a computer system. Antivirus software often runs as a background application, monitoring files (particularly those brought to the computer from the Internet or external drives) for indications of a virus. Because viruses are created continually it is normal to 'subscribe' to virus software, receiving periodic updates that enable the software to fight new viruses and variants. Due to its background operation, it is sometimes necessary (for example, when burning CD-ROMs) to disable virus software to maintain data flow and performance.

2.**076 application/application program** A software program, more often described as a '**program**'. Designed for creating and modifying documents for specific purposes. As such, it is distinguished from operating system software and utilities which improve the functioning of your computer. Typical application groups include those for page layout, graphics, word processing and spreadsheets.
→ 2.162 SYSTEM; 2.167 UTILITY (PROGRAM)

2.**077 Basic Input/Output System (BIOS)** The code, usually residing on a chip placed on the motherboard of a computer, which handles basic hardware input and output operations, such as interactions with a keyboard or hard disk drive.

2.**078 BeOS** A desktop computer operating system designed for consumer-level hardware systems. BeOS is optimized for handling and manipulating streaming media. The company behind BeOS was formed by former employees of Apple Computer and designed to run on Mac hardware, though later versions would also run on Intel computers and dedicated Be hardware known as '**BeBoxes**'. → 6.079 STREAMING MEDIA

2.**079 beta test copy** Version of software released to selected users (generally intensive and dedicated users who use the products but are not part of the creating company) after initial testing (alpha testing) and prior to commercial release. Sometimes called a **beta version**, it is used to find any outstanding operational deficiencies or 'bugs'.

2.**080 C/C++** A family of programming languages that first appeared as 'C' in the early 1970s for programming on UNIX computers. The more versatile C++ appeared a decade later and was adopted by a number of platforms, notably Sun and Apple, and is now the staple programming language for many applications. → 2.076 APPLICATION/APPLICATION PROGRAM

2.**081 cancel/abort** The button in dialogue boxes (or a menu item) that allows you to cancel (**abort**) the action that invoked the box.

2.**082 checkbox** A button in a graphical user interface, such as Windows or Mac OS. Normally comprises a small square. Clicking within the square causes a tick (check mark) to appear, indicating that the corresponding command has been selected.

2.**083 clean install** The process of installing or reinstalling operating system software. A clean install will create new system software components rather than updating existing ones. This ensures that all user adjustable settings are reconfigured with their default or 'factory' settings. A clean install is sometimes necessary to 'flush out' or 'reset' unnecessary or corrupt files that cannot be removed by any other means. → 2.139 OPERATING SYSTEM (OS)

2.**084 clipboard** A memory resource featured in operating systems with a graphical user interface (such as Mac OS or Windows) that provides temporary storage of information that has been cut or copied from a document prior to pasting in another. Cutting or copying further information generally overwrites the original data.

2.**085 code** The instructions in a piece of software that tell the computer what to do. Code can take various forms from basic binary code (the lowest level code, a series of 1s and 0s, which is the form of code the computer understands) through to programming languages and 'scripts'. These are written using English words and phrases. HTML, for example, is a programming code for web browsers. → 2.180 APPLESCRIPT

2.**086 command** A computer instruction delivered either by an application program or the computer user using an input device (a keyboard or mouse). → 2.248 MOUSE

2.**087 command-line interface** Interface that preceded graphical user interfaces, which is still used for some specialist computer applications. Specific text commands are entered against a prompt, followed by the return key, to submit the command to the computer. → 2.116 GRAPHICAL USER INTERFACE (GUI)

2.**088 computer language** The language, or code, devised to make computers perform actions. High level programs are written using English terms and phrases that are subject to very precise syntax rules and can be interpreted by the computer as instructions. 'Low level' languages are little more than binary code which only the computer can readily understand. → 2.076 APPLICATION/APPLICATION PROGRAM; 2.085 CODE

2.**089 control panel (2)** A small application within the Mac OS and Windows operating systems designed for system or software configuration, which enables you to configure system software or to customize various aspects of your computer, such as time, date or appearance.

2.**090 copy-protected software** Software which has been produced in such a way as to prevent its unauthorized use. This is achieved either by software '**encryption**' (embedding it with a unique serial number) or, in extreme cases – and especially where very expensive software is concerned – protecting it with a hardware 'dongle' (a device which must be plugged into your computer in order for the application to work). Difficult to achieve with CD-based software other than by using a software dongle or requiring the use of a subsidiary floppy disk. → 2.025 DONGLE

2.**091 cross-platform** The term applied to software, multimedia titles or anything else (such as floppy disks) that will work on more than one computer platform – that is, those which run on different operating systems. Most commonly used to describe compatibility between Mac OS and Microsoft Windows. → 2.139 OPERATING SYSTEM (OS)

2.**092 cut** A feature of document handling applications (such as word processors or image-editing software) which allows you to remove an item from a location in a document to the clipboard. It can then be pasted to another document or another part of the same document. This is a 'move' command, to be distinguished from 'copy', which places the item on the clipboard while leaving the original where it is. → 2.084 CLIPBOARD; 2.093 CUT AND PASTE; 5.047 COPY

2.**093 cut and paste** The process of removing an item from a document ('cutting' the item, which places it on the 'clipboard') and then placing it elsewhere ('pasting' it),

either in the same or a different document. Originally this term was applied to text but can equally apply to image elements or graphical elements. → 2.084 CLIPBOARD; 2.092 CUT; 5.047 COPY

2.**094 data processing** The systematic processing of information in any way. Applying a software filter to an image involves data processing as does performing a calculation on a spreadsheet.

2.**095 database** Informational data stored on a computer in a systematic fashion for easy retrieval. Databases hold data in separate but consistent categories (called '**fields**') for each type of information, such as names, addresses and telephone numbers. A set of information of this type relating to an individual or an image, for example, are termed 'records'. Relational databases allow complex data manipulation between multidimensional arrays of data. Data management is conducted by a program known as a database manager. → 1.517 PHOTO LIBRARY; 2.096 DATABASE MANAGER; 2.152 RECORD; 4.389 PORTFOLIO; 7.035 IMAGE LIBRARY

2.**096 database manager** An application for constructing databases, allowing you to define, enter, search, sort and output information. Database managers can be 'flat-file', in which information can be created and accessed only in a single, self-contained database, or 'relational', in which information can be shared and exchanged across two or more separate databases. → 2.095 DATABASE; 2.153 RELATIONAL DATABASE

2.**097 debug(ging)** The process of hunting out and correcting programming irregularities in computer software. Normally conducted following tight procedures to limit the number of bugs that remain when a product is signed off for sale. In all but the most basic of programs, there are residual bugs that manifest when that product is released, for which subsequent free patches are supplied. → 2.433 BUG

2.**098 defragment(ing)** The nature of writing files and data to disks in such a way that available free space – whether or not large enough for the total file – is used. If the file is too large for a space it will continue writing to another free space. This makes reading the data back a lengthier process.

2.123 *interface*

Windows 98

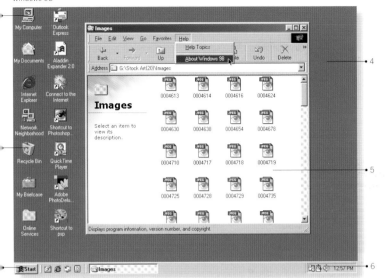

1 *My Computer icon*   4 *Desktop*
2 *Recycle bin*   5 *Folder contents*
3 *Start menu button*   6 *Taskbar*

Mac OS X

1 *Hard drive icon*   4 *Desktop*
2 *Wastebasket*   5 *Folder contents*
3 *Dock*

Defragmenting is the process that reassembles files and data into contiguous areas, speeding up disk access. → 2.467 OPTIMIZE/OPTIMIZING

2.**099 deselect** To deactivate an active item, such as a highlighted image selection or highlighted text, by clicking outside or away from the item. Deselect is available as a menu command in many image editors for removing the selections made on an image.

2.**100 desktop** The metaphorical representation on a computer monitor of a stylised desktop and used as the working environment of a graphical user interface (GUI). → 2.116 GRAPHICAL USER INTERFACE (GUI)

2.**101 dialogue box** Box that opens onscreen when some commands are invoked. The dialogue box provides the user with controls for setting the parameters (control parameters) associated with that command. Many effects filters provide dialogue boxes.

2.**102 drag-and-drop** A feature of some operating systems and applications which enables you to select an item such as a picture box or passage of text in one location, and move or copy it to another simply by 'dragging' it with the mouse button held down and then 'dropping' it in the desired location by releasing the mouse button. This circumvents the use of the clipboard.

2.**103 drawing application** As distinct from most painting and image-editing applications which work on individual picture elements, drawing applications are usually defined as those which are object-oriented (using 'vectors' to mathematically define lines and shapes). Some applications now feature functionality from both the vector drawing and pixel-based painting camps. → 2.141 PAINTING APPLICATION

2.**104 driver/device driver** A small piece of software designed to enable a computer to operate or 'drive' a peripheral piece of hardware, such as a printer ('**printer driver**'), scanner or disk drive. Drivers, once installed, may comprise part of the computer's operating system or be loaded with a program as an application 'plug-in' (as with some scanner drivers, for example). → 2.019 DEVICE; 4.374 PLUG-IN

2.**105 drop-down menu** The menu that appears when you click on a title in the menu bar along the top of your screen. Also called '**pop-down menu**' or '**pull-down menu**'. → 2.130 MENU BAR; 2.132 MENU TITLE

2.**106 Edit menu** A standard menu in most applications (in the Mac OS, one of the three standard menus alongside the 'Apple' and File menus), that contains the fundamental editing commands, such actions as Cut, Copy, Paste and Undo. → 3.117 FILE MENU

2.**107 Enter key** On keyboards, the key that confirms an entry or command. On some computer systems the Enter key is synonymous with the Return key though some applications may also have a specific function for that key. → 2.156 RETURN KEY

2.**108 Esc(ape) key** A standard keyboard key generally used to cancel some action, but with uses that can vary according to the application.

2.**109 Exit** Quit command issued to leave an application on PCs. Usually found at the foot of the File menu.

2.**110 extension** A file which adds functions or functionality to a computer system or application. **Operating system extensions** include such things as hardware 'drivers' which control devices like printers and monitors, whereas application extensions (usually called 'plug-ins') can include any kind of enhancement, from mundane file-handling operations (such as importing and exporting documents) to more exciting special effects. → 2.104 DRIVER/DEVICE DRIVER; 4.374 PLUG-IN

2.**111 extension/init manager** Utility software which enables users to manage system extensions, e.g., turning off redundant or unwanted ones or to test for incompatibilities.

2.**112 firewall** A software security system that protects web sites and networks from unauthorized access. Firewalls can also prevent users downloading information from the Internet either because it is unsuitable or for internal policy reasons. → 2.115 GARDEN WALL

2.**113 freeware** A piece of software that has been made freely available and is in the 'public domain'. Unlike shareware or commercial software there is no fee payable for the use of freeware. → 2.158 SHAREWARE

2.114 function key/s (F key) A set of keys on most keyboards which can be assigned specific functions to carry out a sequence of mouse and keyboard actions.

2.115 garden wall A security feature that can be implemented on computers to restrict Internet access to preferred sites. Normally used to prevent children accessing sites that are deemed unsuitable, but provide them with easy access to appropriate sites. → 2.112 FIREWALL

2.116 graphical user interface (GUI) The feature of most computer operating systems, such as the Mac OS, Windows and Linux, which permits interaction with the computer by means of pointing at graphic symbols (icons) on the monitor screreen with a mouse rather than by typing coded commands. Less commonly known as a 'WIMP' or '**pointing interface**'. → 2.087 COMMAND-LINE INTERFACE; 2.100 DESKTOP; 2.123 INTERFACE

2.117 Help A feature of operating systems and software which provides explanations and advice. Some software packages use application-specific help systems or might use web browsers as the delivery method. An increasing number of applications provide online help. Selecting this option connects to a website featuring specific and often-updated support.

2.118 high-level language A programming language that uses English language and grammar rather than machine code. → 2.127 MACHINE CODE

2.119 icon A graphical representation of an object (such as a disk, file, folder or tool) or of a concept or message used to make identification and selection easier.

2.120 image-editing application A computer application designed for manipulating either scanned or user-generated images. Image-editing applications are advanced **'painting' programs** that edit the individual image pixels of a bitmapped image rather than the vector-based elements of illustration and drawing packages. **Image editors** also provide features for preparing images for process-colour printing (such as colour separations), as well as tools for painting and 'filters' for applying special effects. Sometimes called an **image manipulation program**. Typical image-editing applications inclue Paintshop Pro (Jasc

software), Photoshop (Adobe) and Photo-Paint (Corel).

2.121 input The description of putting (or pulling) data into a computer by whatever means. Typing at the keyboard represents one form of input, pulling a file or document into an image editor another.

2.122 installer A **'shell' program** which enables you to load software on to your hard disk. Installer programs will put the numerous application files in their correct places (including the system folder where appropriate). The location of added files will be stored in the registry or listed in an install log to make uninstalling easier. → 2.451 INSTALL

2.123 interface Software that aids the computer's communication with the user (the '**user interface**') and other application programs. Also the name given to a card or plug that is used to connect peripheral devices with the computer. → 2.087 COMMAND-LINE INTERFACE; 2.116 GRAPHICAL USER INTERFACE (GUI)

2.124 Java A programming language originated by Sun Microsystems for creating small applications ('applets') which can be downloaded from a web server to a user's computer to add dynamic effects such as animations. Java is similar to the C++ language but is more compact and has better memory management. It is also platform neutral, meaning it will run on most platforms and operating systems. → 2.420 APPLET; 6.011 BROWSER

2.125 keyboard character Any character produced onscreen by pressing a key (or combination of keys) on the keyboard. → 2.045 KEYBOARD; 4.108 KEYBOARD SHORTCUT

97

2.126 Linux Operating system derived from UNIX that can be run on a variety of platforms including PCs and Macs. It is 'open sourced', meaning that any user can purchase or download a copy and undertake their own customization or changes, notionally for the benefit of the whole Linux community. Several user interfaces have been developed (making it appear less like UNIX and more like a Mac or Windows operating system) and some 'end user' software has also been developed. Though gaining ground rapidly, it is gaining particular strength with users of Internet servers.

2.126 *Linux*

One implementation of Linux featuring the GIMP image-manipulation program

1 Menu bar
2 Application toolbox
3 Image-editing canvas
4 Desktop
5 Application bar
6 Help

2.146 *preferences*

System preferences can be set by selecting the appropriate icon (here shown with Mac OS X)

2.**127 machine code** The lowest level of programming code; it is easily processed by the computer and is normally generated directly or indirectly by a computer program. → 2.085 CODE

2.**128 macro** A single command (normally issued using a keystroke or keystroke combination) that actions a series of other commands. A macro can be predefined or created by the user (by 'recording' a sequence of commands or keystrokes and assigning it to a key or perhaps a button). Some applications have similar 'events' or '**scripts**'. In Photoshop the Actions feature permits a range of manipulations to be performed using a macro. → 2.114 FUNCTION KEY/S (F KEY); 4.189 ACTIONS

2.**129 menu** List of commands from which a user makes a selection. Applied to both Mac OS or Windows systems, but offered by some earlier systems too. Selections are usually revealed by clicking on the menu header. Pop-up, pull-out and contextual menus also feature in both operating systems.

2.**130 menu bar** The horizontal panel across the top of a computer screen (in Mac OS) or the top of a window in the Windows operating system containing the titles of available menus. → 2.129 MENU

2.**131 menu command** A command given to the computer from a list of choices available within a menu, as distinct from a command made via the keyboard ('keyboard command'). You can, however, make a menu command with a keyboard shortcut, e.g., command (Mac)/control (Windows)+P for Print, +S for Save, +X for Cut, etc.

2.**132 menu title** The title of a menu as it is displayed in the menu bar. → 2.130 MENU BAR

2.**133 message box** Information box that appears in Windows, Mac OS and other graphical user interfaces to advise on a condition, such as an alert or, for example, advising on an action. → 2.417 ALERT

2.**134 modifier key** Key that when pressed (and usually held) modifies the actions of other keys. Keys that perform such modification (not necessarily under all circumstances) include the Control, Alt and Fn keys on Windows keyboards, and Control, Option (Apple key) and Fn keys on Mac OS

keyboards. The Shift key is also sometimes considered a modifier key.

2.**135 MS-DOS** Microsoft **Disk Operating System**, the operating system used on Intel-based personal computers (PCs). MS-DOS (or just plain 'DOS') also provides the skeleton on which Microsoft's 'Windows' operating system hangs. The DOS environment can be run as a 'shell' within Windows from where DOS-based applications can be run. Windows XP finally removes the DOS link. → 2.087 COMMAND-LINE INTERFACE; 2.139 OPERATING SYSTEM (OS); 2.237 WINDOWS XP

2.**136 multithreaded** A feature of operating systems in which operating system activity (or the activity of applications that run on them) divides into smaller 'subtasks', each of which runs in parallel and finally recombines to deliver the intended outcome. Multithreading can deliver substantial time savings for some operations. → 2.465 MULTITASKING

2.**137 NeXTstep** A multitasking operating system created by **Steve Jobs** (after leaving **Apple Computer**) and others for the NeXT computer. NeXTstep had its own graphical user interface, an interface builder, and additional 'kits' for projects such as database indexing. Though the operating system was very advanced, the hardware and software package was expensive and uptake slow. Eventually NeXTstep became **Openstep** and elements of this, in turn, were incorporated in Mac OS X when NeXT was bought by Apple in 1997.

2.**138 Open** A standard operating system command which opens a selected file (or folder) or opens a menu box for the selection of a file to be opened. → 2.456 LAUNCH

2.**139 operating system (OS)** The system software (and in some cases 'firmware') that provides the environment within which all other software operates. The major operating systems are Microsoft's 'DOS' and 'Windows', Apple's 'Mac OS', and **AT&T**'s 'UNIX', the last three of which all use (or can use) GUIs. The open-sourced Linux (a UNIX derivative) provides a further alternative, while the Mac OS has been upgraded to OS X (a Unix-based system) and Windows to Windows XP. → 2.030 FIRMWARE

2.**140 out-of-memory message** A message which tells you that there is not enough memory (RAM) available to perform the task that you require. Typical out-of-memory messages relate to reasons such as having too many system files open (such as fonts) or a particularly memory-intensive task (particularly those involving bitmapped images) exceeding available RAM.

2.**141 painting application** Applications which use bitmaps of pixels to create images rather than the 'vectors' that describe lines in drawing applications (called 'object-oriented'). Image-editing applications are, strictly speaking, painting programs, albeit with additional functionality. → 2.103 DRAWING APPLICATION; 7.077 VECTOR

2.**142 paste** A command (or action) that places a copied item (which might be text, a graphic or image) currently stored in the computer's clipboard in a destination document. → 2.084 CLIPBOARD; 2.093 CUT AND PASTE

2.**143 platform neutral** Term used to describe any software, application or programming language that is not dependent on the operating system of a computer for correct operation. Sun's Java, for example, is a platform neutral programming language.

2.**144 pop-up menu** A menu in a dialogue box or palette that 'pops up' when you click on its title or an icon representing that title.

2.**145 PostScript** Adobe Systems Inc.'s proprietary '**page description language**' (**PDL**) for image output to laser printers and high-resolution imagesetters.

2.**146 preferences** A file that contains the user's preferences for that program. Any user modifications (such as the selection of alternate cursors, preferred palettes or screen layout) are stored here so that those preferences are invoked the next time the program opens.

2.**147 program defaults** Program settings that were configured at the time of installation and usually represent the 'best' settings as proposed by the software creator. Screen layouts, palette positions and colours have default settings which can be modified by the user. Often there is a 'Reset Defaults' option that will reset these settings to their original 'factory' settings. Settings and adjustments are often stored in a dedicated file called 'preferences'. Often the program **defaults** can be reset by deleting the preferences file appropriate to that program. → 2.146 PREFERENCES

2.**148 programming language** Languages devised for writing computer software. Programming languages can be either 'high-level' (based as closely as possible on English), or 'machine code', the lowest level (the least like English but the easiest for a computer to process). Typical languages include Java, C++ and **Pascal**. → 2.118 HIGH-LEVEL LANGUAGE; 2.127 MACHINE CODE

2.**149 push button** A button in a dialogue box which, when clicked, invokes the command specified on the button.

2.**150 Quit** The command, on the Mac OS, by which you 'shut down' an application, as

100

2.144 *pop-up menu*

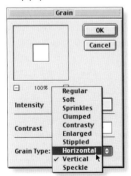

The pop-up menu (here shown in the Grain Filter dialogue box) permits the selection of grain types

2.149 *push button*

2.151 *radio button*

2.176 *alias*

distinct from closing a document within the application, in which case the document disappears but the application remains open.

2.151 radio button A button in a GUI, such as Windows or Mac OS. Comprises a small circle containing another circle. Clicking on the centre selects the button and causes that circle to darken. Designed to look like and operate like station selection buttons on old car radios. → 2.082 CHECKBOX

2.152 record An individual entry on one subject – such as an individual image – in a database and comprising a set of related fields, such as the image title, any associated keywords, exposure information and details on the photographer. → 2.095 DATABASE; 2.096 DATABASE MANAGER

2.153 relational database A database application in which the information resides across multiple separate files rather than from within a single file; distinct from a '**flat-file**' database, in which each file is self-contained and cannot exchange information with another file. As such, relational databases are much more potent and useful for cross-referencing against multiple criteria. Image databases that provide browsing against multiple lists of information are generally relational. → 2.095 DATABASE; 2.096 DATABASE MANAGER

2.154 release version The version of a software application that is made available for sale. An application is normally signed off for release following internal testing (alpha release) and limited external testing (beta release). → 2.079 BETA TEST COPY

2.155 resource A part of a computer system such as a disk drive, memory or other peripheral device that can be allocated to a program or process that is currently running. Also used to describe a small section of code (or data) that can be used across several programs or in several places in one program. A font or a dialogue box are examples of such resources.

2.156 Return key The key on a computer keyboard that once emulated the '**carriage return**' key on an electric typewriter. When used in text-based applications (such as word processors) it performs a similar operation by placing the text insertion point at the start of the next line. However, its principal application is for confirming or

selecting a command highlighted in dialogue boxes. → 2.107 ENTER KEY

2.157 Save dialogue box A box that appears onscreen the first time a document is saved, requiring the user to supply the name and location with which it should be saved. → 2.131 MENU COMMAND

2.158 shareware Software available via the Internet or on magazine cover discs which allows limited free use but demands a nominal payment for continued use. Such payments may be made via registration houses or on the honesty principle. The payment distinguishes this from freeware, where no payment is required. → 2.113 FREEWARE

2.159 Shift key The modifier key used to generate uppercase and other characters on a keyboard.

2.160 shift-click(ing) The process of holding down the shift key while clicking on several items or passages of text on the screen, usually for making multiple selections from a menu list.

2.161 spreadsheet A specialist application designed to provide a framework for complex calculations and to apply the necessary calculations. Spreadsheets use a table of rows and columns into which numerical data or calculations can be entered. Some spreadsheet applications will also generate graphics (three-dimensional ones in some cases) from the data entered into cells. Microsoft Excel and Lotus 1-2-3 are typical commercial examples. → 2.177 APPLE FILE EXCHANGE (AFE)

2.162 system Redundant term for the operating system in a Macintosh (as in System 6). Replaced with the term 'OS' in later versions (OS 9, OS X).

2.163 text editor Any application, such as a word processing application, used to enter and edit text and characters only.

2.164 title bar The bar at the top of the open image document displaying the name of that document, usually with the display magnification and image mode. Any open window in the conventional Windows or Mac OS environment will feature a title bar featuring the file name (and, sometimes, the name of the application that created it). The position of the window onscreen can be adjusted by dragging on this bar. → 2.130 MENU BAR

2.**165 TWAIN** Acronym taken from a ballad by **Rudyard Kipling**. Cross-platform driver interface used particularly for acquiring images from scanners and some cameras.

2.**166 UNIX** An advanced and stable operating system developed by **AT&T**, devised to be multitasking and portable from one machine to another. UNIX is used widely on web servers and also underpins the latest Macintosh operating system (Mac OS X). The open-source operating system, Linux, incorporates much of the UNIX structure. → 2.139 OPERATING SYSTEM (OS)

2.**167 utility program** A program that enhances or supports the way you use your computer. Typical utilities are programs for backup, font management, file-finding, disk management and file recovery, plus plug-ins, screen savers, etc. They are thus distinguished from those programs that enable you to work on a specific project.

2.**168 virus protection utility/program** A utility program designed to offer protection against virus infection of a computer. Such programs will alert and, where possible, remove the 'infection'. → 2.075 ANTIVIRUS SOFTWARE; 2.133 MESSAGE BOX; 2.489 VIRUS

2.**169 What You See Is What You Get (WYSIWYG)** (pronounced 'wizzywig') This acronym refers to any technology which enables you to see images onscreen exactly as they appear when printed. The term is also commonly used to refer to visual HTML editing (for web pages, etc.) in applications such as **DreamWeaver**.
→ 2.116 GRAPHICAL USER INTERFACE (GUI); 4.447 COLOUR MODES; 4.448 COLOUR PICKER (2); 4.456 RGB MODE

2.**170 WIMP** Abbreviation for Windows, Icon, Mouse (or menu) and Pointer. An acronym for the constituent parts of a computer's GUI. → 2.116 GRAPHICAL USER INTERFACE (GUI)

2.**171 window** Part of the GUI of a computer, a window is an area of a computer screen that displays the contents of disk, folder or document. A window can be resized and will be provided with scrolling bars to adjust the position of the contents if those contents are too large to fit within it. → 2.116 GRAPHICAL USER INTERFACE (GUI)

2.**172 word processor** A software application designed for entering and editing text and providing features for checking spelling, indexing, sorting, etc. The term also describes special computers dedicated to achieving the above. More advanced word processors allow the inclusion of images and graphics to provide limited desktop publishing features. A word processor that provides only text features is sometimes known as a text editor.
→ 2.163 TEXT EDITOR

2.**173 X Windows System** Similar in principle to the Windows and the Mac OS interface and one of several GUIs used on UNIX computers and Linux systems. Nominally UNIX is a command-line interface operating system where commands need to be entered as precise alphanumeric strings; X Windows interprets user actions into instructions which UNIX can understand. → 2.116 GRAPHICAL USER INTERFACE (GUI); 2.166 UNIX

2.**174 zapping the PRAM** The term used to describe the resetting of the parameter RAM (**PRAM**) on a Macintosh computer to its 'factory' settings. Achieved by holding down the Option+Command+P+R keys while restarting your computer. Date and time settings are not normally affected, but monitor, keyboard (and mouse or trackpad), Appletalk and memory settings revert to their default values. → 2.310 PARAMETER RAM (PRAM)

2.**175 zoom** A feature of some applications which enables you to enlarge a portion of an image, making it easier to see and work with. → 4.188 ZOOM TOOL

Macintosh interface terms

2.**176 alias** Equivalent to Shortcut in Windows, an alias is a duplicate of a file icon on Mac OS computers. As it is a copy of the icon, but not of the file itself, an alias occupies very little space. It is used as a shortcut to a file that might be buried deep in the file hierarchy or reside on a different, networked computer and is typically placed on the desktop or can be dropped into the startup or Apple menus.
→ 2.231 SHORTCUT

2.**177 Apple File Exchange (AFE)** Feature of the Mac OS. Enables files (and folders and directories) created on Windows PCs (or other computers) to be recognized and opened by a corresponding Mac OS application. Also known as **File Exchange**.

2.178 Apple Guide Online help facility of the Mac operating system that provides specific help and 'walk throughs' of tasks such as setting up a printer. Tutorial screens are used to lead the user through the stages, with dynamic red markers pointing out choices where selections need to be made. A more advanced form of the online Help offered in Windows.

2.179 Apple Menu Customizable menu that drops down from the **Apple logo** on the menu bar. Provides access to systemwide features, irrespective of the application currently running (the launch of Mac OS X has seen the Apple menu somewhat modified in terms of the features offered).

2.180 AppleScript The Mac OS scripting feature enabling users to write scripts for automating common tasks. Rather like macros, AppleScripts can be written for many applications (and for operating systems) in order to perform automatic operations within those programs. In many respects AppleScript can be thought of as the Mac's equivalent to DOS. → 2.128 MACRO

2.181 Application Menu Menu that appears at the right-hand side of the menu bar and identifies the currently active application. This is a pull-down menu that can be pulled down to reveal and select other open applications. In later OS versions a copy or 'alias' of the active application could be pulled 'off' the menu and placed anywhere onscreen. This copy has buttons (and, optionally, application names) enabling rapid selection. In OS 8.5 and later Command-Tab can be used to move sequentially through the open applications.

2.182 Aqua The visual interface used for Mac OS X, equivalent to the 'Platinum' interface of earlier operating systems. The screen layout follows much of the traditional Mac interface 'rules' but adds improved graphics (thanks to Quartz), a 'Dock' for placing frequently used applications and a more fluid appearance. → 2.192 DOCK; 2.200 OS X; 2.204 QUARTZ

2.183 Assistant Walk-through program that provides help in configuring the computer and, for example, setting up Internet connections. Similar to the 'Wizards' in Windows.

2.184 Balloon help Turned on and off by selecting Help > **Show Balloons** or Help > **Hide Balloons** from the menu bar. Uses speech balloons to provide information on a feature or icon currently under the mouse.

2.185 Classic (environment) An operating environment within Mac OS X that emulates the OS 9.1 environment. Enables applications not specifically engineered for OS X to be used on an OS X computer. The Classic environment needs to be used to run all applications not designed for OS X. → 2.200 OS X

2.186 Command key Sometimes called the '**Apple key**' or '**Clover key**' (because of the symbols printed upon it) this is the primary modifier key on a Mac keyboard (the others are the Option and Control keys). It is normally pressed in conjunction with another key to activate additional commands or perform keyboard shortcuts. Used for principal commands such as cutting, copying and pasting selected text. → 4.108 KEYBOARD SHORTCUT

2.187 control key (Mac) Used principally for displaying contextual menus. It is a 'lesser' modifier key than Control on a Windows computer.

2.188 control strip Provides quick access to certain features such as volume control, Internet connection and screen resolutions. Debuting on Mac portables, but now a function of all OS versions prior to OS X, the control strip is a pop-out menu that 'pops' horizontally from a tab (usually) at the bottom left of the screen. Can be customized to add other functions for easy access. Similar to the more basic Tray in the Windows interface. → 2.105 DROP-DOWN MENU

2.189 Darwin The core OS of Apple's OS X operating system. The Darwin component is tasked with providing features such as pre-emptive multitasking and memory protection in order that the principal components (known as **Carbon**, **POSIX** and **Cocoa**) are best placed to take advantage of them.

2.190 desktop picture Picture used to provide the backdrop to the desktop. Can be added or changed using the Desktop Pictures or Appearance Manager control panels (depending on the software version).

2.191 Disk First Aid Standard hard disk repair program. Scans and verifies the disk (or disks) for errors and can verify disk condition.

2.192 Dock Feature of the Mac OS X interface. The Dock sits normally at the bottom of the screen and holds icons that correspond to all folders, applications, documents and more that the user can access (or might like to access) speedily. It is moveable (including an option to be hidden) to enable the workspace to be maximized.

2.193 extensions folder Folder that resides in the system folder, on all Mac operating systems prior to OS X, which holds all the system extensions. → 3.023 FILE EXTENSION

2.194 Finder Fundamental component of the Mac operating system that maintains the Mac desktop and other elements of the interface. Equivalent to the Explorer in Windows.

2.195 Get Info File menu item in the Finder. Information provided varies but normally includes details of the file size, version and location. The front or a subsidiary page includes memory information and in most cases permits the minimum and preferred memory allocations to be reset (usually to provide a larger allocation).

2.196 Launcher A desktop window that features often used icons (or aliases) of frequently used applications. Useful as a shortcut to deeply nested applications and also as a **'simple' interface**, though similar shortcuts can be built into the Apple menu or even left as aliases on the desktop. → 2.179 APPLE MENU

2.197 Mac OS The operating system used on Apple Computer's 'Macintosh' series, which provides the GUI of that system. Mac OS was known as the '**System**' (e.g., System 6 for version 6 of the operating system). Unlike other operating systems, such as Microsoft's 'DOS' and 'Windows', which are entirely software-based, the Mac OS is part software and part 'firmware' (software built into a hardware 'ROM' chip on the Mac's motherboard). It can thus provide a consistent interface with standard control mechanisms, such as dialogue boxes and windows, that allow all software written for the Macintosh to have the same look and feel. Mac OS X introduces substantial new features and a UNIX core. → 2.116 GRAPHICAL USER INTERFACE (GUI); 2.135 MS-DOS; 2.235 WINDOWS

2.198 Mach 3.0 More correctly called the Mach 3.0 kernel, this is the latest version of an open-source programming kernel that has been in intensive development for some years. It is used in the Mac OS X operating system to provide processor 'control' for the computer, handling memory protection, processor scheduling and processor availability. → 2.200 OS X

2.199 Option key Modifier key that can be used to enter special characters (such as the registered trademark ®) or in image-editing applications (in combination with appropriate alphanumeric keys) to provide certain command shortcuts. In Windows the equivalent key is Alt ('Alternate'),

2.181 *Application Menu*

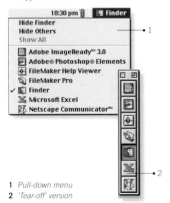

1 *Pull-down menu*
2 *'Tear-off' version*

2.195 *Get Info*

2.197 *Mac OS 9*

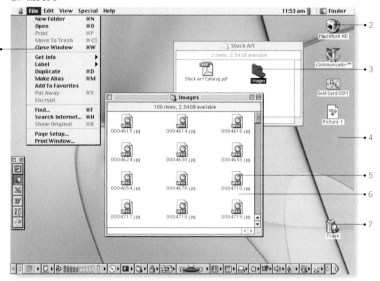

1 Pull-down menu   5 Files
2 Hard disk icon   6 Active window
3 Folder   7 Wastebasket
4 Desktop

2.200 *Mac OS X*

1 Menu bar   4 Desktop
2 Folder contents   5 Dock
3 System resources

which is inscribed on some option keys.
→ 2.074 ALT KEY

2.**200 OS X** Version (10) of the Macintosh operating system; it combines UNIX-based underpinnings with new graphics technologies like Quartz to deliver a potent environment. With robust features (such as memory protection and fully integrated web resources) it offers the most stable and powerful platform but does need a reasonably well-specified Mac to exploit it. As OS X is so fundamentally different from OS 9 and its predecessors, Mac OS X needs to run OS 9 in a 'shell' environment (called 'Classic') to enable software unsuitable for OS X to be run.
→ 2.189 DARWIN

2.**201 Power key** Key on the keyboard of many (but not all) Macintoshes that, when pressed, starts up the computer.

2.**202 Preferences folder** Folder that contains the user preferences (with regard to screen layout, menu preferences and cursor options, for example). Preferences can be reset by deleting the preferences file corresponding to the application. In Windows there is the central Registry database that stores information on user preferences. → 2.146 PREFERENCES; 2.228 REGISTRY

2.**203 PrintMonitor** A fundamental part of the Mac OS up to OS 9, PrintMonitor is a print spooling application that enables 'background' printing, allowing you to print while you carry on working. The advent of OS X has seen the

implementation of a new printing utility.
→ 5.039 BACKGROUND PRINTING

2.**204 Quartz** A 2D-graphics system, based on the portable document format (PDF) designed for dynamic (real-time) rendering of graphics, antialiasing and construction of PostScript graphics to the highest possible quality. Used in Mac OS X, including the Aqua interface. → 2.182 AQUA

2.**205 QuickDraw** Name for the Mac OS routines that enable all display operations onscreen. It is also responsible for outputting text and graphics in a WYSIWYG layout to non-PostScript printers. → 2.145 POSTSCRIPT

2.**206 QuickTime VR** QuickTime 'virtual reality'. An Apple operating system extension which provides extra functionality for creating and playing back 3D objects and panoramic scenes. → 2.110 EXTENSION; 4.393 QUICKTIME

2.**207 ResEdit** A powerful Apple-supplied application for editing resources (icons, sounds, menus, etc.), used for modifying any Macintosh file or software program (system or otherwise). Due to its potency it should only be used under guidance or by those familiar with its operation. → 2.155 RESOURCE; 3.134 RESOURCE FORK

2.**208 scrapbook** Repository of clip art, sound files or text that acts as a 'mini-clipboard'. Multiple elements can be stored here for use in any appropriate application.

2.**209 Sherlock** The 'find' utility for Mac OS computers that enables local disks and the Internet to be searched for files or, if the disk is indexed, content. Different

2.209 *Sherlock*

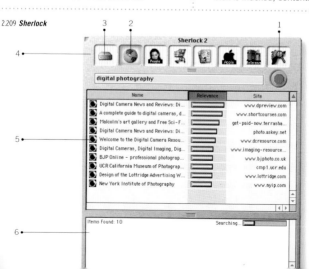

1 *Personal search criteria*
2 *Internet*
3 *Hard disk*
4 *Search 'channels'*
5 *Search results*
6 *Extended search results (where relevant)*

channels can be created to perform Internet searches by linking to appropriate search engines.

2.**210 Simplesound** Basic sound recording and replay feature. Usually used to manage and play the system alert sounds.

2.**211 Simpletext** A basic word-processing application that can be used to read most text-based files. Normally used to display the 'Read me' files supplied with software and needing to be read prior to installation. Equivalent to Notepad or Wordpad in Windows.

2.**212 SoftWindows** Software that emulates the Windows operating system for use on a Mac computer. Virtually all the functionality of Windows is emulated, with Windows running in a 'shell window' on the Mac desktop. The Windows environment uses its own area of the hard disk exclusively and can also share disks and files with the Mac OS. Other emulators, including **Virtual PC** and those featuring hardware solutions, are available.

2.**213 startup screen** Image file stored as a PICT resource file and designed to appear as the Mac starts up and loads extensions.
→ 3.065 PICT RESOURCE

2.**214 Stuffit** The compression, expansion and archiving application created by **Aladdin Systems**. Files created using Stuffit have the suffix .sit. Similar to WinZip and Zip in Windows.

2.**215 system folder** A folder in Mac OS systems that contains all the files, including system and finder files, necessary for running the operating system. Broadly equivalent to the 'Windows' folder on a Windows PC.
→ 2.139 OPERATING SYSTEM (OS)

Windows interface terms

2.**216 Active Desktop** A feature of Windows since Windows 98 (or 95 with Internet Explorer) that enables the Windows desktop to be viewed using a web browser. HTML items can be placed on this active desktop and will be continuously refreshed, as long as an Internet connection is available.

2.**217 briefcase** Feature for carrying files between computers and ensuring synchronization on return and that the most recent copy is pre-eminent.

2.**218 command line** Option in Windows to enter commands and instructions as a text/symbol command. Originates from the 'DOS' operating system which predated Windows. Select Start menu > Run or use the Address toolbar on the Taskbar.

2.**219 control panel (1)** Folder that contains a group of routines for configuring various parts of the computer, such as screen layout, resolution and Internet access.

2.**220 Disk Defragmenter** Utility included in the Windows operating system for defragmenting files and rebuilding them into contiguous files. Defragmentation tended to be more necessary when hard disks were slower than today; contemporary disks are much faster and hence defragmentation is less crucial.

2.226 *Paint*

1 *Menu bar*
2 *Selected tool (pencil)*
3 *Foreground/ background colours*
4 *Image colours*

2.**221 Drive Space** Disk compression utility
designed to compress files and folders to
create more disk space. A **compressed disk**
is, however, slower to read from.

2.**222 End Task** Option presented when the
Control, Alt and Delete keys are pressed
simultaneously. This enables a stalled
application, or one acting erratically, to
be forced to exit. Any unsaved data will
be lost.

2.**223 Find** Command available from the Start
menu that enables files, folders or (in later
Windows versions) Internet information to
be found. Similar to Sherlock in the Mac
OS or the Mac Find command in versions
before OS 8.5.

2.**224 Luna** Interface look for Windows XP.

2.**225 My Computer** Desktop icon that, when
clicked on, opens the My Computer
window. This gives an overview of the
computer and included resources (such as
hard disks, removable discs loaded) and
network resources.

2.**226 Paint** Basic bitmap painting application
provided with Windows but eclipsed by
even the most rudimentary third-party
application.

2.**227 Recycle bin** Repository for unwanted files
or items. By dragging and dropping items
to this bin they can be marked for
deletion, although they are not physically
deleted until the '**Empty Recycle Bin**'
command is issued. Hence when items
are in the bin they can be retrieved (if
dumped accidentally) and still consume
disk space. They can also be retrieved

under certain conditions with utilities,
such as **Norton Utilities**, even after the
recycle/trash bin has been emptied.

2.**228 Registry** Both user preferences and
configuration settings are stored in the
Registry. This is a system-level database
that is addressed by the application
installers. Mac OS computers feature a
Preferences folder where user preferences
for application preferences are stored.
→ 2.146 PREFERENCES

2.**229 right-click** Mouse click for displaying
contextual menus on two-button mice.

2.**230 ScanDisk** Disk scanning and repairing
utility that runs automatically when a disk
crash has occurred or can be started
manually by selecting Start > Programs >
Accessories > System Tools > ScanDisk.

2.**231 shortcut** A feature of Windows (95
onwards) that allows the creation of a
surrogate icon to represent that of the
application. These icons can be placed
anywhere – on the desktop, in a Startup
folder, for example, and clicking on them
will invoke the main application. Equivalent
to 'alias' in the Mac OS. → 2.176 ALIAS

2.**232 Start menu** Fundamental Windows
system menu used to launch programs,
help and access control panels and to
shut down the computer. Normally found
at the bottom left-hand corner of the
screen. In the Mac OS the Apple menu
includes many of the same features and,
like the Start menu, can be customized.

2.**233 Taskbar** Bar across the base of a
Windows computer screen displaying the

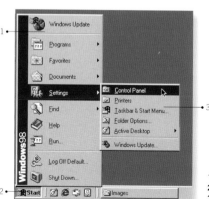

1 *Pop-up menu*
2 *Start button*
3 *Submenu*

open folders/windows and applications and providing the option to switch from one to another. Similar to the Application Menu in Mac OS.

2.**234 Tray** Right-hand end of Taskbar (usually) displaying the time and icons or status indicators (such as printer active, Internet connection established). Clicking on the printer icon, for example, will open the **Printer window**, enabling any printing that is in progress to be halted or deleted.

2.**235 Windows** The PC operating system devised by Microsoft which uses a GUI. Windows has appeared in several versions, offering a more 'friendly' interface than the standard MS-DOS (command-line) interface. Windows 3 was the first to be widely available. Windows 95 brought a more user-friendly appearance to the interface and has since been updated to include workstation variants (NT, 2000) and consumer editions, including Windows 98. The latest versions include **Millennium Edition** (**Me**) and **Experience** (**XP**). → 2.139 OPERATING SYSTEM (OS); → 2.237 WINDOWS XP

2.**236 Windows key** Key found on some Windows computer keyboards that provides a shortcut to the Start menu. Marked with the Windows logo.

2.**237 Windows XP** Windows version previously known by the code name of '**Whistler**' and short for 'Experience'. Principal features are a simplified interface and closer integration of media-handling facilities. It is also designed for multiple users on

shared computers whether in the workplace or at home.

2.**238 wizard** Windows assistant program that walks a user step by step through a process such as installing a printer. The user will be prompted for information at each relevant stage. In the Mac OS wizards are termed 'Assistants'.

2.**239 Zip** The standard format for compressing and compressed files in Windows (also available on Mac).

Input devices

2.**240 card reader** Any device capable of reading – and generally also writing to – a data card (such as a PC card, SmartMedia or CompactFlash card) and found, for example, on digital cameras. Also the name for devices connected to computers to download information stored on these cards. Computer card readers are available that are multi-format (able to read and write to SmartMedia and CompactFlash cards, and possibly PC cards too). Card readers can also be housed in PC cards for use in portable computers. → 2.333 COMPACTFLASH; 2.351 SMARTMEDIA

2.**241 desktop scanner** A small flatbed device for scanning images and text which forms part of a desktop system. The principal feature of the desktop scanner is the glass plate (usually A4 or A3 sized), rather like that of a photocopier. Originals are placed on this and the lid closed. The original is

2.240 *card reader*

1 *CompactFlash*
2 *SmartMedia*

2.241 *desktop scanner*

then scanned by an imager, complete with light source. Some scanners feature an optional transparency adaptor, a replacement 'lid' that is backlit to enable transparent originals to be scanned. This can be used for scanning larger negatives and transparencies (medium-format and larger), but not for 35 mm and APS. For these a dedicated slide scanner is required. Although desktop scanners are becoming increasingly capable, the quality of image generated by them is still somewhat less than that of high-end 'drum' scanners which tend to be used for the most exacting work. Sometimes also called a **flatbed scanner**. → 2.244 DRUM SCANNER; 2.245 FILM SCANNER; 2.251 SCANNER

2.**242 digitizer** A hardware device (usually a scanner or a digitizing tablet) that converts text, graphics or photographed images into digital code that can be read by a computer. → 2.243 DIGITIZING TABLET/PAD

2.**243 digitizing tablet/pad** A hardware device comprising a flat, rectangular pad (normally between A6 and A3 in size) that allows input of brush strokes when drawn upon using a special stylus (a pen-like instrument). Used for precise graphics and image work. Also called a '**graphics tablet/pad**' or '**tablet**'. → 2.252 STYLUS

2.**244 drum scanner** A very high quality and high resolution scanner used for reprographic work. The original artwork (which can be transparencies, negatives or prints) is fixed to the outside of a drum that encloses a halogen light source. The drum rotates at high speed (up to 1000 rpm) while a recording head moves across the surface of the drum scanning the original. As well as the improved resolution, drum scanners offer better dynamic range in the output digital files. → 2.251 SCANNER

2.**245 film scanner/slide scanner** A type of scanner dedicated to scanning 35 mm to medium-format transparencies and negatives. Slides or filmstrips are placed in a holder (similar to that used for placing originals in an enlarger), which is inserted into the scanner. Film scanners work at much higher resolutions than desktop scanners and feature a linear array CCD that scans the slide or negative with a typical resolution of 2500 pixels per inch.

Scanners often feature software that enables limited image editing – such as sharpening – to be performed during a scan. → 1.049 LINEAR ARRAY CCD; 2.251 SCANNER

2.**246 frame grabber** Input device designed to 'grab' a frame (or multiple frames) from an analogue source (for example a television or analogue video) and convert it to a digital format for storage or manipulation.

2.**247 input device** A hardware device specifically designed for, or capable of, inputting data into a computer. Keyboards, mice, scanners and digital cameras can all be regarded as such devices. → 2.019 DEVICE

2.**248 mouse** The small, hand-held, mechanical device which you manipulate to position the pointer on your monitor. Mice may have one, two or three buttons and even a scroll wheel for scrolling through documents or web pages. Buttons can be programmed for special functions.

2.**249 optical mouse** Mouse that uses LEDs in place of a rollerball to determine position and movements. Early optical mice used a dedicated mousepad featuring a grid of fine coloured lines to measure movement, but more recent designs can be used on any smooth surface. → 2.248 MOUSE

2.**250 scan resolution** The resolution at which an original (transparency, negative or flat artwork) is scanned by a scanner, whether desktop, drum or film. Generally quoted in pixels per inch (ppi) or the equivalent lines per inch (lpi); e.g., a 300 ppi image provides sufficent information for halftone reproduction with a 150 lpi screen.

2.**251 scanner** An electronic device that converts artwork, text or photographs into a digital form usually by means of a sequentially moving light beam that scans the surface of the original. The digitized information can then be manipulated by a computer. The simplest scanners are flatbed models, sometimes called a desktop scanner. More sophisticated models capable of higher quality and resolutions are called 'drum scanners'. Hand-held scanners were once popular but are now quite rare; these devices are drawn over the surface of a page of text or graphics and the underlying document is read by the scanner head as it passes

COMPUTER 2 SECTION

2.237 **Windows XP** *My Pictures folder*

1 *Image-use options*
2 *Image search locations*
3 *'My Pictures' folder*
4 *Selected image*
5 *Image gallery*

Windows XP Desktop

1 *Resources*
2 *Start menu*
3 *Task bar*
4 *Control panel window*

111

overhead. These rarely have the quality or accuracy needed for imaging work and are now virtually obsolete. → 2.241 DESKTOP SCANNER; 2.244 DRUM SCANNER

2.**252 stylus** The pen-like pointing device used with digitizing tablets. These are often preferred by graphic designers and photographers for the greater control they offer, particularly as most styli are pressure sensitive. With many selections, darkroom and painting tools you can specify size (with greater pressure relating to a wider stroke), colour (where light pressure applies the background colour, heavy pressure applies the foreground colour and medium pressure applies a blend) and opacity/pressure/exposure. In the last case, the pressure applied is proportional to the effect. Many image editors support styli and digitizing tablets but occasionally plug-ins are needed to confer full functionality. → 2.243 DIGITIZING TABLET/PAD

2.**253 trackball** An alternative input device to the mouse that features a rollerball mounted in a static holder. Mechanically it acts as an upturned mouse. The screen pointer is moved by rolling the ball in its holder and 'clicking' by pressing buttons on the holder. It takes less space than a mouse (in that it does not need to move) but is less precise, particularly for image-editing work. Small trackballs are used as the principal input device on portable computers, though in most cases these have been superseded by trackpads. → 2.248 MOUSE; 2.254 TRACKPAD

2.**254 trackpad** A device found on portable computers that replaces a mouse. The pad is sensitive to finger movements, which control the position of the cursor onscreen. Trackpads can also include areas sensitive to tapping or specific movements that can then be programmed to perform special functions. → 2.253 TRACKBALL

Output devices

2.**255 bubblejet printer** A type of inkjet printer in which minute quantities of liquid ink (measured in picolitres) are heated to boiling point, creating bubbles which eject the ink. → 2.260 INKJET PRINTER

2.**256 DeskJet** Name of a range of printers produced by **Hewlett Packard**.

2.**257 dot matrix printer** Printer that uses a matrix of pins (usually 9 or 24) to strike alphanumeric and shape characters through a ribbon on to the paper. Unsuitable for photographic applications, but sufficient for general text printing. However, with the advent of cheap colour inkjet printers, and superior quality laser printers for text output, dot matrix printers are now rarely used.

2.**258 dye sublimation printer** A printer that uses vaporized ink dyes that are bonded by the printer on to a substrate by heat. The result is near-photographic-quality images. Dye sublimation also allows digital printing of images onto fabric, metal and other substrates. This printing technique is ideal for producing large-format display artwork.

2.244 *drum scanner (desktop)*

2.246 *frame grabber*

2.253 *trackball*

Dye sublimation printers (or **dye subs**) are also known as '**dye diffusion printers**'.

2.**259 film recorder** Device for creating images on photographic film from digital data. Using a laser or LED light source, the image is 'drawn' on the film. Capable of high quality tranparencies these devices are now rarely used, due to the adoption by the reprographic houses (who were the biggest customers for the output) of all-digital techniques.

2.**260 inkjet printer** A printing device that creates an image by 'spraying' tiny jets of ink onto a paper surface at high speed. The liquid ink is stored in a reservoir and channelled through tiny jets in a movable print head that moves horizontally across the page. To achieve different colours, three or more basic ink colours (C, M, Y, and K) are sprayed in a dot pattern called 'dithering' which creates the illusion of different colours. For photo reproduction, certain printers can use special photo-quality inks and papers. Similar in quality and performance to a bubblejet printer.
➔ 2.255 BUBBLEJET PRINTER

2.**261 laser printer** Printer using a laser as part of the process of printing onto paper. The laser alters the properties of a metalized drum electrostatically in response to the signals fed from the computer. This drum then attracts toner powder that is fused by heat onto the paper. LED **page printers** work on a similar principle but use light-emitting diodes rather than a laser for setting the drum. Most laser printers are black and white, but colour printers are increasingly available and can offer virtually photographic quality. Laser printers have traditionally been used as network printers – serving multiple computers, but smaller, slower machines are increasingly available for direct attachment to a single computer. A further advantage of laser printers is their speed; they are typically much faster than inkjets.
➔ 2.265 POSTSCRIPT PRINTER; 7.045 LASER

2.**262 output device** A term for any hardware device that is capable of producing or displaying computer data in a visible form. Monitors and printers are both examples of output devices.

2.**263 phase change printer** Inkjet printer (sometime called a **thermal inkjet**) that uses solid inks, rather than liquid ones. Inks are phase-changed (melted) and sprayed onto the paper where they resolidify, almost instantly.

2.**264 photorealistic** A description applied to output devices, including printers and monitors, that are capable of producing results broadly comparable with those from a conventional photographic source. Some printers include the word 'photorealistic' in their name or description, although this is not a precisely accurate term.

2.**265 PostScript printer** Any printing device which uses the Adobe-licensed 'PostScript' page description language (PDL). These are usually laser printers and the PostScript compatibility usually confers a price premium. However, software RIPs (raster image processors) are available for many mid-market inkjet printers to make them PostScript compatible.
➔ 2.145 POSTSCRIPT

2.**266 printer** An output device that produces a hard copy of your onscreen work. This can be text, graphics or photos. For quality photographic work, photorealistic or photo-quality printers are required. ➔ 2.255 BUBBLEJET PRINTER; 2.260 INKJET PRINTER; 2.261 LASER PRINTER

2.**267 Stylus, Stylus Photo** Range of inkjet printers produced by Epson. Some models are designed with photographic reproduction in mind and given the 'Stylus Photo' name.

2.**268 thermal printer** A device that uses a heat-sensitive paper to produce an image, sometimes found in older fax machines.
➔ 2.263 PHASE CHANGE PRINTER

2.**269 thermal wax transfer printer** Printer that uses coloured wax sheets instead of ink. The wax is melted on to the paper surface using fine heating elements. The printing process tends to be slow as the paper has to pass over the heating elements four times, once for each colour. ➔ 5.017 THERMAL AUTOCHROME (TA)

Display devices

2.**270 16.7 million colours** The number of colours possible on a screen with 24-bit colour display. An option in some monitor control panels or set-up screens, it is sometimes referred to simply as 'millions of colours'.
➔ 2.272 BIT DEPTH

2.**271 256 colours** The number of colours possible on a screen using an 8-bit colour display. An option in some monitor control panels or set-up screens. → 2.272 BIT DEPTH

2.**272 bit depth** The number of bits assigned to each pixel on a monitor, scanner or image file. A bit depth of one (one-bit), for example, produces black and white (the bit is either on or off), whereas a bit depth of eight (eight-bit) will produce 256 greys or colours (256 is the maximum number of different numbers that can be produced from a binary number with eight 0s or 1s). Similarly a bit depth of 24 can give 16.7 million colours (256 x 256 x 256). → 2.429 BIT; 4.498 16-BIT COLOUR

2.**273 cathode ray tube (CRT)** The picture tube of a monitor or television, so named because in the original tubes the then-mysterious '**cathode rays**' (which later proved to be energized electrons) were seen to be emitted from a cathode valve (now known as an '**electron gun**'). A video card is employed in a computer's CPU to convert the binary code into suitable binary signals: one each for the red, green and blue electron beams in the picture tube. The computer screen consists of an array of tiny clusters of R, G and B phosphors. When these colour phosphors are hit by an electron beam, they emit light proportional to the intensity of the signal. The three beams scan the whole screen synchronously so we 'see' the screen image as a whole. → 2.286 PHOSPHOR

2.**274 CCD pitch, CCD element pitch** The linear distance between the centre points of two adjacent picture elements in a CCD array or screen. → 1.011 CHARGE-COUPLED DEVICE (CCD)

2.**275 cinema display** A **widescreen monitor** with an aspect ratio of 16:9; also applied specifically to the 22-inch LCD panel display produced by Apple.

2.**276 composite video** A video-signal delivery method in which all the image information is combined. Hence all the video information can be delivered using a single connector (with single pin) such as the 'video out' RCA jack on older video cassette recorders, and offered on some other video peripherals. Composite video is an easy to engineer solution, but

results in a loss of quality when compared with alternatives such as component video, which keeps video components separate. On computer monitors, quality is maintained by keeping each of the RGB colour signals separate. → 4.552 RGB

2.**277 convergence** A configuration term used for CRT-based colour monitors. These monitors feature three electron beams, one each for the red, green and blue parts of the image. To produce an accurate image all three of these must produce co-incident images onscreen. This is termed achieving convergence. → 2.284 MONITOR; 4.552 RGB

2.**278 flat panel display** Any screen that uses technologies such as liquid crystal or gas plasma to generate the image, rather than a bulky CRT, and is thus comparatively flat. Not to be confused with the term flat screen that refers to a CRT with a flat front (rather than the spherical curve of standard CRTs or cylindrical curve of Trinitron tubes). → 2.296 TRINITRON

2.**279 flat screen** A CRT-based monitor that features a flat front screen. Not to be confused with flat panel display, it features a comparatively flat enclosure. → 2.278 FLAT PANEL DISPLAY

2.**280 gas plasma display** A display panel comprising a large matrix of tiny glass cells, each filled with a combination of gases. The simple structure means that gas **plasma displays** can be made in large sizes, typically ranging from 75 to 250 cm diagonally, enabling viewing from most angles (compared with the more restricted angle of view typical of LCD displays). Gas plasma displays can be used for computer displays but often offer multiple inputs for use as television picture displays as well.

2.**281 interlacing** A technique of 'building' an image on a CRT screen. First, only the odd numbered rows of the image are displayed as one 'field' and then the even numbered rows are displayed at their respective position. Together they build the full image. Interlaced GIFs are frequently used in web pages to promote the appearance of more rapid display of large images. → 3.029 GRAPHICS INTERCHANGE FORMAT (GIF); 3.073 PROGRESSIVE JPEG

2.**282 liquid crystal display (LCD)** A digital display technology first seen on calculator and clock displays, featuring a crystal that liquefies on application of current. When combined with polarizing screens, this results in the tone changes used for colour computer displays, particularly on portables and laptops. LCD monitors tend to be easier on the eye than CRT monitors, but are not as faithful in terms of their absolute colour fidelity.

2.**283 Melzoic** A specialized CRT optimized by image processing and physical design enhancements to reduce digital artefacts, particularly in moving images, making viewing the image more restful. Sometimes referred to as third-generation 100 Hz technology and increasingly used for digital television systems.

2.**284 monitor** The unit which includes the display screen of a computer. Monitors can display images in colour, greyscale or monochrome, and are available in a variety of sizes (measured diagonally) ranging from 9 inch (229 mm) to 21 inch (534 mm) or more. Monitors can use CRTs (like conventional televisions), LCDs (found on most portable computers) or 'gas plasma' (large matrices of tiny, gas-filled glass cells) used for large colour displays. Monitors can be called '**screens**', 'displays', '**VDUs**' (**video display units**) and (historically) 'VDTs' (video display terminals). → 2.273 CATHODE RAY TUBE (CRT); 2.277 CONVERGENCE; 2.279 FLAT SCREEN; 2.280 GAS PLASMA DISPLAY; 2.282 LIQUID CRYSTAL DISPLAY (LCD)

2.**285 onscreen display (OSD)** Strictly, any display on a monitor screen but more usually applied to displays (whether generated by the computer or the monitor control system) that provide monitor information (such as brightness and contrast settings) onscreen.

2.**286 phosphor** The coating on the inside surface of CRTs which glows momentarily when struck by electrons, creating a brief flash of light. This flash depends on persistence of vision in the human eye to retain sight of this flash until the next flash (normally between 25 and 30 flashes a second for each element in the screen image). → 2.273 CATHODE RAY TUBE (CRT)

2.**287 pincushion distortion** The tendency of a monitor image to curve in along its vertical sides. Hence a square reproduced on the screen is narrower midway along a side than at the corner – resembling a well stuffed cushion. The opposite effect (where the edges tend to bulge out) is known as **ballooning distortion**.

2.**288 portrait monitor** A specialized monitor in which the screen is mounted in an upright format, rather than the more conventional landscape format. Portrait monitors can display a full A4 page and hence tend to be used more for text-based editing and other, specialized uses than for imaging. Also most are greyscale (which is sufficient for text) rather than colour. Some monitors can be used in portrait or landscape mode; internal circuitry switches the display when turned from one position to another. → 2.284 MONITOR

2.255 *bubblejet (inkjet) printer*

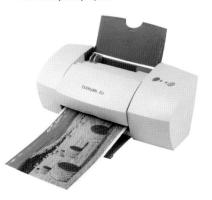

2.268 *thermal printer*

2.261 *laser printer*

2.**289 QVGA** (**Quarter VGA**) A resolution of 320 x 240 pixels and used to describe the window display for small movie files.
→ 2.299 VIDEO GRAPHICS ARRAY (VGA)

2.**290 radiation shield/screen** A glass filter that fits over a monitor screen, designed to reduce the level of radiation being emitted. Can be combined with an antiglare filter that uses camera lens technology to reduce the reflection of ambient light sources from the screen.

2.**291 refresh rate** The frequency at which a screen image or 'frame' is redrawn. It is measured in Hertz (Hz), and a refresh rate of 72 Hz means that the image is 'refreshed' 72 times every second. A screen with a slow refresh rate may produce undesirable flicker. A frequency of 60 Hz or higher will produce increasingly flicker-free results.

2.**292 screen capture** Also called a '**screen shot**', '**screen grab**', '**screen dump**' or '**grab**', this is an exact copy of all items displayed on the screen. PC screens can be grabbed using the PrtScr (Print Screen) key; on Mac computers press Shift-Apple-3 together or Shift-Apple-4 to select the screen area required. A successful screen grab is announced by a camera shutter noise.

2.**293 screen saver/blanker** A means of dimming the screen image or replacing it with a randomly changing pattern after a preset time of inactivity in order to preserve the phosphor coating on the monitor. As newer monitors tend to be more resistant to image 'burn in', screen savers are more commonly employed for aesthetic or security reasons.

2.**294 SuperVGA** (**SVGA**) Super Video Graphics Array. A video display standard which supports 256 colours minimum in resolutions of 800 x 600 or 1024 x 768 pixels. This is the current standard for computer-based imaging. The CRT is non-interlaced and has a high refresh rate to limit flicker. → 2.284 MONITOR; → 2.299 VIDEO GRAPHICS ARRAY (VGA)

2.**295 thousands of colours** The number of colours possible on a screen with a 16-bit colour display. An option in some monitor control panels or set-up screens. → 2.272 BIT DEPTH; 4.498 16-BIT COLOUR

2.**296 Trinitron** A design of CRT produced by Sony in television tubes and also used

extensively by Apple for its computer monitors. Uses an aperture grille of slots (rather than the more conventional dots) to build the image. Trinitron tubes produce pictures where vertical lines are linear, although there is still curvature in horizontal planes. Trinitron tubes tend to be deeper than conventional models.

2.**297 two-page display** (**TPD**) Alternate name for a 21-inch computer monitor (whether CRT-based or an LCD panel) which is capable of displaying two A4 pages (or one landscape A3 page) at full size, side by side. Tends to be used more as a descriptive term in the desktop publishing world.

2.**298 UXGA** Display size of 1600 x 1200 pixels. → 2.294 SUPERVGA (SVGA); 2.299 VIDEO GRAPHICS ARRAY (VGA)

2.**299 Video Graphics Array** (**VGA**) A basic video display standard for PC monitors, with a resolution of 640 x 480 pixels. This is the current minimum graphics display standard on PCs and the minimum resolution for most digital cameras.
→ 1.525 RESOLUTION; 2.284 MONITOR; 2.294 SUPERVGA (SVGA)

2.**300 XGA** Monitors that display above 1024 x 768 pixels or 24-bit colour. → 2.294 SUPERVGA (SVGA); 2.298 UXGA; 2.299 VIDEO GRAPHICS ARRAY (VGA)

Memory terms

2.**301 application memory** Memory reserved for an application.

2.**302 backside cache** A dedicated cache chip that is designed for temporary storage of frequently accessed data. The term 'backside' is used to describe its connection directly to the computer CPU rather than elsewhere on the motherboard (or daughterboard). The direct connection ensures quicker operation as it bypasses the data bus, whose speed and access have a limiting effect on cache access speed. → 2.016 DATA BUS; 2.304 CACHE

2.**303 buffer** An area of memory (normally in a computer but sometimes in a peripheral device) set aside for the storage or processing of data while it is in transit. Buffer memory is normally RAM-based, but can also be a dedicated region on, say, a hard disk (**disk buffer**). Buffer memory within a computer is normally termed a 'cache'. Typical uses of buffer memory include print buffering where print data is stored until the printer is ready to action that data. → 2.304 CACHE; 2.316 RANDOM ACCESS MEMORY (RAM)

2.**304 cache** A small area of RAM or a separate, dedicated memory chip, used for the temporary storage of frequently accessed data. Predictive techniques are used to 'guess' what information is likely to be requested next and keep that data in RAM where it is quicker to access. Disk caches are areas of the hard disk reserved for similar, albeit slower, caching activities. → 2.302 BACKSIDE CACHE; 2.303 BUFFER; 2.316 RANDOM ACCESS MEMORY (RAM)

2.**305 dual inline memory module (DIMM)** One of the two standard types of computer memory chip, DIMMs are higher density boards than SIMMs, holding 6 to 18 memory chips, ranging from 16 to 128 MB. → 2.308 MEMORY; 2.319 SINGLE INLINE MEMORY MODULE (SIMM)

2.**306 dynamic RAM (DRAM)** Pronounced 'dee-ram', RAM that is only active and able to store data when supplied by an electric current. Data is lost when power is turned off. Usually, simply called RAM. Static RAM (SRAM) is able to retain data even when the power is removed but commands a premium price compared with DRAM. DRAM is provided in the form of chips of various megabyte

capacities which plug into the motherboard of your computer.

2.**307 extended data output (EDO) RAM** A type of DRAM chip that makes data available to the CPU while the next sequential memory location is being initialized ready for use. In practice this results in a fast access time.

2.**308 memory** The part of the computer where information is electronically stored. Includes DRAM, the volatile 'random access' memory that is emptied when a computer is switched off and ROM, the stable 'read-only' memory that contains unchanging data, typically the basic startup and initialization functions of some computers (such as Macintoshes). Memory should not be confused with storage, even though both are described in terms of megabytes. → 2.316 RANDOM ACCESS MEMORY (RAM); 2.317 READ-ONLY MEMORY (ROM); → 2.322 VIRTUAL MEMORY

2.**309 memory allocation** The allocation of memory to specific tasks (either automatically by the computer, or by user specification), thus enabling system software, application software, utilities and hardware to operate side by side. For example, the Get Info command in the Mac OS allows users to set Minimum and Preferred memory allocations, over and above those specified by the software. → 2.301 APPLICATION MEMORY

2.**310 parameter RAM (PRAM)** An area of memory – stored in a chip – in Mac OS computers which maintains basic settings such as time and date, even when it is switched

2.282 *liquid crystal display*

2.284 *monitor (CRT)*

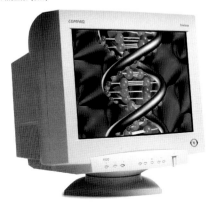

off. The PRAM chip is supplied with power continuously from the onboard lithium battery. Failure of the battery results in erroneous settings appearing when the computer is started. The PRAM can be cleared and default settings restored by pressing Option+Command+P+R as the computer starts.

2.**311 PRAM chip** The hardware chip which stores parameter RAM. → 2.310 PARAMETER RAM (PRAM)

2.**312 programmable ROM (PROM)** A specialized memory chip that can be programmed to perform specific functions, using a hardware device known as a PROM programmer. When a PROM chip has been so programmed it is dedicated to that task (or data) and cannot be reprogrammed.

2.**313 protected memory** A memory management technique that gives a unique address for each application running on the computer. Each application effectively has its own memory space and will not interfere with any other application. Should one application crash it is very unlikely that any other processes will be affected. A regime implemented in Mac OS X.

2.**314 RAM cache** An area of RAM used to store the most recent actions of the computer, saving the need to retrieve these from disk if they are needed again. → 2.304 CACHE

2.**315 RAM disk** A feature of some operating systems (or utility software) in which a part of the RAM can be temporarily assigned as a 'disk drive'. Data retrieval from RAM is considerably faster than from disk operations, and data held on a RAM disk is more speedily accessed and enacted. Care should be exercised with a RAM disk, however, as the contents will disappear when the computer is switched off or in the event of a 'crash'. → 2.316 RANDOM ACCESS MEMORY (RAM)

2.**316 random access memory (RAM)** The 'working space' made available by the computer, into which some or all of an application's code is loaded and remembered while you work with it. When an item is memorized in RAM only for as long as your computer is switched on, so it must be saved to disk to be retained. The amount of memory is important, since not only do some graphics applications require

substantial amounts of memory to operate but also some specific tasks may demand even more. Operating system and application extensions also add to the demand on memory. Most desktop imaging systems start with 64 MB and can go as high as 1 GB RAM. → 2.306 DYNAMIC RAM (DRAM)

2.**317 read-only memory (ROM)** Memory which can be read from, but not written to, as distinct from RAM, in which data can be written to memory but is lost when power to the computer is switched off. CD-ROM represents one form of ROM data. The CD can be read (repeatedly) but cannot be rewritten (CD-RW represents a different form of disk). → 2.316 RANDOM ACCESS MEMORY (RAM)

2.**318 scratch (space/disk)** Disk space set aside as 'virtual memory' for temporary data storage by an application. Image-editing applications typically require substantial space of this type to handle operations on images. → 2.322 VIRTUAL MEMORY

2.**319 single inline memory module (SIMM)** A '**RAM chip**', a computer chip that provides RAM. SIMMs come with three to nine memory chips and are available in densities from 256K to 64 MB. SIMMs and DIMMs are used extensively for computers' RAM requirements but there are often different types of each and compatibility with the intended computer must be verified before purchase. → 2.305 DUAL INLINE MEMORY MODULE (DIMM); 2.316 RANDOM ACCESS MEMORY (RAM)

2.**320 static RAM (SRAM)** Slow and expensive but doesn't need to be refreshed as often to hold information. You can also turn off the computer and on restart, the memory is intact. Used predominantly to retain user-defined configurations and preferences in peripherals. → 2.306 DYNAMIC RAM (DRAM); 2.316 RANDOM ACCESS MEMORY (RAM)

2.**321 video RAM (VRAM)** Specialized RAM dedicated to the support of the video display/monitor. Greater levels of VRAM will normally result in better graphics performance and rendering, subject to the performance of the graphics card.

2.**322 virtual memory** A technique of making non-RAM memory behave as if it were RAM. Typically virtual memory uses a selected amount of hard disk space as surrogate RAM, reading and writing data to it in much the same manner. Theoretically you could set the virtual memory to the size of the free space on the hard disk, but in practice an amount no greater than that of the 'real' RAM is set. The trade-off for this extra memory is speed – virtual memory is only as fast as the data transfer speed of the disk, which is always considerably slower than RAM. Also called 'scratch space' in some applications. → 7.078 VIRTUAL

Storage devices

2.**323 AV drive** A hard disk drive that is particularly fast and, usually, of large capacity. Audio and video files (especially) are large and need fast disk drives for storing in real time. A disk drive rated for AV use will normally command a price premium.

2.**324 Bernoulli drive** A removable disk system that employs the Bernoulli principle. When a flexible magnetic disk is spun at high speeds the air flow creates pressure differentials that cause the disk to rise towards the read/write head. In the event of component or power failure the disk tends to fall away from the head, reducing the risk of damage. Zip disks and drives feature Bernoulli principles.

2.**325 burn (2)** The process of writing data to a recordable CD, CD-R or CD Writer. WORM drives (Write Once, Read Many) burn data permanently into the CD and cannot be

erased or rewritten. → 2.331 COMPACT DISC RECORDABLE (CD-R)

2.**326 CD burner** Common term for a **CD recorder.** The technology for CD burners has developed from write-once read-many (WORM) to writing multiple sessions on the same disc, to completely rewritable discs (CD-RW). → 2.331 COMPACT DISC RECORDABLE (CD-R); 2.332 COMPACT DISC REWRITABLE (CD-RW)

2.**327 CD-ROM** Compact Disc Read Only Memory. Storage medium characterized by a capacity of up to 650 Mb (or higher using compatible discs and drives). Uses optical methods, rather than magnetic, for data reading and cannot be rewritten. → 2.331 COMPACT DISC RECORDABLE (CD-R)

2.**328 CD-ROM/XA** Acronym for Compact Disc Read Only Memory eXtended Architecture.

2.**329 Clik! disk** Small memory storage disk from Iomega designed for use in portable devices (such as some digital cameras and MP3 music players) and with a capacity of 40 MB. Now called a **PocketZip disk**. → 2.330 CLIK! DRIVE; 2.340 JAZ DISK; 2.357 ZIP DISK; 2.452 IOMEGA

2.**330 Clik! drive** Drive that accepts Iomega's Clik! (PocketZip) disks. These drives are sufficiently compact to be incorporated into digital cameras and PC cards and are also available as external devices. PC-card Type III adaptors are available for use in portable computers. → 2.329 CLIK! DISK

2.**331 Compact Disc Recordable (CD-R)** Compact discs that can be written to using a CD recorder (sometimes called a CD burner) and read in a CD-ROM drive. CD-R discs

2.319 *single inline memory module*

2.329 *Clik! disk*

2.344 *memory stick*

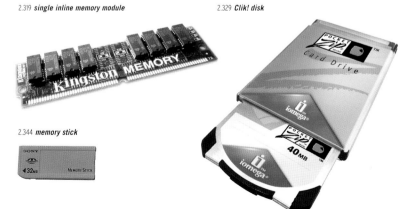

can also be used to copy CD audio discs (where permitted), but recordable CDs for copying audio CDs are not normally suitable for recording computer data.

2.332 Compact Disc Rewritable (CD-RW) CD-based storage medium that can be written to (as with a CD-R disc) but on which the data can also be erased and the disc rewritten. Though these discs are generally compatible with other CD-ROM drives there can be some compatibility issues that lead many manufacturers not to guarantee that a CD-RW recorded on one machine will be usable in another. → 2.327 CD-ROM; 2.331 COMPACT DISC RECORDABLE (CD-R)

2.333 CompactFlash Small memory storage card, resembling a small PC card. Can be slotted into an adaptor card that, in turn, can be slotted into a PC (PCMCIA) card slot for downloading of images. Nikon and Canon tend to prefer the CompactFlash card for their cameras. → 2.351 SMARTMEDIA

2.334 digital versatile disc (DVD) Disc-based storage medium capable of holding up to 17 GB of data. Discs can be double-sided and have multiple data layers. DVD drives can normally also play CD-ROMs. **DVD-R** discs can be recorded in a similar manner to CD-R discs; **DVD-ROM** discs are data storage DVDs offering either 4.7 GB or 8 GB of storage on one or two sides. Recordable DVD technology was introduced by Apple, then adopted by PC companies. DVD discs can also contain video (**DVD-Video**). **DVD-RAM** discs are an alternate recordable format.

2.335 Digital Wallet Portable storage device from **Minds@Work**. Designed for digital photographers, it provides the means for downloading memory cards when away from the computer and storing the images. The unit was launched with a 6 GB hard disk (but other sizes are now available), memory card slot (PC card and CompactFlash by default, plus other media via adaptors), USB connection and LCD panel. Memory cards are inserted in the slot and downloaded using a menu on the LCD panel. On return to home or office the unit is hooked up to a USB cable and downloaded to the computer.

2.336 erasable optical (EO) media Storage media that can be written to, as well as read from, such as the re-recordable CD-ROM format 'CD-RW' (compact disc rewritable) media. → 2.332 COMPACT DISC REWRITABLE (CD-RW); 2.356 WRITE-ONCE READ-MANY (WORM)

2.337 floppy Colloquial name for a floppy disk. Although contemporary floppy disks are not flexible, the actual disk inside the plastic casing is floppy; the name is carried over from the earlier 8-inch and 5.25-inch disks which were housed in soft plastic envelopes. → 2.338 FLOPPY DISK

2.338 floppy disk A flexible circular platter coated with a magnetic medium and housed in a plastic case, on which computer data is stored. Contemporary floppy disks are typically 3.5 inches in diameter and have a capacity of 1.4 MB. These are also known as **FDHD** disks – floppy disk high density – to distinguish

2.333 *CompactFlash*

2.335 *Digital Wallet*

them from earlier, lower density versions. Also called '**diskettes**', the viability of floppy disks is becoming less as the files traditionally backed up on floppies, or transferred between machines on them, become increasingly large. Many computers now do not feature floppy drives, preferring Zip drives or recordable CD drives. → 2.023 DISK/DISC DRIVE

2.**339 floptical** A contraction of 'floppy' and 'optical'. A floptical disc uses 'magneto-optical' (MO) technology on a disc the same size as a common 3.5 inch 'floppy' disk. Floptical discs can contain up to 230 MB (compared with 1.4 MB on a floppy) but their use is more limited than alternative formats such as Iomega's Zip discs. → 2.343 MAGNETO-OPTICAL DISC (MO/MOD)

2.**340 Jaz disk** A removable disk format from Iomega – who also produce the smaller capacity Zip disks and drives – available with a storage capacity of up to 2 GB. Although the disk sizes are similar to those of Zip disks the two formats are not compatible. → 2.341 JAZ DRIVE; 2.357 ZIP DISK; 2.358 ZIP DRIVE

2.**341 Jaz drive** Drive for the 1 GB or 2 GB Jaz disks. Generally an external device connected to the computer via a SCSI connector or via an adaptor to USB or FireWire connections. → 2.340 JAZ DISK

2.**342 magnetic media/storage** Any computer data-storage system which uses a magnetic medium, such as a disk, tape or card, to store information.

2.**343 magneto-optical disc (MO/MOD)** A rewritable disc-based storage medium which combines the technologies of a compact-disc-type laser and an electromagnet for writing and reading data. This combination results in greater data integrity and a far lower chance that data can be corrupted by stray magnetic fields. → 2.023 DISK/DISC DRIVE; 2.338 FLOPPY DISK; 2.339 FLOPTICAL; 2.357 ZIP DISK

2.**344 memory stick** Removable memory card format used by Sony and an alternative to CompactFlash and SmartMedia. Narrower but longer than a SmartMedia card, memory sticks have been employed for memory storage in digital cameras, MP3 music players, for still-image storage in digital video cameras and for general data storage.

2.**345 Microdrive/IBM Microdrive** Miniature hard disc produced by IBM for large scale storage in digital cameras and other portable devices. Based on the dimensions of a CompactFlash Type II card (and compatible with these) it offers capacities of 170 MB, 340 MB, 512 MB and 1 GB. The design specification allows for larger drives in the future.

2.**346 MiniDisc (MD)** Small recordable (and re-recordable) magneto-optical disc housed in a floppy-disk-type caddy and commonly used for audio recording. Forms the recording media for a limited number of digital cameras.

2.**347 optical media** Generic term for media that store data by means of minute pits in the

2.340 *Jaz disk*

2.345 *Microdrive/IBM Microdrive*

surface of a disc-read and written to the disc by a laser beam. Magneto-optical discs, CD-ROMs and DVDs are all types of optical disc. Though some optical media store analogue data (for example, Laservision video discs), computer storage is normally in digital form. The surface pits are of different sizes to indicate the binary digits 1 or 0. These pits are subsequently 'read' by an optical pickup, using a laser which is reflected off a shiny metallic layer on the disc's surface. Optical discs are widely used for audio and video recording and for computer data storage due to their capability of holding large amounts of data. The majority of optical media are CD-ROMs but more recently the digital versatile disc has been introduced with a higher data capacity. DVDs can be double-sided and also multilayered. By using semi-silvered layers the laser can be focused on each of the layers within the disc. → 2.334 DIGITAL VERSATILE DISC (DVD); 2.343 MAGNETO-OPTICAL DISC (MO/MOD)

2.**348 Personal Computer Memory Card International Association (PCMCIA)** A standard format for a type of expansion card used mainly in portable computers for adding features such as external devices, modems and memory. Some digital cameras use **PCMCIA cards**, or adaptors that permit SmartMedia or CompactFlash cards to be used with them. The cumbersome name has been reduced in common usage to '**PC card**' (now used as a trade mark of the PCMCIA), though this term can sometimes cause confusion with mother- and daughterboards used within computers. PC cards are available in three types. **Type I cards** are normally memory devices and have the lowest profile (the flattest). **Type II cards** are thicker and can accommodate the electronics of modem, fax and network cards. The thickest, **Type III cards**, can accommodate mini hard disc assemblies such as IBM's Microdrive. → 2.333 COMPACTFLASH; 2.345 MICRODRIVE/IBM MICRODRIVE; 2.351 SMARTMEDIA

2.**349 RAID** Acronym for **Redundant Array of Inexpensive Drives**. A multiple set of hard disks normally mounted in a single enclosure. Critical data is simultaneously written to multiple disks to improve the read/write performance and reduce the risk of data loss following a single disk failure. Array management software and a disk controller are used to handle error correction.

2.**350 removable media** Any data-storage media that can be physically removed from a computer or peripheral. Certain hard disks, optical discs, CD-ROMs and camera memory cards qualify as removable media.

2.**351 SmartMedia** Small memory storage card used mainly in digital cameras and some MP3 music players. Favoured by, among others, Fuji. Sometimes referred to as **SSFDC (Small Storage for Digital Cameras)**, there are two types. The 3.3v are most common, 5v less so. The correct voltage card must be used with the appropriate camera. → 2.333 COMPACTFLASH

2.**352 storage** Any device in which or on which data can be kept for current or future use. Computers feature two principal categories of storage, RAM and 'non RAM'. The latter category includes internal and external disk drives, tape-based systems and ROM-based media.

2.**353 Syquest** Proprietary name for disk drives and removable disks made by the Syquest Corporation. Syquest disks are available in a range of capacities up to 200 MB. Now largely superseded by Zip disks/drives and CD-RW drives.

2.**354 tape cartridge** A unit (that often resembles a DAT tape cassette) used for storing data from a hard disk usually for backup and archiving purposes. Tape cartridges are comparatively robust media but are not suitable for primary storage as the data stored on them is 'sequential' (recorded in a linear form, from end to end), and cannot be accessed at random, as it can on disks. → 2.355 TAPE DRIVE

2.**355 tape drive** A peripheral or built-in device that reads and writes to tape cartridges. → 2.354 TAPE CARTRIDGE

2.**356 write-once read-many (WORM)** Now largely a redundant term for large capacity storage media such as CD-R discs that can be written to only once and cannot be erased.

2.**357 Zip disk** An evolution of the floppy disk designed and introduced by Iomega. Zip disks are similar in size to floppy disks, but somewhat thicker. The original Zip disks could hold 100 MB of data but a later version has 250 MB capacity. Zip disks have become an unofficial standard for the physical exchange of large data files and are particularly suited to storing and exchanging image files. Note that 100-MB disks can be read by 250-MB drives, but 250-MB disks are not compatible with the smaller drive. → 2.340 JAZ DISK; 2.358 ZIP DRIVE

2.**358 Zip drive** Drive that supports Iomega's 100- and 250-MB floppy-sized Zip disks. Zip drives are available as external and internal devices and as models that are suitable for the media bays of laptop and portable computers.

Connections

2.**359 Apple Desktop Bus (ADB)** The original standard connection on Macintosh computers for keyboard, mouse and desktop peripherals (including some cameras, PDAs and digitizing tablets). Replaced with the launch of the iMac and G3 desktops in 1998 by Universal Serial Bus (USB) connectors. → 2.384 UNIVERSAL SERIAL BUS (USB)

2.**360 crossover cable** A communications cable usually used to link two computers over a short distance. To provide connection between the output pin of one connector and the corresponding input of the other, the wires 'cross over' internally. Sometimes called a null modem cable as it provides connection communications without using a modem.

2.**361 daisy-chain** The linking together, in a line, of computer peripheral devices. Devices such as printers, scanners and external disk drives can be daisy-chained together using appropriate connectors (usually SCSI, USB or FireWire interfaces).
→ 2.402 NETWORK

2.**362 Digital Data Exchange Standard (DDES)** An ANSI/ISO approved standard interface which allows equipment produced by different manufacturers to communicate. → 1.344 INTERNATIONAL STANDARDS ORGANIZATION (ISO); 2.123 INTERFACE; 7.003 ANSI

2.**363 docking station** Small cradle into which a digital camera (or video camera) is placed to effect connection with a computer (or a

television). These sometimes feature 'one touch' buttons that begin downloading images. The use of memory cards, which can be plugged directly into computers or card readers, has made docking stations largely redundant for still cameras.

2.**364 FireWire** Apple Computer's name for the IEEE 1394 bus standard. FireWire is designed for high-speed communications between the computer and peripherals, particularly those such as CD writers and digital movie cameras that require fast data transfer. FireWire connectors are now standard on many digital video cameras and other consumer devices (such as Sony's **Playstation 2**). Data transfer rates with FireWire can be as high as 400 Mbps. Sony designates FireWire connectors and cabling under the proprietary name of '**iLink**'.

2.**365 IEEE 1394** Official name for the connection standard also known as iLink and FireWire. → 2.364 FIREWIRE

2.**366 IrDa** Method and protocol for transferring data from a camera to a computer using infrared signals. Used extensively by **Casio** for their digital cameras.

2.**367 null modem cable** A specially designed cable that allows two computers to connect directly to each other via their communications ports. Useful as a means of connecting a laptop to a larger computer for the exchange of data.
→ 2.360 CROSSOVER CABLE

2.**368 parallel interface** A PC computer connection in which packets of data are transmitted simultaneously in the same direction along a single cable. Compare this with the serial interface in which data packets are transmitted sequentially, one at a time. Although parallel interfaces were once considered 'fast', they are now considered to be of average speed and have been superseded by (or supplemented by) USB and FireWire connectors on many machines. → 2.381 SERIAL INTERFACE

2.**369 parallel port** One of the two standard input/output ports used by the computer to control external peripherals. Parallel ports send data in groups of 16 or 32 bits at a time and are faster than serial ports.
→ 2.382 SERIAL PORT; 2.383 SMALL COMPUTER SYSTEM INTERFACE (SCSI); 2.393 ETHERNET

2.**370 peripheral cable** Any cable used to connect a peripheral device to a computer. Each connection type will need a corresponding peripheral cable (such as SCSI, parallel, serial, ADB, USB and FireWire) though some cables feature interface adaptors to enable devices to be linked to an alternate interface (most typically enabling SCSI devices to be linked to a USB computer).

2.**371 port** A socket in a computer or device into which other devices are plugged.

2.**372 printer port** A computer socket designed for, but not normally exclusive to, a printer. On older Macintosh computers, equivalent printer and modem ports were provided and printers could be connected to either. Newer computers (both PC and Macintosh) tend to offer USB connections to printers.

2.**373 RS232** Formal designation of the PC serial connection used in computers and computer-based equipment for data transfer.

2.**374 SCSI bus** The data path which links SCSI devices to a computer, usually via the cable when devices are linked externally. → 2.383 SMALL COMPUTER SYSTEM INTERFACE (SCSI)

2.**375 SCSI chain** Sequential linking of a number of SCSI devices to a computer. Also called a 'daisy-chain'. → 2.361 DAISY-CHAIN

2.**376 SCSI device** Any peripheral device that can be attached to the computer by means of a SCSI connector. SCSI devices may be inside the computer ('internal device') or outside ('external device'). Such devices can be for input (such as scanners), storage (disks) or output. With the increasingly universal use of USB and FireWire connectors, some SCSI devices can be used with the appropriate interfaces or adaptors.
→ 2.019 DEVICE; 2.383 SMALL COMPUTER SYSTEM INTERFACE (SCSI)

2.**377 SCSI ID (number)** A unique number or 'address' for each SCSI-interfaced device attached to the computer. These numbers are set using on-board switches or may be automatically configured. The unique address makes it possible for commands from the computer to be sent to the correct device. → 2.021 DIP SWITCH; 2.375 SCSI CHAIN; 2.376 SCSI DEVICE

2.**378 SCSI port** The point at which the SCSI chain connects to the computer by means of a connecting plug. SCSI ports can be of the 25-pin or 50-pin variety. The devices themselves almost always have 50-pin ports, while some computers (Macintosh, for example) have 25-pin ports. → 2.383 SMALL COMPUTER SYSTEM INTERFACE (SCSI)

2.**379 SCSI terminator** A device placed at the end of a SCSI chain that protects the SCSI bus and chain from 'signal echo', which can corrupt data transfer. Some SCSI devices are self-terminating and hence when one of these is placed at the end of a SCSI chain no terminator is required. → 2.375 SCSI CHAIN

2.**380 serial** The process of transmitting data sequentially (through a serial port), or consecutively in a sequence, as opposed to simultaneously (by parallel port). → 2.369 PARALLEL PORT

2.**381 serial interface** The connection between computer hardware devices in which data is transmitted sequentially, one bit at a time. Both PC and Macintosh computers feature serial interfaces although they are not directly compatible. In the case of Mac computers, this has now been superseded by USB connectors. The serial interface protocols are RS-232 (PC) and RS-422 (Mac). → 2.368 PARALLEL INTERFACE

2.**382 serial port** The socket, or port, on a computer, used for the connection of devices which use a serial interface – modems or printers, for example. → 2.381 SERIAL INTERFACE

2.**383 small computer system interface (SCSI)** A one-time computer industry standard for interconnecting peripheral devices such as hard disk drives and scanners. SCSI interfaces are robust but computers need to be turned off before any SCSI device is added or removed from the computer or other peripherals daisy-chained to it. Though many high end devices still feature SCSI interfaces, many mass market devices now feature the cheaper USB connection.

2.**384 Universal Serial Bus (USB)** A port (socket) for connecting peripheral devices to your computer that can be daisy-chained together. These can include devices such as scanners, printers, keyboards and hard drives. USB devices can be connected or disconnected from the computer at any time, even with the power on, without risk. Compare this with SCSI devices which can only be added or removed with the computer powered down. → 2.361 DAISY-CHAIN; 2.371 PORT; 2.382 SERIAL PORT; 2.471 PERIPHERAL DEVICE

2.**385 USB-to-SCSI converter** A connector enabling devices originally built for SCSI operation to be connected to and used with a USB-enabled computer. Generally requires special software drivers for correct operation. These allow users of newer computers to retain and use their earlier devices, although performance always tends to be compromised to some degree (the USB data rate is lower than the SCSI data rate). → 2.384 UNIVERSAL SERIAL BUS (USB)

Networking

2.**386 AppleShare** A standard feature of the Mac OS which allows computers to share files across a network. → 2.402 NETWORK

2.**387 AppleTalk** AppleTalk is the basic networking software included in the operating system of a Mac. When you connect a Mac to another Mac or a networked device (such as a shared printer), AppleTalk must be switched on (can be achieved through the Chooser). The physical networking used to connect computers when using AppleTalk can be LocalTalk or Ethernet. → 2.393 ETHERNET; 2.398 LOCALTALK; 2.402 NETWORK

2.**388 bandwidth** The difference between the highest and lowest frequencies that can pass along a communications cable. The broader the bandwidth, the faster data flows. Bandwidth is usually measured in cycles per second (Hertz) or in bits per second (bps).

2.**389 client/server** An arrangement which divides computing into two separate functions, connected by a network. The 'client' is the end user (your computer), while the server is a centralized computer that holds and manages information or multi-user applications, which other computers can access when necessary. → 2.402 NETWORK

2.**390 coaxial cable** Cable type used in network installations. Features a centre conductor (normally made of solid copper) surrounded by an insulator and surrounded in turn by a woven second conductor. The outer conductor shields the inner from interference.

2.**391 download (2)** To transfer data from a remote computer (such as an Internet server) to your own. The opposite of upload. Images copied from a web site are down-loaded. → 2.389 CLIENT/SERVER; 2.414 UPLOAD

2.**392 error correction** A method of checking the integrity of data transmitted from one computer to another.

2.**393 Ethernet** A local area network (LAN) system first developed by Xerox in the mid-1970s. Network nodes (computers or peripherals) are linked either using coaxial cable (similar to that used for TV

2.363 *docking station*

2.400 *modem*

125

aerial/antenna cabling), fibre optic cabling or twisted-pair cables. → 2.397 LOCAL AREA NETWORK (LAN); 2.402 NETWORK; 2.413 TWISTED-PAIR CABLE

2.**394 file server** A computer (normally) on a local area network (LAN) that provides a central resource for the storage and retrieval of files and applications. Specialized controlling software enables the file server to handle simultaneous requests from multiple computers. Compare this with a **disk server** that is merely a shared disk drive and cannot handle multiple requests. → 2.402 NETWORK

2.**395 file transfer** The transmission of a file from any computer to another. This can be effected by a network or may involve communications via a telephone line (such as Internet file transfers). → 2.400 MODEM; 2.402 NETWORK

2.**396 gateway** A device used to connect networks that may have different communication protocols to enable data to be successfully and meaningfully passed on. The gateway provides the 'translation' facilities to enable the communication. → 2.402 NETWORK; 6.041 INTERNET

2.**397 local area network (LAN)** A network in which all the nodes are directly linked and (usually) are in one location. The simplest LAN can be a computer linked to a printer. → 2.402 NETWORK; 2.415 WIDE AREA NETWORK (WAN)

2.**398 LocalTalk** Apple's proprietary networking system introduced in the early days of Macintosh computers. Uses the modem or printer ports and telephone-type cables for (generally) low-speed networking between Macs and compatible printers. Although all recent Macs feature Ethernet networking as standard, it has only been with the introduction of the iMac, iBook and G3 ('blue and white') computers that LocalTalk has been dropped in favour of the faster standard.

2.**399 log on** The process of connecting a user to a network. Most logging on procedures require that the user enter a username and a secure password.

2.**400 modem** Acronym for **modulator-demodulator**. An internal or external device that converts digital data from a computer to an analogue signal for transfer between computers using

standard telephone lines. A modem at the receiving end converts the signal back to a digital one. The term is often incorrectly used to describe other computer–telephone line interfaces such as the terminal adaptors used for all-digital ISDN and ADSL.

2.**401 multiplexing** The simultaneous transmission of many messages concurrently along a single channel. The device designed to combine signals is known as a multiplexer.

2.**402 network** A set of computers and shared peripherals that are connected by an appropriate communications cabling. Can also involve a dial-up or Internet connection to other devices and can be permanent or temporary. Local area networks (LANs) are networks within (typically) a single building; wide area networks (WANs) are spread across multiple sites (e.g., geographically separate company sites).

2.**403 network link** The element in a computer network that links the computer (or other device) to the network cabling.

2.**404 offline** Work done on a computer with access to a network or the Internet while not actually using data from the network. The opposite of online. → 2.405 ONLINE

2.**405 online** In network terms, any activity taking place on a computer or device involving communication with a network such as the Internet. When the connection is not in use, the system is described as being offline. → 2.404 OFFLINE

2.**406 parity bit** An extra bit of data appended to a set of data bits to verify that the bits received are correct and identical to those transmitted. → 2.429 BIT

2.**407 peer-to-peer** A network system in which there is no central server to which all computers have access for storage and retrieval of data and applications. Instead files are spread around different computers to which all the users have mutual access.

2.**408 shared disk** Any hard disk on a networked computer to which other computers on the network have access. → 2.402 NETWORK

2.**409 start bit** A single data bit used in data communication to indicate the beginning of transmission. → 2.410 STOP BIT; 2.429 BIT

2.**410 stop bit** The data bit which indicates the end of one byte in data transmission. → 2.409 START BIT

2.**411 synchronous communication/transmission** High-speed data transmission whereby data is sent in blocks between anchored electronic synchronizing signals, such that the complete data arrives at the same time, e.g., an image on a monitor.

2.**412 token ring** A method of linking computers in which each node makes a single connection to the ring. Information is sent from one device to the next in a fixed sequence. Only the computer which holds the 'token' is permitted to transmit. → 2.397 LOCAL AREA NETWORK (LAN); 2.415 WIDE AREA NETWORK (WAN)

2.**413 twisted-pair cable** Cable comprising two separate wires insulated from each other but twisted together. It offers good performance and resilience from interference. Normally used for networking (such as Ethernet), one wire carries the signal while the other is earthed.

2.**414 upload** The sending of data from a desktop computer to a remote one (such as a server or an Internet site). An email message, for example, is uploaded when sent to an email server. The recipient then downloads the email to his or her computer.

2.**415 wide area network (WAN)** Local area networks (LANs) can be connected (either by terrestrial or satellite links) to create a wide area network. Commercially WANs often comprise a series of LAN installations at the separate sites of an organization. → 2.397 LOCAL AREA NETWORK (LAN); 2.402 NETWORK

Miscellaneous terms

2.**416 AirPort** Wireless technology used in, or available to, all Macintosh computers built since 2000 (and many before that). Comprises a card installed in the computer that enables the computer to communicate with a base station (within 45 m). The base station can enable that computer to connect with other AirPort-enabled computers within range and without wires and connect to the Internet, again without wires. → 2.431 BLUETOOTH

2.**417 alert** An audible or visible warning on a computer alerting you to a specific situation. Usually used to alert the user to a required input or action, or an error.

2.**418 algorithm** A predetermined step-by-step mathematical procedure for solving a specific problem.

2.**419 analogue** The continuously variable range of values used to describe colour, tone, video or sound. A photographic print is a continuous tone (i.e., analogue) image. For image manipulation on computer, the analogue image has to be converted to digital data. → 1.001 A/D CONVERTER

2.**420 applet** Any small application designed for a specific task. Also used to describe a small application, written in the Java programming language, which is downloaded by an Internet browser to

Connectors

1 *Parallel* → *2.369*
2 *Ethernet* → *2.393*
3 *USB (A type socket)* → *2.384*
4 *Firewire* → *2.364*

2.416 *AirPort base station*

perform specific tasks. → 2.124 JAVA; 6.011 BROWSER; 6.041 INTERNET

2.**421 archive** A file or collection of files which has been backed up for storage or compressed to free up disk space. → 2.424 BACKUP, ARCHIVAL

2.**422 background processing** The processing of computer commands from one application while also responding to user activities in the 'foreground'. → 2.303 BUFFER; 5.039 BACKGROUND PRINTING

2.**423 backup** The action of making a copy of files as protection against a computer failure. Also the general name for the items generated as the result of backing up, or copying, the files on your hard disk. A backup is used to restore damaged, lost, or archived files to your hard disk. Different regimes can be employed (either alone or together) to ensure data safety. Such regimes include **archival**, global, incremental, same-disk and **mirror-image** backups. → 2.424 BACKUP, ARCHIVAL; 2.425 BACKUP, INCREMENTAL; 2.426 BACKUP, SAME DISK; 2.427 BACKUP SET

2.**424 backup, archival** A backup routine which copies selected files while preserving previously backed-up copies of those files. As such, archival backups tend to grow increasingly large, but can be critical in enabling past versions and historical information to be retrieved with relative ease. → 2.423 BACKUP

2.**425 backup, incremental** A copy to a backup set of only those files on your hard disk that have been modified since the last time you backed up the disk. Use an archival backup routine if you need to preserve earlier copies of files, as incremental backups sometimes replace files with newer versions. → 2.423 BACKUP; 2.424 BACKUP, ARCHIVAL; 2.427 BACKUP SET

2.**426 backup, same disk** A backup of a file on the same disk as the original. In effect this is what is created when a file is saved using the 'Save As' command. A same-disk backup is easy to perform but does not provide protection if the disk, or the computer, fails. → 2.423 BACKUP

2.**427 backup set** The collection of disks, tapes, files, etc., which form the backed-up copy of your hard disk. Sometimes called a storage set. → 2.423 BACKUP

2.**428 batch processing** Actioning a command or series of commands on a set of documents (image files, for example) sequentially.

2.**429 bit** Acronym for binary digit, the smallest piece of information a computer can use. A bit is expressed as one of two values – a 1 or a 0, on or off, plus or minus. Each alphabet character is written in 8-bit binary code. Eight bits are one byte. → 2.272 BIT DEPTH; 2.434 BYTE; 2.439 DIGIT; 4.399 BITMAP; 6.009 BIT RATE; 7.005 BINARY

2.**430 bitstream** A sequence of binary digits representing a flow of information being transferred from one digital device to another. → 7.005 BINARY

2.**431 Bluetooth** Semistandard communication protocol designed to permit computers, peripherals and communications devices to exchange data, normally over a short range. Typically used to enable GSM mobile phones to communicate with computers or computers within LANs. → 2.416 AIRPORT

2.**432 boot/boot up/booting up** Contraction of the term '**bootstrapping**' and sometimes called startup. The starting up of a computer or computer-based device wherein the operating system is loaded and resources (disks, memory and, where appropriate, peripherals) are allocated. The term **'cold' boot** describes starting the computer from 'power up' whereas a **'warm' boot** describes the restarting of a computer to activate changes introduced by, e.g., a software installation.

2.**433 bug** Sometimes referred to as an '**operational deficiency**', a bug is an unintentional and often unpredictable programming error not foreseen when the program was being constructed and tested. The term is thought to originate from early phonograph recordings, when a real bug that was discovered in the mechanism was attributed with causing erroneous recording and failure. → 2.079 BETA TEST COPY

2.**434 byte** A single group of eight binary bits (0s and 1s) which is processed as one unit. It is possible to configure eight 0s and 1s in only 256 different permutations, so a byte can represent any value between 0 and 255, one byte being required for each. → 2.429 BIT; 3.002 ASCII

2.**435 clock speed** Sometimes called **clock rate**, the clock speed is often (and somewhat erroneously) quoted as the measure of a performance of a computer. It indicates the rate at which an **oscillator 'clock'** in the computer vibrates. Described in MHz, or, as speeds have increased, GHz.

2.**436 computer graphics** Specifically a term used to refer to a particular genre of computer-generated imagery but also (more generally) any graphic item produced or output from a computer.

2.**437 data** From the plural of 'datum', meaning a piece of information, 'data' is now used as a singular or plural noun to describe any information that can be stored and processed via a computer. Text, bits or images can all be described as data and can all be expressed in binary code, the basis of digital technology.

2.**438 data transfer rate** The speed at which data is transferred from one device to another, but generally referring to its transfer from a disk drive into computer memory; usually measured in megabytes per second. → 2.281 INTERLACING; 2.308 MEMORY; 2.460 MEGABYTE (MB, MBYTE, MEG)

2.**439 digit** Any single numeral from 0 to 9 in Arabic numerals, or a binary 'digit' of 1 or 0. → 2.429 BIT

2.**440 digital** Data in which varying 'analogue' values are converted to binary values. The term is also used to describe any device that handles digital data. → 1.001 A/D CONVERTER; 2.429 BIT

2.**441 digital device** Any piece of equipment which operates by means of instructions or signals represented by binary digits, such as a computer. → 2.019 DEVICE; 2.429 BIT; 2.440 DIGITAL

2.**442 digitize** The conversion of any media or text into digital (binary) format so that it can be processed, manipulated, stored, and reconstructed. Sometimes described as analogue to digital conversion. → 2.429 BIT; 2.440 DIGITAL

2.**443 document (1)** Any data file containing text, graphics or an image.

2.**444 external device** Any item of hardware that is connected to a computer but resides externally. Scanners and printers are external, whereas disk drives can be either internal or external according to the model.

2.**445 factory settings/presets** Settings to which a device (computer, peripheral or software) has been set at the factory or assembly plant. Also known as 'defaults' or 'program defaults'. These settings can be changed by the user and reset using 'restore factory settings' or 'restore defaults' options. → 2.147 PROGRAM DEFAULTS

2.**446 flow chart** A diagrammatic representation of a process. Also used as a diagrammatic representation of a computer program's actions.

2.**447 formatting** The system process of preparing a new disk so that it can be used with a computer for organizing and storing data. When a disk is formatted, the 'blank' magnetic surface is divided into sectors, tracks and empty directories. When a disk containing data is formatted or reformatted, any data on it is usually erased. → 1.008 CARD FORMATTING; 3.128 INITIALIZE

2.**448 gigabyte (GB, G, gig)** One thousand million bytes.

2.**449 hardware** The physical components of a computer system along with all peripheral devices. The information stored on the computer includes the software and firmware. → 2.030 FIRMWARE

2.**450 information technology (IT)** Term originally used to describe computer-based data (information) handling but now used generically to describe all aspects of computer and communications technology.

2.**451 install** To load software from the supplied disks to the computer, an installer program (unique to the software, or part of the operating system) is used to perform the installation and ensure that all appropriate files are loaded in the correct locations. → 2.122 INSTALLER

2.**452 Iomega** Producer of the popular Zip, Jaz and Clik! (now PocketZip) disks and drives. → 2.329 CLIK! DISK; 2.340 JAZ DISK; 2.357 ZIP DISK

2.**453 kilobit (kb, kbit)** One thousand bits. As computers work on the binary system one kilobit is equal to 1,000 bits. An upper case 'K' represents 'kilobyte' while the lower case form means 'kilobit', although usage is inconsistent. Used for communications, modem speed is often described as 56 K, when what is actually

meant is 56 kilobits – which should accurately be expressed as 56 kbps.
→ 2.429 BIT; 2.455 KILOBYTE (K, KB, KBYTE)

2.**454 kilobits per second (kbps)** A measurement of the speed at which data is transferred from one computer to another, usually via a modem. A speed of 56 kbps is therefore a rate of 56,000 bits per second. → 2.453 KILOBIT (KB, KBIT)

2.**455 kilobyte (K, KB, Kbyte)** One kilobyte is equal to 1,024 bytes (8,192 bits). Since one byte represents a single character, a kilobyte is roughly equivalent to 170 words. Correctly, an upper case 'K' represents 'kilobyte' while the lower case form means 'kilobit'. → 2.448 GIGABYTE (GB, G, GIG); 2.460 MEGABYTE (MB, MBYTE, MEG); 2.485 TERABYTE; 7.044 KILO

2.**456 launch** The action of starting a computer software application. Can be performed by double clicking on the application's icon (or an alias/shortcut, depending on the operating system), highlighting the icon and choosing 'Open' or 'Start' from the File menu. Some applications can be opened by double clicking on a document created with that application. This relies on the file type of the document being one that is associated (or linked to) that application.

2.**457 locked disk** A removable or floppy disk which is **write-protected** and is thus read-only. Proprietary CD-ROMs are usually locked and when used in Mac OS systems, a small lock symbol will appear in the window of any item from that disk.

2.**458 locked file** A data file which cannot be modified or deleted. A file can be locked either using software commands or by virtue of being on a disk that is locked. Important files should be locked. Typically most software applications will not allow changes to be saved to a locked file, but permit a copy that includes the changes to be saved using the 'Save As' command.
→ 2.457 LOCKED DISK

2.**459 megabit (Mb, Mbit)** 1,000 kilobits or 1,000,000 bits of data.

2.**460 megabyte (MB, Mbyte, meg)** One million bytes. Because this is based on the binary system, a megabyte actually comprises 1,024 KB (kilobytes) or 1,048,576 bytes of data. → 2.448 GIGABYTE (GB, G, GIG); 2.455 KILOBYTE (K, KB, KBYTE); 2.485 TERABYTE

2.**461 megaHertz (MHz)** One million Hertz (or cycles, occurrences, or instructions per second). Used to indicate the 'speed' of a computer's CPU and is sometimes called the 'clock speed'. As the actual performance of a computer depends upon other elements within the computer architecture, this clock speed is not a precise indication of the absolute performance of a computer. For example, the differing structures of CISC chips (as used in Windows computers) and RISC chips (Macintosh computers) means similar clock speeds on chips do not relate to similar performance.

2.**462 mobile communications** In respect of digital imaging, mobile communication systems can be used (as with a conventional land-based telephone line) to send images direct from certain camera models or to send images for downloading to, or uploading from, a computer. Such systems are used extensively in news photography as an expedient way of delivering images to a news desk or broadcast facility. Some **PDAs** – personal digital assistants – can be configured (using add-on modules) to act as digital cameras and mobile telephony devices. Captured images can be sent directly from the device or stored for later transmission.
→ 2.416 AIRPORT; 2.431 BLUETOOTH

2.**463 multi-user** With regard to software, a software package that can be installed for multiple users. Subject to the terms of the licence, this may comprise several stand-alone installations or one installation on a network. In the latter case the number of concurrent users can often be monitored by the software via network management software.

2.**464 multisession** A recording technique for CD-ROMs and used extensively with PhotoCDs. It allows a disc to be partially filled and then used in any CD-ROM drive. Additional material can then be added and the Table of Contents for the disc updated to identify the new material. → 2.482 SESSION; 2.484 TABLE OF CONTENTS

2.**465 multitasking** The ability of a computer to do many things at once, such as run several applications simultaneously. Although many computers may appear to be doing this, few are actually true multitasking machines. Many PCs can switch very rapidly from one application to another (sometimes called '**time-slicing**'). Mac OS X offers pre-emptive multitasking, which is not actually multitasking. → 2.474 PRE-EMPTVE MULTITASKING

2.**466 noncontiguous space** The typical layout of space on a computer disk. As files are written to disk and deleted, space for subsequent saves may not be continuous and hence files can be broken over several free spaces. As more documents are saved, resaved and deleted the space gets increasingly fragmented and noncontiguous. Reading from, and writing files to, noncontiguous space is less efficient than with contiguous space, hence many utilities (such as Norton Utilities) help defragment space to improve efficiency. → 2.098 DEFRAGMENT(ING)

2.**467 optimize/optimizing** The technique of speeding up disk operations (**disk optimizing**) by using special 'utility' software. Using this software, fragmented files (scattered in small pieces across the disk) are rebuilt as contiguous units, speeding up the time taken to read the file from the disk. → 2.098 DEFRAGMENT(ING)

2.**468 original equipment manufacturer (OEM)** The actual manufacturer of a hardware item that is normally sold under the name of another manufacturer. Commonly used with disk drives and some other peripherals. OEMs are common in the PC world where computers may be built from components supplied by a number of

OEMs. The practice does not imply that parts supplied are substandard and many 'big names' produce equipment that is 'badge engineered' with the name of another.

2.**469 output** Any data or information extracted from a computer, by whatever means, but typically via a monitor, printer or storage device.

2.**470 partition/partitioning** The division of a hard disk into smaller 'volumes', each of which behaves as if it were a separate disk. On a PC, for example, such partitioning may result in a 'C drive' becoming a 'C' and 'D' drive. So-called 'real partitions' (or 'SCSI partitions') are created when the disk is formatted; 'file partitions' (also called 'disk images') are large files created on an existing disk drive and do not require reformatting. The use of an emulator program, such as SoftWindows on a Mac, creates a file partition which acts as a C drive for the PC software. → 3.024 FILE FORMAT

2.**471 peripheral device** Any device attached to a computer that is not normally crucial to the computer's operation. Scanners, digitizing tablets and film recorders would be obvious examples. Even though they are pretty much essential to the computer's operation, printers and backup devices are also usually classed as peripheral devices. → 2.019 DEVICE

2.**472 personal digital assistant (PDA)** Small, hand-held device used to store personal data and enact (usually cut-down)

2.447 *formatting*

1 *Disk size* 2 *Format options*

131

2.457 *locked disk*

Clip Art & Images SVG Sa

Registration

1 *Indicates locked disk*

versions of desktop computer applications. Typical PDAs offer notepads, address books, diaries and 'micro' spreadsheets as standard, though additional applications can be downloaded to many versions. PDAs can be 'synchronized' with computers in order to back up information written to the PDA by the user and to transfer relevant information (such as emails) to the PDA. Digital camera modules are available for some PDAs that enable the combined unit to function as a basic camera, using the PDA screen as a viewfinder and display. Similarly modems can be added that offer connection via a landline or a mobile communications network. → 2.431 BLUETOOTH; 2.462 MOBILE COMMUNICATIONS

2.**473 plug and play** Descriptive term also used as a marketing description of computer or hardware devices that can be connected and function almost immediately. Although Macintosh computers have always featured plug and play, the architecture of PCs is such that complex configurations were often required when adding additional equipment. Only with the advent of Windows 95 was some element of plug and play introduced. → 2.047 MACINTOSH

2.**474 pre-emptive multitasking** A form of multitasking wherein the processor periodically passes control to a waiting application, preventing any single process from monopolizing the processor. Tasks are prioritized to ensure every task gets the appropriate resources at the right time. It is most effectively featured in Mac OS X. → 2.465 MULTITASKING

2.**475 random access** General term for data that can be written or retrieved at random on request, usually from a hard disk or random access memory, rather than that which can only be retrieved sequentially, such as from a tape.

2.**476 raster image processor (RIP)** A hardware device or (more commonly now) a software emulation that converts data generated by a page description language, such as PostScript, into a form which can be output on a conventional printer (i.e., one not specified for PostScript printing). Though RIPs can be coupled with high-resolution imagesetters for use in commercial printing, they are frequently

provided for mid-range bubblejet printers enabling these devices to output PostScript pages economically. → 2.265 POSTSCRIPT PRINTER

2.**477 read only** Any disk, memory or document which can only be read from, and not written to. These can be set to read only through a software setting or, in the case of some rewritable disks, a switch or slider on the disk casing. SmartMedia cards are rendered read only by applying a small silver disc (supplied with the cards) at a marked position on the card.

2.**478 reboot** The process of reloading a computer's operating system into memory. This can be achieved by either switching the power off ('shutting down') and switching it on again ('cold boot'), or by using the 'Restart' command, if available ('warm boot'). Also referred to as a 'restart'. → 2.066 STARTUP DISC; 2.432 BOOT/BOOT UP/BOOTING UP

2.**479 restore** Generally the action of returning settings or data to their original values, such as 'restore factory settings', which restores settings to those set when the product was installed. Also applies to copying files from a backup set to their original locations after the computer-based originals have become damaged or been deleted.

2.**480 scan(ning)** An electronic process that converts an image into digital form by sequential exposure to a moving light beam such as a laser. The scanned image can then be manipulated by a computer or output for printing as separated film or direct to plate (CTP). → 2.241 DESKTOP SCANNER; 2.244 DRUM SCANNER; 7.045 LASER

2.**481 sector** The smallest storage units on a disk with a typical size of 512 bytes. Disks are conventionally divided into sides (top and bottom for each of the physical disks that comprise the hard disk), tracks (annular rings) and sectors, which are parts of these rings. → 2.486 TRACK

2.**482 session** Time during which a computer application runs. Also a term used to describe a mode of recording data on to a recordable CD. When using a CD recorder, data can be recorded either as sessions or as a complete disc. When recorded as a complete disc, no further data can be added even if there is recordable space available. When sessions are recorded, further sessions can be added, space permitting. The disc will subsequently need to be 'finished'. Finishing involves writing an index to the start of the disc called a 'table of contents'. The table of contents advises the computer of the locations of all elements recorded on the disc (or the start points of tracks on an audio CD). Multisession discs allow material to be added to a disc but for the disc to be used meantime in any CD-ROM drive. ➔ 2.464 MULTISESSION; 2.484 TABLE OF CONTENTS

2.**483 sleep mode** Computer activity state. Allows most computer circuitry including the screen or monitor and disk drives to power down. By hitting a key (such as the space bar or the return) the computer powers up ready for use. Waking from sleep is quicker than starting the computer from scratch and any open applications or documents will remain open, ready for use.

2.**484 table of contents** The index or 'directory' of a CD. Whether an audio CD or CD-ROM the table of contents is recorded at the start of the disc after all other data has been recorded. It gives the position of all important features on the disc (such as files or audio tracks, depending on the disc type). ➔ 2.482 SESSION

2.**485 terabyte** A million megabytes of data. One terabyte is equal to 1,024 GB (gigabytes) or 1,048,576 MB (megabytes) of data (slightly greater than one million megabytes due to the use of the binary system for counting units). ➔ 2.448 GIGABYTE (GB, G, GIG); 2.455 KILOBYTE (K, KB, KBYTE); 2.460 MEGABYTE (MB, MBYTE, MEG)

2.**486 track** The concentric 'rings' on a formatted computer disk (typically a hard disk drive), on which data is stored. Each track is divided into radial 'sectors' in order to make data access more rapid. ➔ 2.481 SECTOR

2.**487 upgrade** An enhancement or modification to a computer, such as an increase in

memory, the addition of a new graphics card or even an improved peripheral. Software upgrades are issued periodically and can offer improved functionality or features (but may require an upgraded computer to run).

2.**488 user-specified defaults** Program settings (such as cursor types in image-editing applications or measurement units) that have been either specified or modified by the user. As such they are no longer the original 'factory' defaults. In most programs there is a command 'Reset Defaults' or 'Reset Settings' which restores all settings to their original conditions.

2.**489 virus** A computer program that is deliberately and maliciously written to disrupt the normal operation of any computer it is exported to (from a disk or via the Internet). A virus may infect some files, but not others (an application, perhaps, but not documents), and they manifest themselves in different ways, from the annoying (perhaps altering the computer display in some minor way) through to the disruptive (rendering the host computer useless pending a complete reinstallation of all software). The most destructive can propagate themselves onwards using the email addresses from email utilities. ➔ 2.168 VIRUS PROTECTION UTILITY/PROGRAM

2.**490 volume** A disk or tape used to store computer data. A partitioned disk will comprise multiple volumes corresponding to the number of partitioned areas.

2.**491 word** or **codeword** represents the number of binary 'words' (actually characters) that can be expressed in binary encoding. A 4-bit word (24) can only provide 16 distinct binary codewords; 7-bit (27) ASCII code provides 128 characters. The most commonly used codewords are 8-bit (28) or 256 characters which allows for the standard alphabet and punctuation, plus accented, specialist characters and international character sets. ➔ 2.429 BIT; 2.434 BYTE

3

FILE MANAGEMENT

File formats

3.001 animated GIF A GIF file comprising multiple, normally sequential 'still' images that can be played one after another as an animation when viewed using a web browser. Used for animation effects on Internet-delivered images.

3.002 ASCII 'American Standard Code for Information Interchange', a code that assigns a number to the 128 letters, numbers and symbols (including carriage returns and tabs) which can be typed on a keyboard. Designed in the US in the 1960s in order to standardize data transmission, its origins are revealed by the lack of a £ sign or other international character sets. For this reason, 8-bit codewords were introduced providing 256 characters. The first 128 follow the ASCII code, with an '0' added before the first digit; the second 128 are used for other symbols. Images can be stored as ASCII code or as binary files. → 2.091 CROSS-PLATFORM; → 3.005 BINARY FILE

3.003 Audio Video Interleave (AVI) The standard format for audio and video data in Windows environments. Uses the Microsoft RIFF (Resource Interchange File Format) specification. ImageReady can create (and edit) files in this format. → 3.092 CODEC; 4.393 QUICKTIME

3.004 base resolution The fundamental resolution of a PhotoCD. The 512 x 768 pixel resolution corresponds to that of US and Japanese NTSC standard televisions. The standard PhotoCD records five different resolutions, from a small screen resolution to 18MB or multiples of the base resolution (**base/16**, **base/4**, **base**, **4base**, **16base**); **64base** features on Pro PhotoCD. This multiresolution file system makes it easier to choose the optimum file size. → 3.058 PHOTOCD; 3.072 PRO PHOTOCD

3.005 binary file A file in which data is described in binary code rather than text. Binary files can represent pictures, sounds, or a complete application program. → 3.006 BINHEX; 7.005 BINARY

3.006 BinHex An acronym for BINary to HEXadecimal, a file format which converts binary data files to ASCII text. This is a convenient format for sending some files via email and the Internet as some computer systems can handle only ASCII text characters, especially if the data originates on, or is destined for, a Macintosh computer. → 3.002 ASCII; 3.005 BINARY FILE

3.007 BMP Standard Windows image format derived from the term 'bitmap'. The BMP format actually supports bitmap, RGB, indexed colour and greyscale colour modes but does not recognize alpha channels. Bit depths can be specified by the user when saving for either Windows or OS/2 operating systems. Images stored in the clipboard are also bitmapped but usually have the extension .CLP. Run Length Encoding can be used to compress certain BMP files but some applications (such as MS Paint) are unable to read or interpret compressed files. Some non-mainstream applications will append the file extension .DIB for bitmap files rather than the more conventional BMP.

3.008 CGM Computer Graphics Metafile.

3.009 CIFF Camera Image File Format: designed as a 'semi-standard' format for image storage in digicams, it has not gained universal acceptance.

3.010 CLP Clipboard bitmap format. → 3.007 BMP

3.011 CMX Corel Clipart format.

3.012 CompuServe GIF Little-used 'full' name for Graphic Interchange Format files; named after CompuServe, who developed it for use in their Internet service. → 3.028 GIF89A

3.001 *animated GIF*

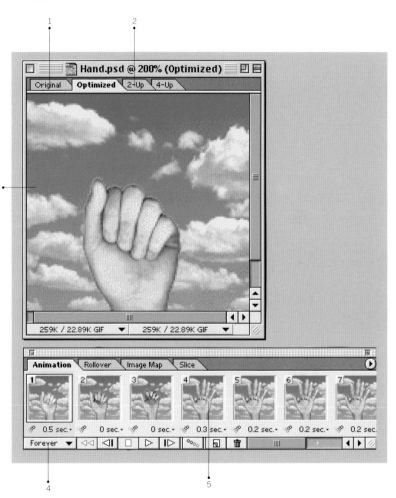

1 *Original-image view selector*
2 *2-up view (original and optimized images)*
3 *Currently selected image*
4 *Looping options (play once, for ever, specified number)*
5 *Animated GIF frames*

3.**013 CPT** The file format used in Corel's Photo-Paint and also the file extension for files created in that format.

3.**014 CUT** An 8-bit colour file format used by Dr Halo software. → 2.084 CLIPBOARD; 2.093 CUT AND PASTE; 5.047 COPY

3.**015 DCX Zsoft** Multipage Paintbrush format (1-bit).

3.**016 DIB** RGB encoded file format (with 1-, 4-, 8- or 24-bit colour) used with the OS/2 operating system. Can also be used with Windows computers with RGB or Run Length Encoding (RLE). → 3.104 RUN LENGTH ENCODING (RLE)

3.**017 DRW Micrografx Draw format.**

3.**018 EMF Enhanced Windows Metafile.**

3.**019 Encapsulated PostScript (EPS)** Standard graphics file format used for 'object-orientated' or vector graphics files that are produced by drawing applications such as Adobe Illustrator and Macromedia FreeHand. An EPS file usually comprises two parts: the PostScript code (which tells the printer how to print the image) and an onscreen preview (which can be in PICT, TIFF or JPEG format). The EPS format can be used to store bitmapped images, particularly those used for desktop colour separation ('DCS'); these EPS files are encoded as either 'ASCII' (a text-based description of an image) or 'binary' (which uses numbers rather than text to store data). The coding method used in EPS files does vary according to the computer platform. To print bitmapped EPS files from a Windows-based system, ASCII encoding is used, whereas those to be printed from the Mac OS are usually saved with binary encoding. → 3.002 ASCII

3.**020 EPS TIFF Preview Format** A format option found in later Photoshop versions that enables you to open files that create previews but are not supported by Photoshop. Such preview files can be edited conventionally but often only at comparatively low resolution. Likewise there is an equivalent **EPS PICT Preview format** for which the same conditions apply.

3.**021 Exchangeable Image Format (EXIF)** A JPEG-based file format that can embed supplementary information (such as camera settings and exposure information) within a file. This information can be

retrieved later when EXIF-compatible applications are used for the editing or storage of the applicable files. EXIF is extensively used by many digital camera manufacturers, notably Fujifilm. → 3.043 JPEG

3.**022 file** A collection of data which is stored as an individual item on a disk. A file can be a document, a folder, an application or a resource. The file is the smallest unit of collected information that enables a computer to distinguish it from another set. → 3.024 FILE FORMAT

3.**023 file extension** The abbreviated suffix at the end of a filename and usually separated from the filename by a full stop(.). The file extension describes either its type (such as EPS or JPG) or origin (the application which created it, such as PSD for Photoshop, PSP for Paintshop Pro). A file extension usually comprises three letters and must be specified at the end of a Windows filename. Mac file extensions can be longer and are not usually displayed.

3.**024 file format** The data structure within a file that determines how that file is stored or displayed onscreen. Simple files comprise ASCII text. More complex files (such as CorelDraw's **CDR**) will include instructions for screen layout and how it should interface with an application. Common file formats for images include PICT, BMP, TIFF and JPEG.

3.**025 file type** In the Mac OS, the four-letter code assigned to every file when it is created to identify its kind or format, such as 'APPL' for an application, 'TEXT' for text files, and so on. Special software such as ResEdit is generally required to identify the file type. In Windows the file type is normally indicated by the file extension. → 3.022 FILE; 3.023 FILE EXTENSION

3.**026 FlashPix (FPX)** File format designed by Kodak, Microsoft, HP and Live Picture for the 'consumer' market and designed originally for a 'cheap' CD-based alternative to PhotoCD. FPX files feature multiple resolutions. Image data is stored as a series of arrays where each array represents a unique spatial resolution. FPX file sizes tend to be around 30% larger than the equivalent TIFF file but have the benefit of requiring less RAM for viewing (typically 20% of that for the corresponding TIFF file). → 3.058 PHOTOCD; 3.067 PICTURECD

3.**027 GIF87a** A bitmapped graphics format originally devised by Internet company CompuServe (now part of AOL) in order to permit the easy transfer of graphics or images over the web. Sometimes referred to as 'CompuServe GIF'. This original specification (GIF87a) was later superseded by GIF89a which permits (among other refinements) transparent backgrounds. → 3.029 GRAPHICS INTERCHANGE FORMAT (GIF)

3.**028 GIF89a** Version of the GIF file format that allows image transparency in web pages. Images can also be rendered progressively, in the same manner as progressive JPEG files. Using the GIF89a format, multiple images can be stored sequentially and then replayed in that sequence as an animation (the result is known as an animated GIF). It has been named after 1989, the year of its inception. → 3.001 ANIMATED GIF; 3.029 GRAPHICS INTERCHANGE FORMAT (GIF); 3.073 PROGRESSIVE JPEG; 3.085 TRANSPARENT GIF

3.**029 Graphics Interchange Format (GIF)** A graphics file format designed principally for the delivery of raster images over the Internet. A standard GIF image uses 8-bit colour and can thus contain up to 256 colours (including a transparent one). Ultimately the size of a GIF file will depend on the number of colours used in the actual image and the compression used. GIF can use the LZW compression method. GIFs are supported by most browsers and can be used for creating images for web pages and exchanging images over the web. Due to the limited number of colours, GIF files are not normally used for high quality images, although web-based image thumbnails (that give a quick preview of an image) can often use this format successfully. → 3.001 ANIMATED GIF; 3.037 INTERLACED GIF; 3.085 TRANSPARENT GIF; 3.086 WEB IMAGE FORMATS; 3.102 LZW COMPRESSION

3.**030 Hexadecimal (hex)** A computer term for a 16-digit numbering system which uses 0 to 9 and substitutes the letters A, B, C, D, E and F for the numbers 11 to 15. → 3.006 BINHEX; 7.005 BINARY

3.**031 High Sierra standard** Principal data format for CD-ROMs. Specifies the layout of the data in tracks and sectors on the disc, subsequently adopted by the ISO as ISO 9660. Discs conforming to the High Sierra format can be read on any compatible computer platform. → 3.039 ISO 9660

3.**032 Hybrid format** Also known as the **Mac/ISO Hybrid** format, a recording format for CD-ROMs that includes the cross-platform ISO 9660 and Mac HFS/HFS+ formats on a single disc. Discs recorded in this format allow Mac data to be only visible to Mac computers and the ISO data to other users. It is typically used to create discs for software for Mac and PC that needs to be delivered on a single CD.

3.**033 image file** Any digital file containing the data corresponding to a graphic or image. Image files can be saved in a variety of formats both generic (such as JPEG, TIFF or BMP) for use with multiple applications or computer platforms, or specific ones such as Photoshop. Often the data stored in an image file comprises ASCII characters, but these can only be interpreted within an application. → 3.002 ASCII

3.**034 Image Pac** Kodak's proprietary system for PhotoCD image storage, including all the PhotoCD resolutions from base/16 through to 64base. The latter, used only in the Pro PhotoCD, is contained within the Image Pac Extension (IPE). → 3.058 PHOTOCD

3.**035 IMG** Format used by GEM paint (1-, 4- or 8-bit colour)

3.**036 Interchange File Format (IFF)** A little used file exchange format used to transfer files to and from Commodore Amiga systems.

3.**037 interlaced GIF** A GIF89a format image in which the image, when delivered to a host computer (on a web page, for example), reveals itself at increasing detail as it downloads. Similar to the progressive JPEG format. → 3.085 TRANSPARENT GIF

3.**038 IPE Image Pac Extension**. The 64base component of a Pro PhotoCD (professional) featuring the largest (highest definition) files on these discs. → 3.004 BASE RESOLUTION; 3.058 PHOTOCD

3.**039 ISO 9660** Cross-platform standard for CD-ROM recording that incorporates the High Sierra standard. Disks recorded in the ISO 9660 format can be read by computers running Mac OS, DOS, Unix, Linux and Windows. → 3.031 High Sierra standard

3.**040 IVUE** Proprietary file format devised by Live Picture Inc. for their **FITS (functional interpolating transformation system)** process. FITS image edits are stored as corresponding mathematical expressions in a FITS file, while the original image data is stored in the IVUE file. Ultimately an output file is produced which is based upon the original IVUE files but with the FITS modifications incorporated. It scores by requiring only the pertinent part of the image being edited to be manipulated thereby saving systems resources.

3.**041 JIF** Image compression format using Huffmann coding. → 3.098 Huffmann coding

3.**042 Joint Photographic Experts Group (JPEG)** A division of the ISO responsible for defining compression standards for bitmapped colour images. The JPEG compressed file format is widely used but is a 'lossy' format: image data is lost forever when a file is compressed. Such losses are cumulative when a compressed file is opened, edited and resaved. As the level of compression (which relates to the file size) can be controlled by the file creator, it makes the format particularly suitable for web delivery, where the compression level/file size ratio can be varied. High ratios give poor quality images that can be emailed fast, while lower ratios give better quality images but require longer delivery times. → 3.024 File format; 3.029 Graphics

Interchange Format (GIF); 3.096 file compression; 3.101 lossy compression

3.**043 JPEG** An ISO standard for the storing of compressed images. One of two formats (the other is GIF) that are used extensively for web graphics. The compression routine breaks the image into square pixel blocks and reduces the data defining each block. Under extreme compression, this blocking becomes pronounced, producing characteristic JPEG compression artefacts. Some software (such as Paintshop Pro, from Version 7) includes software filters to remove these artefacts, or at least render them so that they are less pronounced. Digital cameras use JPEG compression to enable more effective use of the available memory, often permitting several levels of compression to be selected by the user. The compression algorithms have been updated and incorporated into the JPEG2000 specification. → 3.042 Joint Photographic Experts Group (JPEG); 3.045 JPEG2000; 3.073 progressive JPEG; 3.086 web image formats

3.**044 JPEG File Interchange Format (JFIF)** A standard for JPEG compressions which ensures that files can be viewed on any computer platform and in any appropriate application. → 3.043 JPEG

3.**045 JPEG2000** The image compression standard developed with the Joint Photographic Experts Group (part of ISO). It uses **Wavelet technology** to improve upon the existing standard and offer improved compression that accommodates higher

3.043 **JPEG**

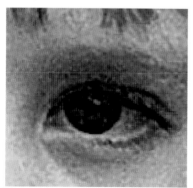

Low JPEG compression (higher quality)

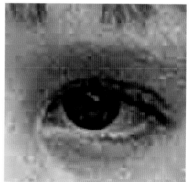

High JPEG compression (lower quality)

resolutions and richer content.
Other enhancements include greater
error resilience to enable successful
transmission in 'noisy' environments (such
as the Internet). For the user the best
feature of this revision is the ability for the
recipient of an image to determine what
bit depth and what resolution the final
decompressed image should have.
It therefore adds a whole new level of
flexibility to image compression.

3.**046 KDC Kodak Digital Camera**, 24-bit format.

3.**047 LBM** Compressed or uncompressed files
created in **Deluxe Paint**.

3.**048 MAC** 1-bit file format that is used
with **MacPaint**.

3.**049 MacBinary** A file format that allows
Macintosh files to be transferred via
modem or shared with non-Mac
computers retaining the resource and data
forks (and their data). → 3.108 DATA FORK;
3.134 RESOURCE FORK

3.**050 Motion Picture Experts Group (MPEG)** A set
of compression formats for digital video
files and animations, providing heavy
compression ratios of up to 200:1. MPEG-
2 is commonly used for digital television
transmissions. Differing formats define the
degree of intra-frame compression
(compression of individual frames of a
video) and/or interframe compression
(compression between individual frames).

3.**051 MOV** Format of a movie file created in
Apple's Quicktime and the file extension
for these files .MOV. → 4.393 QUICKTIME

3.**052 MPEG Level 3** The audio format used for
sound on DVD video discs. Offers sound
comparable to CD quality but with greatly
reduced file sizes. Some cameras can
record and play MPEG Level 3 and some
can replay music tracks recorded in this
format (now more commonly referred
to as **MP3**).

3.**053 MSP** Microsoft Paint format, 1-bit colour.

3.**054 NEF** Format used to store raw image
data on the Nikon DI digital camera.

3.**055 PBM Portable Bit Map** (UNIX).

3.**056 PCX** PC-based file format supporting
bitmap, RGB, indexed colour and
greyscale colour modes. Image bit depth
can be 1, 4, 8 or 24. Originally devised
to support Z-Soft's PC Paintbrush
application, the files can support a modest
degree of compression.

3.**057 PGM** Portable Greymap ASCII or binary
file (UNIX).

3.**058 PhotoCD (Kodak PhotoCD)** A proprietary,
cross-platform technology developed by
Kodak for scanning and storing photographs
on CD-ROM. PhotoCD files (**PCD format**)
can be opened and edited with most
image-editing applications. PhotoCDs
contain images at multiple resolutions,
referred to as base/16, base/4, base,
4base, 16base. The largest resolution,
64base, is found only on professional
PhotoCD (Pro PhotoCD). → 3.004 BASE
RESOLUTION; 3.072 PRO PHOTOCD; → 4.571 YCC

3.**059 PhotoCD Portfolio** A further modification
of the PhotoCD format (coming after
the Pro PhotoCD and the Image Pac
extension). Designed to deliver multimedia
presentations on computers using
dedicated players. Up to 680 images of
low to medium resolution can be stored,
one hour of sound, or a combination of
both. → 3.058 PHOTOCD

3.**060 Photoshop DCS 1.0** Specialized file format
(Desktop Colour Separation) that permits
the saving of the four separate (CMYK)
channels as separate PostScript files. If a
file contains a spot colour channel it can
be saved as **DCS** 2.0.

3.**061 Photoshop DCS 2.0** Desktop colour
separation file format that additionally
supports (and retains) a single alpha
channel and multiple spot channels.
Colour channel information can be stored
as multiple files (as in Photoshop DCS 1.0)
or as a single, more compact file. → 3.060
PHOTOSHOP DCS 1.0

3.**062 Photoshop format (PSD format)** The default
file format for images and graphics created
in Photoshop. By using the Photoshop
format (with the .PSD file extension, where
this is shown) all the Photoshop image
modes (RGB, CMYK, bitmap, greyscale,
duotone, indexed colour, Lab and
multichannel) will be supported along with
all other image features such as layers
(including adjustment, type and effects
layers), alpha and spot channels and
image guides. Data can, however, be lost if
an image that has been created in a
particular Photoshop version is opened
and edited in an earlier version. Features
from the later version will be lost in
this case.

139

3.**063 PICS animation** A Macintosh animation format that uses sequences of individual PICT format images to create a sequence. → 3.064 PICT

3.**064 PICT** Contraction of 'picture', PICT is a standard file format for storing bitmapped and object-oriented images. Although originally introduced on Macintosh computers, it can now be used on many Windows PCs with appropriate applications. The original PICT format supported only eight colours, but a newer version, PICT2, supports 32-bit colour. PICT files can be stored in compressed form using the JPEG regime. → 3.065 PICT RESOURCE

3.**065 PICT Resource** A Mac OS-only file format, so called because it is a PICT file that is contained in the resource fork of a Mac OS file. The resource fork is where, typically, images from the scrapbook and application splash screens are stored. To use an image as a Mac OS splash screen (an image to replace the Mac OS screen as the extensions load) it needs to be saved as a PICT resource and saved in the System Folder under the name 'Startup screen'. → 3.108 DATA FORK

3.**066 PICT2** 'Formal' name of the extension of the PICT file format that can save 32-bit colour images. → 3.064 PICT

3.**067 PictureCD** CD-based image storage format devised by Kodak and Intel. Designed as an expedient and cost-effective alternative to PhotoCDs, PictureCDs are produced at the time a film is processed. In addition to being produced as conventional prints, images are recorded in JPEG format onto CD, so that a reasonable quality A4 print can be produced. Additional features provided on the CD include basic image-editing software, and viewing, emailing and printing applications. This additional content varies according to the PictureCD release version, which is denoted by volume and issue numbers. Original PictureCDs provided only Windows-based additional content, although images can be opened on any platform.

3.**068 PIXAR** File format designed for image file exchange with PIXAR computers. These are used for high-end graphics and (particularly) three-dimensional graphics,

rendering and animation. Supports RGB and greyscale images with a single alpha channel.

3.**069 Portable Document Format (PDF)** A cross-platform format that allows files and documents to be created and retain all text and picture formatting, irrespective of whether the destination computer is able to support original file formats or fonts. Requires Adobe Acrobat to create the file and Acrobat Reader on host computers to read. Acrobat Reader is offered as a free stand-alone application and as a plug-in to the major web browsers. Generic PDF files, created using Adobe Acrobat (or some other applications such as Adobe Illustrator), can contain multiple pages and images. Some image editors can open these documents as image files (by rasterizing) and convert each page to a separate document (e.g., **Photoshop PDF**).

3.**070 Portable Network Graphics (PNG)** A file format for images used on the web originally designed as a replacement for the GIF format (to circumvent certain legal restrictions with the CompuServe registered GIF format). PNG files can be compressed by up to 30% without any loss of data (30% lossless compression). Variable transparency (in the manner of GIF89a) can be introduced using Alpha channels. PNG supports 24-bit images (**PNG-24**) and background images with 'smooth-edged' transparency. Greyscale and RGB colour modes with a single alpha channel are permitted, along with an indexed-colour mode with no alpha channel. An alternate, smaller file version **PNG-8** is sometimes encountered. Not all web browsers can handle PNG file formats, but the level of acceptance is increasing.

3.**071 PPM Portable Pixel Map** file (UNIX).

3.**072 Pro PhotoCD** 'Professional' version of Kodak's PhotoCD technology. Adds additional high-resolution 64base files to the 'consumer' resolutions. 64base files yield a file size of 72 MB per image and are capable of supporting much more detail. The 64base extension is sometimes referred to as the Image Pac extension → 3.038 IPE; 3.058 PHOTOCD

3.**073 progressive JPEG** A JPEG file whose image is displayed in its entirety first with

very low resolution and then at increasing
resolution as more data is downloaded to
the web browser (rather than the alternate
method, which displays the top part of the
image at full resolution and then builds the
complete image at this full resolution).
Sometimes called '**proJPEG**'. → 3.037
INTERLACED GIF; 3.043 JPEG

3.074 PSP Default file type for files created in
Paintshop Pro. Can be uncompressed,
feature run length encoding or LZW
compression. → 3.104 RUN LENGTH
ENCODING (RLE)

3.075 QuickTime Movie A cross-platform format
for audio, video or audiovideo data.
Images and animations can be saved as
QuickTime Movie format files (QuickTime
movies) and existing QuickTime movies
can be edited and optimized in
applications such as ImageReady.

3.076 Raster Image File Format (RIFF) A little-used
proprietary image file format originally
devised by Letraset.

3.077 RAW File format that saves image data
as a data stream that defines the colour
information in the file and supports RGB,
CMYK and greyscale colour modes with
alpha channels, and multichannel,
indexed-colour, Lab and duotone
modes without.

3.078 Scitex CT Scitex Continuous Tone format
files. Specialized file format generated by
the Scitex computers used for high-end
image processing. Files saved to Scitex CT
format in applications such as Photoshop
will not necessarily run on Scitex

environments without additional utilities.
These are needed to enable the files to
migrate to the Scitex platform. The format
supports RGB, CMYK and greyscale colour
modes but not alpha channels. Scitex files
and platforms are usually restricted to
use with high-quality reprographics
(such as glossy magazine covers) but are
increasingly being replaced with more
conventional machines as their power and
quality increase.

3.079 self-extracting archive (SEA) Extension
applied to a group of Macintosh files that
have been compressed using Aladdin
System's Stuffit utility. Files automatically
unpack when loaded to the computer
(from an Internet transfer or CD-ROM).
→ 3.096 FILE COMPRESSION

3.080 SIT The suffix of files that have
been compressed using Stuffit, a file
compression utility common on Macintosh
computers and similar in use to the
Windows 'Zip' compression system.
→ 3.096 FILE COMPRESSION

3.081 Tagged Image File Format (TIFF, TIF) A
standard graphics file format originally
developed by Aldus Corporation (now
merged with Adobe) and Microsoft. The
TIF format can be used for black-and-
white, greyscale and colour images
that have been generated on different
computer platforms. One version includes
LZW compression, which is not compatible
with all programs.

3.082 Targa File format (with the TGA file
extension) designed for computers that are

3.067 *PictureCD*

3.073 *progressive JPEG (three pass)*

1 Final pass
(full resolution)
2 Middle pass
3 First pass (lowest
resolution)

3.043 *JPEG compression*

Image after five open/save cycles

Image after ten open/save cycles

3.100 *lossless compression*

Lossless TIF (LZW) compression

JPEG compression

3.099 *image colour reduction*

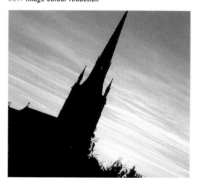

Original image

Reduced colour

equipped with the **TrueVision** video board. Supports 24-bit RGB images and 32-bit images (8 bits per channel for the red, green and blue channels and 8 bits for a single alpha channel). Targa files can be either compressed or uncompressed.

3.**083 text file** Any file containing only ASCII characters and not featuring any formatting. As such it can be read or interpreted by any operating system. In some circumstances image and graphics information can be sent as such a text file for interpretation on the host computer.
→ 3.002 ASCII

3.**084 TGA** Uncompressed TrueVision file format (8-, 16- or 32-bit colour).
→ 3.082 TARGA

3.**085 transparent GIF** A feature of the 'GIF89a' file format which supports transparency. GIF89a files featuring areas of **transparent background** are also known as 'transparent GIFs'. With transparency, a non-rectangular image can be placed on the background of a web page; this allows the background colour to show through the transparent pixels and the image maintains its rectangular shape. → 3.028 GIF89A; 3.037 INTERLACED GIF

3.**086 web image formats** For images that are destined for the web it makes sense to select a format that can readily be handled by any web browser for any application on destination computers. Realistically this means a choice between JPEG and GIF formats. Use JPEG: (i) when saving a 'normal' photograph. JPEG images can contain more than 32 million colours. (ii) when you need to compress a file for sending or use on a web page. Although JPEG is a lossy format is usually possible to strike a good balance between compression and the appearance of image artefacts. (iii) when you want to create a background for a web page. Because JPEG files can contain a larger range of colours and tone, they can handle the possible low contrast regions that may appear in an image prepared for use as a backdrop. Use the GIF format: (i) for images with very limited colours. If an image contains less than 64 colours you will probably find the file size is smaller

than the corresponding JPEG. With certain subjects and small image sizes you may find that even this limited palette can give acceptable results. (ii) if text is included. JPEG files can 'lose' the information that keeps the edges of text distinct and readable. Use neither JPEG nor GIF if you are exchanging images (either via email or a website) for image editing. It is better to use a file format such as TIFF or PICT, even though the file size is inevitably larger. Sending a smaller image size is often preferable to an overly compressed one. → 3.029 GRAPHICS INTERCHANGE FORMAT (GIF); 3.043 JPEG

3.**087 Windows Run Length Encoded file format** A format based on the Windows BMP format that permits a small amount of image compression. With computers that are running Windows it can be used to produce compressed screen wallpaper files and is the format in which a file needs to be stored if it is to replace the default Windows splash screen at startup. → 3.007 BMP; 3.104 RUN LENGTH ENCODING (RLE)

3.**088 WMF** Microsoft Windows Metafile.

3.**089 WPG** Word Perfect graphics file.

File compressions

3.**090 Animation codec** A lossless compression setting (codec) used by QuickTime designed to be used for graphics and images of all bit depths. → 2.272 BIT DEPTH; 3.092 CODEC; 4.393 QUICKTIME

3.**091 CCITT encoding (Comité Consultatif International Téléphonique et Télégraphique).** A lossless compression technique that tends to be limited now for use with black-and-white images. This compression is supported by EPS and PDF file formats.

3.**092 codec** Acronym for **COmpressor/ DECompressor** or in some descriptors COder/DECoder. Hardware or software designed to compress or decompress sequences of video (or audio) data such as those used for QuickTime and AVI movies. → 3.075 QUICKTIME MOVIE; 4.393 QUICKTIME

3.**093 Component Video codec** A QuickTime compression setting (codec) which generates a 2:1 compression. It is limited to 16-bit colour depth and hence cannot deliver the highest of qualities. Typically it is used for archiving movies. → 3.075 QUICKTIME MOVIE; 3.092 CODEC; 4.393 QUICKTIME

3.**094 compressor** Algorithms comprising part of a codec responsible for compressing the data. → 3.092 CODEC

3.**095 decompressor** Algorithms comprising part of a codec and responsible for restoring the compressed data to a form that can be interpreted by the host application. → 3.092 CODEC

3.**096 file compression** The process of **data compression**, reducing the size of a file (or application) so that it occupies less disk space or can be sent across a network (or by Internet) more expediently. There are also many regimes for compressing files depending on the original information and the means of delivery or storage. When compressing applications, for example, the compression method must not lose any of the information in the uncompressed files. Image and movie files, however, can be compressed by 'throwing away' some of the data without this adversely affecting the look of the images. There are many regimes and utilities for compressing data, but those most frequently encountered for image compression are the lossless LZW and the lossy JPEG and GIF. The latter two are used extensively when images are sent over the Internet. Compression systems that do not lose any data are described as 'lossless' systems, whereas those where some data is lost are described as 'lossy'. Digital-movie and audio formats use compression techniques called codecs (short for COmpression/DECompression). → 3.043 JPEG; 3.075 QUICKTIME MOVIE; 3.092 CODEC; 3.102 LZW COMPRESSION; 4.393 QUICKTIME

3.**097 Graphics codec** Formerly called **Apple Graphics**, the Graphics codec is a QuickTime compression codec designed for use with still images of limited colour depth. → 3.075 QUICKTIME MOVIE; 3.092 CODEC; 4.393 QUICKTIME

3.**098 Huffmann coding** Coding regime that is used for file compression, particularly image files. The JIF format uses Huffmann coding.

3.**099 image colour reduction** The process, either manually instigated or produced by imaging software, of reducing the total number of colours in an image. Although the removal of colours can cause the image to be degraded (and in particular to take on a semi-posterized effect), some missing colours can be simulated by dithering techniques (where adjacent colours are 'mixed' onscreen). An image with a limited number of colours is easier to compress.

3.**100 lossless compression** File compression techniques designed to reduce the size of a file but without reducing the image information or compromising image quality when the image is subsequently restored. Typical examples are RLE, LZW and CCITT. → 3.102 LZW COMPRESSION

3.**101 lossy compression** Methods of file compression in which some data is physically discarded from a file during compression. When the file is decompressed, interpolated or repeated, data is used to 'fill' the areas from which data has been discarded. JPEG is a lossy compression format. → 3.043 JPEG; 3.100 LOSSLESS COMPRESSION

3.**102 LZW compression** Lempel–Ziv–Welch compression, a widely used 'lossless' compression method for bitmapped images, giving a compression ratio of 2:1 or more depending on the range and extent of colours in an image. Typically an image featuring large areas of flat or continuous colour can be more highly compressed than one with a greater range of colour and a greater number of image elements. LZW uses repeating strings of data in the compression of character streams into code streams; this is the basis of the compression used in GIF files. → 3.029 GRAPHICS INTERCHANGE FORMAT (GIF); 3.096 FILE COMPRESSION

3.**103 None codec** QuickTime compression codec that does not feature any compression. → 3.092 CODEC; 4.393 QUICKTIME

3.**104 Run Length Encoding (RLE)** A lossless compression technique that can be used with Photoshop and TIFF format files. Windows RLE files are a variation on the Windows BMP format. → 3.100 LOSSLESS COMPRESSION

3.110 *directory structure*

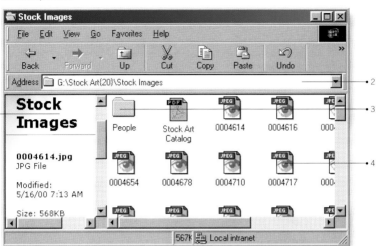

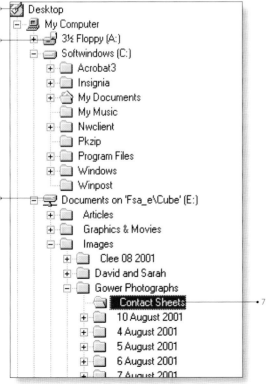

1 *Directory details*
2 *Directory/folder name*
3 *Subdirectory*
4 *Files*
5 *Top-level folder*
6 *Drives*
7 *Lowest-level folder*

3.125 *hierarchical structure*

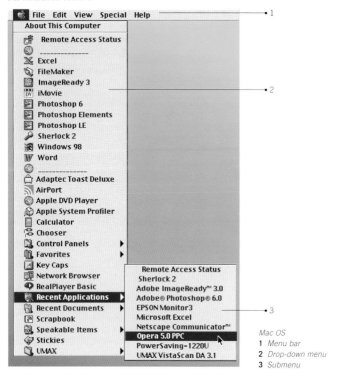

Mac OS
1 *Menu bar*
2 *Drop-down menu*
3 *Submenu*

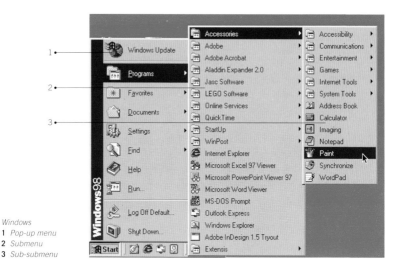

Windows
1 *Pop-up menu*
2 *Submenu*
3 *Sub-submenu*

3.105 **Video codec** Sometimes called **Apple Video**, this is a QuickTime full-motion video compression codec that offers fast compression but only average picture quality. It is also limited to 16-bit colour depth. → 3.092 CODEC; 4.393 QUICKTIME; 4.509 COLOUR DEPTH

3.106 **visually lossless compression** Image compression technique (used particularly with Kodak PhotoCD systems) that uses deficiencies in the human eye and image perception to create compressed files using lossy techniques, but without any perceived loss in the quality of the image. The system discards some colour information but retains the detail. As the eye perceives detail more precisely than the colour detailing, there is no obvious visual degradation. → 3.058 PHOTOCD

3.107 **zip (file)** A compression system used to compress Windows files and directories to provide smaller files (for example, for sending by email). With suitable software, zip files can be created and opened on Mac computers, but the more usual method for Mac file compression is Stuffit.

File handling

3.108 **data fork** One of the two '**forks**' of a Mac OS file that contains the user-created files. The other is the resource fork that contains resources such as icons, sounds and certain imagery. This is typically text, graphics or image. Some document files may contain only a data fork; application files will always have a resource fork and may have a data fork too. → 3.134 RESOURCE FORK

3.109 **directory** A term for the collection of files and sub-folders (those of a lower hierarchical level) now commonly referred to as a folder.

3.110 **directory structure** The underlying hierarchical structure of all the files on a hard disk. → 3.109 DIRECTORY; 3.125 HIERARCHICAL STRUCTURE

3.111 **disk image/disc image** A single file that can represent an entire volume such as a floppy disk, hard disk, or CD-ROM. Disk images are typically used for making copies of 'installer' disks and also for creating partitions for recording data to CD-Rs. If software needs to be restored to a hard drive, a disk image can be used. → 3.033 IMAGE FILE

3.112 **export** To save a file for export into another application. → 3.126 IMPORT; 3.127 IMPORT/EXPORT FILTER

3.113 **FAT files** Because FATs can become corrupted, most disk utilities have a program which duplicates the FAT each time the computer boots up and stores it on the hard drive. → 3.114 FILE ALLOCATION TABLE

3.114 **file allocation table (FAT)** A method used by computer operating systems to keep track of files stored on a hard disk. When a file is stored non-contiguously the file allocation table keeps track of the position of the segments. This is not to be confused with 'Fat' or 'Fat Binary' executable files, which contain both native PowerPC and 68K Mac instructions, allowing them to run optimally on any type of Macintosh system.

3.115 **file association(s)** The linking of a data file (such as an image or text file) with an application. When a file is created by an application in a format exclusive to that application (such as a .psp file in Paintshop Pro, or .psd file in Photoshop) that file is linked to the creating application. If the file is opened (by clicking or double clicking on it) the appropriate application is opened. In the case of non-specific file types, they can be manually linked to an application (by using a command such as the Associate command in PhotoImpact) or all files of a particular type can be associated with an application using an association table. → 2.177 APPLE FILE EXCHANGE

3.116 **file conversion software** Software designed to enable files of one format to be opened in another, or on a different computer platform. Commercial products include **Debabelizer** and **Dataviz Conversions Plus**.

3.117 **File menu** One of three standard menus appearing in the menu bar of most applications (and almost all conventional image-editing applications) from where commands are invoked which allow files to be created, opened, saved, printed and closed. → 3.022 FILE

3.118 **file recovery** The process of recovering a file for use after it has become damaged or erroneously deleted. When a file is deleted, the data from that file remains on the disk (unless it is overwritten by

147

subsequent file writing and saving activity). Deleting a file involves removing the file 'title' from the invisible directory that monitors and keeps track of all files on the disk. It is therefore possible (subject to it not being overwritten) to recover the file using a file recovery utility (such as those included in applications such as Norton Utilities or some shareware products). Recovering corrupted files is more problematic and will very much depend on the degree of corruption and the place where that corruption occurred. The best remedy for corrupted files is to replace the disk copy with one from a backup set, hence it is very important that backups are regularly taken!

3.**119 filename** The name given to a file (either by the user or generated sometimes automatically by an application or operating system). Macintosh filenames can be up to 31 characters long, whereas Windows filenames can be up to 255 characters. It is normally safer to restrict Windows filenames to eight characters if compatibility with older (DOS-based) computers is required. Filenames can contain alphanumeric and symbolic characters with certain limitations: Windows users should avoid the characters: / \ | : * ? " < >. Macintosh users should avoid: • : / \ as these have special meaning within the operating system. → 3.023 FILE EXTENSION

3.**120 folder** An alternate name (particularly on Macintosh computers) for a file directory. This is interpreted by the literal depiction of directories as folders on the desktop into which files can be placed for organizational purposes. One folder can be placed inside another (when it is said to be 'nested'). Folders form the basis for the organization of all data on your computer. → 3.109 DIRECTORY

3.**121 foreign file** A document created in a different application or computer system to the one you are using.

3.**122 fragmented file** A file on a hard disk that is not stored as a continuous block of data but is split into several non-contiguous chunks. As files are written and deleted from a disk, the space available for new file writing becomes non-contiguous. Although saving a file across several of

these areas does not affect the integrity of the file it does increase the time needed to read that file. Applications exist to defragment hard disks by rebuilding files contiguously. → 2.098 DEFRAGMENT(ING); 2.467 OPTIMIZE/OPTIMIZING

3.**123 hierarchical file system (HFS)** The method used by the Mac OS to organize and store files and folders so they can be accessed by any program. Files are organized inside folders which may, in turn, be inside other folders, thus creating a hierarchy.

3.**124 hierarchical menu** A menu containing items which, when selected, generate their own menus, or submenus. The Start menu in Windows or Apple menu in the Mac OS feature menu and **submenus** characteristic of hierarchical menus. → 3.123 HIERARCHICAL FILE SYSTEM (HFS)

3.**125 hierarchical structure** The arrangement of files, folders and directories in an orderly manner that enables a user to find a path to the data required. Rigorous hierarchical structures are used extensively in networking, databases and in file management. → 3.123 HIERARCHICAL FILE SYSTEM (HFS)

3.**126 import** To bring text, pictures or other data into a document. → 3.112 EXPORT

3.**127 import/export filter** A feature for translating a file from the host format to another format, and vice-versa. In image-editing applications, such filters can be used to import image files that are in a different format to that normally handled by the program and usually involves converting that image to a file format acceptable to the application. → 3.112 EXPORT; 3.126 IMPORT

3.**128 initialize** The process of clearing a disk (a hard disk or a floppy disk) of all directories so that it is effectively 'clean' and contains no obvious information. When a disk is initialized it usually involves removing only the file information rather than the data in those files so that, with the right utility software, the file data could be recovered. Some initializing processes also format the disk by laying a new format upon it. In this case all data is normally removed. → 2.447 FORMATTING

3.**129 invisible file** Any file on a disk that is normally concealed from the computer user. This is often because the information contained in these files is required by the operating system and should not be deleted by the user. Using utility software, files can be deliberately made invisible for security or practical reasons. It is common practice to make the support files of multimedia applications invisible.

3.130 key frame A single animation frame in a QuickTime sequence in which information is stored as a reference, so that subsequent frames only store changes in the frame ('differences') rather than the whole frame each time, thus making the file smaller. The frames based on changes are called 'delta frames' or 'difference frames'.

3.131 legacy files Files created in, and worked upon, in a previous version of an application. When the file is opened in a more recent version of that application some of the functionality is limited (especially for new features in the application) unless the file is resaved in a newer format. In Photoshop 5 and later the term specifically applies to files created without embedded profiles.

3.132 nested folder A folder that is placed inside another folder. Equivalent to a subdirectory of a directory. → 3.120 FOLDER

3.133 object linking and embedding (OLE) Microsoft technology in which a linked object – an image created in a graphics application, for example – that has been 'embedded' into another application, such as a page-layout application, will be updated each time it is altered in the source application. An embedded object will, when 'double-

clicked', fire up the source application in anticipation of further editing.

3.134 resource fork The part of a Mac OS file that contains resources such as icons and sounds. Resources contained in the resource fork of a file can be modified with resource editors such as 'ResEdit'. → 2.207 RESEDIT; 3.108 DATA FORK

3.135 root directory/level The first level at which files and folders are placed. In DOS-based computers this was typically the C: directory. In Windows and Mac OS desktops, the root directory is that represented by the window which appears when you double-click on (open) a disk icon.

3.136 subdirectory Any directory that is secondary to the principal, or 'root', directory. A subfolder or 'nested folder'. → 3.135 ROOT DIRECTORY/LEVEL

3.137 swap file A temporary file created on a PC into which the contents of the RAM memory is transferred (or 'swapped') to free up that RAM for other actions. Swap files tend to be created by image-editing applications when the file being manipulated is larger than the available free memory. Although this permits large files to be handled, the transfer of information to and from the swap file means computer operation can be slow. Hence swap files are not a substitute for good provision of RAM memory. → 2.322 VIRTUAL MEMORY

3.138 temp file A temporary file, usually created by the operating system to be used for storage of temporary data (such as that from a 'swap file').

3.122 *fragmented file*

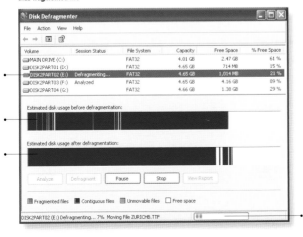

1 Disk selected for defragmentation
2 File fragmentation map before defragmentation
3 Predicted fragmentation after defragmentation
4 Progress bar

4

IMAGE MANIPULATION

Programs

4.001 Art Dabbler (Corel) Image editor and art creation tool that uses the metaphor of an artist's sketch pad for the interface. On-screen drawers are used to house palettes and painting/drawing tools. The latter follow their real-world counterparts very closely in their action. This is more a tool for creating artwork from images than an image editor per se. ➔ 4.010 PAINTER

4.002 Bryce (Corel) Not an image-editing product, but rather a landscape and skyscape rendering product. Convincing landscapes can be produced from a range of primitive shapes and used subsequently for image backgrounds. Data from actual landscapes can also be used to produce forms based on real landforms.

4.003 Canvas/Deneba Canvas Comprehensive image editor/drawing package/layout/web graphics application. Canvas is distinguished from other applications in the fluidity of creating and manipulating images using multiple tools normally considered the preserve of a single application. Hence an image can be manipulated and combined with vector graphics, and the result used to create a web page complete with web functionality (such as GIF animations, rollover buttons) that automatically generates the JavaScript programming code required to support it. Very well specified, the interface includes an array of features that can be bewildering for even the intermediate user but will ultimately deliver the finest of images. ➔ 4.001 ART DABBLER; 4.010 PAINTER

4.004 CorelDRAW! Extensive and well-regarded graphics application from Corel, available for Mac, PC and Linux platforms. Photo-Paint is the pixel-based image editor and is bundled with the CorelDRAW! vector-based product along with other utilities.
➔ 4.014 PHOTO-PAINT; 4.023 PHOTOSHOP ELEMENTS

4.005 GIMP/The GIMP Acronym for GNU Image Manipulation Program, the GIMP is the principal image-editing application for the Linux operating system. Originally created in 1995, the first 'stable' release was Version 1 in mid-1998. It is a freely distributed product that can be used as image editor, paint program, image format converter and more. Principal features include: multiple undo/re-do; layer and channel support; full suite of image-editing tools; plug-in compatibility. Variations to this program exist (as is the nature of many Linux products) and test versions have been run under the OS/2 and Mac OS X operating systems.
➔ 4.381 COMPUPIC

4.006 guided activities A feature of some image editors that provide a logical step-by-step approach to image editing. The user is taken from stage to stage in a rigorous way. Typical stages would include acquiring an image, cropping, making colour corrections and so on. Such applications often feature project-based activities that follow on from the image editing for creating albums, calendars and more from the images.
➔ 4.035 PROJECT-BASED SOFTWARE

4.007 image analysis software Software designed to extract quantitative information from an image. Though image-editing packages emulate some of the techniques and can give some similar results, this is a specialized field designed for studying the texture or characteristics of the subject of an image.

4.008 ImageReady (Adobe) Adobe's Photoshop sibling optimized for the creation of web graphics. First appeared bundled with Photoshop 5.5 in 1998. Version 3 came out with Photoshop 6 in late summer 2000. Many of the features of ImageReady are directly comparable with those of Photoshop and the two products can be used independently. Macromedia's

4,001 *Art Dabbler*

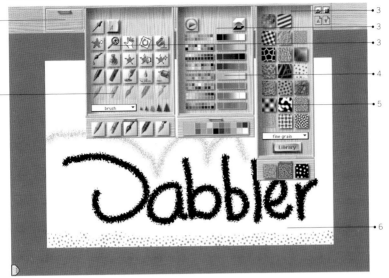

1 Tool drawer	4 Colour drawer
2 Closed drawer	5 Texture/pattern drawer
3 Open drawers	6 Canvas

4,011 *Paintshop Pro*

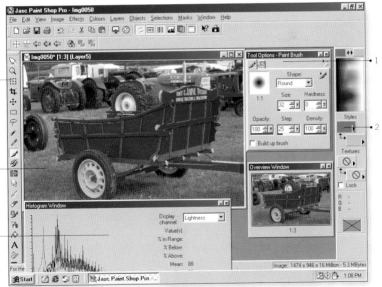

151

1 Tool options palette	3 Histogram window
2 Foreground/ background colours	4 Image canvas
	5 Toolbar

4.014 *Photo-Paint*

1 *Tool settings palette* 4 *Image canvas*
2 *Tool options* 5 *Colour palette*
3 *Toolbar* 6 *Colour selector*

4.022 *Photoshop*

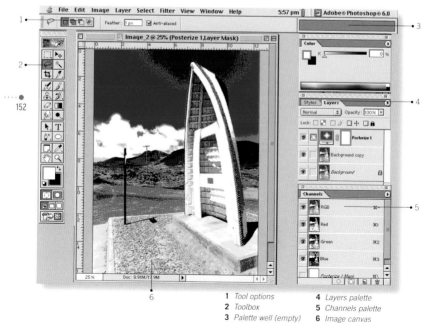

152

1 *Tool options* 4 *Layers palette*
2 *Toolbox* 5 *Channels palette*
3 *Palette well (empty)* 6 *Image canvas*

Fireworks is an alternative product that offers a comprehensive suite of image-editing tools, along with web graphics functionality. It also integrates with other Macromedia products (including graphics application **Freehand**).
→ 4.022 PHOTOSHOP

4.**009 Mr Photo/Mr Photo Gold Edition** An image editor from **NewSoft** suited to the needs of the beginner to intermediate user. Offers basic editing features in a browser-type interface that displays files and directories along with thumbnails of images in selected image directories.

4.**010 Painter (Corel/procreate)** Image editing and painting application. Setting the application apart from Corel's Photo-Paint is the ability to use synthesized natural media such as pastel on cartridge paper and oil on canvas. You can thus create realistic looking artwork from images. The interface is individual and (almost) unique in having no toolbar; expanding menus are used instead. This format makes it more difficult for those familiar with other applications to pick up and run with this product, but this does not hide the power of the tools offered and quality of the results.

4.**011 Paintshop Pro (Jasc)** Image-editing program from Jasc Software. Originally distributed over the Internet as shareware, it was seen as an alternative 'paint' utility to MS Paint. Successive releases have produced a product that has much of the functionality of Photoshop but at a much reduced cost. Companion product Animation Shop produces web graphic animations.

4.**012 Photo Easy (Ixla)** Image-editing and cataloguing software, designed for the casual user and those wanting to share photos. Features include customized downloading from digital cameras and scanners, an image cataloguing and management system, retouching tools (including quick fix tools) and projects. Web-based image exchange is also featured. The Ixla digital camera interface is also used with some other image editors, notably Corel Photo-Paint Digital Camera Edition → 2.120 IMAGE-EDITING APPLICATION; 4.035 PROJECT-BASED SOFTWARE; 4.143 QUICK FIX TOOLS

4.**013 Photo Express (Ulead)** Project-based image editor from the creators of PhotoImpact. With a more limited range of web tools than its stablemate, it has a very comprehensive interface that can tend to look cluttered with smaller resolution monitors. Also features basic album creation and image management.

4.**014 Photo-Paint (Corel)** Image editor from the Corel stable, which began life as a pixel-based editor element of the extensive and highly regarded CorelDRAW! application. By Version 7 it had become a credible image editor and by its next release became a viable Photoshop contender. It is now available for PC and Mac and is available as a stand-alone product as well as remaining a component of CorelDRAW! Variations on the basic project have appeared, most notably **Photo-Paint Digital Camera Edition** that adds comprehensive support for a range of digital cameras as well as ancillary support.

4.**015 Photodeluxe (Adobe)** Consumer-level program that offers image-manipulation tools along with an additional tier of projects. Projects are designed to help the user perform quick fixes to images (remove red-eye, perform a crop) and use images creatively to create posters and greeting cards. Photodeluxe features two modes. The basic mode offers guided activities, where the user is guided through a series of stages to produce an edited image. The other mode (depending on the version), is called 'On Your Own' or 'Advanced Menus', and permits conventional image editing using more conventional menu selections. Like MGI's Photosuite, Photodeluxe offers templates for creating projects based on your images. → 4.035 PROJECT-BASED SOFTWARE

4.**016 PhotoExpert** A comprehensive image editor that is designed more for getting fun from images rather than for either detailed or precise manipulations. The interface features large fluid buttons and controls that in many ways echo those of Photosuite.

4.**017 Photofactory** 'Bundled' package containing three stand-alone packages: Photosoap 2, PowerGoo and PowerShow. The latter is a presentation and slide show product from the same group responsible for Soap and Goo, MetaCreations. → 4.025 PhotoSoap/PhotoSoap 2; 4.037 SuperGoo

4.018 PhotoFantasy (ArcSoft) Application from the creator of PhotoStudio, billed as an 'image entertainment' application. Designed to produce specialist montages of personal photos of friends and family combined with a range of humorous or absurd background images.

4.019 PhotoGenetics Image editor from **QBeo** (www.qbeo.com) that uses image surrogate approach to editing. Rather than extensive commands and options, surrogates of the selected image are produced that vary in some way (such as having slightly different colour balance) from the original. The user then rates the variation as a little better or a lot better and the change is applied to the image. Through an iterative process of alterations the user arrives at the 'perfect' image.

4.020 PhotoImpact (Ulead) Comprehensive and versatile image editor and web graphics application. Unique to this application is the extensive EasyPalettes feature that provides a range of drag and drop effects that are particularly useful for those unfamiliar with certain effect results. The web functionality extends to the creation of complete web pages from within the application.

4.021 PhotoMontage (Arcsoft) Application from the creator of PhotoStudio that creates image montages. A single image is rebuilt using thousands of tiny sub-thumbnail micro-images. Each micro-image is selected according to its tonal, contrast and brightness level so that the final image, when viewed from a distance, appears 'normal'. The same effect can be created in MGI's Photosuite using the Phototapestry feature. → 4.026 PhotoStudio (ArcSoft)

4.022 Photoshop (Adobe) Pixel-based images editing program, and an industry standard tool. Photoshop was launched at Version 1 in 1990 as a Macintosh product and designed for use by desktop publishers and artists. Layers were introduced with Version 3 four years later, while Version 4 brought actions and adjustment layers. Multiple undos and the History palette arrived with Version 5 in 1998. With Version 5.5 Adobe added ImageReady 2.0, the parallel image editor designed for creating and editing web imagery. Some web functionality also appeared in the main Photoshop application. Version 6, in Autumn 2000, added more web features to Photoshop and enhanced capabilities to ImageReady (now updated to Version 3). Added text functionality and vector tools have also been added.

4.023 Photoshop Elements (Adobe) Version of Adobe's Photoshop released in 2001 to supersede Photoshop LE (Limited Edition). 'Elements' is designed to sit between Adobe's consumer program Photodeluxe and the 'full' Photoshop; it offers functionality designed for the amateur photographer and enthusiast. In practice this means that some of the pre-press

4.027 *Photosuite*

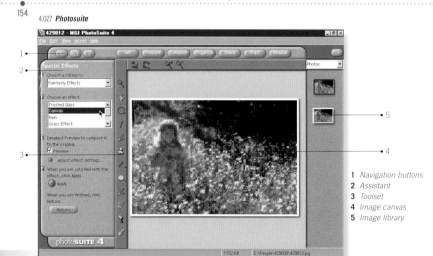

1 Navigation buttons
2 Assistant
3 Toolset
4 Image canvas
5 Image library

elements have been sacrificed but this shortfall is made up for in terms of comprehensive help and tutorial support. The interface is almost identical to that of 'full' Photoshop, but differs in some of the tools and functionality that are designed for a 'serious amateur' marketplace.

4.**024 Photoshop LE (Adobe)** Adobe's Photoshop version featuring a trimmed down specification. With advanced (especially pre-press) features removed, this version was designed more for the photographer who needed the power of Photoshop. The last release, based on Photoshop 5, has now been superseded by Photoshop Elements. Copies of Photoshop LE (both of current and earlier vintages) are often found in the 'bundled' software provided with scanners and digital cameras.

4.**025 PhotoSoap/PhotoSoap 2** Image editor devised by software guru Kai Krause and marketed through MetaCreations. Subsequently made available from ScanSoft following the dismantling of much of MetaCreations. Soap uses a unique and fluid interface that is identical in both the original Macintosh implementation and Windows. Images are moved between metaphorical rooms (such as 'Clean' and 'Compose') where different commands and effects become available. Version 2 added additional features and updated the interface to ape that of Apple's iMac. Also known as **PowerSoap**.

4.**026 PhotoStudio (ArcSoft)** Image editor suitable for the novice and intermediate-

level user. The well specified image-editing features are supported by an Album palette (providing cataloguing, sorting and filing features), web graphics, creation tools and online photo sharing using the PhotoIsland.com website.

4.**027 Photosuite (MGI)** Image-editing application from MGI software. Photosuite first appeared as a conventional image editor that, by the time it had reached Version 8, was the most widely used. The next upgrade saw a change of direction with the product being rebuilt as an Internet Explorer browser-based product. It also swapped the traditional interface for a project-led one. Users are led step-by-step through the principal stages of image editing and can then use their manipulated images as the basis of a graphic – such as calendars or greeting cards. → 4.035 PROJECT-BASED SOFTWARE

4.**028 PhotoVista (MGI)** Panorama-creating software marketed and developed by MGI Software (following the acquisition of the product from Live Picture). PhotoVista 'stitches' individual images comprising a panorama by identifying common elements in adjacent shots. The user need only enter the images and the lens type (or equivalent) used for taking them for an accurate panorama to be produced. Equivalent products include **Spin Panorama** and ArcSoft's **Panorama Maker**. Also several image-editing packages (including MGI's own Photosuite and Photoshop Elements) include panorama creation options.

4.028 *PhotoVista*

155

1 *Lens selection icon*
2 *Image window*
3 *Panorama creation icon*

4.**029 Picture It** Image editor from Microsoft. Uses an approach similar to that of Photodeluxe in having a two-level approach, offering Workbench and Project activity areas. At the Workbench, conventional image manipulation is performed, while the Project section creates a range of 'products' using templates and the edited images.

4.**030 Picture Publisher** Broad image editor and web graphics creator from **Micrografx (iGrafx)**. Designed to be a one-stop resource for all elements of image editing and graphics production, it houses a powerful image editor and is supported by a large raft of media (templates, stock photos and fonts) to enable non-photographers to start work immediately after installation.

4.**031 Picture Window** Image-editing application from **Digital Light and Colour** (www.dl-c.com) designed for the enthusiast and professional photographer rather than the graphic designer and artist. Hence, much of the language used in the application refers to common terms in photography. Feature list includes comprehensive image editor, printing facilities and tools to create multimedia slide shows.

4.**032 pixel-based image editor** Generalized term for image editing based on performing changes (manipulations or painting) to individual pixels or groups of pixels. This is distinguished from the vector-based editing that underpins some drawing and design packages such as Adobe Illustrator. Photoshop is substantially a pixel-based image editor, although new features in Photoshop 6 add vector-based editing functionality.

4.**033 Professor Franklin's Instant Photo Artist** An image editor by **StreetWise Software** that is designed more to create artistic effects than 'real' photographic results. Features an 'Art Room' where an image can be converted into a 'painting' or even converted to an outline for recolouring. The second area, the Design Studio, provides the collateral for calendars, cards, newsletters and the like.

4.**034 Professor Franklin's Instant Photo Effects** Image editor companion to Professor Franklin's Instant Photo Artist. Uses a simple but effective approach to image manipulation that combines basic image surrogates for quick results with some powerful filters. Plenty of help is provided (making this ideal for newcomers to digital imaging) and the program features links and compatibility to Microsoft Office.
→ 4.033 PROFESSOR FRANKLIN'S INSTANT PHOTO ARTIST

4.**035 project-based software** Feature of some image editors which enables edited images to be used as the basis of a creative item, such as a calendar, greeting card or poster. The software may only provide the templates for such items or it may walk the user step-by-step through the stages required to complete the project. Archetypes of the software featuring projects include Adobe's Photodeluxe and MGI's Photosuite.
→ 4.015 PHOTODELUXE; 4.027 PHOTOSUITE

4.**036 Satori PhotoXL** High-level image editor for Windows that offers non-destructive editing: images are referenced by the program and are preserved. Edits are saved separately, resulting in compact file sizes and efficient performance and high compatibility with Photoshop, including import of Photoshop PSD files.

4.**037 SuperGoo** Morphing and collaging software from the same group that is responsible for PhotoSoap. Using a similar fluid interface the software is designed to produce caricatures of faces, using a range of distorting tools. Libraries of embellishments can be used to add glasses, wigs and other elements to the faces. → 4.025 PHOTOSOAP/PHOTOSOAP 2

Interface tools

4.**038 Airbrush tool** Painting tool that simulates the behaviour and effect of a mechanical airbrush. The airbrush applies gradual tones where the edges of the stroke path are increasingly more diffuse. The speed of application and the final density can be controlled using the airbrush tool controls.

4.**039 Aligned Clone, Clone Aligned** Rubber stamp option in Photoshop. With Aligned selected, the cloning point and painting point move in parallel. Don't check this box if you want to clone repeatedly from the same source point.

4.**040 Angular Gradient** Option of most Gradient tools which shades in an anticlockwise direction around the start point. → 4.092 GRADIENT TOOL

4.**041 annotation tools** Tools that provide the means of linking annotations (which can be text- or audio-based) with an image. When that image is opened, an annotation command can be selected to display or play the annotation. Called the **Notes tool** in Photoshop, where it enables notes and audio to be added anywhere on an image canvas. Notes or audio annotations can be added 'live' by selecting the appropriate tool and positioning on the canvas, or existing text or audio can be appended.

4.**042 artefact removal** Quick fix tool that helps remove the image artefacts normally introduced by high levels of JPEG compression (hence '**JPEG artefact removal**'). Usually provided with a control slider to vary the extent of the correction, the artefact removal tool removes the colour bleed and blockiness that are characteristic of this compression technique.

4.**043 auto colour balance** Quick fix command/feature. Provides an instant adjustment of the colour balance. Such modifications typically analyse the colour balance of an image, compare this with an 'ideal' and make any necessary adjustment. Though this can be very effective, the ideal comparison may not be appropriate to some shots. For example, some sunset shots might become desaturated as the colour balance is adjusted to reduce the predominant red elements. → 4.143 QUICK FIX TOOLS

4.**044 auto contrast tool** Quick fix command/feature. Adjusts the contrast of an image (normally) to provide a pre-determined average spread of contrast values in the shot. Will work successfully for those images that should have an average spread but can give unpredictable results otherwise. → 4.143 QUICK FIX TOOLS

4.**045 auto enhance tool/feature** Quick fix command/feature, provided as a single press-button or single adjustable control on some software packages. Auto enhance tools adjust several parameters (typically brightness, contrast and sometimes colour balance) to bring them within acceptable levels. The degree of correction applied depends on how far the print is from the 'ideal' values of these parameters. Like many of these quick fix tools, correction is made on the basis of a set of average 'ideal' values. Where the spread of values in the print differs, correction may be unsuccessful but for the majority of prints, auto enhance is an effective way of correcting exposure-type deficiencies in the original image. → 4.143 QUICK FIX TOOLS

4.**046 auto histogram adjustment** Quick fix command/feature which adjusts the histogram to reflect the spread of brightness values within an image, stretching the values where necessary such that the brightest value becomes white and the darkest black. → 4.047 AUTO LEVELS; 4.098 HISTOGRAM

4.038 *Airbrush tool*

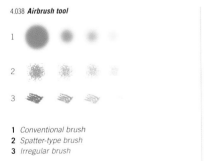

1 Conventional brush
2 Spatter-type brush
3 Irregular brush

4.051 *Bleed control*

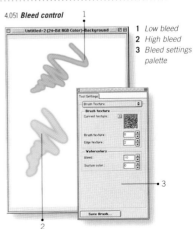

1 Low bleed
2 High bleed
3 Bleed settings palette

4.**047 auto levels** Quick fix command/feature. Automatically adjusts the histogram sliders (that determine highlight and shadow positions) and defines the lightest and darkest pixel in the image (or in each channel) as white and black respectively. The most extreme pixels at either end are usually ignored in order that the levels are adjusted according to the greater part of the image rather than extreme values that may be exceptional. → 4.046 AUTO HISTOGRAM ADJUSTMENT

4.**048 auto scratch remover** Quick fix command/feature. Strictly a filter, but offered as a quick fix command in many image editors and also provided as a feature of some scanner software (enabling the removal of scratches during the scan). This **scratch removal tool** identifies small black or white marks that differ from the composition of the image background and overwrites them with that background. The size and type of blemish that can be removed can often be set by the user. Selecting a large size can also remove fine detail from within the image, as with the Dust & Scratches filter. → 4.248 DUST & SCRATCHES FILTER

4.**049 background (1)** The base layer in an image, over which other objects and/or layers are placed.

4.**050 background colour** The colour that appears when part of an image is erased. Both foreground and background colours are usually displayed on the workspace; in the case of Photoshop this is in the lower part of the Toolbar. → 4.085 FOREGROUND COLOUR

4.**051 Bleed control** Setting in Photo-Paint and some other image editors that can be used to determine the way that paint is applied through a paintbrush stroke. The effect of setting a modest level is that the paintbrush will run out of paint during a stroke and then drag through the background colour.

4.**052 Brush options** Menu, palette or interface option for defining options and parameters for brushes such as brush diameter, hardness, angle, roundness and spacing.

4.**053 Burn tool** Tool that simulates the tool used in hand-enlarging to intensify part of an image by giving it more exposure.

4.**054 canvas** The term canvas is used in many image editors to describe the editable image area. → 4.187 WORKING CANVAS

4.**055 Circle Mask tool** Circular/oval selection tool in Photo-Paint that performs the same action as the elliptical marquee in Photoshop. → 4.118 MARQUEE TOOL

4.**056 clone tool** Tool that duplicates the pixels in one part of an image used to overwrite the pixels in another area of the image. Cloning is used to 'hide' elements of an image or to add features to that image. In most image-editing applications the clone tool can also be used to copy elements from one image to another. The clone tool is known as the Rubber Stamp tool in Photoshop. → 4.152 RUBBER STAMP TOOL

4.**057 Colours menu** Menu in Paintshop Pro (and some other image editors) that

4.063 *Crop tool*

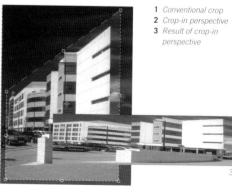

1 *Conventional crop*
2 *Crop-in perspective*
3 *Result of crop-in perspective*

1

2

3

4.040 *Angular Gradient*

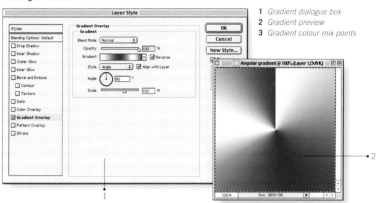

1 *Gradient dialogue box*
2 *Gradient preview*
3 *Gradient colour mix points*

4.113 *Linear Gradient*   ### 4.067 *Diamond Gradient*

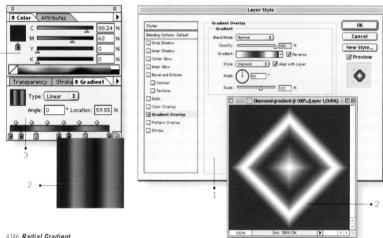

4.146 *Radial Gradient*

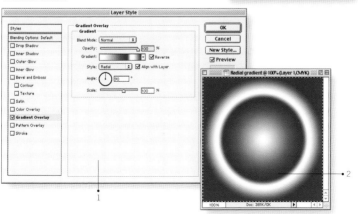

groups together features and commands
relating to colour. The Paintshop Pro menu
includes colour adjustment commands,
posterize and solarize commands, and
colour palette creation/editing tools.

4.**058 context-sensitive menus** Menus that
change (depending on the item currently
selected) to display the options for tools or
palettes in use.

4.**059 crispener** A redundant term in digital
imaging (but still used in some graphics
applications) for the sharpening feature.
In some respects it is a more appropriate
term to describe the action of sharpening
filters that 'crisp' the image rather than
produce genuine sharpness.

4.**060 crop** To trim or mask an image (either
digitally, onscreen or as a print) so that it
fits a given area, or to discard unwanted
portions of an image.

4.**061 Crop (in Perspective)** Photoshop 6 feature.
An enhancement of the Crop tool that
enables objects to be cropped and
displayed using perspective controls.
For example, a painting on a wall
photographed obliquely (and with
receding horizontals) can be cropped
and displayed rectilinearly.

4.**062 Crop Marquee** The selection boundary
marker produced when the crop tool
is used, prior to performing the crop.
→ 4.063 CROP TOOL

4.**063 Crop tool** A Crop tool is used to trim an
image of superfluous or unwanted
elements from the edges of an image. It
features a marquee that is dragged over

the portion of the image that is to be kept;
double-clicking within the selected area
applies the crop. Advanced crop tools
(such as the Deskew Crop tool in Photo-
Paint) can also be used to correct some
perspective effects when cropping.

4.**064 Define Brush** Brushes palette pull-out
option. Use Define Brush to create a
custom brush shape from an image
selection. Your custom brush can be up to
1000 pixels by 1000 pixels in extent.

4.**065 Defringe** In effect rather similar to a
Feather command, it helps reduce the
prominence of any join seams when
objects are pasted onto one layer from
another, or from another image. Colours at
the edge of the selection are coloured
along with those pixels adjacent to a
specified pixel radius. Not available in all
image editors.

4.**066 Deskew Crop tool** Photo-Paint tool that is
nominally used to perform image crops
(in a similar manner to the Crop tool in
Photoshop or Paintshop Pro) but can also
be used to straighten crooked images.
→ 4.063 CROP TOOL

4.**067 Diamond Gradient** Option of most Gradient
tools. Similar to the Radial Gradient, the
diamond gradient is defined by drawing a
line from the centre of the diamond to one
of the corners. The gradient is defined as a
diamond pattern based on the axis of the
diamond. → 4.092 GRADIENT TOOL

4.**068 Distort** Pull or push any image handles
to distort the image at will. Though
sometimes included with transform tools,

160
4.070 *effects browser*

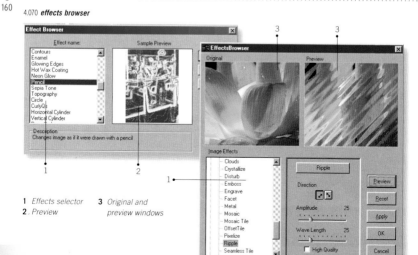

1 Effects selector
2 Preview
3 Original and
preview windows

the distort command permits a greater range of distortions than the transform tool strictly permits.

4.**069 EasyPalette** Palette feature of Ulead's PhotoImpact. EasyPalettes are galleries of effects filters and other features that can be applied to an image by dragging the appropriate thumbnail from the gallery to the image. Similar (though less extensive) features can be found in other applications such as the drag-and-drop filter effects of Photoshop Elements.

4.**070 effects browser** Feature of several image editors (including Paintshop Pro and Photoshop Elements) that allows the installed range of effects filters to be reviewed so that the effect offered can be compared with an original image. Some effects browsers allow the user to 'drag and drop' a selected effect on to the image to apply that effect (or open a dialogue box for that filter if any settings or adjustments need to be made first).

4.**071 Effects (Photoshop Elements)** In Photoshop Elements, the term Effects has been used to describe effects achieved through the pre-programmed automatic sequencing of program functions, layer styles and filters. A range of effects are shown on the Effects palette and can be dragged and dropped onto a selected image. Effects are similar to Styles in later Photoshop versions and ImageReady.

4.**072 Elliptical Marquee tool** Marquee option accessed by clicking and holding on the Marquee icon in the Toolbar and dragging down until the elliptical option is highlighted. Allows the selection of elliptical shapes, including circles. An options palette on the associated menu allows the user to set an amount of feathering (to soften the edges of the selection), a fixed size or a constrained-aspect ratio (useful for defining circles and ellipses of a particular section). The circular mask tool in Photo-Paint has much the same effect.

4.**073 Equalize** Acts on the brightness values of pixels in an image. The brightest and darkest values in an image are assigned to white and black, and the intermediate pixels are distributed as evenly as is feasible between them. A typical use can be in 'lightening' a dark PictureCD image

or scanned image. Called **Auto Equalize** in some applications. → 3.067 PictureCD

4.**074 equalize/equalization** The process of digitally enhancing an image by increasing its tonal range. Most image editors feature an equalize command that performs automatic equalization of an image.

4.**075 Eraser tool** A tool, or more commonly a set of tools, designed to rub out pixels from a layer to reveal those below.
The **Background Eraser tool** is used to erase pixels on a layer to transparency; tolerance and sampling options can be adjusted using an options palette or selection option. **Magic Erasers** erase all similar pixels in a layer to transparency, after clicking on a representative sample point. Use the tolerance setting in the Magic Eraser Options palette to determine the range of pixels that will be erased. A low tolerance will remove pixels in the layer with a colour value close to the selected one; a higher tolerance will erase pixels with a greater range of colour values.

4.**076 Extract** Photoshop 5.5 (and onwards) command that makes the selection of difficult foreground subjects from backgrounds much easier. A sophisticated development of the 'magnetic' lasso-type tools, Extract makes the selection of intricate detail (such as foliage and hair) simple. The Extract dialogue box (which is unique among Photoshop offerings) enables you to define the edge of your subject using a highlighter pen tool. Next you define the interior of the selection and can preview the extraction. Extraction parameters can be varied and the process repeated until a satisfactory preview is achieved. When the extraction is performed, the background is erased leaving only the foreground subject.

4.**077 Eyedropper tool** Conventionally used to select the foreground or background colour from those colours in the image or in a selectable colour swatch set. Eyedroppers can normally be accurate to one pixel or a larger area (such as a 3 x 3 pixel matrix) which is then averaged to give the selected colour.

4.**078 fade correction** Quick fix command/ feature. Alters the contrast, colour saturation and balance to compensate for

161

'typical' fading characteristics. A dialogue box control can be used to adjust the degree of correction applied. Also known as '**auto fade correction**'. → 4.143 QUICK FIX TOOLS

4.**079 Feather** Command or option that blurs or softens the edges of selections. This helps blend these selections when they are pasted into different backgrounds, giving less of a 'cut-out' effect.

4.**080 Filter menu** Image manipulation filters are grouped in this menu. Basic filters are normally grouped under subheadings such as Artistic, Distort and Texture. Plug-ins – additional filters provided by third parties – usually appear in a separate group either by the name of the filter or the name of the filter set (such as Xenofex or Eye Candy). In some applications the Filter menu is known as the **Effects menu**.

4.**081 Flatten Image** A command in applications that feature layers. Decreasing the number of layers in an image decreases the file size. An image is normally flattened when all image editing on the individual layers is complete. A flattened file is smaller (often much smaller) than the original but it is impossible then to perform edits on the elements that were formerly in separate layers. Some colour modes do not support layers; hence converting between modes can result in automatic flattening. → 4.447 COLOUR MODES

4.**082 flip** The action of rotating an image 180° around a horizontal axis. The resultant image is reversed from top to bottom. → 4.084 FLOP

4.**083 floating palette** A description of any palette that can be moved around the workspace and thus placed conveniently where work is currently in progress. Floating palettes can sometimes be 'docked' with the main toolbar or, in the case of Photoshop 6, dropped into a palette 'well'. → 4.130 PALETTE

4.**084 flop** The rotation of a digital image in image-editing software 180° around a vertical axis such that right and left edges are reversed. → 4.082 FLIP

4.**085 foreground colour** The 'active' colour that will be used by default when a painting tool is selected. The current foreground colour is normally shown on-screen, along with the background colour. The foreground colour may be selected or changed from a Colour Picker or the Eyedropper tool. → 4.050 BACKGROUND COLOUR; 4.170 SWITCH COLOURS

4.**086 Foreground/Background Color selector** Part of the main image-editor interface in most applications. Shows foreground and background colours. Additional controls may allow foreground and background colours to be reversed or for these to be reset to black and white.

4.**087 Fountain fill** Feature in Photo-Paint that fills a selected area with a gradient from one colour to another or across a range of colours. Similar to the gradient feature in Photoshop and other image-editing applications. → 4.092 GRADIENT TOOL

4.**088 Free Transform** Command that permits the free transformation of an image, layer, path or selection. Transformation is achieved by pulling, pushing or rotating the selection handles. Transformations are usually performed on the basis of a mathematical transformation which distinguishes the results from those of distortion effects that are usually totally freeform and user-determined.

4.**089 Frequency** Option associated with the 'magnetic' tools such as the Magnetic Lasso and Magnetic Pen. Ranging from 0 to 100, it determines how often fastening points are placed as the selection is made. Use a high frequency (which creates a greater number of points) to select irregular objects. The **Edge Contrast** feature operates in a similar way. Again ranging between 0 and 100, it determines the amount of contrast needed between objects for an edge to be recognized. Use higher levels of edge contrast in higher contrast images.

4.**090 Gamma control panel** Mac OS control panel provided in Photoshop prior to version 5 to assist in the calibration of monitors (version 5 onwards features the replacement Adobe Gamma control panel).

4.**091 Grabber hand/tool** Tool that enables the repositioning of a picture inside its box or the moving of a page around in its window. When an image is enlarged (perhaps by using the zoom tool) so that it is larger than the space available in the on-screen window, the hand is useful in manoeuvering the image to an appropriate position for editing.

4.092 Gradient tool Tool permitting the creation of a gradual blend between two or more colours within a selection. There are several different types of gradient fills offered, those of Photoshop are typical: Linear, Radial, Angular, Diamond and Reflected. A selection of gradient presets are usually provided, but user-defined options can be used to create custom gradients. In Photo-Paint the Gradient tool is called the Interactive fill tool. → 4.040 ANGULAR GRADIENT; 4.067 DIAMOND GRADIENT; 4.113 LINEAR GRADIENT; 4.146 RADIAL GRADIENT; 4.149 REFLECTED GRADIENT

4.093 grid Usually sets of non-printing lines (or, alternatively, dots) that can be placed over an image to ensure that image elements and perspective are correctly set. A menu selection permits the grid display to be toggled on or off. → 4.095 GUIDES

4.094 Grow Photoshop command. Expands a selection to include further areas of similar colour. This might typically be used following a selection with the Magic Wand tool. A selection can be enlarged in a contiguous manner based on the current tolerance setting for the Magic Wand. → 4.160 SIMILAR

4.095 guides Lines that appear to float over the entire image space but do not print. Unlike a grid, guide lines can be manually positioned vertically or horizontally across any part of the image. Not all applications provide both grid lines and guides. → 4.093 GRID

4.096 Hand tool Editing or manipulating small elements within an image often involves zooming in to a specific region. You can move the image relative to the viewable window area using the Hand tool while holding down the space bar. This is often quicker than zooming out and then zooming in on a new area.

4.097 Help menu The place to come for help and assistance. Access to help files, context-sensitive help, tutorials and online help, where available, can be found from here.

4.098 histogram A graphic representation of the distribution of brightness values in an image, normally ranging from black at the left-hand vertex to white at the right. Analysis of the shape of the histogram (either by the user or an automatic algorithm) can be used to evaluate criteria, such as tonal range, and establishes whether there is sufficient detail to make corrections.

4.099 History Photoshop feature that enables you to selectively undo any of up to 99 previous stages of an image-editing session. Each of these stages is referred to as a state. Using the History Brush tool you can selectively restore areas of an image to a chosen previous state, either by filling a selection with a previous state, or by erasing the current state to reveal a previous one.

4.100 History Brush Photoshop History feature tool. Brush tool that can be used to paint over the current edit-state image with

4.098 *histogram*

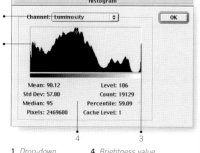

1 Drop-down channel selector
2 Black
3 White
4 Brightness value characteristics of selected histogram point

4.105 *Impressionist Brush tool*

163

pixels from a previous state of that image taken from the History palette. Note that this tool cannot be used on an image that has been resized or rescaled. → 4.101 HISTORY BRUSH TOOL

4.**101 History Brush tool** This tool, to be found in the more recent versions of Photoshop, lets you paint over a mistake in an image using an earlier selected state from the History palette. Pixels from that earlier state will overwrite the current ones. Note that an image that has been resized in any direction cannot be edited using the History Brush as the process depends on direct correspondence between pixel positions. It is impossible to make such correlations between resized images.

4.**102 image area** The area in a program interface where the image to be manipulated sits. Also a term in desktop publishing to describe the area within which a particular image or group of images is to fit in a final document.

4.**103 Image menu** Menu group that provides fundamental image functions (depending on the image-editing application), including Mode (for image mode selection), Adjust (for basic colour/contrast/brightness control), Canvas Size (for adding areas to or removing them from the workspace) and Image Size (for modifying an image's file resolution, dimensions or size).

4.**104 Image-editing application interface** Image-editing applications desktop interfaces usually feature similar elements. The exceptions are those (such as PhotoSoap and Photosuite) that feature bespoke environments better suited to their individual approaches. The principal 'active' elements are the Toolbar (which is surprisingly similar in layout across many applications) and the floating palettes. The palettes can move about the screen or be docked onto other palettes. In most applications the whole of the desktop (apart from the fixed title bar and menu bar) is available for the image (or images). → 4.121 MENU BAR (IMAGE-EDITING APPLICATION)

4.**105 Impressionist Brush tool** Brush introduced with Photoshop Elements that enables painting with stylized strokes. Impressionist painting styles can be simulated by varying the tool controls (style, size and fidelity).

4.**106 input resolution** The degree of definition with which an image is 'captured', or recorded, and which determines the final quality of output. Final output quality depends on three aspects of input: the scan resolution, the size of the original image as compared with its final size (in which case the resolution of the scanning device itself may also be significant), and the resolution of the output device. → 1.515 OPTICAL RESOLUTION; 5.079 OUTPUT RESOLUTION

4.**107 Ixla Digital Camera Interface** Interface that enables the downloading of digital cameras to image-editing software. Used by some third parties (such as Corel) to provide an enhanced and comprehensive link to digital cameras.

4.**108 keyboard shortcut** A keystroke (or more often a combination of keystrokes) that invokes a function normally selected via the mouse and menus. For example in Photoshop the 'L' key will make the currently displayed lasso option active; 'W' will activate the magic wand. Tables of shortcuts are supplied with software as an aide-mémoire. → 2.131 MENU COMMAND

4.**109 Lasso** The freehand selection tool usually indicated by a lasso icon/graphic in the Toolbar. More recent versions of image editors feature variations on the basic lasso, such as the **Magnetic Lasso** (that can identify the edges nearest to the selection path, aiding accurate selection of discrete objects) and the Polygon Lasso (that allows straight-edged selections to be made). In the case of the latter, to draw a straight line, place the cursor point at the end of the first line and click. Place the cursor at the end of the next line and click again to select the second segment.

4.**110 Lasso Mask tool** Lasso tool in Photo-Paint for freehand selections that also allows a selection that includes pixels of similar colours. → 4.109 LASSO

4.**111 Layer menu** Menu dedicated to layer manipulations. Options allow you to create, delete or duplicate layers, link, group and arrange layers and flatten an image. In Photo-Paint, layers are represented by Objects and the functions of this menu are available through the broadly equivalent **Object menu**.

4.**112 Line tool** Line tools draw straight lines, normally in the foreground (or a selected)

colour. In Photoshop and some other applications double-clicking on the Line tool will display its Options palette. The lines can be constrained to multiples of 45° by holding down the shift key when dragging the line. Note that in some image-editing applications, the Line tool describes a freehand drawing tool.

4.**113 Linear Gradient** Option of most Gradient tools. Shades uniformly along a line drawn across the selection. The start point is coloured in the first colour (or foreground colour, in a foreground to background gradient) and the end point in the last colour (or background). A gentle gradient is achieved by drawing a long line over the selection (which can extend beyond the selection at either extreme); a harsher gradient will result from drawing a short line within the selection. → 4.092 GRADIENT TOOL

4.**114 Liquify** Photoshop 6 feature. An image distortion 'filter' or filter set that allows a series of tools to be used to alter the characteristics and linearity of an image. Distorting tools include **Twist**, **Bloat** and **Pucker**, the last giving a pinched, pincushion effect. Reconstruction modes are provided to undo or alter the effect of the distorting tools. The three modes of reconstruction are known as **Amplitwist**, **Affine** and **Displace**. A Warp Mesh is drawn over the surface of the image to enable distortions to be easily seen and monitored. Image areas can also be masked at any point (prior to distorting,

prior to reconstruction or otherwise) to prevent the tools taking effect in those areas. In Liquify this masking, and the consequent unmasking, is known as **freezing** and **thawing**. → 2.287 PINCUSHION DISTORTION; 4.122 MESH WARP

4.**115 Magic Wand tool** Basic selection tool shown in the Toolbar as a magician's wand that makes selections on the basis of colour value. By setting a tolerance value for this tool you can limit the selection to those pixels with brightness and colour levels very close to the selected one (low tolerance level) or, by setting a higher value, to a much broader range of levels. Selection can also be made in an individual colour channel. → 4.193 CHANNELS

4.**116 Magnify tool** Tool that enables the whole (or part) of an image to be magnified to assist in the examination or editing. Though some magnifying tools enable an 'instant close-up' others act in the manner of a Zoom tool, allowing progressive enlargement of the image. → 4.188 ZOOM TOOL

4.**117 marching ants** Colloquial description for an active marquee. The moving alternate white/black bands look like ants walking around the selection. → 4.157 SELECTION; 4.158 SELECTION MARQUEE/RECTANGLE/BOX

4.**118 Marquee tool** One of the principal selection tools usually found at the prime position on the Toolbar. Provides an easy way to make rectangular, elliptical, single column or single row selections. The marquee selections are user-determined

4.114 *Liquify*

1 *Warp-type selections*
2 *Image window*
3 *Brush parameters*

positional selections, in that, unlike the Lasso or Magic Wand tools, there is no interaction with the image itself. Circular and rectangular mask tools perform a similar role to the marquee tool in Photo-Paint.

4.**119 mask** In the printing industry a mask was a material used to protect all or part of an image or page in photomechanical reproduction, photography, illustration or layout. Image-editor applications feature a digital equivalent that enables users to apply a mask to all or selected parts of an image. Such masks are often stored in an 'alpha channel'. → 4.191 ALPHA CHANNEL

4.**120 Measure tool** Measures the distance between any two points in the working image. Results are shown in the Info palette. All measurements are shown in the measurement units currently set (those shown on the rulers, if displayed).

4.**121 menu bar (image-editing application)** Virtually all image-editing applications (with the exception of unique products like Kai's PhotoSoap) feature a reasonably consistent menu bar where identical (or equivalent) menu items are similarly placed. This makes it relatively easy to move from one image editor to another. Only when it comes to some of the detailed commands does the regime differ between applications. File, Edit, Image, View, Window and Help tend to be common features; most also have Effects (or Filters) for effects filter selection and Layer (or Objects).

4.**122 mesh warp** In some applications, the facility to distort an image by means of dragging 'handles' at the intersections of the lines of a grid ('mesh') placed over the image. Also called '**rubber sheeting**'. Photoshop 6's Liquify command works on similar principles.

4.**123 Modify** Photoshop command, that expands or contracts a selection by a specified number of pixels. Use this if your selection includes a boundary you wish to exclude (by contracting the selection), if you have drawn freehand with a lasso and not been able to keep entirely to the object boundaries. You can also smooth a boundary (to remove unsteady selection) and place a border of specified width around the selection.

4.**124 Move tool** Allows a selection, feature or layer to be dragged to a new position. → 4.157 SELECTION; 4.198 LAYERS

4.**125 Object Picker tool** Photo-Paint tool used to select and transform objects. Masks can be similarly handled by the **Mask Transform tool**.

4.**126 origin** The fixed or **zero point** of horizontal and vertical axes, or of the rulers featured in image-editing (and most other) applications from which measurements can be made. Hence also '**ruler origin**'.

4.**127 Paint Bucket tool** The Paint Bucket tool floods selected pixels with the foreground colour, and also colours adjacent pixels that are similar in colour value (determined by setting a Tolerance level in the Options palette). The Paint

4.115 *Magic Wand tool*

4.118 *Marquee tool*

Bucket tool is called the **Fill tool** or **Bucket tool** in many image-editing applications.

4.**128 Paintbrush tool** Along with the Airbrush tool and the Pencil tool, used to apply colour directly to an image layer or to the background. Shown in the Toolbar as an artist's sable brush. Creates soft strokes of colour nominally in the foreground colour. The size and texture depends on the **brush** type selected from the Brushes palette. Use the Paintbrush Options palette to fine-tune the paintbrush performance.

4.**129 painting tools** Set of tools used for painting pixels onto the current image. Comprises the Paintbrush (soft strokes), Airbrush (emulating traditional airbrushes and aerosols) and the hard-edged Pencil. Some image-editing applications (particularly those with enhanced 'art' features) include a greater array of painting tools that can include crayons, pastel sticks and more.

4.**130 palette** A window, often 'floating' (movable), that contains features such as tools, measurements, or other functions. Palettes can be hidden or revealed as required, generally using the Window menu along with the **Show/Hide commands**. Floating palettes can also be docked onto menu bars or toolbars.

4.**131 Palette Well** Photoshop 6 feature of the Tool Options bar (also new to Photoshop 6). Palettes can be 'dropped' into the well to clear the desktop workspace. Clicking on a palette in the well opens that palette

allowing changes to be made to the parameters of that palette. Afterwards the palette disappears back into the well.
→ 4.083 FLOATING PALETTE

4.**132 pattern removal** Effects filter designed to remove **Moiré fringe** and wave patterns that occur when two halftone screens are superimposed. Sometimes called **Moiré pattern removal** or **Remove Moiré filter**.

4.**133 Pattern Stamp** Clone tool option that transforms a selection into a pattern tile.

4.**134 Pen tool** Tool used to create paths. The basic Pen tool is used to draw around an intended selection, adding anchor points that are connected to make the path. You can add as many or as few **anchor points** as required to draw the path; simple, basic shapes will require few anchor points, while more complex selections will need more. **Closed paths** are completed by clicking on the original starting point. **Open paths** (for example, a straight line) are completed by clicking in the Pen tool icon in the Toolbar. The **Magnetic Pen** uses the same technique as the Magnetic Lasso: it identifies the 'edge' closest to the track being described by the user and snaps the path to it. Anchor points are automatically added as the path progresses and can be added, removed or moved later. The **Freeform pen** provides a means of drawing a freeform path. Use this to draw paths when the selection outline is not critical or you are confident of your drawing abilities. Again, anchor points are added along the path

167

4.119 *mask*

4.130 *palette*

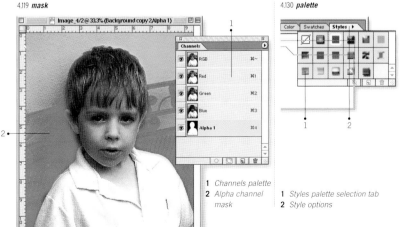

1 Channels palette
2 Alpha channel mask

1 Styles palette selection tab
2 Style options

automatically. Additional options for these tools (that appear in dialogue boxes or on pull-out menus) include the **Add/Delete Point tools**, **Direct Selection tool** (selects points on a path) and **Convert Point tool** (converts corner points into curve points and vice versa). ➔ 4.202 PATH

4.**135 Perspective** Command used principally to aid the correction of perspective effects in images, but also for the introduction of such effects for creative effect. The most common use is to remove converging verticals in buildings when the original image was taken with a conventional lens (relatively) close up.

4.**136 picture tubes** Painting tool offered by Paintshop Pro that permits painting with discrete sets of graphic or image elements. Typical picture tubes include elements such as fish (for filling an aquarium scene) or coins. The appearance of the elements can be controlled by altering settings in the Picture Tube dialogue box.

4.**137 Polygon Lasso** A version (or option) of the standard lasso selection tool that permits accurate freehand selection of rectilinear objects. The polygon is defined by clicking on corner (or turn) points, and 'closed' by clicking on the start point.

4.**138 Posterize** Creates an image with large flat areas of colour. Specify a number of levels in the dialogue box. Modest numbers (4 to 8) work best. Setting four levels in an RGB image will result in four tonal levels for each of the three colour channels – 12 in all.

4.**139 Precise Cursor** Cursors in most image editors show the tool in use; selecting the alternate setting of Precise Cursors (usually in the Preferences menu option) changes the cursor from the default shape to a precise cross-hair graticule. Essential for determining the exact start point for the tool action. A second option, **Brush Size cursor**, displays a cursor the size (and shape) of a selected brush.

4.**140 Preserve Transparency box** A feature of the Layers palette in Photoshop and some other image editors. Selecting Preserve Transparency restricts any painting or editing to those parts of that layer that already contain pixels. An object in an otherwise transparent layer can thus have its colour balance altered, be recoloured or have a filter applied without compromising the remainder of the layer.

4.**141 Pressure** Parameter in some painting tool options palettes. Set a percentage figure here to determine the strength of the painting tool applied. Normally 100% is required for full (opaque) coverage. Equivalent to the Opacity settings found in some palettes, it is the virtual equivalent of applying pressure to a brush or pen. ➔ 4.201 OPACITY

4.**142 Purge** Menu command in many image editors designed to clear data that otherwise hogs valuable space in buffers or RAM, including (but not limited to) Undo histories and the clipboard.

4.**143 quick fix tools** Feature of many image-editing applications that permits certain

4.135 *Perspective*

1

2

3

1 *Original image (converging verticals)*
2 *Adjusting the crop*
3 *Corrected image*

image corrections (such as redeye removal, colour correction or contrast/brightness adjustments) to be made automatically using a single key-stroke or menu selection. The quality and effectiveness of such 'fixes' will depend upon the quality of the underlying algorithm, and is generally good, but the more accomplished user will be able to get better, more controlled results using conventional tools.

4.**144 Quick Mask** Provides a quick method of creating a mask around a selection. The mask can be drawn and precisely defined by using any of the painting tools or the eraser respectively.

4.**145 radial fill** An option of gradient fill tools that provides a fill comprising a pattern of concentric circles of graduated tints. Although multiple colours and spectra can be created for any fill, shades typically begin with the foreground colour (if selected) from the starting point and change through to the background colour at the end point. → 4.092 GRADIENT TOOL

4.**146 Radial Gradient** Option of most Gradient tools. Shades along a radius line in a circular manner. The start point of the line is the 'origin' and is coloured in the first, or start, colour, while the end point defines the circumference and is coloured with the end colour. → 4.092 GRADIENT TOOL

4.**147 Recipe** Feature of Photoshop Elements that gives directions, as in a conventional recipe, for performing certain tasks such as redeye removal or cleaning up an image.

4.**148 Rectangle Mask tool** Rectangular selection tool in Photo-Paint that performs the same action as the Rectangular Marquee in Photoshop. In Photo-Paint the Rectangle Mask tool is also used to make single row selections, equivalent to the single row (or single column) marquee in Photoshop. → 4.118 MARQUEE TOOL

4.**149 Reflected Gradient** Option of most Gradient tools. Produces a symmetrical pattern of linear gradients to either side of the start point. The effect is one of a '**ridge**' or '**furrow**'. → 4.092 GRADIENT TOOL

4.**150 remove video interlace lines** Feature (provided as an effects filter or a transform effect) designed to remove artefacts (i.e., **remove scan lines**) in images that originate as video images.

4.**151 Rotate** Command that rotates an image or selection around a central point.

4.**152 Rubber Stamp tool** Sometimes called the cloning tool (on account of its action), the Rubber Stamp tool is often considered by newcomers to be the fundamental tool, in as much as it provides the image-editing principle of 'removing unwanted image elements'. Later Photoshop versions (and some other editors) feature two Rubber Stamp tools, the basic tool and the Pattern Stamp. The basic tool is normally used as a brush (and shares the common Brushes palette for brush type selection) but 'paints' with image elements drawn from another part of the image, or a separate image. Choose the point you wish to use as the origination point for painting and

---

169

4.139 *Precise Cursor*

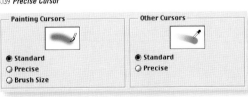

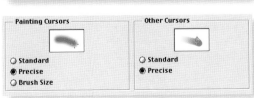

4.144 *Quick Mask*

Alt-click or Option-click on it. Now move to the image element you wish to cover or remove and click the mouse to paint on the pixels from the origination point. When you click and drag the selection point can be set to move also, thus providing an exact copy of the original area. Careful use of the opacity setting in the Rubber Stamp Options palette can provide more subtle results and further options. → 4.056 CLONE TOOL; 4.133 PATTERN STAMP

4.**153 Rulers** Rulers can be optionally made to appear along the top and left edge of the active window, with the current cursor position indicated by dash marks on each ruler. Depending on the application the ruler units can be set to metric, imperial, points or others.

4.**154 screen display mode** Many image editors provide multiple viewing options for their interface as a Toolbar feature. The default standard screen mode displays your image, menus and tools on the conventional desktop (along with any other open windows and the desktop image itself). Other modes might, for example, hide palettes and tools to provide a clear view of the image, and still others might show only the image. In Photoshop three buttons on the Toolbar provide rapid selection of three modes. The default is assigned to the first. The second button, the **full screen mode with menus**, shows only the Photoshop environment against a plain grey background. The final button, **full screen mode**, dispenses with menus, displaying only the tools, palettes and image.

170

4.**155 select(ing)** The choosing of an item (such as a piece of text, graphic symbol or icon), in image-editing terms part of an image, by using one of the selection tools in order to alter, move or manipulate it. Selection tools include the Marquee, Lasso and Magic Wand. Commands exist (which vary according to the image editor) to add or subtract areas to or from a selection, or to select multiple areas.

4.**156 Select menu** The management of selections can be made from this menu. In Photoshop, the primary options allow you to **Select All** (the entire image or layer), to **Deselect** (have nothing selected), **Reselect** (restore the last selection) and **Select Inverse** (swap selected and unselected

areas). Further commands allow you to smooth, enlarge or decrease selections, feather selection edges (to make montages more convincing) and save selections from channels. The **Color Range** command pemits the creation of a selection based on colour parameters. In other image editors some of these features are also found in other menus; Photo-Paint distributes them through the Mask and Object menus.

4.**157 selection** Any image, or part of an image, that is selected for editing. A selection might be determined by physical location, or by parameters relating to its pixels (brightness, colour value). Selections are made using the selection tools (such as the Marquee, Lasso or Magic Wand) or, for example, by means of colour range selection commands.

4.**158 selection marquee/rectangle/box** A dotted line which forms a rectangle, oval or array. The line is drawn by means of the Marquee tool, and becomes a selection. → 4.118 MARQUEE TOOL

4.**159 signal strength meter** Enables the robustness of a digital watermark created using the Digimarc process to be evaluated. Digital watermarks are designed to withstand copying and transmission of images, but the more robust the encoding, the greater the degradation of the image. The method of display of the signal strength meter (if available) varies according to the application but often comprises a bar along the bottom edge of the image. Note that this feature is usually only enabled when an image with an embedded watermark is open.

4.**160 Similar** Photoshop command that allows the selection of non-contiguous areas of colour based on, e.g., the tolerance setting of the Magic Wand tool, if that has previously been used to make the original selection. → 4.094 GROW

4.**161 Skew** Command for skewing an image selection; pulling or pushing a side handle will skew the selection along the current vertical or horizontal axis.

4.**162 Slice tool** Tool that appears in image editors with web creation features. It enables complex graphics and imagery to be created from, and within, a single document, as well as saving different areas at different resolutions to reduce file size. A slice is a distinct rectangular area of an image that is assigned as a cell in an HTML table in the corresponding HTML file for that image. When slices are created using ImageReady, further slices are created automatically, such that the entire image is assigned to cells in the HTML table. Slices drawn in an image are known as user-slices. Auto-generated slices created by the host application are usually described as **auto-slices**.

4.**163 Smooth** The Smooth command adds or removes pixels from a selection within a specified radius. Used in conjunction with a tool, such as the Magic Wand, to absorb small unselected areas in a scene whose colour (perhaps due to noise or other artefacts) falls outside the tolerance setting of that tool.

4.**164 Smudge tool** Tool simulating the dragging of a finger through wet, viscous paint. Colour is drawn from the first point of contact and dragged through with the 'finger'. Smudging can be used to give motion effects by drawing parallel smudges to one side of an object. Called Blur tool (as distinct from Blur effects filter) in some applications.

4.**165 Snapshot** Photoshop command that saves a copy of the image (in its current edit state) to the list of snapshots shown at the top of the History palette. You can later work with a copy of the image in that edit state by clicking on the appropriate snapshot. This is a temporary storage facility; snapshots are lost when the image is closed.

4.**166 Sponge tool** A toning tool, the sponge can be used to introduce subtle changes to the colour saturation of an image area. It can be set to either increase or decrease colour saturation or, in greyscale mode, move tone towards, or away from, the mid-grey level.

4.**167 standard cursor** Cursor option that shows cursors that normally mimic the shape of the corresponding tool icon. Standard cursors are useful as a reminder of which tool is in use but are often too imprecise for accurate selection work, in which case the alternate precise cursor setting should be used. → 4.139 PRECISE CURSOR

4.**168 Stroke Path** The Stroke Path command in Photoshop enables a previously constructed path to be painted using one of the painting tools.

4.**169 Styles** A set of layer effects that can be saved and applied to a chosen layer or image. Styles can be used to create button effects, textures, image effects or text effects. Suites of predefined styles are included in Photoshop 6 and can be selected from the Styles palette. Similar Styles are featured in ImageReady from version 2.0.

4.**170 Switch Colours** Command or icon that swaps round the foreground and background colours.

4.**171 Threshold** Creates a high-contrast 'lith film' effect from greyscale or colour images. A dialogue box asks for a threshold level. Any levels below will be represented as black, those above as white.

171

4.164 *Smudge tool*

4.171 *Threshold*

Original

Threshold applied

4.**172 Tolerance** The range of pixels within which a specific tool operates. Specifies, for example, the range of colours the Magic Wand selects, or the range of colours the Paint Bucket tool floods.

4.**173 tool** The features in image-editing applications that provides selections, drawing and painting, and copying. Tools are generally represented by icons in a toolbox or tool palette.

4.**174 Tool palette** Palette, either fixed (in the case of applications such as Photosuite) or floating, that contains the image-editing tools. In some applications it may be called the Toolbar or Toolbox. → 4.083 FLOATING PALETTE; 4.175 TOOLBAR, TOOLBOX

4.**175 Toolbar, Toolbox** The main feature of most image-editing application workspaces that holds the main tools and controls and generally, by default and convention, appears down the left-hand edge of the workspace. Also known as the Toolbox. The Toolbar is divided into several areas (although the exact make-up does vary according to software). Usually the uppermost section is devoted to the Selection tools, including the Lasso, the Magic Wand and the Marquee. Next come the Painting tools (such as Airbrush and Paintbrush, Clone/Rubber Stamp tool and Brushes). Darkroom (Dodge/Burn, Sponge) and **Text tools** come next, followed by the Navigation and Utility tools where these are available. → 4.173 TOOL

4.**176 Transform** Command that provides a set of tools to transform an image, including rotations, scaling, horizontal and vertical flips and perspective control. → 4.088 FREE TRANSFORM

4.**177 Transform Selection** Command that permits a selection to be transformed. Handles appear around the selection to enable an image to be flipped, rotated, skewed or rescaled. Note that the transformation applies only to the selection marquee: it does not normally rescale the object originally selected. → 4.088 FREE TRANSFORM; 4.176 TRANSFORM

4.**178 transformation tool** The generic name given to tools that change the location or appearance of an item, by scaling, reflection or a three-dimensional transformation.

4.**179 Trim** Alternate crop-type command. Use Trim in preference to Crop to discard a border around an image based on transparency or edge colour rather than the arbitrary method of Crop.

4.**180 Type Mask tool** The Type Mask tool lets the user produce selection borders in the outline of text type characters. Type selections will appear in the active layer from where they can be moved, filled, stroked or copied in the same manner as any other selection. A **Vertical Type Mask tool** provides the same function for vertical text.

4.**181 Type tool** Tool for overlaying text on an image. The implementation of the Type tool varies considerably between image editors. In some, text overlays the image and is indelibly printed onto the image. In older versions of Photoshop the text was produced in a dialogue box called up from the Type tool icon. The most recent versions of Photoshop permit the text to be placed directly on the canvas and edited in situ or subsequently. Additional text layout controls are also provided. → 4.180 TYPE MASK TOOL

4.**182 Variations** Photoshop command that displays variations in colour balance and brightness. Select Variations to open the Variations dialogue box. Perhaps the most visual of the colour adjustment features, Variations illustrates your current image as a thumbnail, surrounded by others that are identical except for having a slightly different colour balance. These are denoted appropriately by, for example, More Red, More Blue, etc. Another part of the display shows thumbnails lighter and darker than the original. By clicking on the appropriate icon, that colour (or brightness) value is applied to the image. You can make multiple applications and a comparative pair of thumbnails, Original and Current Pick, allows you to monitor your progress.

4.**183 View menu** View menu commands, where this menu is provided, are principally concerned with the presentation of images and canvases within the interface. For example, in Photoshop, New View permits the display of the working image in a second window. This allows you to zoom in on the detail in one window while

4.175 **Toolbox (from Photoshop)**

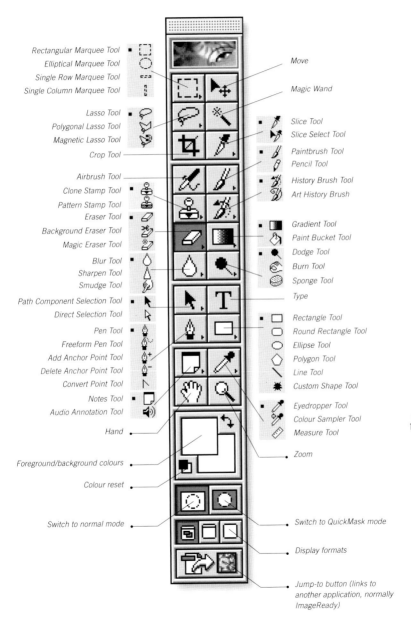

Rectangular Marquee Tool
Elliptical Marquee Tool
Single Row Marquee Tool
Single Column Marquee Tool

Lasso Tool
Polygonal Lasso Tool
Magnetic Lasso Tool
Crop Tool

Airbrush Tool
Clone Stamp Tool
Pattern Stamp Tool
Eraser Tool
Background Eraser Tool
Magic Eraser Tool

Blur Tool
Sharpen Tool
Smudge Tool

Path Component Selection Tool
Direct Selection Tool

Pen Tool
Freeform Pen Tool
Add Anchor Point Tool
Delete Anchor Point Tool
Convert Point Tool

Notes Tool
Audio Annotation Tool

Hand

Foreground/background colours

Colour reset

Switch to normal mode

Move

Magic Wand

Slice Tool
Slice Select Tool

Paintbrush Tool
Pencil Tool

History Brush Tool
Art History Brush

Gradient Tool
Paint Bucket Tool

Dodge Tool
Burn Tool
Sponge Tool

Type

Rectangle Tool
Round Rectangle Tool
Ellipse Tool
Polygon Tool
Line Tool
Custom Shape Tool

Eyedropper Tool
Colour Sampler Tool
Measure Tool

Zoom

Switch to QuickMask mode

Display formats

Jump-to button (links to
another application, normally
ImageReady)

173

monitoring the full image in the second. Gamut Warning displays those colours in the image that will not print using a conventional four-colour process. Hide/Show options are provided for Edges, Paths, Rulers, Guides and Grids.

4.184 **watermark** Digital images are, by their nature, easy to copy. Hence digital watermarks have been devised that add an invisible watermark to an image. It becomes visible only when that image is viewed with software including the appropriate plug-in. Most image-editing applications have standardized on the Digimarc system. This stores the watermark as digital noise in the image. Its presence is not immediately apparent and can survive most image edits – it can even be traced when an image is printed and rescanned. It is important, when images are received, that the copyright of the image is with the person who is supplying the picture. Analysing for watermarks can verify such ownership.
→ 4.382 DIGIMARC

4.185 **white point** Point on a histogram denoting where those pixels that define white are. Though nominally at the extreme end of the histogram, the white point should normally be moved to the position of the first 'white' pixels. → 4.098 HISTOGRAM

4.186 **Window menu** Principally devoted to the showing or hiding of interface features and providing an easy way of switching between concurrently open palettes and canvases.

4.187 **working canvas** The working canvas (or work canvas) describes the current working document. → 4.054 CANVAS

4.188 **Zoom tool** Generally indicated by a magnifying glass in the Toolbar, the Zoom tool will enlarge or reduce an area of the current active window. Sometimes called a '**reduction tool**' or '**reduction glass**'. Place the Zoom tool over the part of the image you wish to enlarge and press the mouse (or the return key). Press and hold a modifier key (such as the Alt or Option key) and press return to zoom out. The zoom percentage is usually shown. The notional 100% view of the document is based on monitor and image resolution rather than actual linear dimensions, so, e.g., a 300 ppi image will appear at 24% on a 72 ppi monitor.

Layers, channels and paths

4.189 **Actions** Term used in Photoshop to describe macros, or scripts, which apply a series of predefined commands to an image. Though a number of preconfigured actions are provided (including creating a sepia-toned print, a vignette and frames), the power of Actions comes from using the provided 'recorder' that enables an often-used sequence of commands to be saved as your own action. It can then be applied to future images. Actions are displayed in the Actions palette either as the series of commands (which is editable) or as a one-touch button.

4.189 *Actions*

1 *Button mode*
2 *Menu mode*

4.192 *Bézier curve*

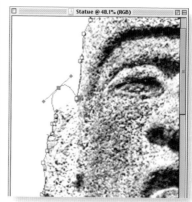

4.**190 adjustment layer** A specialized layer that can be handled as a conventional layer but designed to enact effects upon all those layers below it in the **image 'stack'**. Effects that can be applied via an adjustment layer include changes in levels, brightness/contrast, colour balance and even posterization. These changes do not actually affect the underlying pixels. If the adjustment layer is removed the image will revert to its previous appearance. Conversely, an adjustment layer's adjustments can be permanently embedded in the image (or in the underlying layers) by selecting the appropriate layer merge command (such as Merge Down). → 4.198 LAYERS

4.**191 alpha channel** A specific channel type in which information regarding the transparency of a pixel is kept. In image files, alpha channels can be stored as a separate channel additional to the standard three RGB or four CMYK channels. Image masks are stored in alpha channels. → 4.119 MASK; 6.013 CHANNEL

4.**192 Bézier curve** A curved line between two **Bézier control points** (**BCP**). Each point is a tiny database, or 'vector', which stores information about the line, such as its thickness, colour, length and direction. Complex shapes can be applied to the curve by manipulating 'handles', which are dragged out from the control points. In image-editing applications, Bézier curves are used to define very precise shapes on a path; graphics applications make

extensive use of them for drawing shapes. → 4.195 CLIPPING PATH; 4.202 PATH

4.**193 channels** A conventional RGB colour image is usually composed of three separate single-colour images, one each for red, green and blue, called channels. Each colour channel contains a monochrome representation of the parts of the image that include that colour. In the case of the RGB image channels containing the red, green and blue colours, images are combined to produce a full-colour image, but each of these individual channels can be manipulated in much the same way as a complete image. Channels can be merged or split using the **Merge Channels** or **Split Channels** commands. Additional channels exist to perform specific tasks: greyscale channels that save selections for masking are known as alpha channels; **spot colour channels** are used to provide separate channels for specific ink colours known as spot colours (premixed inks used either in addition to or in place of CMYK inks). → 4.191 ALPHA CHANNEL; 4.203 SPOT CHANNEL

4.**194 clipping group** A stack of image layers that produce a resultant image or effect that is a net composite of the constituents. For example, where the base layer is a selection shape (say, an ellipse), the next layer a transparent texture (such as craquelure) and the top layer a pattern, the clipping group would produce a textured pattern in the shape of an ellipse. → 4.119 MASK; 4.198 LAYERS

4.193 *channels*

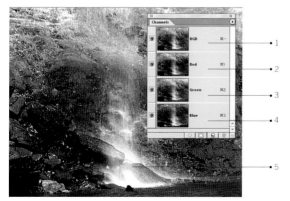

1 *RGB channel composite*
2 *Red channel*
3 *Green channel*
4 *Blue panel*
5 *Image canvas*

4.**195 clipping path** A **Bézier outline** that can be drawn around a subject or image element to determine which areas of an image should be considered transparent or 'clipped'. Using a clipping path, an object can be isolated from the remainder of the image, which is then rendered transparent, enabling background elements in an image composite to show through. A particular application is when cut-out images are to be placed on top of a tint background in a page layout. When a clipping path is created it can be embedded into the image file, normally when saved to the EPS format. → 4.192 BÉZIER CURVE

4.**196 layer effects/layer styles** Series of effects, such as Drop Shadow, Inner Glow, Emboss and Bevel, enacted on the contents of a layer.

4.**197 layer mask** A mask that can be applied to the elements of an image in a particular layer. The layer mask can be modified to create different effects but such changes do not alter the pixels of that layer. As with adjustment layers (of which this is a close relation), a layer mask can be applied to the 'host' layer (to make the changes permanent) or removed, along with any changes.

4.**198 layers** Method of producing composite images by 'suspending' image elements on separate 'overlays'. It mimics the method used by a cartoon animator wherein an opaque background is overlaid with the transparent 'cells' (layers) upon which pixels can be painted or copied.

Once layers have been created they can then be re-ordered, blended and have their transparency (opacity) altered. The power of using layers is that effects or manipulations can be applied to individual layers (or to groups of layers) independent of the others. When changes need to be made to the image only the relevant layer need be worked upon. Adjustment layers are specialized layers that perform modifications to the underlying layers without being visible themselves. → 4.190 ADJUSTMENT LAYER

4.**199 montage** An assembly of several different images, forming a single original. A montage of photographs is often described as a **photomontage** or composite. → 7.008 COLLAGE

4.**200 object** A term that describes an image layer in some image-editing applications, including Corel's PhotoPaint.

4.**201 opacity** The degree of transparency that each layer of an image (or object, in certain image-editing applications) has in relation to the layer beneath. Layer opacities can normally be adjusted using an opacity control in the Layers palette or Layers option palette, depending on the application. → 4.198 LAYERS

4.**202 path** A line curve or shape drawn using a Pen tool. Paths typically comprise anchor points linked by curved (or straight) line segments. The anchor points can be repositioned to alter a path if required. Each anchor features a direction line (Bézier line) and (normally) a pair of

4.196 *layer effects/layer styles*

4.202 *path*

direction points. These can be pulled and moved to smoothly reshape the curve. Closed paths can be converted into selections and vice versa. → 4.192 BÉZIER CURVE; 4.204 WORK PATH

4.**203 spot channel** An additional image channel that contains the channel information for elements in an image to be represented by a colour outside the normal CMYK. Spot colours are specially mixed colours that are normally printed in addition to (or instead of) the conventional CMYK colours. Using a spot colour can also be a cheap way to print that colour in artwork (a brochure, for example) without resorting to full-colour printing: an image can be created using only black and a spot colour. With the prevalence of 5-, 6-, 8- and 10-colour printing presses, it is possible to add spot colours and specials to printed materials without unacceptable cost implications.

4.**204 work path** Path created (initially) from an image selection or by using the Pen tool. In the latter case the path appears as a **temporary work path** until saved. → 4.202 PATH

Filters

4.**205 3D Stereo Noise filter** Effects filter that produces a dithered noise pattern that can, under the right viewing conditions, deliver a three-dimensional effect to an image. The noise introduced is designed to be viewed by focusing your eyes at a greater or lesser distance than the actual plane of the image, rendering the actual image elements at a different plane to the noise. One of the set of Render filters in Photo-Paint.

4.**206 3D Transform filter** Render filter that converts a flat image into a cube, sphere or cylinder, by mapping the conventional rectangular coordinates of points in the image to the corresponding coordinates of the three-dimensional body.

4.**207 Accented Edges filter** Brush-stroke-type filter. Adds emphasis to edges in an image. The dialogue box for this filter permits the accent edge brightness to be set at a high level, in which case the emphasis is gentle and resembles pastels, or low, when an India-ink-like outline is created.

4.**208 Adaptive Unsharp filter** Sharpen filter that increases edge detail by analysing the corresponding values of neighbouring pixels. Similar in effect to the Unsharp Mask filter. → 4.316 SHARPEN FILTERS; 4.346 UNSHARP MASK filter

4.**209 Add Noise filter** Adds random discrete pixels to the image, simulating levels of broadband noise or film grain (though many applications feature an alternate 'Add Grain' filter designed to add noise that specifically resembles film grain). This filter serves several purposes. By setting the noise levels to low, it can be used to conceal banding and dithering in images (particularly in gradient areas such as skies), and helps conceal the joins when image elements are pasted on a background. The default setting delivers **panchromatic noise**. Click on the Monochromatic button to base the noise on underlying tonal values: Uniform for a random pattern and Gaussian for a result (based on Gaussian statistics) that is often more speckled. Photo-Paint's implementation includes a Spike option that provides coloured noise from a narrow selection of colours. → 4.287 NOISE FILTERS

4.**210 Aged Newspaper filter** Simulates the effect of a newspaper that has yellowed with age. The image is given a soft brown tone and is further softened by allowing the ink to 'run' slightly. Artistic filter found in some later versions of Paintshop Pro.

4.**211 Angled Strokes filter** A useful filter from the Artistic range (or Brush Strokes in Photoshop). Adds a painted texture comprising diagonal strokes. Image areas lighter than 50% grey are painted with strokes in one direction; darker areas are painted in the opposite direction. A useful filter for imparting informal texture where there is to be no underlying 'canvas' texture. → 4.212 ARTISTIC FILTERS; 4.219 BRUSH STROKES FILTERS

4.**212 Artistic filters** General term for effects filters designed to produce effects that emulate specific painting methods or techniques such as 'watercolour', 'impressionist' and 'oil painting'. Others that fall into this category produce art effects that might be difficult to achieve with conventional media. Often artistic filters are grouped under the heading

177

'Artistic' in the Filters or Effects menu.
→ 4.253 EFFECTS FILTERS

4.**213 Band Pass filter** Effects filter that permits a range of frequencies to pass. The user can determine where the high and low pass points of the filter are set. High frequency data contains sharp detail while low frequency contains areas of low contrast and slow variation in tone. Hence unwanted image elements can be screened out. → 4.270 HIGH PASS FILTER; 4.277 LOW PASS FILTER

4.**214 Bas Relief filter** Artistic/Sketch filter which creates texture from image elements. This results in an image that appears to be carved into lino-like material and lit semiobliquely to emphasize the texture. The foreground colour is applied to dark areas of the image and the background colour to lighter parts.
→ 4.319 SKETCH FILTERS

4.**215 Bit Planes filter** Emphasizes tonal changes by reducing the image to basic RGB colour components. Typically, a clear sky would appear as a solid block of blue, but areas of steep gradients of colour will appear as steps of colour. A colour transform filter in Photo-Paint.

4.**216 Blur filter** The conventional blur effect filter, designed to detect noise around colour transitions and remove it. It does this by detecting pixels close to boundaries and averaging their values, effectively eliminating noise and random colour variations. Blur More is identical but applies the effect more strongly. Somewhat crude, the Blur filter is now joined in many image-editing filter sets with more controllable filters such as the Gaussian Blur and Smart Blur filters. → 4.217 BLUR FILTERS; 4.262 GAUSSIAN BLUR FILTER; 4.320 SMART BLUR FILTER

4.**217 blur filters** Effects filters designed to soften and smooth edges in a manner similar to soft focus or blurring. Certain blur filters can also create motion effects. The blur filter family includes Blur More, Gaussian Blur, Motion Blur, Radial Blur and Jaggy Despeckle, Smart Blur, Soften and Directional Smooth filters. → 4.218 BLUR MORE FILTER; 4.262 GAUSSIAN BLUR FILTER; 4.274 JAGGY DESPECKLE FILTER; 4.285 MOTION BLUR FILTER; 4.306 RADIAL BLUR FILTER; 4.320 SMART BLUR FILTER; 4.325 SOFTEN FILTER

4.**218 Blur More filter** An extreme form of the Blur filter, which can create an effect several times stronger than the normal 'Blur'. Adobe describe the effect of Photoshop's Blur More as being four times greater than that of Blur. → 4.216 BLUR FILTER; 4.217 BLUR FILTERS

4.**219 Brush Strokes filters** A set of filters that can make an image emulate brush-and-ink stroke effects. In Photoshop such filters have their own category (Brush Strokes) whereas in other applications some may be found under the Artistic heading or even Drawing effects. Textured strokes feature prominently in the filter set, which includes effects such as Accented Edges, Crosshatch and Ink Outlines.

4.**220 Canvas filter** Applies a textured surface to an image. Canvas types can usually be selected from a preset range or additional textures created using the filter. Canvas filters are usually considered either Artistic or Texture filters. → 4.212 ARTISTIC FILTERS

4.**221 Chalk & Charcoal filter** Sketch/Artistic filter. Uses black as the foreground colour and white as the background colour to translate an image into a bold graphic with a hand-drawn appearance. Highlight areas are replaced with diagonal chalk strokes, shadows are textured charcoal-black and midtones are represented by a mid-grey ground. By substituting different foreground and background colours for black and white, unusual effects can be achieved including some strong 'luminous' effects. → 4.319 SKETCH FILTERS

4.**222 Charcoal filter** Sketch/Artistic filter. Similar to the Chalk & Charcoal filter but with only 'charcoal' as the drawing medium. Edges are clearly defined while midtones comprise short diagonal strokes. Charcoal thickness, level of detail and light/dark balance can be adjusted. Like Chalk & Charcoal, this filter delivers authentic results with black as the foreground colour and white as the background, but any other colours can be used. → 4.319 SKETCH FILTERS

4.**223 Chrome filter** One of the more extreme sketch filters, Chrome converts an image into a polished metal moulding. Image highlights become raised bright areas while shadows become 'valleys'. Altering the control parameters delivers surface effects that range from mild undulations to a finely detailed representation of the original image. Chrome tends to flatten contrast in the image and hence it is usually necessary to boost contrast afterwards to restore the contrast range of the original. → 4.319 SKETCH FILTERS

4.224 Clarify filter A subtle sharpening filter that can add apparent focus to an image without the normal artefacts. Also improves detail in old, faded images and can be used to pep-up images taken in flat lighting conditions. Available in Paintshop Pro from version 7.

4.225 Clouds filter Render filter. Creates a cloudscape using random values between those of the foreground and background colours. Care is therefore needed in selecting sensible colours in order to create a realistic effect. When aiming to create a realistic sky, background and foreground colours are completely interchangeable. This filter does not depend on the currently active image, unlike the Difference Clouds filter, which subsequently blends the clouds with the underlying image. → 4.239 DIFFERENCE CLOUDS FILTER; 4.308 RENDER FILTERS

4.226 Coloured Pencil filter Artistic filter that redraws the image using a solid background colour and a pencil-like texture for the image elements. Crosshatching effects are used to emphasize details and edges.

4.227 Colour Halftone filter Creates the effect of a printer's halftone screen on each channel of the image. The image is broken down into rectangles, then for each channel the rectangle is replaced with a circle (with a radius proportional to the luminosity value of the rectangle). Called Halftone filter in some applications. → 4.298 PIXELATING FILTERS; 5.004 HALFTONE (1)

4.228 Coloured Edges filter Enhances and colours the edges within an image.

4.229 Coloured Foil filter Applies several colours to the image and gives a three-dimensional look.

4.230 Conté Crayon filter Sketch/Artistic filter that simulates a dense-textured conté crayon. For an accurate conté crayon effect, set the foreground colour (which is applied to the darker areas of the image) to black or deep brown. A Texture control

allows you to select the base texture (**brick**, **burlap**, painters' canvas or stone) upon which the conté crayon image will be drawn. → 4.319 SKETCH FILTERS

4.231 Craquelure filter Texture filter that produces an image 'canvas' backing that looks like blown polystyrene wallpaper. Fine, rounded cracks echoing the principal features of the image, broken up by small or large cracks, the size of which can be set in the dialogue box.

4.232 Crosshatch filter A filter from the Brush Strokes or Artistic categories, depending on application. Adds a texture to edges simulating coloured pencil hatching. The details of the original image are retained making this a good choice for detailed and exceptionally small images. → 4.212 ARTISTIC FILTERS; 4.219 BRUSH STROKES FILTERS

4.233 Crystallize filter Pixelating filter that breaks an image into polygons of solid colour (the 'crystals'). The hue and luminosity of each polygon is calculated on the averaged values of the pixels in the space occupied by the polygon. → 4.298 PIXELATING FILTERS

4.234 Cutout filter Artistic filter type that converts the image to a '**paper collage**' Contrast is increased and colour values flattened to produce images that appear to have been built from layers of coloured paper. → 4.212 ARTISTIC FILTERS

4.235 Dark Strokes filter Brush stroke filter that paints short, tightly packed strokes in dark image areas and longer, white strokes across lighter image areas. The result is a heavier image than that created with angled strokes or Crosshatch filters. → 4.219 BRUSH STROKES FILTERS

4.236 Deinterlace filter A video filter found in Photoshop under Filter>Video>Deinterlace that detects interlaced lines in a moving video image and discards them to give a smoothed image. The discarded lines can be replaced by interpolation or by duplicating the neighbouring **scan lines**. A similar filter is available in PaintShop Pro, Virtual Dub and other digital video-editing applications.

4.237 Descreen Filter, usually part of a scanner's software or image acquire software, that reduces or removes dot screen artefacts in images scanned from books, magazines or newspapers. In an

179

4.206 *3D Transform filter*

4.206 *3D Transform filter*

4.206 *3D Transform filter*

4.207 *Accented Edges filter*

4.209 *Add Noise filter*

4.210 *Aged Newspaper filter*

4.211 *Angled Strokes filter*

4.214 *Bas Relief filter*

4.220 *Canvas filter*

4.221 *Chalk & Charcoal filter*

4.222 *Charcoal filter*

4.223 *Chrome filter*

4.217 *blur filter (original picture)*

4.262 *Gaussian Blur filter*

4.285 *Motion Blur filter*

4.320 *Smart Blur filter*

4.306 *Radial Blur filter (zoom mode)*

4.225 *Clouds filter*

4.226 *Coloured Pencil filter*

4.227 *Colour Halftone filter*

4.228 *Coloured Edges filter*

4.229 *Coloured Foil filter*

4.230 *Conté Crayon filter*

image editor's filter palette, filters such as Moiré removal or pattern removal perform a similar role. → 4.132 PATTERN REMOVAL

4.238 Despeckle filter A useful Noise filter that removes noise and unwanted fine detail but preserves the main image details. Edge-detection techniques determine the fundamental image edges (i.e., the important ones where major colour changes occur) and blurs the rest of the image.

4.239 Difference Clouds filter A Render filter like the 'Clouds' filter, Difference Clouds creates cloudscapes using random colour values between those of the foreground and background colours. It then blends these 'clouds' with the underlying image using the same technique as the Difference blending mode. → 4.225 CLOUDS FILTER; 4.460 BLENDING MODE; 4.466 DIFFERENCE

4.240 Diffuse filter Defocuses an image by moving pixels either randomly or according to their colour values. Depending on the level of diffusion selected this filter can be used to remove noise or produce a soft-focus effect. Photoshop includes additional parameters in its Diffuse filter. Lighten Only replaces darker pixels with lighter ones, Darken Only replaces lighter pixels with darker ones. → 4.335 STYLIZE FILTERS

4.241 Diffuse Glow filter A Distortion filter in Photoshop. Adds a Softar-like diffusion filter effect to the image. This effect is created by adding transparent white noise across the entire image, with the intensity being brighter at the image (or selection) centre. → 4.245 DISTORT FILTERS

4.242 Directional Sharpen filter Sharpen filter that identifies edges then analyses the adjacent pixels. It then determines to which side of that line sharpening should be applied. Prevents the artefacts that sometimes occur when a line is sharpened (and particularly when a line is over-sharpened).

4.243 Directional Smooth filter Blur effects filter that blurs areas of an image that feature gradual changes in contrast, preserving detail in the edges and texture. The result is an image that maintains critical focus but has a softer overall appearance. Somewhat similar to a 'Softar' soft focus filter. → 4.217 BLUR FILTERS

4.244 Displace filter Distortion filter that displaces or distorts an image according to the characteristics of a displacement map image (a special image containing displacement information) or, in some applications, in a freeform manner. → 4.245 DISTORT FILTERS

4.245 Distort filters General name for filters that introduce geometric distortions to an image. In some applications, transformation filters are classed as Distort filters but in strict terms they are a separate category. Adobe are the only software manufacturer to correctly advise that Distort filters are very memory-hungry.

4.246 drop shadow Effect (available as a filter, plug-in or layer feature) that produces a shadow beneath a selection conforming to the selection outline. This shadow (depending on the filter) can be moved relative to the selection, given variable opacity or even tilted. In the last case a drop shadow can be applied to a selection (say, a person) and that shadow will mimic a sunlight shadow.

4.247 Dry Brush filter Artistic filter type using the dry brush technique (where a loaded brush has most of the paint removed before being brushed firmly on the canvas) to give an effect of paint drawn over the surface. Though colour variation tends to be reduced by blending, additional brush texture is added. → 4.212 ARTISTIC FILTERS

4.248 Dust & Scratches filter A common filter usually found in the Noise category. Reduces the overall noise level in an image. Fine dust particles and scratches in the image are identified by the filter and treated in the same way as finer noise artefacts. Careful setting of Radius and Threshold parameters are required to ensure that the settings are just sufficient to remove dust and scratches actually present. If it is set any higher, there is a risk that the whole image will become soft and ill-defined as genuine image element edges are also removed. → 4.287 NOISE FILTERS

4.249 dynamic effects General term for image manipulation effects that involve changes to the entire image. Those that involve flipping and reversing, resizing, distortions and warps are classed as dynamic effects.

4.**250 Edge Detect filter** Finds the edges in an image (as with the Find Edges filter) but then places them on a plain colour background. → 4.259 FIND EDGES FILTER

4.**251 Edge effects** A term used generally to describe effect filters that perform some manipulation on edges (such as Sharpen Edges, Edge Detect and Find Edges) but also to describe a group of effects in Paintshop Pro. This offers the following effects:

– **Dilate**: enhances the light areas of an image

– **Erode**: enhances the dark areas of the image

– **Enhance**: increases contrast along the edges in an image

– **Enhance More**: provides a stronger contrast along the edges in the image

– **Find All**: increases contrast between light and dark areas by darkening the image and then highlighting the edges

– **Find Horizontal**: enhances the horizontal edges in the same way as Find All

– **Find Vertical**: enhances only the vertical edges in the same way as Find All

– **Trace Contour**: traces a series of single pixel lines around the contrasty areas then turns all remaining pixels white. → 4.250 EDGE DETECT FILTER; 4.259 FIND EDGES FILTER; 4.314 SHARPEN EDGES FILTER

4.**252 edge enhancement** General term for techniques that enhance detail (mostly edges) to give the perceived effect of greater focus. Filters in the Sharpen group are edge enhancement features. → 4.316 SHARPEN FILTERS

4.**253 effects filters** Effects filters offer image enhancement and manipulation functions that are applied across an image or an active selection within an image. Basic filters emulate traditional photographic filters (hence the name). Most image-editing applications feature effects filters as standard, often arranged into collections such as 'Artistic' (emulating painting and drawing techniques), 'Sketch' (pencil/crayon effects) and 'Stylize' (more extreme), along with 'corrective' types (blur and sharpen). Many image editors also accept additional filters (called plug-in filters) that, when installed, operate seamlessly with the host application. → 4.374 PLUG-IN

4.**254 Emboss filter** Widely available Stylize filter. Identifies principal edges and raises or depresses the enclosed selection. The fill colour becomes grey and the edges coloured. The embossing angle can be changed through 360° and the surface of the emboss altered between a depression and a raised platform. This results in images that appear to be carved in grey stone. → 4.335 STYLIZE FILTERS

4.**255 Enamel filter** Gives an image the appearance of being created on shiny enamel.

4.**256 Extrude filter** A Stylize filter that creates a three-dimensional effect of the image being extruded through a grille; image elements become square prisms or pyramids, 'bursting' from the image centre. Its extreme nature limits its effectiveness and it is best used on selections within an image to draw attention to other (non-selected) elements. → 4.335 STYLIZE FILTERS

4.**257 Facet filter** Pixelating filter that creates blocks of continuous colour from groups of pixels. The size and shape of the irregular blocks are determined by the underlying tone and the brightness levels. Delivers a result that can look hand painted or over-blocked depending on how control parameters are set. → 4.298 PIXELATING FILTERS

4.**258 Film Grain filter** Categorized as an Artistic or Texture filter depending on the application. Restores characteristics to an image that the film manufacturers have struggled long and hard to remove! An even, specular pattern is laid over the dark and midtones, and a similar saturated pattern is laid over the lighter areas. Used subtly, this filter is excellent at removing 'image banding' (stepwise changes in colour gradients) and can also conceal 'joins' in image montages. → 4.212 ARTISTIC FILTERS

4.**259 Find Edges filter** Effects filter that appears (depending on the application) under the headings of Stylize or Sharpen. Identifies and then increases the emphasis of edges in an image. → 4.253 EFFECTS FILTERS; 4.316 SHARPEN FILTERS; 4.335 STYLIZE FILTERS

4.**260 Fragment filter** Pixelating filter. Offsets four copies of the image, with the pixels in each copy averaged. Can create blurred

183

4.231 *Craquelure filter*

4.232 *Crosshatch filter*

4.233 *Crystallize filter*

4.234 *Cutout filter*

4.235 *Dark Strokes filter*

4.238 *Despeckle filter*

4.239 *Difference Clouds filter*

4.240 *Diffuse filter*

4.241 *Diffuse Glow filter*

4.244 *Displace filter*

4.247 *Dry Brush filter*

4.248 *Dust & Scratches filter*

4.254 *Emboss filter*

4.255 *Enamel filter*

4.256 *Extrude filter*

4.257 *Facet filter*

4.258 *Film Grain filter*

4.259 *Find Edges filter*

4.260 *Fragment filter*

4.261 *Fresco filter*

4.263 *Glass Block filter*

185

4.264 *Glass filter – 'button' glass*

4.264 *Glass filter – rippled glass*

4.265 *Glowing Edges filter*

effects that can be used to simulate rapid vibration effects. → 4.298 PIXELATING FILTERS

4.261 Fresco filter Artistic filter that applies large loose dabs of colour based on the underlying colours. Tends to create bold graphics when used on images with simple forms. → 4.212 ARTISTIC FILTERS

4.262 Gaussian Blur filter Blur filter that applies a weighted average (based on the bell-shaped curve of the Gaussian distribution) when identifying and softening boundaries. It also introduces low-frequency detail and a mild 'mistiness' to the image which is ideal for covering (blending out) discrete image information, such as noise and artefacts. A useful tool for applying variable degrees of blur and a more controllable tool than conventional blur filters. → 4.217 BLUR FILTERS.

4.263 Glass Block filter Filter that makes an underlying image appear as if it were being viewed through a glass block. Glass textures and patterns can often be applied for additional effects. → 4.212 ARTISTIC FILTERS; 4.321 SMOKED GLASS FILTER

4.264 Glass filter Distortion filter that simulates different glass types placed over the image. Preset glass types are provided, but custom 'glasses' can be created and saved. Photo-Paint offers variations on the glass theme with its Smoked Glass and Glass Block filters, the latter being very similar to the basic glass filter. → 4.245 DISTORT FILTERS; 4.263 GLASS BLOCK FILTER; 4.321 SMOKED GLASS FILTER

4.265 Glowing Edges filter A Stylize filter that identifies image edges and paints them with a bright, fluorescent-like glow. The glow width, edge brightness and smoothness can be adjusted from the dialogue box. → 4.335 STYLIZE FILTERS

4.266 Grain filter A texture filter that works in many respects like the Add Noise filter. A straightforward filter for adding texture in the form of fine or medium film grain. Additional options can create stippling, horizontal and vertical lines rather than simple grain. → 4.209 ADD NOISE FILTER; 4.339 TEXTURE FILTERS

4.267 Graphic Pen filter Sketch filter. Simulates the use of a graphic or technical drawing pen with fine, parallel ink strokes picking out the original image. Stroke length, light/dark balance and light direction may

be manipulated for best effect. → 4.319 SKETCH FILTERS

4.268 Halftone filter Transforms image into a colour halftone. A greyscale halftone image can be created using an alternate filter such as Photoshop's Halftone Pattern filter. → 4.227 COLOUR HALFTONE FILTER; 4.269 HALFTONE PATTERN FILTER

4.269 Halftone Pattern filter Converts the image to a greyscale halftone screened image, resembling a newspaper image. The Photoshop implementation of this filter includes an optional Line setting which simulates a black and white TV picture (with prominent scan lines), while the Circle setting overlays the image with concentric rings. → 4.227 COLOUR HALFTONE FILTER; 4.268 HALFTONE FILTER; 4.319 SKETCH FILTERS

4.270 High Pass filter A Sharpen filter that removes low-frequency data from an image. Low-frequency data corresponds to areas of low contrast and slowly varying data. Tends to emphasize the highlights of the image. Setting a low percentage in the dialogue box results in the highlighted areas being enhanced; higher percentage settings result in the virtual removal of low frequency areas. → 4.277 LOW PASS FILTER

4.271 Hot Wax Coating filter Gives an image the appearance of being coated in a layer of hot wax.

4.272 Impressionist filter An Artistic filter that converts the image to dabs of colour to emulate the technique of the Impressionist painters. → 4.105 IMPRESSIONIST BRUSH TOOL; 4.212 ARTISTIC FILTERS

4.273 Ink Outlines filter Brush Strokes filter. Repaints the entire image (or selection) to give the appearance of a **pen-and-ink drawing**. → 4.219 BRUSH STROKES FILTERS

4.274 Jaggy Despeckle filter Softens an image by scattering the colours. This filter works best when used with sharp or high contrast imagery.

4.275 Lens Flare filter A Render filter that introduces (controllable) lens flare into images that previously had none (through good practice on the part of the photographer). Lens flare can often be simulated for a variety of lenses (for example, using multiple artefacts for multi-element zoom lenses). → 4.308 RENDER FILTERS

4.276 Lighting Effects filter Powerful set of rendering filter effects that can be used to alter or introduce new lighting effects into an image. Most of these include an extensive range of tools to achieve credible effects. For example, the Photoshop implementation uses four sets of light properties, three light types and 17 styles to produce endless variations of lighting effects. '**Bump Maps**' (texture greyscale files) can be linked to the image to create contour-line three-dimensional effects.

4.277 Low Pass filter Removes the sharp edges and detail from an image (elements of an image that correspond to 'high-frequency' data). Areas of low contrast and gradual change correspond to low frequency; these pass unhindered through this filter. Where this filter is available, it is usually offered as one of the 'blur' filters, being used to smooth away fine blemishes by reducing the intensity or levels of high-frequency information.

4.278 Map to Object filter Effects filter in Photo-Paint that wraps the image around the surface of a three-dimensional cylinder.

4.279 Maximum filter Noise filter that effects noise removal by adjusting the colour value of pixels based on the maximum colour values of adjacent pixels. Can cause blurring when used at high levels.
→ 4.282 MINIMUM FILTER; 4.287 NOISE FILTERS

4.280 Median filter Noise filter that can be used to reduce motion artefacts from hand-held images taken at long exposures. It can also help remove compression artefacts from areas of similar tone. Flesh tones respond particularly well. Median works by blending pixel brightness values to reduce the noise level in an image. Pixels that differ markedly from surrounding ones are discarded and replaced with those of median value (based on the value of pixels in their immediate environment).
→ 4.287 NOISE FILTERS

4.281 Mezzotint filter Pixelating filter that produces an image built from fully saturated coloured dots. These 'dots' can be large, medium or fine. In alternate settings they can be drawn into short or long strokes giving a slight copperplate engraving look to the image. → 4.298 PIXELATING FILTERS

4.282 Minimum filter Noise filter that reduces or removes noise by adjusting the colour values of pixels based on the minimum colours of neighbouring pixels.

4.283 Mosaic filter Pixelation filter that recreates square tile mosaics by creating new square 'pixels' of solid colour representing the average of the underlying pixels. The size of the mosaic tiles can be adjusted between 2 and 200 pixels. In combination with other filters (such as Blur or soften) it can be used to create needlepoint tapestry effects. In some implementations, the Mosaic filter can be used to create less regular mosaic effects.
→ 4.298 PIXELATING FILTERS

4.284 Mosaic Tiles filter A Texture filter that breaks the image into rough square tiles with depressions between them. By reducing the brightness of the cracks, dirty groutwork can be simulated. Without care this filter can look more like crazy paving! Don't confuse this with the Mosaic filter, which breaks the image into enlarged single-coloured pixel tiles, with no gaps between them. → 4.283 MOSAIC FILTER

4.285 Motion Blur filter One of the blur filters, Motion Blur creates a linear blur (implying movement) at any angle. The degree of blur can be altered between arbitrary levels that introduce mild through to excessive blurs. Works most effectively when applied to an inverted selection: a selection is made of an object (say, a car, a runner or a train), the selection is inverted (to select the surroundings) and the filter applied to the inverse selection.
→ 4.217 BLUR FILTERS

4.286 Neon Glow filter Artistic filter that applies amorphous neon tube-like glows to objects, often creating brightly coloured haloes. → 4.212 ARTISTIC FILTERS

4.287 noise filters Set of effects filters that add or remove noise (and noise-like) artefacts from an image. Typical filters (depending on the image-editing application) include 'Add Noise', 'Dust & Scratches', 'Remove Noise' and 'Median' filters.

4.288 Note Paper filter Sketch filter that reduces images in tone so that they appear to become layers in highly textured handmade paper. Though the effect is similar to that of the Emboss filter, the

187

4.266 *Grain filter*

4.267 *Graphic Pen filter*

4.268 *Halftone filter*

4.269 *Halftone Pattern filter (circles)*

4.269 *Halftone Pattern filter (line)*

4.269 *Halftone Pattern filter (large dots)*

4.270 *High Pass filter*

4.271 *Hot Wax Coating filter*

4.272 *Impressionist filter*

4.273 *Ink Outlines filter*

4.275 *Lens Flare filter*

4.276 *Lighting Effects filter*

4.279 *Maximum filter*

4.280 *Median filter*

4.281 *Mezzotint filter*

4.282 *Minimum filter*

4.283 *Mosaic filter*

4.284 *Mosaic Tiles filter*

4.286 *Neon Glow filter*

4.288 *Note Paper filter*

4.289 *NTSC Colors filter*

4.290 *Ocean Ripple filter*

4.291 *Offset filter*

4.292 *Page Curl*

more pronounced use of texture makes for a more interesting end result. → 4.319 SKETCH FILTERS

4.**289 NTSC Colors filter** Video filter that alters the colour gamut to that of NTSC colour television. This restricted gamut prevents oversaturated colours from the original image bleeding when they are displayed using the NTSC colour television system. → 4.544 NTSC

4.**290 Ocean Ripple filter** Distort filter that places random ripple effects across the image, simulating the appearance of an object through the media of a changing refractive index, as distinct from 'ripple' filters. The latter create the effect of ripples on the surface of water, such as when a pebble is dropped in an (idealized) stream. Also useful for creating image edge effects. → 4.245 DISTORT FILTERS; 4.310 RIPPLE FILTER

4.**291 Offset filter** A selection-based filter that moves the selection a specified amount horizontally and/or vertically. An empty space is left at the original selection location that can be filled with the current background colour or another selected part of the image.

4.**292 Page Curl** Features in several image-editing applications and as a plug-in filter. Creates the effect of a corner of the image having curled up to reveal the background. The degree of curl can be set in the corresponding dialogue box.

4.**293 Paint Daubs filter** An Artistic filter that produces a daubed paint effect using fine to medium brush sizes (1 to 50 pixels). In Photoshop the daub type can be selected from simple, light rough, light dark, wide sharp, wide blurry and sparkle. → 4.212 ARTISTIC FILTERS

4.**294 Palette Knife filter** One of the more traditional Artistic filters, the Palette Knife filter simulates painting with a fine, narrow palette knife. For a more effective result the paint is sometimes applied very thinly so that a texture representing an underlying canvas is revealed. → 4.212 ARTISTIC FILTERS

4.**295 Patchwork filter** A Texture filter that creates an effect more like needlepoint embroidery or tapestry than patchwork. The image is broken into small squares, each of which adopts the most prominent colour of the underlying pixels. The

190

squares are given curved edges and are raised or lowered randomly in order to simulate highlights and shadows. → 4.283 MOSAIC FILTER; 4.337 TAPESTRY FILTER; 4.339 TEXTURE FILTERS

4.**296 Photocopy filter** Sketch filter. Creates the effect of old high-contrast photocopying. Dark areas are principally defined by their edges (with a sharp fall-off to white or the background colour within the borders). → 4.319 SKETCH FILTERS

4.**297 Pinch filter** Distort filter that squeezes or pulls an image. Depending on the actual filter, pinch effects can either be conducted 'live' on the image (squeezing or pulling the image edges) or can be controlled via settings – usually percentages – in a dialogue box. A squeeze of 100% pinches a selection towards its geometric centre; a squeeze (pull) of –100% balloons the selection outwards. → 4.245 DISTORT FILTERS

4.**298 pixelating filters** Group of filters that add or exaggerate pixelation (and pixelation-like effects) by grouping pixels into larger units of similar colour values. Typical **Pixelate filters** include Colour Halftone, Crystallize, Facet, Fragment, Mezzotint, Mosaic and Pointillize. → 4.233 CRYSTALLIZE FILTER; 4.257 FACET FILTER; 4.260 FRAGMENT FILTER; 4.268 HALFTONE FILTER; 4.281 MEZZOTINT FILTER; 4.283 MOSAIC FILTER; 4.301 POINTILLIZE FILTER

4.**299 Plaster filter** Sketch filter used to create embossed effect that is similar to the Notepaper filter but stronger and with different textures. The precise result will depend on the foreground and background colours. → 4.319 SKETCH FILTERS

4.**300 Plastic Wrap filter** Curious Artistic filter that gives an image the appearance of a three-dimensional image vacuum-packed in shiny plastic, emphasizing surface features. Similar to the Hot Wax Coating filter → 4.212 ARTISTIC FILTERS; 4.271 HOT WAX COATING FILTER

4.**301 Pointillize filter** Pixelation that emulates the effect made famous by the pointillist group of painters. The image is broken into random dots (of adjustable diameter) based on the colour of the underlying pixels. Gaps between the dots are filled with the background colour. → 4.298 PIXELATING FILTERS

4.**302 Polar Coordinates filter** Distort filter that converts an image's coordinates from conventional rectangular x–y axis to polar, and vice versa. The rectangular-to-polar conversion produces cylindrical anamorphoses – images that make no obvious logical sense until a mirrored cylinder is placed over the centre, when the image is displayed in conventional form again. → 4.245 DISTORT FILTERS

4.**303 Poster Edges filter** Artistic filter that first posterizes an image then emphasizes image edges with black lines. → 1.444 POSTERIZE; 4.212 ARTISTIC FILTERS

4.**304 Psychedelic filter** Alters the colours in an image to bright semi-fluorescent colours. A colour transform filter in Photo-Paint.

4.**305 Puzzle filter/jigsaw filter** Filter that divides the image into jigsaw puzzle-like pieces. Size and number of pieces can be set by the user. Some plug-in filter sets include such a filter, as do mainstream applications such as Photo-Paint.

4.**306 Radial Blur filter** Blur-type filter that can be used to create either **Spin** or **Zoom** blurs. The Spin option blurs around a central axis: the central point remains sharp while points around are blurred to concentric arcs (the degree of rotation can be specified). The Zoom option simulates a time exposure during which the zoom control is operated. The central point of the blur again remains sharp but points around are drawn into radial lines, which increase in length with distance from the image centre. There is an implication of movement to or from the camera along the axis of the lens. → 4.217 BLUR FILTERS; 4.285 MOTION BLUR FILTER

4.**307 Remove noise filter** Noise filter. Softens an image and reduces the speckling due to noise. Noise can be introduced when an image is scanned or captured. The filter works by averaging a pixel with its neighbours. Normally a threshold level is set and any pixel whose brightness level exceeds this is removed or set to a median value. → 4.287 NOISE FILTERS

4.**308 Render filters** Filters from this group can be used to render textures such as cloud effects, refraction patterns and even perform three-dimensional transformations. The group includes 3D Transform, Clouds, Difference Clouds, Lens Flare, Lighting Effects and Texture Fill. → 4.206 3D TRANSFORM FILTER; 4.225 CLOUDS FILTER; 4.239 DIFFERENCE CLOUDS FILTER; 4.275 LENS FLARE FILTER; 4.276 LIGHTING EFFECTS FILTER; 4.338 TEXTURE FILL FILTER

4.**309 Reticulation filter** A Sketch filter that can duplicate the 'wrinkled' effect that results when a conventional film emulsion is processed in chemicals at high temperature or can give the impression of crazed porcelain, depending on the degree of application. → 4.319 SKETCH FILTERS

4.**310 Ripple filter** Distort. Simulates random pond-like ripples. The Wave filter provides similar results but provides more control. → 4.245 DISTORT FILTERS; 4.351 WAVE FILTER

4.**311 Rough Pastels filter** Artistic filter that builds up the image from broad and roughly textured strokes of coloured pastels. A degree of underlying texture is usually allowed to appear through, especially in the darker areas. → 4.212 ARTISTIC FILTERS

4.**312 Salt and Pepper filter** A Paintshop Pro filter designed to remove fine black or white specks from an image due to dust. The filter identifies light or dark areas from the background and replaces them with an average of the background colour.

4.**313 Sepia filter** Filter that emulates a sepia camera filter, imparting a warm brown look to any underlying image. Images can be converted to greyscale and then lowered in contrast to create an antique sepia-toned effect.

4.**314 Sharpen Edges filter** This variation of the Sharpen filter determines 'edge points' where there are major changes in colour values, and sharpens them. Edges are thus sharpened but the remaining regions of the image are left in an unsharpened state. Similar to the Unsharp Mask filter, but less controllable. → 4.346 UNSHARP MASK FILTER

4.**315 Sharpen filter** Improves apparent focus in a selection. Works by identifying rapid changes in pixel values that indicate edges and emphasizing them. Colour and tone transitions are narrowed and hence appear sharper. → 4.316 SHARPEN FILTERS

4.**316 sharpen filters** Set of effects filters that create increased sharpness in the image. Though these filters are often used to 'focus' blurred images they do not in fact

4.293 *Paint Daubs filter*

4.294 *Palette Knife filter*

4.295 *Patchwork filter*

4.296 *Photocopy filter*

4.297 *Pinch filter – 'bloating'*

4.297 *Pinch filter – 'puckering'*

4.299 *Plaster filter*

4.300 *Plastic Wrap filter*

4.301 *Pointillize filter*

4.302 *Polar Coordinates filter*

4.302 *Polar Coordinates filter*

4.303 *Poster Edges filter*

4.304 *Psychedelic filter*

4.305 *Puzzle filter*

4.309 *Reticulation filter*

4.310 *Ripple filter*

4.311 *Rough Pastels filter*

4.313 *Sepia filter*

4.316 *sharpen filter (original picture)*

4.314 *Sharpen Edges filter*

4.315 *Sharpen filter*

193

4.317 *Sharpen More filter*

4.346 *Unsharp Mask filter*

4.318 *Shear filter*

focus, but rather increase the perception of sharpness. Even digital imaging cannot restore image detail that was not recorded at the time of exposure due to imprecise focus or camera shake. Sharpen filters include Sharpen, Sharpen More, Sharpen Edges and Unsharp Mask. ➜ 4.208 ADAPTIVE UNSHARP FILTER; 4.242 DIRECTIONAL SHARPEN FILTER; 4.314 SHARPEN EDGES FILTER; 4.315 SHARPEN FILTER; 4.317 SHARPEN MORE FILTER; 4.346 UNSHARP MASK FILTER

4.**317 Sharpen More filter** Applies a focusing-type effect more strongly than the basic Sharpen filter. It accentuates boundaries by making transitions more marked and narrower in effect. Like the corresponding Blur More filter, the Sharpen More filter in Photoshop offers sharpening two to four times greater than that of the Sharpen filter. ➜ 4.316 SHARPEN FILTERS

4.**318 Shear filter** Distortion filter. Creates a distortion along the path of a curved line that can be pulled or dragged using the dialogue box. The undistorted areas of the image can be filled with the original background image, wrapped around from other parts or filled with a 'stretched' image. ➜ 4.245 DISTORT FILTERS

4.**319 Sketch filters** A separate group of filters in Photoshop, though, due to their conceptual similarity, often included with Artistic filters. Sketch filters comprise a somewhat eclectic group, some of which give the effect of sketching media while others impart new textures to selections. They comprise Bas Relief, which creates three-dimensional effects, Chalk & Charcoal, Charcoal, Chrome, Conté Crayon, Graphic Pen, Halftone Screen, Note Paper, Photocopy, Plaster, Reticulation, Stamp, Torn Edges and Water Paper. ➜ 4.214 BAS RELIEF FILTER; 4.221 CHALK & CHARCOAL FILTER; 4.230 CONTÉ CRAYON FILTER; 4.268 HALFTONE FILTER; 4.299 PLASTER FILTER; 4.342 TORN EDGES FILTER; 4.349 WATER PAPER FILTER

4.**320 Smart Blur filter** An 'intelligent' blurring tool. By setting a blur radius (a pixel distance for pixels to be included in the blur), a threshold level (below which pixel values will not be blurred) and a blur quality, customized blurs become possible that appear more convincing than generally applied blurs. ➜ 4.217 BLUR FILTERS

4.**321 Smoked Glass filter** Effects filter that applies an overall tint to an image. Despite the name the tint can often be adjusted to almost any colour. ➜ 4.212 ARTISTIC FILTERS; 4.263 GLASS BLOCK FILTER

4.**322 Smooth filter** By reducing the differences between adjacent pixels, an image can be smoothed without unduly affecting the detail. Smooth filters come into their own on 'dithered' images, where an intermediate colour has been created from two adjacent tones. Applying the Smooth filter reduces the differences between dithered colours. ➜ 4.216 BLUR FILTER; 4.325 SOFTEN FILTER

4.**323 Smoothing filter** Filter that smooths the overall texture of an image while keeping the edge detail. Typical applications include the reproduction of maps and improving images of faces: skin blemishes can be suppressed while detail in the eyes and hair is retained. Offered in Paintshop Pro versions from 7.

4.**324 Smudge Stick filter** Artistic filter that uses short diagonal strokes to smudge the darker parts of the image. Lighter areas become brighter but tend to lose definition.

4.**325 Soften filter** A more gentle implementation of the Smooth filter. ➜ 4.322 SMOOTH FILTER

4.**326 Solarize filter** Emulation of the traditional photographic technique of solarization by an effects filter. The image and its negative are combined, simulating a semireversal process due to exposure of film to light during processing. In some applications this is considered a stylized filter type (such as in Photoshop) whereas applications like Photo-Paint regard it as a colour transform filter. ➜ 4.335 STYLIZE FILTERS

4.**327 solarize/solarization** An effect involving the 'simplification' of colour differences. Subtle changes in colour become flat tones, or are replaced by different colours. Photoshop features a Solarize filter (one of the Stylize group) but in many image editors it is considered a feature rather than an effects filter. ➜ 1.444 POSTERIZE

4.**328 Spatter filter** A Brush Strokes group filter in Photoshop, a Texture filter in some other applications. Simulates an airbrush with a minor blockage or poor aerosol dispersal. Effects can vary from a mildly grainy finish through to abstract. Using extreme settings with this filter a pseudo pointillism effect can be achieved. → 4.219 BRUSH STROKES FILTERS

4.**329 Spherize filter** A Distortion filter that wraps the image over a curved surface that can be spherical (concave or convex) or cylindrical (horizontal or vertical). Similar to the Map to Object filter in Photo-Paint. → 4.245 DISTORT FILTERS; 4.278 MAP TO OBJECT FILTER

4.**330 Spiky Halo** Deformation filter found in Paintshop Pro that can be used to produce radial patterns of waves.

4.**331 Sponge filter** Artistic filter that should not be confused in action or effect with the saturate/desaturate Sponge tool. The Sponge filter creates a highly textured image that appears to have been painted using colour dabs applied with a natural sponge. → 4.212 ARTISTIC FILTERS

4.**332 Sprayed Strokes filter** A Brush Strokes filter that repaints the image using angled sprayed strokes in a limited palette of colours based on the dominant colours in the image. → 4.219 BRUSH STROKES FILTERS

4.**333 Stained Glass filter** A Texture filter that converts the image to a series of cells that take their colour from the predominant colour of the pixels enclosed. Each cell is then outlined in 'lead' using the foreground colour. → 4.339 TEXTURE FILTERS

4.**334 Stamp filter** Sketch filter that turns any image into a black-and-white-only (or foreground and background colour only) image that resembles a decorator's woodcut or **linocut stamp**. Most effective when used with simple images. → 4.319 SKETCH FILTERS

4.**335 Stylize filters** Set of filters that, when used directly (rather than selectively or with transparency), create graphic image results. Filters in this group include Diffuse, Emboss, Extrude, Find Edges, Glowing Edges, Solarize, Tiles, Trace Contour and Wind. → 4.240 DIFFUSE FILTER; 4.254 EMBOSS FILTER; 4.256 EXTRUDE FILTER; 4.259 FIND EDGES FILTER; 4.326 SOLARIZE FILTER; 4.343 TRACE CONTOUR FILTER; 4.353 WIND FILTER

4.**336 Sumi-e filter** Brush Strokes filter found in Photoshop and some third party plug-in filter sets. Replicates the Japanese technique of using a fully loaded chisel-tipped brush on rice paper. Delivers deep blacks with soft edges. → 4.219 BRUSH STROKES FILTERS

4.**337 Tapestry filter** Emulates the look of needlepoint tapestry by breaking the image into close-packed squares that can be altered in size through the filter dialogue. A softer version of the Mosaic filter. A similar Patchwork filter is offered in some packages. → 4.283 MOSAIC FILTER; 4.295 PATCHWORK FILTER

4.**338 Texture Fill filter** A Render filter that fills the selection with texture provided from a separate greyscale texture file. Using this filter automatically prompts you to locate the required texture file.

4.**339 Texture filters** Filters that impart or create textures. In Photoshop they include Craquelure, Grain, Mosaic Tiles, Patchwork, Stained Glass and the freeform Texturizer. → 4.231 CRAQUELURE FILTER; 4.266 GRAIN FILTER; 4.284 MOSAIC TILES FILTER; 4.295 PATCHWORK FILTER; 4.333 STAINED GLASS FILTER; 4.340 TEXTURIZER FILTER

4.**340 Texturizer filter** Texture-creating filter that applies one of four standard textures (stone, burlap, brick or canvas) at a variable scale and relief. You can also load your own texture which can then be similarly adjusted and applied. → 4.339 TEXTURE FILTERS

4.**341 Tiles filter** A Stylize filter in which the image is broken into tiles, each of which is then moved slightly (and randomly) from its original position. The space between the tiles can be filled with foreground or background colours, the original image, or its inverse. Similar in appearance to a basic **Hockney 'joiner' picture**. → 4.335 STYLIZE FILTERS

4.**342 Torn Edges filter** Sketch filter that first reduces an image to only foreground and background tones, and then represents the image elements as roughly torn pieces of paper. Works best with simple images.. → 4.319 SKETCH FILTERS

4.**343 Trace Contour filter** Stylize filter that produces a polychromatic contour map by analysing brightness changes in the image and drawing thin lines for each colour channel. The result is a **polychromatic contour map**. → 4.335 STYLIZE FILTERS

4.**344 Twirl filter** Distortion filter that twists a selection about a central axis.

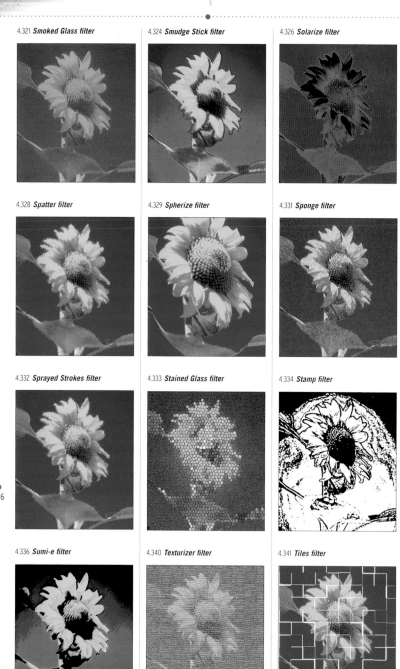

4.321 *Smoked Glass filter*

4.324 *Smudge Stick filter*

4.326 *Solarize filter*

4.328 *Spatter filter*

4.329 *Spherize filter*

4.331 *Sponge filter*

4.332 *Sprayed Strokes filter*

4.333 *Stained Glass filter*

4.334 *Stamp filter*

4.336 *Sumi-e filter*

4.340 *Texturizer filter*

4.341 *Tiles filter*

4.342 *Torn Edges filter*

4.343 *Trace Contour filter*

4.344 *Twirl filter*

4.345 *Underpainting filter*

4.348 *Vignette filter*

4.349 *Water Paper filter*

4.350 *Watercolour filter*

4.351 *Wave filter*

4.352 *Wet edges filter*

197

4.353 *Wind filter*

4.353 *Wind (Stagger) filter*

4.354 *Zigzag filter*

The selection edges are fixed, so the result is an image that coils progressively more tightly around its centre. → 4.245 DISTORT FILTERS

4.**345 Underpainting filter** An Artistic filter that gives the effect of an image painted on both surfaces of textured glass, where the textured surface is the lower, the plane surface uppermost. A textured image is therefore seen through a translucent top 'flat' image. → 4.212 ARTISTIC FILTERS

4.**346 Unsharp Mask filter** One of the most potent Sharpening filters, Unsharp Mask can sharpen edges whose definition has been softened by scanning, resampling or resizing. Differing adjacent pixels are identified and the contrast between them increased. The Unsharp Mask uses three control parameters: **Amount**, **Radius** and **Threshold**. Amount determines the amount of contrast added to boundary (edge) pixels. Radius describes the number of pixels adjacent to that boundary that are affected by the sharpening and Threshold sets a minimum value for pixel contrast below which the filter will have no effect. Once mastered it is a powerful filter and can achieve more subtle, but more effective, results than any other normal sharpening filter. → 1.486 UNSHARP MASKING (USM); 4.316 SHARPEN FILTERS

4.**347 Video filters** Specialized filters designed for video-based work. In Photoshop, these filters include Deinterlace and NTSC Colors. → 4.236 DEINTERLACE FILTER; 4.289 NTSC COLORS FILTER

4.**348 Vignette filter** Effects filter that creates a vignette around an image. Vignettes can be oval, rectangular (or any freehand shape), with soft or hard edge. In many ways this is a 'quick fix' rather than a filter as it performs a series of actions within a single dialogue box. → 4.253 EFFECTS FILTERS

4.**349 Water Paper filter** A Sketch filter which reduces the image to paint daubs laid on damp paper. The 'paint' bleeds along the grain of the paper to give a soft image with a faint grid pattern that tends to make it look like a hazy tapestry. → 4.319 SKETCH FILTERS

4.**350 Watercolour filter** Traditional Artistic filter that converts the image to look like a soft, watery watercolour painted onto a lightly textured heavyweight paper. The edges of discrete coloured areas are increased in colour saturation to simulate wet edges typical of this technique. → 4.212 ARTISTIC FILTERS

4.**351 Wave filter** Version of the Ripple Distortion filter that features customizable controls. Using 'wave generators', ripples are created. The number of wave generators can be specified, as can wavelength and wave height. Though waves are conventionally sinusoidal, i.e., following the shape of a sine curve, they can also be triangular or square. → 4.245 DISTORT FILTERS

4.**352 wet edges** A painting effect used with some effects (such as the Watercolour filter) that makes the edges of the painted area more dense, giving the impression that it has been painted with watery paint.

4.**353 Wind filter** A Stylize filter that gives a 'cartoon' wind effect by drawing out the left or right edges of the image as short horizontal strokes. In Photoshop, a Blast option provides a stronger effect, while the Stagger option offsets the wind slightly. → 4.335 STYLIZE FILTERS

4.**354 Zigzag filter** Distortion filter that produces radial distortions in the manner of pebble-in-the-pond ripples, but with more flexibility, control and customization options. → 4.245 DISTORT FILTERS

Plug-ins

4.**355 Alien Skin** Manufacturer of Photoshop plug-in sets. The original filter set, the Mac-based 'Black Box', was followed by the highly regarded Eye Candy. The latter has been updated to Eye Candy 4000 and the set has been augmented by the parallel Xenofex set. Alien Skin filters have a common characteristic interface look that features an extensive range of controls. Most useful of these is 'Random Seed' that virtually ensures uniqueness in the application of many of the filters. → 4.359 EYE CANDY; 4.376 XENOFEX

4.**356 Andromeda** Creator of Photoshop plug-in filter sets, generally quite extreme in nature, such as **Mezzo Line-Screen** which transforms images to black and white mezzo line art, **Rainbow (spectral effects)** and **Velocity** (multiple ghosting, highlight smears, fade-out effects). → 4.374 PLUG-IN

4.**357 Auto F/X** Creator of plug-ins mainly (but not exclusively) dedicated to edge effects and frames. **Photo/Graphic Edges** add traditional or contemporary frames to digital images while **Photo/Graphic Patterns** produce background textures.

4.**358 Extensis** Creator of image filter and other Photoshop compatible plug-ins. Principal products include the intelligent enhancement tool Intellihance, Intellihance Pro and PhotoTools, and which add extra functionality to the Photoshop interface. Some Extensis plug-ins are provided in Adobe Photodeluxe.
→ 4.364 INTELLIHANCE PRO; 4.368 MASK PRO; 4.370 PHOTOFRAME; 4.373 PHOTOTOOLS; 4.374 PLUG-IN

4.**359 Eye Candy** First major release of effects filters from Alien Skin software following their **Black Box** product. Now revised and known as **Eye Candy 4000** it features many of the 'classic' original filters along with some newcomers. Eye Candy filters – like all Alien Skin offerings – feature extensive controls to make effects as authentic or outlandish as required. Notable Eye Candy filters include **Antimatter** (creates an image negative but preserves the luminosity values of the original), **Fire** (produces realistic flame effects) and **Water Drops**. The latter can be used to deliver convincing dew drops. Eye Candy effects are also available for creating video effects (**Eye Candy for After Effects**). After Effects is Adobe's digital video effects package.

4.**360 Genuine Fractals** Plug-in for Photoshop designed to speed up operations by allowing medium-sized files to be edited but for a corresponding large file to be used for final output. Uses fractal mathematical techniques to extrapolate the results from one resolution to another.

4.**361 Genuine Fractals Print Pro** Photoshop plug-in that can encode CMYK, RGB, CIE L*a*b*, Multichannel and Greyscale images as scaleable files. An encoded file is small enough to edit easily using small to medium amounts of RAM memory (and other system resources) but can be scaled up to provide high quality output at large sizes.

4.**362 ImagePort** A plug-in or extension for page-layout program QuarkXPress that enables users of this program to import native Photoshop files directly into Quark documents without losing the layer, channel and path features. This overcomes the need to 'flatten' an image (which loses the layer and associated information) and lets the user manipulate the layers, channels and paths from within the program. → 4.392 QUARKXPRESS

4.**363 ImageWorks/PDF ImageWorks** Plug-in for Adobe Acrobat (full application, rather than the Reader) that permits manipulation of PDF images. Import, move, resize, rotate, extract, and move forwards/backwards are among the manipulations featured. Further enhancement – colour space conversions, downsampling and defect removal – is also possible. → 4.377 ACROBAT

4.359 *Eye Candy*

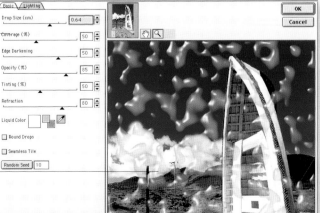

1 *Lighting type selection*
2 *Filter parameters*
3 *Image preview*

4.**364 Intellihance Pro** A Photoshop plug-in from Extensis designed for performing rapid image and colour corrections. Intellihance Pro analyses the image to determine the optimal corrections, but also provides a range of fine-tuned variations from which the user can select. Up to 25 different variations (using multiple corrective parameters) can be viewed at one time. Later versions of Photoshop include the Variations command that, in some respects, is similar to some of Intellihance Pro's functionality. → 4.182 VARIATIONS; 4.358 EXTENSIS

4.**365 Julia Set Explorer** Plug-in filter set also known as **Fractal Explorer** and supplied as part of the plug-in set with Photo-Paint. Compliant with the Photoshop plug-in architecture, it lets the user explore Julia Set fractal patterns and create intriguing patterns based on these both as given and mixed with the user's own images. Built by a team that includes Kai Krause (PhotoSoap, PowerGoo) it includes an early version of his fluid interface, offering idiosyncratic controls and an extremely large number of options. → 4.361 GENUINE FRACTALS PRINT PRO

4.**366 Kai's Power Tools (KPT)** Set of Photoshop plug-in effects filters that can also be used with other image-editing applications that accept Photoshop-compatible plug-ins. Originally created by Kai Krause for MetaCreations, KPT filters are characterized by unique, organic dialogue box interfaces that are similar in their look and fluid operation to Kai's PhotoSoap.

KPT filters tend to range from the subtle through to the extremely odd. A number of the most recent offerings (KPT5 and KPT6) rely on fractal algorithms for effect generation. → 4.374 PLUG-IN

4.**367 Knockout** Advanced masking plug-in that both speeds up mask creation and renders more accurate results. Useful for isolating and masking elements with difficult edges such as hair, smoke and shadows. Formerly known as **Ultimatte Knockout**.

4.**368 Mask Pro** Masking plug-in for Photoshop from Extensis. Designed to make the action of image masking simpler. Mask Pro achieves this with advanced edge-detection techniques to help create perfect edges to masks and edge blending to prevent many of the usual disruptive artefacts that adversely affect masks.

4.**369 Paint Alchemy** Set of Photoshop plug-in filter effects from software house Xaos. The principal filters convert photographic images into painterly effects using tools analogous to painting styles such as Pencil, Impressionist and Pastel. These effects score highly on the degree of control offered, and many are quite unique without being overtly gimmicky.

4.**370 PhotoFrame** Interactive Photoshop plug-in for creating edge and border effects. Along with an extensive range of presets, **Instant Edge** and **Instant Frame builder** functions aid in the creation of unique custom effects. → 4.358 EXTENSIS

4.**371 PhotoGraphics** Photoshop plug-in set from Extensis that adds graphics illustration

4.366 *Kai's Power Tools (KPT)*

1 *Image preview*
2 *Brush controls*
3 *Lighting controls*

tools to the Photoshop palette. Vector shapes can be created and manipulated from within the host application. Some of the most used features, such as text manipulations and vector shapes, became somewhat redundant with the arrival of Photoshop 6; coupled with compatibility problems with Mac OS 9.1, and later versions, has meant this product is not undergoing any further development.
→ 4.358 EXTENSIS

4.372 **Photolab** Plug-in set included with Photo-Paint (most versions) and compatible with Photoshop. Includes filters that sport conventional interfaces like **Gradtone** (adds or replaces colours based on the luminance of the image), **HueSlider** (slides an image towards a target hue colour), **MonoChrome** (converts image into a coloured monochrome image) and Levels (adjusts levels to make them more like that of a 'normal' image). Photolab filters tend to be among the less extreme and include many useful features.

4.373 **PhotoTools** Suite of plug-ins from Extensis enabling many additional filter effects to be added to Photoshop. These do, however, lean towards the needs of graphics and web graphics designers rather than the pure photographer. Effects like **PhotoTexture** permit infinitely variable textures to be created; others enable special effects for web graphics buttons and shadows. → 4.358 EXTENSIS

4.374 **plug-in** Small software module designed to integrate with a larger application. The plug-in blends seamlessly with the host, delivering new or enhanced functionality. Plug-ins are common in image-editing and page-layout applications for such things as special effects filters. They are also common in web browsers. Many third-parties now provide filter plug-ins for image editors that, in general, adopt the architecture for integration created for adding plug-ins to Photoshop. When effects filter plug-ins (or plug-in sets) are added to a host program, they can be accessed from the Filter or Effects menu, just as one of the basic filter sets. Plug-ins are not limited to effects filters. Some scanner manufacturers, for example, provide plug-ins to make image acquisition more effective and to enable their scanner to work from within an image-editing application. Note that although most plug-ins are Photoshop compatible, and many alternate applications describe themselves as accepting Photoshop plug-ins, some plug-ins are Photoshop specific and will not operate with other products. It is essential to check compatibility before purchase.

4.375 **Xaos Tools** Manufacturer of the popular Photoshop plug-in filter set, Paint Alchemy. Xaos also produces **TypeCaster** (a plug-in that turns text in Photoshop into 3D features) and **Terrazzo**, a plug-in that converts image segments into symmetrical tiles for use in backgrounds. **Segmentation** converts Photoshop images into vector-based line art. Xaos also produces

4.376 *Xenofex*

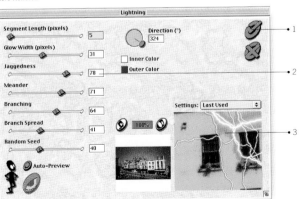

1 Apply button
2 Effect adjustment parameters
3 Image preview (zoomed)

products for the Silicon Graphics Irix system such as Pandemonium, an image-processing engine, and title creating tool, nTitle. → 4.369 PAINT ALCHEMY

4.**376 Xenofex** Set of Photoshop-compatible plug-in effects filters that also work with other image-editing applications. Created by Alien Skin Software (who had earlier produced the regarded Eye Candy filter set), the Xenofex suite includes filters such as Lightning (adds convincing bolts of lightning to an image), **Baked Earth** (a crazed surface texture), **Flag** (distort-type filter) and **Puzzle** (a jigsaw-creating effect) among the collection of 17 filters.

Graphics and associated terms

4.**377 Acrobat** An Adobe application for producing documents that can subsequently be viewed on any computer or computing platform that is equipped with the Acrobat Reader software, irrespective of the operating system or font availability. Files created by Acrobat are called PDF files (portable document format). Documents can include text, images and graphics. Fonts not supported by the host computer can also be reproduced. Plug-ins are available that permit limited (but useful) image manipulations to be performed upon PDF images from within Acrobat. → 4.363 IMAGEWORKS/PDF IMAGEWORKS; 4.374 PLUG-IN

4.**378 Adobe Type Manager (ATM)** Utility software that (transparently to the user) improves the display of font characters onscreen. The Deluxe version of ATM also assists in font management, making it easy to organize PostScript® Type 1, OpenType®, and TrueType fonts in ways that will help workflow. It enables fonts (or groups of fonts) to be activated and deactivated when they are needed. → 4.395 ANTIALIASING

4.**379 Canoma** Application originally from MetaCreations (Bryce, PhotoSoap, PowerGoo) that can transform perspective and viewing positions of ordinary images. The image is modelled in 3D using preformed templates after which the perspective relative to these elements is changed; changes are reflected in the image which is recompiled for this new viewpoint.

4.**380 Canto Cumulus** Cataloguing software from the German Canto company that provides image and media storage and cataloguing. Versions of **Cumulus** are included in some CorelDRAW! editions.

4.**381 CompuPic** CompuPic for Linux is a digital media-management program that is often run in parallel with the GIMP. As well as being able to manage most file formats (including those of font, video and sound resources) CompuPic also features limited image-editing capabilities. CompuPic is produced by **Photodex**. → 4.005 GIMP/ THE GIMP

4.**382 Digimarc** Proprietary plug-in that permits the digital watermarking of images. → 4.184 WATERMARK

4.384 *Illustrator*

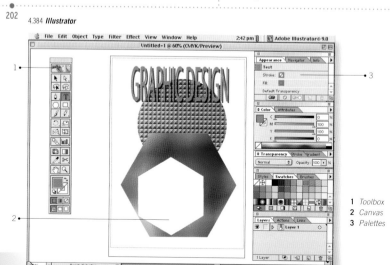

1 *Toolbox*
2 *Canvas*
3 *Palettes*

4.**383 Flash (Macromedia)** A vector-based graphics package that can combine bitmap images, audio and animation with interactive features in order to create effective websites and web features. Features created using Flash, delivered over the Internet, can be viewed by anyone with a Flash player. This can be downloaded from the Macromedia website free of charge.

4.**384 Illustrator** Adobe's vector-based graphics program. It shares many elements of its interface with Photoshop and many items (images, clipping paths) can be moved between the two applications. → 4.022 PHOTOSHOP

4.**385 InDesign** A powerful desktop publishing and page-layout program from Adobe, designed as a competitor for the long-established QuarkXPress package. Using a similar structure and common interface elements to other Adobe products (especially Photoshop and Illustrator), it provides for very tight integration with these for publishing projects.

4.**386 PageMaker** A page-layout and desktop publishing program from Adobe. The program was originally created by Aldus but came under the Adobe umbrella following that company's acquisition of **Aldus**. The appearance and widespread adoption of Adobe's InDesign has pushed PageMaker somewhat into the background. → 4.385 INDESIGN

4.**387 PhotoRecall** Image cataloguing, album creating and image-editing application from **G & A Software**. The product uses very literal and graphic methods to display albums and catalogues. Though the application is very effective, the interface may not give the professional appearance serious users expect. Image-editing tools are also effective, if a little less than comprehensive.

4.**388 Pixology Piccolo** An image-management application that, in version 2, has flourished and developed into a complete digital-imaging resource for the consumer market. Users can easily view, manage and edit digital pictures and have the option to transform them into professionally printed glossy photos via Internet links to certain qualified photofinishers. Pixology's Piccolo software also provides the software used in online photo-printing services for many well-known operators.

4.**389 Portfolio** Image-management software (**'Media Asset Management'**) from Extensis. Advanced and powerful software application for cataloguing, databasing and retrieving images. The current version is available as a stand-alone version (Desktop Edition) designed for the single user needing to locate and preview digital files, and a Network Edition for distributed use (also available as the more powerful Server Edition). → 4.358 EXTENSIS

4.**390 Premiere** Adobe's video-editing program, designed for desktop digital-video editing and for creating video (including streaming video) for the web.

4.385 *InDesign*

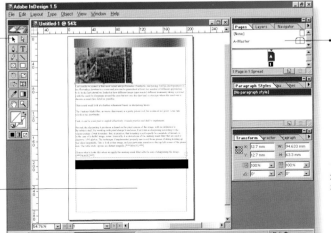

1 *Toolbox*
2 *Document*
3 *Palettes*

4.**391 Presto Photo Album** Low-cost consumer-level digital image album-creating application. Users can create multiple albums and personalize them appropriately by adding image borders, page backgrounds, etc. Organizational tools help users keep track of their images. Other options include an email feature that enables a completed album to be emailed to friends and family.

4.**392 QuarkXPress** Industry-standard publishing tool that provides advanced page-layout features in an architecture that, like Photoshop, offers users the opportunity to add plug-ins to extend and enhance the basic functionality. QuarkXPress Passport extends the basic QuarkXPress program into a multilanguage publishing tool. Pertinent plug-ins permit image files to be imported into QuarkXPress and, in some cases, retain image information such as layers, channels and paths.
→ 4.362 IMAGEPORT

4.**393 QuickTime** Name of Mac OS and Windows application for viewing image, movie or sound files. Used extensively for distributing such media via CD-ROM and the Internet. A 'Pro' version permits transforming a DV movie into a QuickTime movie and back for use in Apple's iMovie (DV movie editing application) for example. QuickTime features automatic compression and decompression of image files. → 3.092 CODEC

Common image manipulation terms

4.**394 aliasing** The jagged appearance of lines and edges in bitmapped images (particularly when curved or crossing the image diagonally) due to the square pixels making up the image becoming visible to the eye. Sometimes called 'jaggies', 'staircasing' or 'stairstepping'. The effect is often visible with on-screen fonts. The effect can be reduced by using antialiasing techniques. → 4.395 ANTIALIASING

4.**395 antialiasing** A technique that eliminates or reduces the visibility of lines and edges in an image that take on a jagged appearance due to the screen resolution. This is achieved by blending the colour at the edges of the object with the background colour by averaging the density of the range of pixels involved. The aliasing on fonts can be reduced by using such utilities as Adobe Type Manager. → 4.394 ALIASING; 4.399 BITMAP

4.**396 area process** Processing groups of pixels in an image rather than individual pixels. Image-editing techniques are almost all area-processing techniques. Also known as '**neighbourhood processing**'.

4.**397 aspect ratio** The ratio of the width of an image to its height, expressed as x:y. For example, the aspect ratio of an image measuring 200 x 100 pixels is 2:1. The aspect ratio of 35 mm full-frame shots is 3:2 – 36 x 24 mm. Conventional television pictures have the ratio 3:4 while widescreen television (and the HDTV

4.389 *Portfolio*

1 Database records
2 Keywords applied to selected image
3 Details of selected record

Advanced Photo System format) aspect ratio is 16:9.

4.**398 bicubic interpolation** When an image is resampled (for example, to change its size or resolution), and new pixels are created, Photoshop uses interpolation to determine the colour values for these newcomers. It does this by judging the colours of the neighbouring pixels and applying an interpolation algorithm. Bicubic interpolation gives the highest quality result, with the best tonal gradations. The penalty is that it is the slowest method. Use bicubic interpolation when quality is paramount, and bilinear or nearest neighbour when speed is more important.

4.**399 bitmap** A description of graphics displayed on a computer monitor where that display is pixel-based. → 2.429 BIT; 7.005 BINARY; 7.060 PIXEL

4.**400 clip art/clip media** Media specifically designed for incorporating in other documents for illustrative purposes. Originally these comprised diagrams, graphics or photographs for adding to desktop publishing documents, but today clip media can include sound clips and movies designed for adding effects or visuals to home videos. Clip art is conventionally delivered in three formats. Paper delivery, where the artwork is designed to be cut and pasted onto a layout, is becoming less common. Instead CD-ROM or web delivery is becoming more favoured, both for the range offered and the immediacy (particularly via web

delivery). The quality of clip art collections can vary enormously from crude graphics through to high quality, professional artwork and imaging. The licensing requirements for use also vary, and it is important to check these against your intended use before purchasing. Though clip art collections are often referred to as being 'copyright-free', this merely grants you the licence to use the images without payment of further fees. This is a bit of a misnomer and care should be exercised over your subsequent use of the images. Similarly, '**royalty free**' means no further royalties are required to be paid for future use, but this use may be restricted to personal or non-commercial use. → 4.401 COPYRIGHT-FREE; 4.412 IMAGE RESOURCE

4.**401 copyright-free** An ambiguous term used to describe image or media resources such as clip art. Despite the term, this does not usually give the purchaser the right to unlimited further use of the product: it is only the licence to use these products that is granted by purchase. The precise scope of this should be checked before purchase; violation of the terms of the licence, even unintentionally, can render the user liable to prosecution. → 4.400 CLIP ART/CLIP MEDIA; 4.412 IMAGE RESOURCE; 7.011 COPYRIGHT

4.**402 destination image** An image to which elements of a source image are to be copied. Conventionally in image-editing applications, both images can be opened and displayed on the desktop.

205

4.390 *Premiere*

1 *Project palette*
2 *Timeline*
3 *Video and audio tracks*
4 *Transitions palette*
5 *Movie window*

A destination image may have more than one corresponding source image. → 4.433 SOURCE IMAGE

4.**403 digital image** Image converted to (or created in) the digital domain. Elements of the image are represented by pixels with discrete colour and brightness values. → 7.018 DIGITAL DOMAIN

4.**404 dithering** An interpolation technique that calculates average values of adjacent pixels. The technique is used to add pixels (for example, to create smoother edges using antialiasing) or to reduce the number of colours. In the latter case the removed colours are replaced with those of average value that match those of a predetermined palette of colours. A 24-bit colour image could be resampled to a 256 colour image in which case a dithered palette of intermediate colours will 'fill' the remaining colours. → 4.413 INTERPOLATION

4.**405 downsampling** The reduction in resolution of a digital image. Samples (measures of pixel characteristics) are made over groups of pixels which are then merged to comprise the pixels of the smaller image. → 4.427 RESAMPLE

4.**406 downsize** The reduction in size of an image usually by reducing the resolution by downsampling. → 4.405 DOWNSAMPLING

4.**407 electronic image** Any image that is created electronically, but a term usually reserved for the image formed on an electronic viewfinder such as those of some video cameras. → 4.403 DIGITAL IMAGE

4.**408 gamma** A measure of contrast in a digital image, photographic film or paper. When referring to a monitor, gamma describes the way colour and light are displayed, e.g., brightness level and contrast. → 4.409 GAMMA CORRECTION

4.**409 gamma correction** The adjustment by compressing or expanding the range of the midtones of an image. On a monitor, gamma correction involves adjusting the highlight, midtone and shadow values in the curve dialogue box. The result is a change in the image contrast. Sometimes known as tone correction. → 4.408 GAMMA

4.**410 global change** An image manipulation or colour change applied to an entire image rather than a selection.

4.**411 image resolution** The degree of definition (or clarity) at which an image is either reproduced or displayed. → 1.525 RESOLUTION

4.**412 image resource** Any resource of images that can be external (such as royalty-free image libraries, clip art and those distributed digitally on various media such as CD-ROM and the Web) or 'internal', a photographer's own collection of available images. → 4.400 CLIP ART/CLIP MEDIA; 7.035 IMAGE LIBRARY

4.**413 interpolation** A computer calculation used to estimate unknown values which fall between known values. This process is used, for example, to redefine pixels in bitmapped images after they have been modified in some way, such as when an image is resized (called 'resampling'), rotated or if colour corrections have been made. In such cases, the program makes estimates from the known values of other pixels lying in the same or similar ranges. Interpolation is also used by some scanning and image-manipulation software to enhance the resolution of images that have been scanned at low resolution. However, interpolation merely creates new pixels based on an average of those either side and hence no new detail is added. It is always preferable to scan at the highest possible optical resolution. The insertion of animation values between two keyframes of a movie sequence also involves interpolation. Some applications allow you to choose an interpolation method – Photoshop, for example, offers '**Nearest Neighbor**' for fast but imprecise results that may produce jagged effects, '**Bilinear**' for medium-quality results, and '**Bicubic**' for smooth and precise results, but with slower performance. → 4.404 DITHERING; 4.427 RESAMPLE; 5.049 DESCREEN(ING)

4.**414 IT8 Calibration** Calibration process for scanners that involves using a specially supplied transparency (the **IT8 compliant target**) that, combined with the calibration software, can help produce scans of very high colour accuracy. → 4.415 IT8 TARGET

4.**415 IT8 Target** Target images used to calibrate scanners (and some other colour imaging devices). Normally transparencies (though print versions are also available), IT8 targets are high quality photographic images that include a set of colour patches that conform to international colour

standards CIE L*a*b*. → 4.414 IT8
CALIBRATION; 4.489 COLOUR SPACE

4.**416 joiner** Image composed of two or
more images with common elements.
Most commonly used in panoramic
photography where separate views of the
panorama are digitally combined by
identifying and blending common features
at adjacent edges.

4.**417 kernel** A group of pixels (usually a
square of odd-numbered pixels) to which
image manipulations are applied. → 4.396
AREA PROCESS

4.**418 library** A feature of some applications
which provides a facility for storing
frequently used items or attributes (such
as colours) that you have created so that
you can access them immediately from
within any document.

4.**419 morphing** Image-manipulating technique
that enables one image object to 'evolve'
seamlessly into another that is often quite
different. The effect is achieved by
mapping points between the before
and after objects and animating the
positional changes.

4.**420 multiple selected items** The selection of
two or more items so that they can be
modified (or moved) as one. Using a
selection tool, other areas of the image
(such as those of equal colour) can be
added to create a multiple selection.
→ 1.212 GROUP

4.**421 noise** The undesirable fluctuations or
interference that usually affects the whole
image, reducing detail representation and

giving an effect similar to film grain.
Small amounts of noise can be artificially
added to images for creative and
compositional purposes using relevant
noise (or grain) filters.

4.**422 online image editing** Some websites offer
image-editing facilities. In order to edit an
image using such a site it is necessary to
first upload an image to the editing site
(there is often a limit to the file size, which
may be as low as 250 kilobytes and there
is usually a restriction of the file types
accepted, GIF being the most widely
accepted, closely followed by JPEG). Once
the image is at the website, manipulations
can be performed. These are often in a
more prescribed way than is possible with
conventional image-editing applications –
for example, cropping may have to be
performed using image coordinates rather
than dragging a selection. Online editing is
designed more for creating images and
image-based graphics for websites than as
an alternative to conventional editing, but
online editors are a useful facility for when
'caught short' without your favoured
application available.

4.**423 picture skew** The distortion of an image
by slanting the two opposite sides of a
rectangle away from the horizontal or
vertical. Commands and options for
various (and multiple) skews are provided
in image editors as basic commands or
plug-in effects filters. → 7.057 PERSPECTIVE

4.**424 pixelation/pixelization** An image that has,
either intentionally or otherwise, been

4.394 *aliasing*

207

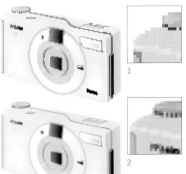

1 Aliasing
2 Anti-aliasing

4.421 *noise*

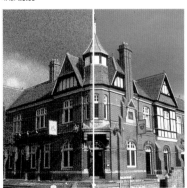

With noise   Without noise

broken up into square blocks that look like oversized pixels, giving it a 'digitized' look. Can be done for deliberate creative reasons. The effect is used occasionally on television or still images to selectively hide the identity of a person featured in a photo without rendering the remainder of the image distorted. → 4.394 ALIASING

4.**425 render** Wrapping a surface texture over a three-dimensional body created as a 'wire frame'. Typically used to create realistic landscapes or turn wire-frame figures into 'characters'. The wrapping is usually combined with other effects (such as lighting effects) to increase the realism. Render filters create effects such as clouds and lighting effects. → 4.308 RENDER FILTERS

4.**426 replication** A technique used when an image is enlarged by resampling, but specifically when the resolution is being increased by factors of two in each direction. Rather than being interpolated, new, identical pixels that are added take on the exact colour and brightness values of their neighbours.

4.**427 resample** Altering an image by modifying the number of pixels to either increase or decrease its resolution. Increasing the number of pixels is called 'resampling up', while reducing the number is called 'resampling down' or 'downsampling'. Resampling does not just involve adding (or removing) pixels but rather 'redrawing' the image over a new pattern of pixels (for example, a matrix of 10 by 10 pixels can

be replaced by a resampled array of 11 by 11). → 4.404 DITHERING; 4.413 INTERPOLATION

4.**428 rescale** Amending the size of an image by proportionally reducing its height and its width.

4.**429 restore (revert)** To restore something to its original state or, in the case of a document, to its last 'saved' version. Also called 'revert'. In the case of image editing, restore generally refers to 'undoing' all edits since the image was last saved.

4.**430 Rubylith** Proprietary name for a widely used type of peelable masking film used for film make-up. Due to its colour it is opaque to the UV light used to expose the film. The red colour applied when using masks in image-editing applications is sometimes colloquially referred to as a rubylith. → 4.119 MASK

4.**431 scanned image** An image that has been recorded by a scanner and converted to a suitable form for reproduction, such as film or a digital file. → 2.480 SCAN(NING)

4.**432 smoothing** The refinement of bitmapped images and text by a technique called 'antialiasing' (adding pixels of an 'in between' tone). Smoothing is also used in some drawing and 3D applications, where it is applied to a path to smooth a line, or to 'polygons' to tweak resolution in the final render. → 4.395 ANTIALIASING

4.**433 source image** An image from which image elements, selections or pixels are to be copied, usually to a destination image. → 4.402 DESTINATION IMAGE

4.424 *pixelation/pixelization*

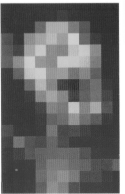

4.435 *thumbnail*

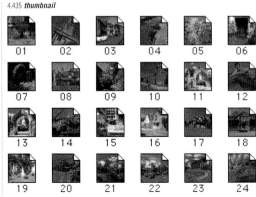

4.**434 spatial frequency** The brightness value in a digital image. Where there are large changes between adjacent (or near-adjacent) pixels there is a high spatial frequency, while more gentle changes give low spatial frequencies. Band pass filters can remove or reduce (attenuate) selected spatial frequencies. Using a low pass filter, for example, smooths away fine detail and forms the basis for Blur and Dust & Scratches type filters.

4.**435 thumbnail** A small representation of an image used mainly for identification purposes in image directory listing or, within image-editor palettes, for illustrating channels and layers. Thumbnail print displays are also produced to accompany PictureCDs, PhotoCDs and most APS and 35 mm films submitted for processing.

4.**436 transpose/transposition** To exchange the position of any two images, either by design or because they are in the wrong order. For example, image layers may be transposed when a lower layer and higher one are positionally reversed. Animation cells can be transposed in a similar way.

Colour models

4.**437 Adaptive colour** The adaptive palette in the indexed colour mode, which allows you to select the number of colours (relating to bit depth) for the image.
→ 2.272 BIT DEPTH; 4.452 INDEXED COLOUR

4.**438 additive colours** Colour model describing the primary colours of transmitted light: red, green and blue (RGB). Additive colours can be mixed to form all other colours in photographic reproduction and computer display monitors, but the alternate CMYK model is used to define printed image colours. → 4.446 COLOUR MODEL; 4.552 RGB; 4.558 SUBTRACTIVE COLOURS

4.**439 bitmap mode** Mode that uses only one of two values (0 or 1, white or black) to define a pixel in an image. They have a bit depth of 1 and are often called 1-bit images (or bitmapped 1-bit images).

4.**440 CIE L*a*b* colour space** Three-dimensional colour model based on a system devised by the CIE organization for measuring colour. The **L*a*b* colour** model is designed to be device independent when it comes to maintaining consistent colour. Results should be consistent regardless of the device used, whether scanner, monitor or printer. L*a*b* colour consists of a luminance or lightness component (L) and two chromatic components: a (green to red) and b (blue to yellow). → 4.503 CIE

4.**441 CMY** Cyan, magenta and yellow, the primary colours of the 'subtractive' colour model. The complete model also includes the black component, K. These colours are created when red, green or blue colour components are subtracted from white light. For example, if a leaf reflects blue and green light but absorbs red, it will appear cyan. The red colour is 'subtracted'. Black, cyan, magenta and yellow comprise the basic process printing colours. → 4.442 CMYK; 4.446 COLOUR MODEL; 4.552 RGB; 4.558 SUBTRACTIVE COLOURS

4.**442 CMYK** Cyan, magenta, yellow and black are the four **process ink** printing colours based on the subtractive colour model. CMYK colour reproduction is an optical illusion which is achieved by separating the original colour image into the four process colours as halftone dots. The dots vary in size according to the colour density. Each colour separation prints with a different screen angle. If you look at a printed image under a 'glass', you see a pattern of colour dots. These dots do not actually overprint (except in areas of flat colour). The black plate is usually a ghost image which adds definition to the other colours. The density of the CMY separations can also be reduced through a technique known as 'undercolour removal' (UCR) and replaced by the black plate. Note that black is represented (here and elsewhere) by the letter 'K' representing the 'key' plate, a term from printing technology. → 4.441 CMY; 4.446 COLOUR MODEL; 4.552 RGB; 5.043 COLOUR SEPARATION

4.**443 CMYK mode** Mode typically used in image-editing applications when preparing an image for printing. An RGB image is converted to CMYK to create colour separations. Most image editing is done in RGB mode and the image converted prior to printing. Some applications feature a CMYK preview to enable the image to be viewed in CMYK mode while still available for edit in RGB mode. → 4.442 CMYK; 4.444 CMYK MODEL

209

4.**444 CMYK model** Colour model based on the properties of printing inks. Ink printed on paper absorbs light from certain parts of the spectrum, reflecting back others that we perceive as the colour of that ink. When cyan, magenta and yellow inks are printed they produce blue, green and red, and when all three have similar densities they make black. Hence these colours are known as subtractive colours.
→ 4.442 CMYK

4.**445 CMYK255** Subtractive colour model produced when different densities of cyan, magenta, yellow and black ink or pigments are printed. The values of each colour range from 0 to 255.

4.**446 colour model** The method of defining or modifying colour. There are many proprietary colour models, such as PANTONE, **FOCOLTONE**, **TRUMATCH**, **TOYO** and **DIC** that have been created for specific purposes (usually connected with printing processes) but two generic models are those most commonly encountered in image editing. These are based on the way light is transmitted and are known as the 'additive' and 'subtractive' colour models. The additive colour model used, for example, in computer monitors, transmits varying proportions of red, green and blue (RGB) light that are interpreted as different colours. When 100% of each are combined white light is produced; 0%, black. Varying the combinations produces intermediate colours of all hues. The subtractive colour model is based on the absorption (i.e. subtraction) and reflection of light; for example, consider the printing inks cyan, magenta and yellow – if you subtract 100% values of either red, green or blue from white light, you create cyan, magenta or yellow. This is the CMYK model. In image editing the most common models are the RGB, CMYK and hue, saturation, brightness (HSB) models.
→ 4.438 ADDITIVE COLOURS; 4.441 CMY; 4.442 CMYK; 4.552 RGB; 4.558 SUBTRACTIVE COLOURS

4.**447 colour modes** The colour mode determines the colour model to be used when displaying and printing images. Modes tend to be built around common colour models such as RGB, HSB, CMYK and CIE L*a*b. Additional modes are configured for specific uses such as duotones, bitmap, greyscale, multichannel and indexed colour.

4.**448 colour picker (2)** A colour model when displayed on a computer monitor. Operating systems and image-editing applications tend to have their own default colour pickers. In an application, double-clicking on the foreground or background colour will often open the current default colour picker. → 4.446 COLOUR MODEL

4.**449 duotone** An image mode that creates two colour images. Special effects can be achieved by using the same technique and printing with different coloured inks. The term is sometimes used erroneously to describe a '**duplex halftone**', or '**false duotone**' (a duplicate halftone printed in

4.438 *additive colours*

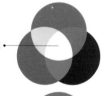

1 *Additive*

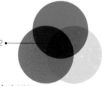

2 *Subtractive*

4.439 *bitmap mode*

4.450 *greyscale (image mode)*

two colours). Although a duotone precisely defines a two-colour image, the duotone option in many image-editing applications also permits the creation of three-colour **tritones** and four-colour **quadtones**. Duotones can also be used to increase the tonal range of a greyscale mode image. Greyscale images can include 256 levels of grey but even the most precise printing presses can offer only around 50 levels of grey per ink. Using multiple inks (each capable of 50 levels) creates a better overall image.

4.**450 greyscale (image mode)** Image mode that renders the image in a maximum 256 levels of grey (using 8-bits) from pure white to pure black. Monochrome monitors (which are rarely used nowadays) can only display black pixels, so greys are achieved by varying the number and positioning of black pixels using a technique called 'dithering'. Images scanned using greyscale scanners (or black and white scanners) typically produce images that are displayed in greyscale mode. Images can be converted from a colour mode to greyscale, in which case the colour information is discarded. If the image is subsequently converted back to a colour mode, then the colour values for each pixel will be based on the grey value from the greyscale image. → 2.429 BIT; 4.404 DITHERING; 7.001 8-BIT

4.**451 hue, saturation, brightness (HSB)** Colour model based upon the light transmitted in an image and that most closely based on the human perception of colour. Hue describes the spectral colour (which might be the actual pigment colour or that of the image phosphors on a computer monitor); it is measured by its position on the standard colour wheel and expressed as a degree between 0° and 360°. Saturation (sometimes called chroma) describes the intensity of that pigment. Using the colour wheel model the saturation increases from the centre to the edge. Saturation is usually expressed as a percentage where 0% is grey and 100% is fully saturated. Brightness describes the strength of luminance (that is, the amount of black or white that is present). This too is measured as a percentage ranging from 0% (black) to 100% (white). Although HSB is the preferred term in many applications, the equivalent terms '**HSL**' (**hue, saturation, lightness**) and '**HLV**' (**hue, lightness, value**) are sometimes encountered. → 4.518 COLOUR WHEEL; 4.530 HUE; 4.553 SATURATION

4.**452 indexed colour** Image mode that can comprise a maximum of 256 colours. Indexed colour modes are commonly used to reduce the file size of RGB images for use in multimedia presentations or on web pages, where file size is critical. The diminution of the file size is achieved by using an indexed table of colours (a colour lookup table, or CLUT) to which the original colours in an image are matched. Should a particular colour not appear in

4.440 *CIE L*a*b* colour space*

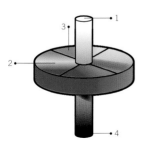

1 *Luminance = 100 (white)*
2 *Blue to yellow component*
3 *Green to red component*
4 *Luminance = 0 (black)*

4.449 *duotone*

the table, the nearest colour is used or else the colour is simulated by dithering. → 4.404 DITHERING; → 4.437 ADAPTIVE COLOUR; 4.512 COLOUR LOOKUP TABLE (CLUT); 7.001 8-BIT

4.**453 Lab colour** Lab colour (as opposed to the CIE L*a*b* colour model) is the internal colour model used by Adobe Photoshop when converting from one colour mode to another. 'Lab mode' is useful for working with Kodak PhotoCD images.

4.**454 Multichannel mode** Colour mode in which images contain multiple channels of up to 256 levels of grey. A typical use is to assemble channels from different original images to create an image that will ultimately be converted to a colour mode. When an RGB colour image is changed to Multichannel mode the red, green and blue channels are changed to cyan, magenta and yellow.

4.**455 NTSC (1953)** Colour-space model based on the television and video standard used mainly in the United States and Japan. The television standard here is based on a screen display of 525 lines displayed at 30 frames per second (as opposed to the 625 lines at 25 frames per second used for PAL and SECAM television). It would typically be used only if an image is primarily intended for broadcast in NTSC format.

4.**456 RGB mode** Colour mode that uses the RGB model. Each pixel in an image is assigned an intensity value (ranging from 0 for black to 255 for white) for each of the colours red, green and blue. For example, a vivid blue pixel will have values such as 10 for red, 30 for green and 240 for blue. All computer monitors display RGB images, even when editing those of another colour mode (such as CMYK). Data is converted to RGB for the screen display. → 4.447 COLOUR MODES; 4.457 RGB MODEL

4.**457 RGB model** Colour model based on the primary colours of red, green and blue. Where these overlap they produce cyan, magenta and yellow (and white where all three colours overlap in equal amounts). The term additive colours is used to describe RGB, due to further colours being produced by addition. Cyan, magenta and yellow are often termed secondary colours.

4.**458 Society of Motion Picture and Television Engineers (SMPTE)** A US organization which defines broadcast standards such as HDTV (high-definition television) and has been responsible for certain colour spaces, including SMPTE-240M and SMPTE-c. → 4.494 SMPTE-240M; 4.495 SMPTE-c

Colour (blend) modes

4.**459 Behind** Modifications are made to the transparent parts of an image and the base colour pixels are not affected. Due to the nature of this mode it will only work on images that have the Preserved Transparency option (or equivalent) turned off. → 4.460 BLENDING MODE

4.**460 blending mode** When using certain image editors, individual layers can be blended with those underneath using blending modes. Blending modes feature in Photoshop, Paintshop Pro (from version 6) and virtually identical merge modes featured in Photo-Paint. There are a number of regimes, but 17 of these are common to several applications – Normal, Behind, Clear, Dissolve, Multiply, Screen, Soft Light, Hard Light, Color Dodge, Color Burn, Darken, Lighten, Difference, Exclusion, Overlay, Saturation, Color and Luminosity. Blending modes enact changes upon the original pixels in an image (sometimes called the base layer) by means of an applied blend colour (or 'paint' layer). This produces a resultant colour based on the original colour and on the nature of the blend. Many users find that blending mode results can be unpredictable and use trial and error to get the desired effects.

4.**461 Clear** Specialized mode that can only be applied to multilayer images when the Preserve Transparency option is turned off. Using the Fill or Stroke commands, the line or paint bucket tool, each base colour pixel is made transparent by the application of the blend colour. → 4.460 BLENDING MODE

4.**462 Color** The luminance levels of the base colour are preserved and combined with the hue and saturation of the blend colour to produce a 'tinted' result. By preserving grey levels in the image a monochrome image can be coloured and colour images can be tinted; it is hence a useful mode for colouring images or creating pseudo hand-tinted effects. → 4.460 BLENDING MODE

4.**463 Colour Dodge** Uses the blend colour to brighten the image. Using a light paint over a base colour has a lightening effect, whereas a darker colour produces only a tint in the base colour. Black has no effect at all. → 4.460 BLENDING MODE

4.**464 Colour Burn** Uses the blend colour to darken the image. A light colour will tend to tint the base colour while using white produces no effect. → 4.460 BLENDING MODE

4.**465 Darken** First compares colour information in base and blend paint layers. Paint colour is only applied when the blend colour is darker; hence the paint colour chosen should be darker than the base colours to be changed. → 4.460 BLENDING MODE

4.**466 Difference** Creates a 'negative' effect by subtracting the paint blend colour from the base colour or the base colour from the paint blend colour, depending on which has the greatest brightness level. Use white as a paint colour to invert the base colour (black does not have any effect). If a duplicate layer is created and combined with the background (at 100%) using Difference, the result is a black image. → 4.460 BLENDING MODE

4.**467 Dissolve** Creates a 'video' dissolve effect proportional to the pressure (or opacity) set. Blend layer and base are combined using a random pixel pattern. The blend layer is unaffected when the opacity is set to 100% but the diffusion becomes increasingly pronounced as the opacity is reduced. → 4.460 BLENDING MODE

4.**468 Exclusion** Similar to the Difference mode but with lower contrast. Base colour is converted to a grey when the paint colour is dark and inverted when light. Using white as the blend colour will simply invert the image. → 4.460 BLENDING MODE; 4.466 DIFFERENCE

4.**469 Hard Light** Creates an effect similar to directing a bright light at the subject. Depending on the base colour, the paint colour will be multiplied or screened. Base colour is lightened if the paint colour is light, and darkened if the paint colour is dark. Contrast tends to be emphasized and highlights exaggerated. Somewhat similar to Overlay but with a more pronounced effect. → 4.460 BLENDING MODE

4.**470 Hue** The hue of the blend colour is applied to the luminance and saturation values of the base colour. The result is often a strongly colourized image that appears like a television picture stripped of the luminance component. → 4.460 BLENDING MODE; 4.501 CHROMA; 4.545 PASTEL SHADES; 4.553 SATURATION

4.**471 Lighten** Compares the base and blending colours and applies colour only if the blend colour is lighter than the base. Achieves an overall lightening effect. → 4.460 BLENDING MODE

4.**472 Luminosity** Luminosity values in the base colour are replaced with the corresponding luminosity value from the paint colour.

4.451 *hue, saturation, brightness (HSB)*

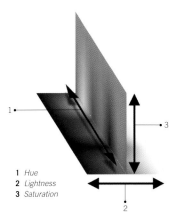

1 *Hue*
2 *Lightness*
3 *Saturation*

4.460 *blending mode*

A layered, unblended image of a flower (base image) and a coin (blend image), shown overleaf with different blending effects

4.462 *Color*

4.463 *Colour Dodge*

4.464 *Colour Burn*

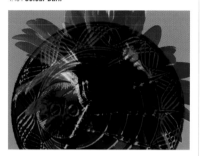

4.465 *Darken*

4.466 *Difference*

4.467 *Dissolve*

214

4.468 *Exclusion*

4.469 *Hard Light*

4.470 *Hue*

4.471 *Lighten*

4.472 *Luminosity*

4.474 *Multiply*

4.476 *Overlay*

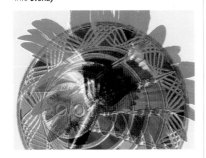

4.477 *Saturation*

215

4.478 *Screen*

4.479 *Soft Light*

The hue and saturation remain unchanged. → 4.460 BLENDING MODE

4.**473 merge modes** A range of different modes for producing blends between a source colour and base colour. Similar to the colour blending modes of Photoshop. Also called **paint modes**. The complete list comprises Normal, Add, **Subtract**, **Difference**, **Multiply**, **Divide**, **If Lighter**, **If Darker**, **Texturize**, Colour, Hue, Saturation, **Lightness**, **Invert**, **Logical AND**, **Logical OR**, **Logical XOR**, **Behind**, Screen, Overlay, Soft Light, Hard Light, Colour Dodge, Colour Burn, Red, Green, Blue, Cyan, Magenta, Yellow and Black → 4.460 BLENDING MODE

4.**474 Multiply** Useful tool for creating or enhancing shadow effects. Uses the paint pixel values to multiply those of the base. The resultant colour is always darker than the original except when white is the paint colour. A light paint imparts a gentler, but similar, effect to darker colours. → 4.460 BLENDING MODE

4.**475 Normal** The default mode, which is called Threshold in bitmap or indexed colour mode images. Every pixel is edited to create a resultant mixed colour that can be modulated by altering the transparency (opacity) of the paint layer. → 4.460 BLENDING MODE

4.**476 Overlay** Retains black and white in their original forms but darkens dark areas and lightens light areas. The base colour is mixed with the blend colour but retains the luminosity values of the original image. → 4.460 BLENDING MODE

4.**477 Saturation** Produces an image where the luminosity and hue of the base image are preserved but the saturation is derived from the paint layer. There is no change in areas with zero saturation (i.e., those with shades of grey). → 4.460 BLENDING MODE

4.**478 Screen** Calculates the inverse of the blend and multiplies this with the base pixel values. The resultant colour is always lighter than the original with the darkest parts of the base removed to give a bleached effect. There is no bleaching only if the blend colour is black. This mode has been likened to printing a positive image from two negatives sandwiched together. → 4.460 BLENDING MODE

4.**479 Soft Light** A more gentle, but similar, effect to Overlay. A light paint or layer colour lightens the base colour, a dark one darkens the base colour. Luminosity values in the base are preserved. If the blend paint or layer is lighter than 50% grey, the image is lightened in the same manner as would result from photographic dodging. Blends darker than 50% produce a burned effect. → 4.460 BLENDING MODE; 4.476 OVERLAY

Colour management systems

4.**480 Adobe Gamma control panel** A control panel produced by Adobe, principally for Adobe products, designed to assist in the accurate calibration of a monitor. It first appeared in Photoshop version 5 as a replacement for the Gamma control panel (Mac OS) and monitor control dialogue (Windows) offered in earlier versions. The user is stepped through the calibration process adjusting, in turn, the contrast, brightness, gamma, colour balance and white point of your monitor. Additional adjustments to Photoshop's colour-conversion settings ensure that an image is displayed consistently from one monitor to another. Though specifically tailored to Photoshop, much of the calibration applies across the board. → 4.408 GAMMA

4.**481 Apple RGB** Colour space that was once the default in Photoshop and used heavily in the desktop printing industry. It was based around the Macintosh's once-ubiquitous 13-inch Trinitron monitor.

4.**482 CIE Colour Rendering Index** The CIE authorized method of monitoring the comparison of colour fidelity when an object is illuminated under a test illumination source, as compared with a reference source. → 4.503 CIE

4.**483 CIE RGB** Colour space capable of handling 16-bit colour channels and boasting a wide gamut, but offering poor handling of certain colours, notably cyan and blue. → 4.446 COLOUR MODEL; 4.489 COLOUR SPACE

4.**484 Colormatch RGB** A colour space that features an expanded RGB gamut. Colormatch RGB was originally defined by monitor manufacturer Radius for use with their PressView monitors and is mostly restricted to use with these devices (once

the mainstay of prepress environments).
→ 4.486 COLOUR GAMUT; 4.489 COLOUR SPACE

4.**485 ColorSync** A colour management system (CMS) designed to provide colour consistency and conversion options, originally across Macintosh systems and Apple hardware, but now applicable to third-party devices too. The ColorSync CMS (or 'ColorSync' for short) converts the colours used in one application or device so that they can be accurately reproduced on another. Normally these have to be ColorSync compatible. The mechanics of ColorSync are such that a ColorSync profile is embedded in an image file when it is saved in TIFF, JPEG or PICT format. When the time comes to print that image, ColorSync compares the characteristics of the display monitor with those of the printer and applies changes to the printer/ink profiles to ensure that the screen and printer images match as closely as possible. → 4.488 COLOUR MANAGEMENT SYSTEM (CMS)

4.**486 colour gamut** A **gamut** is the full range of colours that a colour system or device can display. There are different gamuts for different colour models and modes, all of which tend to offer a smaller range of colours than that of the human eye. Also, the colour range possible on a monitor is substantially greater than that possible on the printed page. To allow for and compensate for these variations, different 'colour management systems' (CMS) have been devised to maintain the consistency of colour gamuts across various devices.
→ 4.487 COLOUR MANAGEMENT MODULE (CMM); 4.488 COLOUR MANAGEMENT SYSTEM (CMS)

4.**487 colour management module (CMM)** Profile used for managing and matching colours accurately across different platforms and devices. CMMs conform to a specific colour management system (CMS) such as that defined by the International Colour Consortium (ICC). In this case the CMMs will interpret the ICC colour management profiles, which describe the RGB and CMYK colour spaces on your computer. Standard profiles are usually installed by image-editing applications (the number and variety will depend on the application) but in many cases you can create your own. This would normally be important if

specific or unusual devices were in use that are not accommodated by the standard modules. The selected profile is then embedded in the image you are working on so that it can later be used as a reference by other devices in the production process. → 4.442 CMYK; 4.485 COLORSYNC; 4.488 COLOUR MANAGEMENT SYSTEM (CMS); 4.492 ICC PROFILE; 4.552 RGB

4.**488 colour management system (CMS)** A colour management system is used in image-editing applications as a method of achieving colour accuracy and consistency between all devices in the colour reproduction chain. Due to the different characteristics of devices such as scanners, monitors, printers, imagesetters, and so on, the colours intended by the user to be printed out can often be represented by different tones in each. By adopting a CMS such differences may be removed or reduced. Most principal image editors use the colour management system devised by the International Colour Consortium (ICC), although other systems (Kodak's Digital Science Color Management System, Apple's ColorSync, and Microsoft's ICM) may be encountered or used for specific purposes. → 4.485 COLORSYNC; 4.486 COLOUR GAMUT; 4.487 COLOUR MANAGEMENT MODULE (CMM)

4.**489 colour space** Three-dimensional interpretation of a colour model, illustrating all variations possible with that model.
→ 4.446 COLOUR MODEL; 4.448 COLOUR PICKER (2)

4.**490 custom colour space** A colour space in which gamma, white point and phosphor level settings can be made by the user. Usually only required by the more advanced user and those with particular needs and requirements in their colour space. Inexperienced users are often advised to use preconfigured colour spaces due to the unpredictable nature of the results from making custom settings.
→ 4.489 COLOUR SPACE

4.**491 Digital Science CMS/Kodak CMS** A colour management system devised by Kodak and automatically installed when you choose to install the Kodak PhotoCD acquire plug-in. → 4.488 COLOUR MANAGEMENT SYSTEM (CMS)

4.**492 ICC profile** Colour management system from the ICC (International Colour

Consortium). The ICC profile is essentially a colour space designed for cross-platform and cross-application use and hence to help produce consistent results across many applications. It can also be used for colour management in hardware devices. A CMM (colour management module) is invoked by an image-editing application to interpret ICC profiles appropriate to the colour spaces (either RGB or CMYK) in current use. This interpretation then becomes part of the current image and is available for other systems and devices to enable them to ensure correct colour output or management.

4.**493 Monitor RGB** ICC profile for a specific monitor. Unlike other colour spaces, those resulting from this profile are not device independent and, if two monitors are attached to one computer, the results (and the Monitor ICC profiles) are unlikely to be the same on each. ➔ 4.492 ICC PROFILE

4.**494 SMPTE-240M** RGB colour space devised by the Society of Motion Picture and Television Engineers for high-definition television (HDTV) in the US and Japan. Although it features a large gamut (and is suitable for prepress and where high quality is required), the alternate Wide Gamut RGB offers an even wider gamut. ➔ 4.497 WIDE GAMUT RGB

4.**495 SMPTE-c** Colour space with a very limited gamut and tending to be used for very specialized applications (such as with images used with North American NTSC television).

4.**496 sRGB** A colour space pioneered by Hewlett Packard and Microsoft and designed to be an Internet standard. The space assumes the characteristics of an 'average' PC monitor that, in aiming to be universal, has a compromised (restricted) gamut. ➔ 4.446 COLOUR MODEL; 4.489 COLOUR SPACE

4.**497 Wide Gamut RGB** A colour space that uses pure wavelengths of red, green and blue to give an exceptionally wide gamut. Unfortunately because of the restriction of printing inks and monitor screen phosphors, much of the gain in this colour space is lost when an image is directed to either.

Colour terms

4.**498 16-bit colour** A facility in some higher level image-editing applications that allows images to be edited in 16-bit-per-channel mode rather than the more normal 8-bit mode. RGB images usually use three 8-bit channels (totalling 24 bits and described as 24-bit), whereas CMYK images use four 8-bit channels (totalling 32 bits). A 16-bit per channel image provides finer control over colour but, because an RGB image then totals 48 bits (16 x 3) and a CMYK image totals 64 bits (16 x 4), the resulting file sizes are considerably larger than for 8-bit-per-channel images. ➔ 2.272 BIT DEPTH

4.**499 bilevel, bilevelled** Images comprising only black and white tones, with no intermediate grey levels.

4.489 *colour space*

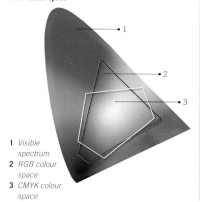

1 *Visible spectrum*
2 *RGB colour space*
3 *CMYK colour space*

4.506 *colour cast*

4.**500 brightness** The relative lightness or darkness of the colour, usually measured as a percentage from 0% (black) to 100% (white).

4.**501 chroma** The intensity, or 'quality', of a colour, defined by hue and degree of saturation. In some definitions the terms saturation and chroma are used interchangeably. The term is generally used by printers. → 4.530 HUE

4.**502 chrominance (c)** The component of a video signal carrying the colour information (as opposed to the luminance signal which carries brightness information) in the component video transmission system. → 4.501 CHROMA

4.**503 CIE** Commission Internationale de l'Eclairage. The international organization responsible for the creation and definition of the visual colour model that forms the basis for colorimetric measurements of colour and is commonly referred to as L*a*b* colour space. → 4.440 CIE L*A*B* COLOUR SPACE

4.**504 colour** The visual interpretation of the various wavelengths of reflected or refracted light.

4.**505 colour atlas** Collection of printed colours used for choosing or specifying colours. Often called a colour picker, though that term is now increasingly used to identify the software-based colour selector.

4.**506 colour cast** A bias in a colour image which can be either intentionally introduced or the undesirable consequence of a lighting problem. Intentional colour casts tend to be introduced to enhance an effect (such as accentuating the reds and oranges of a sunset, or applying a sepia tone to imply an aged photo) and can be done via an appropriate command in an image-editing application. Alternatively it can be done at the proof stage to enhance the colour in an image. Undesirable **casts** arise from a number of causes but are typically due to an imbalance between the lighting source and the response of the film (or that of the CCD in the case of a digital camera). Using daylight film under tungsten lighting causes an amber colour cast while setting the colour balance of a digital camera for indoor scenes can give a flat blue cast outdoors.

4.**507 colour checker** Chart comprising selected colours that include 'typical' tones of real objects such as sky and skin tones. Used to calibrate monitors and certain video cameras. **Test cards**, such as **Card F**, can be used as colour checkers: they include neutrals, primary and secondary colours, and the central image provides skin tones. → 4.536 MACBETH CHART

4.**508 colour correction (image term)** Altering the colour characteristics of an image to correct for colour bias or to alter the **colour balance**. This may be to alter a colour cast to provide a neutrally lit result. In image editing, colour corrections can sometimes be achieved by using 'quick fix' tools or by using colour adjustment controls.

4.**509 colour depth** The number of bits required to define the colour of each pixel. A black and white image requires only one bit – it is either off (black) or on (white) – whereas a colour depth of 8 bits can display either 256 greys or 256 colours. A 24-bit image can display 16.7 million colours – 8 bits each for red, green and blue (256 x 256 x 256). → 2.429 BIT

4.**510 colour difference signals** The two chrominance channels of the YCC colour model (which forms the basis of the PhotoCD system). In this model there are three channels: the luminance (Y) channel and two chrominance (CC) colour difference signal channels. These carry information relating to red minus luminance and blue minus luminance. → 3.058 PHOTOCD

4.**511 colour difference unit** Unit used to measure the difference in colour when using the CIE L*a*b* system and employed in the formulaic calculations of this colour space.

4.**512 colour lookup table (CLUT)** A preset table of colours (to a maximum of 256) which the operating system uses when in 8-bit mode. CLUTs are also attached to individual images saved in 8-bit 'indexed' mode – that is, when an application converts a 24-bit image (one with millions of colours) to 8-bit it draws up a table ('index') of up to 256 of the most frequently used colours in the image (the total number of colours depends on where the image will be viewed – Mac, Windows or the web, for example). If a colour in the original image does not appear in the table, the application chooses the closest one or simulates it by 'dithering' available colours in the table. → 2.139 OPERATING SYSTEM (OS); 4.404 DITHERING; 4.452 INDEXED COLOUR

4.**513 colour measurement** The process of determining the colour of a sample. In print this can be done by comparing with a colour swatch, atlas or picker. In digital applications, the colour can be selected and then analysed by the applications (for example, by using the eyedropper tool).

4.**514 colour picker (1)** A book of printed colour swatches that are defined according to their make-up in terms of ink components. Colour pickers generally conform to a colour model, such as PANTONE, in order that consistency can be maintained between the originator and any printer. Computer systems and image-editing applications include colour pickers for users to select specific colours. A colour chart is similar, but specifically reproduces the colours made up from the process-colour inks. → 4.446 COLOUR MODEL; 4.448 COLOUR PICKER (2); 4.515 COLOUR SWATCH; 5.041 COLOUR CHART

4.**515 colour swatch** A sample of a specific colour, taken from a colour chart, colour picker or some other printed example, and used as a guide for specification or reproduction of spot colours or process tints. Image-editing applications feature swatch palettes, **Color Swatches**, that include commonly used colours or a set of specific tones compiled by the users for specific purposes (such as recolouring the sky in a scene). → 4.514 COLOUR PICKER (1); 5.041 COLOUR CHART

4.**516 colour table** A predefined table (or list) of colours used to determine a specific colour model, e.g. for converting an image to CMYK. A colour lookup table, or 'CLUT', also describes the palette of colours used to display an image. → 4.442 CMYK; 4.446 COLOUR MODEL; 4.487 COLOUR MANAGEMENT MODULE (CMM); 4.492 ICC PROFILE

4.**517 colour value** The tonal value of a colour related to a scale of greys from white to black. → 4.534 LIGHTNESS (2)

4.**518 colour wheel** The complete spectrum of visible colours represented as a circular diagram and used as the basis of some colour pickers. The HSB (hue, saturation, brightness) colour model determines hue as the angular position on the colour wheel and saturation as the corresponding radial position. → 4.448 COLOUR PICKER (2); 4.514 COLOUR PICKER (1)

4.**519 colourants** Pigments and dyes that absorb light (selectively) of particular frequencies. Includes, for example, cyan, magenta and yellow dyes and transparent dyes used in filter manufacture.

4.**520 complementary colours** Any pair of colours directly opposite each other on a colour wheel, that, when combined, form white (or black depending on the colour model, subtractive or additive). → 4.438 ADDITIVE COLOURS; 4.446 COLOUR MODEL; 4.518 COLOUR WHEEL; 4.558 SUBTRACTIVE COLOURS

4.508 *colour correction (image term)*

Before   *After*

4.522 *desaturate*

Before   *After*

4.521 Cyan (C) Along with magenta and yellow, cyan comprises one of the three primary colours in the subtractive model, and one of the three process colours used in four-colour printing. Cyan is sometimes referred to as 'process blue'. → 4.442 CMYK; 4.558 SUBTRACTIVE COLOURS; 5.003 FOUR-COLOUR PROCESS

4.522 desaturate The process of reducing the saturation of a colour and making it more grey. In image-editing applications, the Desaturate command can be used to remove the colour from an image or a selection. When an image is desaturated it becomes monochrome, but retains the original (colour) image mode. More subtle desaturation (less than total colour removal) can be achieved using the desaturation tool, which is most commonly presented as the Sponge tool. This tool can also be used to increase the saturation. → 4.166 SPONGE TOOL; 4.553 SATURATION

4.523 desaturated colour Colour which either contains a low proportion of colour relative to grey or a colour that has had the colour component reduced so that the amount of grey in proportion to hue is increased. → 4.522 DESATURATE; 4.553 SATURATION

4.524 device-independent colour The colour produced from a colour management system that can be accurately reproduced on any device or computer platform. The L*a*b model is an example of a model designed to deliver device-independent colour. → 4.440 CIE L*A*B* COLOUR SPACE

4.525 embedded profiles Profiles (usually ICC profiles) embedded in an image file (i.e., included in the image file data but only 'visible' to the application) indicating the correct colour space used during image creation or editing. → 4.492 ICC PROFILE

4.526 four-bit/4-bit The allocation of four bits of memory to each pixel, giving an image or screen display of 16 greys or colours (a row of four bits can be written in 16 different combinations: 0000, 0001, 1001, 0110, etc.). → 2.429 BIT; 7.001 8-BIT

4.527 green One of the three additive primary colours (the other two being red and blue). → 4.438 ADDITIVE COLOURS; 4.552 RGB

4.528 grey Any perfect neutral tone between black and white that has no colour or colour bias. Warm greys are greys to which 'warm' colours (such as reds and oranges) have been added. Cool greys have blues added.

4.529 grey balance/balanced grey The proportions of yellow, magenta and cyan (inks or colours) that together produce a neutral grey.

4.530 hue Pure spectral colour. The hue value distinguishes one colour from another. The hue of a colour can remain the same even if the amount of black or white is varied. For example, a shade of pink and maroon may be based on the same hue of red. → 4.460 BLENDING MODE; 4.501 CHROMA; 4.545 PASTEL SHADES; 4.553 SATURATION

4.531 ideal tone reproduction curve A graph featuring a 45° line relating the tones in an original image and those of the

4.514 *colour picker (1)*

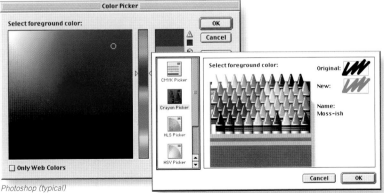

Photoshop (typical)

Mac Crayon picker

reproduced image. This is an 'ideal' due to the shortcomings of reproduction media that means the reproduced hues are always inferior to the originals.

4.**532 International Colour Consortium (ICC)** An organization responsible for defining cross-application colour standards. The ICC colour management system is widely used and often referred to as simply the ICC model. → 4.488 COLOUR MANAGEMENT SYSTEM (CMS)

4.**533 lightness (1)** One component of the L*a*b colour model, also known as the luminance component, which contains the information relating to the image luminosity.

4.**534 lightness (2)** The tonal measure of a colour relative to a scale running from black to white. Also called 'brightness' or 'value'. → 4.451 HUE, SATURATION, BRIGHTNESS (HSB)

4.**535 luminance (y)** The strength of a greyscale video signal. A high luminance signal produces brighter output than a low signal. → 4.472 LUMINOSITY

4.**536 MacBeth Chart** A card-mounted colour chart produced by **Gretag MacBeth**. This professional standard chart has become the international standard reference card, both for colours and for greyscale. By photographing the MacBeth chart alongside an object, advanced and precise colour corrections can be made. The chart includes 24 squares, with the additive primary colours, the subtractive primary colours and the specialist colours that

relate to 'real world' colours such as sample skin tones.

4.**537 Magenta (M)** With cyan and yellow, one of the three subtractive primaries, and one of the four process colours that are used in four-colour printing. Sometimes called 'process red'. → 4.442 CMYK; 5.003 FOUR-COLOUR PROCESS

4.**538 mean noon sunlight** An arbitrary colour temperature to which most daylight colour films are balanced, based on the average colour temperature of direct sunlight at midday in Washington, DC (5,400 K).

4.**539 midtones/middletones** The range of tonal values in an image anywhere between the darkest 'shadow' tones and lightest 'highlights'. Usually refers to the central band of a histogram. → 4.098 HISTOGRAM

4.**540 minus colour** Description of a colour by the colour it absorbs, rather than what it reflects. Cyan, for example, is described as minus red, as red is the colour a cyan dye absorbs.

4.**541 mono(chrome)/monochromatic** An image of varying tones reproduced in a single colour. Black and white images are only one form of monochromatic image; an image featuring red and white (including all intermediate shades of pink) is also monochromatic. → 4.542 MONOTONE

4.**542 monotone** A single colour, or in printing terms the reproduction of a single colour image, without tonal variation.

4.**543 Munsell System** A system of ordering colour, such that colours are arranged with perceptual equal spacing. Colours are

4.518 *colour wheel*

4.520 *complementary colours*

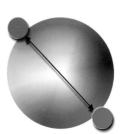

defined according to the Munsell hues, values and chroma values. Munsell specifies five principal hues, namely red, yellow, green, blue and purple. Values range from 10 (for a perfect colour diffuser) through to 0 (for a black with a reflectance of 0%). Chroma ranges from 0 for perfect neutrals to 16 for fully saturated colours.

4.**544 NTSC** The US National Television Standards Committee. Responsible for defining and monitoring television standards in the US The analogue NTSC standard is 525 lines, 30 frames per second. The NTSC (1953) colour space has been defined for images intended for broadcast on NTSC systems.
→ 4.455 NTSC (1953)

4.**545 pastel shades** Lighter shades of a colour, created by the reduction of saturation.
→ 4.553 SATURATION

4.**546 phase alternation by line (PAL)** A western European (except France) colour television standard which uses 625 lines and displays images at 25 frames per second.
→ 4.544 NTSC; 4.554 SECAM

4.**547 pixel depth** The number of shades that a single pixel can display. Pixel depth is determined by the number of bits used to display the pixel. One bit equals a single colour (black), so four bits (any permutation of four 1s and 0s, such as 0011 or 1001) produce 16 shades, and so on up to 32 bits (although actually only 24 are available) producing 16.7 million colours, the other eight being reserved for functions such as masking. → 4.509 COLOUR DEPTH

4.**548 preferred tone reproduction curve** An ogive ('s' shaped) curve defining the tonal relationship between an original image and the reproduced image. → 4.531 IDEAL TONE REPRODUCTION CURVE

4.**549 primary colours** Sets of three pure colours from which all other colours can be mixed. The primary colours that are used in printing are cyan, magenta and yellow, the so-called 'subtractive' pigment primaries. The primary colours of light, or the 'additive' primaries, are red, green and blue. In the 'real world' we find that colours, inks and pigments are not sufficiently pure for all colours (and particularly black or white, depending on

which primary set is used) to be synthesized. → 4.438 ADDITIVE COLOURS; 4.558 SUBTRACTIVE COLOURS

4.**550 profile** The colour (and contrast) characteristics of a device or process that is used by a colour management system to achieve faithful colour reproduction. The most common profile is the ICC profile, which is a cross-application (and cross-device) standard. → 4.492 ICC PROFILE

4.**551 Red** One of the three additive primary colours, along with green and blue.
→ 4.438 ADDITIVE COLOURS

4.**552 RGB** Abbreviation for red, green, blue, the three primary colours of the 'additive' colour model. Also used to describe the signals fed to a monitor. In an RGB feed separate red, green and blue signals are fed to the monitor, as opposed to, say, the composite feed where all video signals are sent along one wire. → 4.438 ADDITIVE COLOURS

4.**553 saturation** The degree to which a colour of fixed tone varies from the neutral, grey tone. The variation stretches from none (grey) through pastel shades (low saturation) to pure colour with no grey (high saturation, or 'fully saturated').
→ 4.460 BLENDING MODE

4.**554 SECAM** Système Electronique pour Couleur avec Mémoire, the colour television standard used in France, Eastern Europe and Russia. Like PAL, it features 625 lines and displays images at 25 frames per second. A variation used in the Middle East is known as Middle East SECAM or MESECAM. PAL and SECAM broadcast images are not compatible, but high band video recordings (SVHS or Hi8) made in either format will replay on equipment designed for the other.
→ 4.544 NTSC

4.**555 separation table** When you create artwork that is to be printed at a print shop, you'll first create an RGB to CMYK conversion and receive colour proofs showing the parameters for the colour separations. You can save the conversion information in colour separation tables so that any future work undertaken with that print shop can be appropriately calibrated.

4.**556 sepia** An amber/brown colour. Also the colour of a monochrome print in which the normal shades of grey appear as shades of

brown. Due originally to the effects of ageing and oxidation on a print, the tone can be simulated chemically using sepia toners, and in image-editing applications by altering the hue of a colourized image or by the application of an effects filter.
→ 1.482 SEPIA TONING; 4.449 DUOTONE

4.**557 spectrum** The dispersion of electromagnetic radiation. The degree of dispersion is dependent on the wavelength of the incident radiation. The extent of the dispersion also depends on the dispersive device (typically a prism or diffraction grating). The visible spectrum includes that part of the electromagnetic spectrum between red and violet which is visible to the human eye.

4.**558 subtractive colours** The colour model describing the primary colours of reflected light: cyan, magenta and yellow (CMY). The subtractive colours, plus black, form the basis for printed process colours (CMYK). → 4.438 ADDITIVE COLOURS; 4.442 CMYK; 4.446 COLOUR MODEL

4.**559 swatch** In digital imaging terms, a sample of a colour or texture. → 4.515 COLOUR SWATCH

4.**560 tertiary colour** The colour resulting from the mixing of two secondary colours.

4.**561 tint** A light shade of lower saturation produced by reducing the saturation of a solid colour. Pink is a tint of red. The term is sometimes used to describe the base colour of photographic paper, which can be, among others, 'cream white' or 'cold (blue) white'.

4.**562 tonal range** The range of tonal values within an image. When using an image-editing application, the histogram feature displays tonal range: when an image has a full tonal range there will be pixels represented across the whole of the histogram. Analysis or identification of variation and deficiencies within the histogram distribution forms the basis of making tonal corrections.

4.**563 tonal reproduction** A measure of the tones reproduced (in a print, or on a monitor) as compared to those of the source image. It is usual for the tonal reproduction to be less than that of any original.

4.**564 tonal value/tone value** The relative densities of tones in an image.

4.**565 trichromatic** Comprising three colours. In photography the trichromatic process involves working with three emulsions, each sensitized to one of red, green or blue wavelength. A full-colour image is compiled from images drawn from each emulsion.

4.**566 twenty-four-bit/24-bit colour** The allocation of 24 bits of memory to each pixel, 8 bits for each of the primary colours R, G and B. For each colour there are 256 shades; overall, the total number of colours displayed is 256 x 256 x 256 or 16.7 million colours. For CMYK colour separations 24-bit colour is also required.
→ 4.509 COLOUR DEPTH

4.**567 unique hue** Any hue (colour) that cannot be described by any hue names other than

4.545 *pastel shades*

4.549 *primary colours*

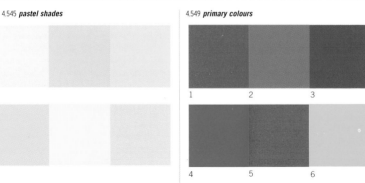

1	Red	4	Cyan
2	Green	5	Magenta
3	Blue	6	Yellow

its own. There are four unique hues, red, yellow, green and blue.

4.**568 warm colours** Any colour with a hue veering towards red or yellow, as distinct from cool colours which veer towards blue or green. ➔ 4.528 GREY

4.**569 white light** The colour of light that results from red, blue and green being combined in equal proportions at full saturation. If the saturations are anything less than full (and the proportions remain equal), then the colour grey results. ➔ 4.438 ADDITIVE COLOURS

4.**570 white point (monitor)** The colour measure of white light when the intensities of the red, green and blue components are equal. With gamma and phosphors, this measure is one of three monitor setup parameters. Normally it should be left to the default value of 6500K which represents 'typical' cool daylight. Alternate settings can be made and viewed 'live'.

4.**571 YCC** Colour model that forms the basis of the PhotoCD system. ➔ 3.058 PHOTOCD; 4.510 COLOUR DIFFERENCE SIGNALS

4.**572 Yellow (Y)** With cyan and magenta, one of the three subtractive primaries, and one of the four process colours used in four-colour printing. Sometimes called 'process yellow'. ➔ 4.442 CMYK; 5.003 FOUR-COLOUR PROCESS

4.**573 status bar** The Photoshop status bar is shown at the base of the active window (Mac OS) or at the base of the Photoshop window (Windows). It is always visible on Macintosh computers but can be toggled on or off with Windows computers: choose Hide/Show Status Bar from the Windows menu. Depending on the operating system, the status bar displays the zoom percentage, document sizes, scratch sizes (RAM currently accessible to Photoshop), efficiency (percentage of that RAM that is currently being used), timing, and short comments relating to the current tool or command. Pressing and holding the status bar will show an image thumbnail. Option-press (Mac OS) or Alt-press (Windows) on the status bar to display resolution and dimension information. ➔ 4.188 ZOOM TOOL

4.**574 Tool Options bar** Photoshop 6 feature (similar features are found in some other applications). Comprises a strip (34 pixels deep) across the monitor immediately below the menu bar (default setting). Provides essential information and controls for the selected tools, in the manner of the corresponding Tools palette in earlier versions of Photoshop. The Options bar can be moved by dragging the title bar on the left edge. When selection tools are chosen, the Options bar features new buttons enabling Boolean operations to be carried out on the selection, including adding to, removing from and intersecting with the selection. The Options bar also includes an area to dock palettes. This area, however, is only available when the Options bar is docked at the top or bottom of the screen and when the screen resolution is 800 x 600 pixels or greater.

4.563 *tonal reproduction curves*

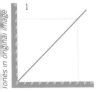

Reproduced tones

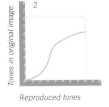

Reproduced tones

1 *Ideal reproduction curve*
2 *Actual reproduction curve*

4.556 *sepia*

5

PRINT TERMS

Printers and printing types

5.001 colour printing Printing process(es) that uses inks other than black; also used to describe printing that uses coloured inks with black. The principal commercial colour printing processes today are offset lithography (either sheet- or web-fed) and web gravure. For smaller runs on special substrates, screen printing is used. → 5.014 PRINTING PROCESSES; 5.016 SCREEN PRINTING

5.002 flexography Flexographic printing is the most common application of the relief printing process used today, predominantly for long-run newspapers and packaging. Flexo printing plates are made from resilient, light-sensitive photo-polymers which are exposed to ultraviolet light through a film negative which hardens the image area. The unexposed areas are washed away by means of a solvent, leaving the printing areas in 'relief'. Digital **flexo plate-imaging** technology uses a high-power infra-red laser to cut through the top layer of the plate leaving the image areas in relief. → 5.008 LETTERSET; 5.009 LITHOGRAPHY

5.003 four-colour process A **process colour printing** method designed to render and reproduce full-colour images from the four-colour separations: cyan, magenta, yellow and black. The black plate adds density and depth to the image and prints the black linework, e.g., text. → 4.442 CMYK; 5.019 THREE-COLOUR PROCESS; 5.043 COLOUR SEPARATION; 5.107 UNDERCOLOUR REMOVAL (UCR)

5.004 halftone (1) The reprographic technique, developed in the 1880s, of reproducing a continuous tone image on a printing press by breaking it up into a pattern of equally spaced dots of varying size. This determines tones or shades – the larger the dots, the darker the shade.

5.005 halftone (2) The description of any image reproduced by the halftone process or printed digitally using a halftone effect or filter. → 5.004 HALFTONE (1)

5.006 intaglio Printing process, known commercially as gravure, used for the high speed production of long print runs, usually for the magazine, direct mail and catalogue market, where accurate colour reproduction is essential. **Gravure** has the

5.003 *four-colour process colours*

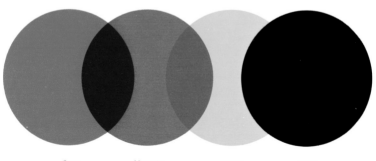

| Cyan | Magenta | Yellow | Black |

greatest resemblance to photography. Ink is controlled by different sizes of cells, either chemically etched or electronically engraved into the surface of the 'plate', commonly a copper-coated cylinder. The cells can have the same area and can vary in depth, or vary in both area and depth, giving a smooth transition of tones, thereby replicating the continuous tone of a photographic image. → 5.007 LETTERPRESS; 5.012 OFFSET LITHOGRAPHY; 5.016 SCREEN PRINTING

5.**007 letterpress** The name of a process and printing device, now used predominantly for private press work and jobbing printing. Letterpress printing is based on a plate featuring a raised surface (relief) of that to be printed. This surface is inked and the plate pressed onto the paper (or other surface). The plate is wrong reading because the paper comes into direct contact with the plate. → 5.002 FLEXOGRAPHY; 5.006 INTAGLIO; 5.012 OFFSET LITHOGRAPHY; 5.016 SCREEN PRINTING

5.**008 letterset** Term derived from a contraction of letterpress and offset. Printing process that uses a relief plate but prints using the offset method. Sometimes referred to as relief offset or indirect letterpress.

5.**009 lithography** A '**planographic**' printing process based on the chemical repulsion of oil (ink) and water. Aloys Senefelder developed the process by etching images onto flat stone. Between each 'impression', a film of water was applied to the stone. The greasy image areas would accept ink and the porous **stone** accepted the water. Like letterpress, the image was wrong reading as the paper was applied directly to the 'plate' or 'stone'. → 5.002 FLEXOGRAPHY; 5.006 INTAGLIO; 5.007 LETTERPRESS; 5.012 OFFSET LITHOGRAPHY; 5.016 SCREEN PRINTING

5.**010 mezzotint** An intaglio-type technique that reproduces tones rather than lines. Image-editing effects filters can reproduce mezzotints although the range of effects often exceeds those of true mezzotints. → 5.006 INTAGLIO

5.**011 nonimpact printing** Printing processes in which the ink is delivered to the paper surface without the printing press or printing device striking the surface. Laser printers, which lay ink on the surface of the paper (prior to it being 'fixed' by heat), and inkjet printers (which make no contact at all) are two examples of nonimpact printing.

5.**012 offset lithography** Now dominant, the modern lithographic process follows the principles of lithography, but instead of transferring the image directly to the paper, the inked plate cylinder transfers the image to a blanket; the paper passes between the blanket and the impression cylinder, i.e., the image is offset during the printing process. As a result, the original artwork is right-reading. → 5.002 FLEXOGRAPHY; 5.006 INTAGLIO; 5.007 LETTERPRESS; 5.009 LITHOGRAPHY; 5.016 SCREEN PRINTING

5.004 *halftone (1)*

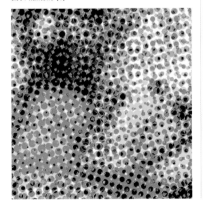

5.010 *mezzotint*

5.**013 Pictrography** Printing system introduced by Fuji that uses a laser printer to transfer an image onto a '**donor sheet**' that has been dipped in silver halide and other chemicals. This donor sheet is combined with a transfer sheet that accepts the chemicals when heated in the presence of a small amount of water. Donor sheets remain in the printer where the unused impregnated chemicals can be removed along with the silver halide.

5.**014 printing processes** There are four generic printing processes: 'intaglio' (e.g., gravure), 'planographic' (e.g., lithography), '**relief**' (e.g., letterpress and flexography) and '**stencil**' (e.g., screen printing).
→ 5.002 FLEXOGRAPHY; 5.006 INTAGLIO; 5.007 LETTERPRESS; 5.009 LITHOGRAPHY; 5.016 SCREEN PRINTING

5.**015 proofing press** A small mechanical (usually hand operated) press used for small numbers of proofs. Often these are used to provide additional proofs to a Cromalin (if, for example, it is required to see how a 'real' print would look). Proofing presses are increasingly being replaced with digital imaging devices which offer accurate guides to the printer, particularly if they are calibrated to match the printing press to be used. → 5.110 CROMALIN

5.**016 screen printing** A printing process in which ink is forced by using a squeegee through a porous mesh screen stretched across a frame. The frame was traditionally made of silk (used for its ultra-fine mesh structure) but is now more likely to be of a more robust (but equally structured) synthetic material. An image is laid on the screen by photomechanical means for a complex image or by a hand-cut stencil for simpler, graphic images. When these are bonded to the screen they act as a block to the ink. Screen printing can be used to produce high-quality four-colour printing with additional specified Pantone® or special colours for branding, packaging and large-format printing.

5.**017 Thermal Autochrome (TA)** Printing system that uses a composite paper that contains three dye layers embedded under a conventional-appearing white surface layer. In each layer the dyes are suspended in microcapsules that only release the dye at a precise temperature. The printing head delivers this temperature to specific regions releasing the dye. By varying the heat profile the different colours are released and different saturations achieved producing, ultimately, a photographic-quality image.

5.**018 thermal printing** General term for printing methods that use heat as a principal part of the image-forming process. Typical thermal print processes include thermal transfer printers and Thermal Autochrome, but laser printers (that use heat to bond an image onto the paper substrate) are not normally considered to be in this class.
→ 5.017 THERMAL AUTOCHROME (TA)

5.**019 three-colour process** Printing method that uses only cyan, magenta and yellow inks, synthesizing black from a combination of

5.007 *letterpress*

5.009 *lithography*

5.016 *screen printing*

5.006 *intaglio*

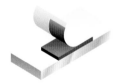

1 *Paper*
2 *Ink*
3 *Printing surface*
4 *Stencil*
5 *Screen mesh*

all three. Used now only on the most basic of inkjet printers due to the inability to achieve a perfect deep black. Also, the use of high densities of three inks can lead to the overwetting of the paper and bleeding.

5.**020 blad** Publishing term used to describe printed advance sales material usually consisting of a number of representative spreads wrapped (or bound) in the jacket proof.

Print finishing

5.**021 coated paper** A general term describing papers which have had some type of coating (normally a mineral compound) applied to their surface after the paper itself was made. Most papers used for printing images that have colour fidelity and ink integrity are coated. The surface finish (whether gloss, matt or otherwise) is determined by the type of tree or fibre used in the paper pulp, the fillers added during the papermaking process, and the coating and finishing process applied to the paper during drying.

5.**022 colour bar** The colour device printed on the edge of colour proofs or in the trim area of press sheets which enables the repro house and printer to check – by eye or with instruments – the accuracy of printing. The colour bar helps to monitor such things as ink density, paper stability, dot gain, trapping, and so on. Settings in the Page Setup menu of an

image-editing application usually include options for printing these.
→ 5.023 CORNER MARKS; 5.035 REGISTRATION MARKS; 5.043 COLOUR SEPARATION

5.**023 corner marks** Light, precise marks in the corner of an image (or a page of artwork) that indicate the **trimmed page size** (**TPS**). Can also be used as a positioning guide or for registration during make-up or printing. Also called 'crop marks' or '**trim marks**'.
→ 5.035 REGISTRATION MARKS

5.**024 crop marks** Short lines that can be included on a proof print (or other prints) to indicate to a print shop where the page should be trimmed. → 5.023 CORNER MARKS

5.**025 dry mounting** Technique, now largely superseded, which was used to mount traditional photographs onto display board using heat-sensitive adhesive tissue. The tissue is warmed with an iron to tack it down; then the iron is used to press the print and board together (specialized presses are also available to create the bond). The strangely named '**dry mounting sprays**' provide a similar adhesive that can be used hot or cold, depending on formulation.

5.**026 enamel** A coating that provides a glossy surface on paper.

5.**027 film coating** A lightweight protective film applied to paper on press (**machine seal** or **UV varnish**), often on the fifth unit of a five-colour press. Creative uses of varnishes include spot varnish directly on image areas of the page and matt lamination with spot varnish applied later to pick up

5.010 *mezzotint*

5.024 *crop marks*

highlights of the design. → 5.028 FILM LAMINATION/LAMINATING

5.028 film lamination/laminating A thin, protective, plastic film that is bonded to a printed paper under pressure and heat. Laminates can have a glossy or matt finish and have a variable effect on UV/sunlight resistance.

5.029 finishing All operations that take place after printing, such as mounting, collating, **folding**, **gathering**, **stitching**, **trimming** and, in the case of published books and magazines, **binding** and **packing**.

5.030 gsm Abbreviation for grams per square metre; measure of the density of paper (in Europe). In the US the measure of paper weight is in pounds (lbs.), written as # and refers to the weight of one **ream** (500 sheets) in the paper's basic size, measured in inches. Standard printing papers are between 80 and 130 gsm, although Bibles are often printed on papers as low as 30 gsm. Heavyweight papers start at around 160 gsm.

5.031 heat sealing A technique in which two materials, usually plastic, are fused together under heat and pressure. Where this involves the sandwiching of a paper or card sheet between the process, this is also known as laminating. → 5.027 FILM COATING; 5.028 FILM LAMINATION/LAMINATING

5.032 matt art A coated paper with a dull, smooth finish which gives excellent results in four-colour printing, without the glare associated with gloss art papers. In the US it is described as '**cameo coated paper**'.

5.033 matt/matte A flat, slightly dull surface. Matt finish photographic paper (or the equivalent) for use in laser or inkjet printers, typically used as an alternative to glossy surfaces where surface reflections might be an issue.

5.034 photo quality paper Paper (normally for an inkjet printer, or colour laser) that has a surface capable of accepting photorealistic (photo quality) images. The surface can be glossy, matt or of intermediate finish, but in all cases is usually heavyweight (greater than 200 gsm). → 5.030 GSM

5.035 registration marks Marks that can be printed on the margins of an image to determine whether, when printed as colour separations, all four components print in register. Some image-editing applications can be set (usually via the Page Setup command) to print registration and other marks.

5.036 varnish A liquid that dries with a hard surface and is generally insoluble in water. It is used in the manufacture of printing inks, in some drying agents and often used as an overcoating protector for finished printwork, particularly on matt or silk papers.

Printing terms

5.037 absorbency/absorption The property of a paper, or other substrate, to absorb liquids such as ink. In desktop printing, absorption is not only determined by the fibre structure of the paper, but also by the surface coating properties and constituency of the ink. Incorrect absorption can lead to printing problems such as show through and drying failure. Visually this leads to effects such as **surface blooming**, reticulation, mottling and poor definition. Many desktop printers (such as inkjets) can adapt their printing methods, and the ink quantities delivered, to accommodate different substrate types. Typically, an inkjet will differentiate between plain paper, coated inkjet paper, photographic (quality) paper and plastic films (used for transparencies and lightboxes).

5.038 air A large area (or areas) of white space in a layout. It can also be used to describe a large area of white space around a subject in an image, sometimes done deliberately to make the addition of text or a caption easier when constructing a layout. → 5.073 LAYOUT

5.039 background printing A computer printing option (that is usually enabled) that allows a printer to print while the computer remains available for other operations in the foreground. The effectiveness of background printing sometimes depends on how well the printer is buffered. → 2.303 BUFFER

5.040 banding An artefact of some printers where areas of continuous tonal gradient are reproduced by discontinuous steps in the levels of tone. Although this deficiency can be used creatively (it can create

5.043 *colour separation*

Blue filter

Green filter

Red filter

Yellow printer film

Magenta printer film

Cyan printer film

Black printer film

Yellow proof

Magenta proof

Cyan proof

Black proof

Yellow proof

Yellow + magenta

Yellow + magenta
+ cyan

Yellow + magenta
+ cyan + black

posterized effects) it is generally to be avoided. It tends to occur more with printers not specifically designed for photographic or photorealistic output and unable to mix or dither colour appropriately. ➔ 1.444 POSTERIZE; 4.404 DITHERING

5.**041 colour chart** A printed reference chart used in colour reproduction to select or match colour tints made from percentage variations of the four process colours. Though standard colour charts are produced (such as the Pantone set) it is usual to use a set produced by the printing company chosen to undertake the respective printing if absolute accuracy is required. The chart should also be printed on a paper stock that is identical (or at least has similar characteristics) to that of the intended job. ➔ 4.514 COLOUR PICKER (1); 4.515 COLOUR SWATCH; 5.080 PANTONE®

5.**042 colour correction (reproduction)** The process of adjusting colour values in reproduction in order to achieve the desired result. Although this can occur at the scanning or image-manipulation stages, colour correction is generally carried out after wet proofing (proofs created using process colour inks).

5.**043 colour separation** The process of dividing a colour image into the four individual process colours (hence its alternative name '**process colour separation**') – cyan, magenta, yellow and black – for reproducing on a printing press. The traditional method for this (using a

'process' camera) has now been superseded by high-end scanners. The majority of image-editing applications are able to generate **separations** directly. ➔ 2.251 SCANNER; 4.442 CMYK

5.**044 colour separations** The set of four films (or in the case of digital imaging, four images), one for each of the four process colours – cyan, magenta, yellow and black – generated as a result of the colour separation process. ➔ 2.266 PRINTER; 4.442 CMYK; 5.043 COLOUR SEPARATION

5.**045 continuous feeder** Attachment on a sheet-fed printing press or some high-end inkjet printers that enables the sheet-fed media to be replaced with a continuous roll. Such media is normally provided in rolls which have greater capacity than a sheet feeder and also offer greater flexibility in printing.

5.**046 contrast ratio** A term used as a measure of paper (or equivalent substrate) opacity. A contrast ratio of 100% is regarded as being totally opaque.

5.**047 copy** Any original document (manuscript, typescript, transparency or computer disk) that is to be used for reproduction.

5.**048 cutout** A halftone image in which the background has been removed to provide a freeform image. Also called an '**outline halftone**'. ➔ 5.004 HALFTONE (1)

5.**049 descreen(ing)** The technique of removing a halftone dot pattern from a printed original to avoid an undesirable 'moiré' pattern which may occur if a halftone screen is reapplied. This can be achieved in image-editing applications using built-in

5.049 *descreen(ing)*

before

after

'filters' (effects) to slightly blur the image and then sharpen it. Scanners feature descreening routines that will remove the pattern during the image-acquisition process. → 4.132 PATTERN REMOVAL; 4.413 INTERPOLATION; 5.004 HALFTONE (1)

5.050 desensitize Chemical treatment of a lithographic plate using an 'etch' to make the non-image areas water-receptive. In desensitizing these areas they repel ink, leaving the ink only on the image areas. → 5.009 LITHOGRAPHY; 5.012 OFFSET LITHOGRAPHY; 5.113 ETCH

5.051 desktop publishing (DTP) The process of document creation and publishing (i.e., printing) using desktop computers. The term originated with the launch of the Macintosh computer (and, to a limited extent, with its predecessor, the Apple Lisa) which boasted a GUI that enabled projects to be visualized accurately on the computer desktop. The subsequent advent of precise printing technologies such as PostScript and RIP have enabled professional results from DTP. The term 'electronic publishing' tends to be used for more sophisticated DTP installations. → 2.018 DESKTOP COMPUTER; 2.047 MACINTOSH; 4.392 QUARKXPRESS

5.052 digital print process Any printing that is produced directly from digital data without any intermediate film or plate output, e.g., Computer-to-Plate (CTP) or computer file to a digital printer.

5.053 digital printing Any print produced from digital data. → 5.052 DIGITAL PRINT PROCESS

5.054 dot pattern The pattern created by halftone dots after all colours are printed. If the image is printed in perfect registration the dots from the separate colours will produce a 'rosette' pattern. → 4.132 PATTERN REMOVAL; 5.049 DESCREEN(ING)

5.055 dots per inch (dpi) A unit of measurement used to represent the input resolution of devices such as scanners, or output resolution of imagesetters and printers. → 5.074 LINES PER INCH (LPI); 5.083 PIXELS PER INCH (PPI)

5.056 double-tone ink A specialized printing ink that produces a secondary tone (while maintaining the original colour) as it dries. The result is artwork with the illusion of two-colour printing in a single pass.

5.057 drum The print or image-transfer mechanism in a laser printer or drum scanner. Also a term for the cylinder of a printing press.

5.058 dye-based ink Any ink in which the colour is produced from aniline dyes. As such they are distinguished from the alternate pigment-based inks. The latter are more permanent but can be more problematic in use.

5.059 finished page area The area on a computer layout or printed sheet that will form the page after the sheet is trimmed. Once printed, the finished page area is delineated by corner marks ('trim', or 'crop' marks).

5.060 first generation copy A duplicate of an item, such as a photograph, made directly from the original (as distinct from a copy made from another copy of the original). → 1.499 DUPE

5.061 flat colour A uniform colour of consistent hue with no variation or gradient of luminosity or density. In digital printing, flat colours over large areas caused problems, but these have been overcome in the new generation of digital printers. → 5.099 SPOT COLOUR

5.062 full colour Alternate name for 'four colour' and also a term used to describe colour reproduction for printing (conventionally using cyan, magenta, yellow and black inks) where the final result is reproduced with a full range of colours. → 5.003 FOUR-COLOUR PROCESS

5.063 greyness A measure of the contamination of the cyan, magenta or yellow inks. A higher greyness value indicates a lower level of colour purity and saturation.

5.064 Greyscale Component Replacement (GCR) One of two methods (the other is Undercolour Removal) used in prepress to produce an effective black on press. Black ink is used in place of some of the cyan, magenta and yellow in both neutral and coloured image areas. This leads to deep, saturated colours that are more accurately defined than with Undercolour Removal and have a better grey balance. The final choice of method will be determined by the twin requirements of the paper stock and the preferences of the print shop. → 5.107 UNDERCOLOUR REMOVAL (UCR)

233

5.**065 greyscale (printing)** A tonal scale from white to black (usually in equal increments) printed at the edge of an image or document for the purpose of controlling the quality of both colour and black-and-white photographic processing (and assessing quality in a halftone print).

5.**066 halftone dot** The smallest basic element of a halftone. The term 'dot' can describe a round, square, elliptical or any other shape. The number, or frequency, of halftone dots is measured traditionally in lines per inch (lpi). → 5.005 HALFTONE (2)

5.**067 hexachrome** A printing process based upon six inks rather than the conventional four inks of the CMYK process. True Hexachrome (capital 'H') adds orange and green ink to CMYK. Other six-ink systems often go by the name of hexachrome but should properly be called six-colour systems. These usually add pale magenta and pale yellow to offer improved skin tones.

5.**068 ink penetration** The degree to which ink penetrates a substrate. Knowledge of the characteristics of ink penetration (which will depend on the ink used, substrate and the printing mechanism) is important to avoid problems such as smudging, feathering or bleeding.

5.**069 ink receptivity** The degree to which a substrate such as paper or plastic-coated film will absorb printing ink. → 5.068 INK PENETRATION

5.**070 knockout (printing)** An area of background colour that has been masked ('knocked out') by a foreground object, and thus does not print. The opposite of 'overprint'. Similar masks are used by image-editing applications to restrict or prevent the action of commands or filters applied to the image. → 4.367 KNOCKOUT

5.**071 landscape format** An image or page format in which the width is greater than the height. Sometimes called horizontal format. → 5.085 PORTRAIT FORMAT

5.**072 lap** Shortened form of '**overlap**', a term describing those colours which overlap to avoid registration problems ('trapping'). → 5.105 TRAPPING

5.**073 layout** A drawing which gives the general appearance of a design, indicating the position of text and illustrations. In DTP, a layout is created digitally. The designer sets up a master grid with all the page attributes and text stylesheets. Also known as '**page layout**'.

5.**074 lines per inch (lpi)** A reproduction and printing measurement for the resolution of a halftone, calculated as half the dpi of the scanned image. A 300 dpi scan is therefore 150 lpi.

5.**075 master** An original item from which all copies are made, or upon which any changes are marked or made.

5.**076 medium** A solvent, usually a viscose substance such as linseed oil, gum arabic or a synthetic equivalent, which is used with a pigment or dye to create printing ink or artist's paint.

5.**077 mock-up** A first rendering of a project (such as a page, a book or composite

5.066 *halftone dot*

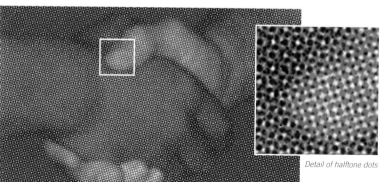

Detail of halftone dots

Typical reproduced image

image) in which the main elements are represented by simulation of low resolution images (that may or may not be based on the final images) produced to assess and evaluate the anticipated final effect rather than to show the result in detail. A mock-up will show the appearance of a font, for example, rather than the exact words that will appear. Based on the mock-up, changes can be made to aid legibility or the layout altered to achieve a better 'balance'. Mock-ups are also known as '**presentation visuals**' or '**finished roughs**'.

5.**078 orientation** The print direction of a page, or the format of an image (portrait or landscape).

5.**079 output resolution** The resolution of a printer, monitor, imagesetter or similar device, usually measured in dpi (dots per inch). The relationship between output resolution and halftone screen ruling determines the tonal range that can be printed. The following formula should be used to calculate the optimum number of greys that can be achieved (remembering that 256 is the PostScript maximum): (output resolution ÷ screen ruling)2 + 1 = shades of grey. Therefore an image output at 1,200 dpi and printed with a screen ruling of 90 lpi will produce 178 shades of grey. Increasing the screen ruling creates smaller halftone dots and adds detail to an image but it also reduces the number of greys, so the same image output at 1,200 dpi and printed with a screen ruling of 175 lpi will produce only 48 shades of grey. The screen ruling in four-colour process work is usually 150 lpi, so for an image to print with the maximum number of 256 greys it will need to be output with an imagesetter resolution of 2,400 dpi. A typical resolution for a monitor is 72–90 dpi, for a laser printer 600 dpi, and for an imagesetter anything upward of 1,000 dpi. → 4.106 INPUT RESOLUTION; 5.074 LINES PER INCH (LPI)

5.**080 PANTONE®** The proprietary trademark for a system of colour standards created by Pantone Inc. In the PANTONE® system, each colour bears a description of its formulation (in percentages) for subsequent printing in order that colours can be accurately mixed and remixed. The PANTONE MATCHING SYSTEM (**PMS**)

is used extensively and means that the colour or colours specified by the originator of artwork can have his (or her) work produced with colour accuracy by any printer. However, PANTONE colours are produced for four-colour printing by mixing the correct percentages of the CMYK inks specified in the PANTONE swatch. They are not supplied pre-mixed.

5.**081 photomechanical transfer (PMT)** A method of transferring images onto paper, film or metal litho plates by means of photography. An image produced by this method is also known as diffusion transfer, chemical transfer or velox.

5.**082 photoresist** A coating impervious to acid or other etching medium that is selectively applied to a printing plate to protect it from attack between printing. At one time litho plates were stored; however, with the improvements in recovery and recycling techniques and the reduction in material costs, it is cheaper to remake the plates if a reprint is called for.

5.**083 pixels per inch (ppi)** A measure of the resolution in an image (or, less commonly used now, in a CCD imaging chip). Normally measured horizontally. Also a measurement of the ability of a scanner to discern detail in a scanned image. → 5.074 LINES PER INCH (LPI); 7.060 PIXEL

5.**084 plate** A sheet, originally metal but now also plastic, resin or paper, from which an image is printed at, or via, a commercial printer. The plate can be generated by the user or, more usually, is produced by the printer from origination material (including digital files).

5.**085 portrait format** An image or page in a vertical format. Sometimes called upright format. → 5.071 LANDSCAPE FORMAT

5.**086 press** Any machine that transfers (prints) an impression, originally from a block or plate onto paper or some other material.

5.**087 process ink gamut (PIG) chart** A chart used to compare the different colours (hues) that are produced by a range of ink and substrate combinations: the same colour may print in quite different ways with differing substrates. Using a PIG chart is recommended for critical applications to assess colour fidelity for a chosen combination.

5.**088 register** Colour plates printed sequentially, wet on wet, directly over each other so that equivalent elements in each are overlaid. Any error is described as misregistration, being 'out of register' or 'out of fit'.

5.**089 registration colour** In many graphics applications, a default colour that, when applied to items such as crop marks, will print on every separation plate in order to ensure perfect registration.

5.**090 rich black** A very dense black produced by underprinting black ink areas with another colour (usually magenta) at a density of between 20% and 40%.

5.**091 rotary press** Description of any printing press in which the printing surface is on a rotating cylinder or drum.

5.**092 rough** An early drawing of a proposed design showing the principal components positionally, rather than in any detail. Sometimes known as a '**visual**' or '**scamp**'. → 5.073 LAYOUT

5.**093 secondary colour** Sometimes known as an overprint colour, secondary colours are produced when one primary colour overprints another.

5.**094 separation artwork** Artwork which consists of separate layers for each of the colours used. → 5.043 COLOUR SEPARATION

5.**095 separation filters** The filters used to separate colours photographically in order that each colour can be printed individually. Each nominally transmits about one-third of the spectrum. → 5.043 COLOUR SEPARATION

5.**096 service bureau** The general printing equivalent of a photofinisher. Service **bureaux** provide printing services for digital images (to professional standards and to large sizes, as compared with the 'consumer' level services provided by a photofinisher), and other work such as colour scanning and high-resolution imagesetting.

5.**097 solid** An image element or area of a printed page printed with 100% of a colour.

5.**098 source document** Any original used as a master for reproduction.

5.**099 spot colour** Any colour used for printing which has been 'custom mixed' for the job, as opposed to one of the four standard process colours. Spot colours need not be used in addition to the four standard colours; adding a spot colour with black is a cheap way to introduce high-impact colour to an otherwise monochrome project.

5.**100 spread** A technique used in print preparation to ensure that two abutting areas of ink print without gaps (trapped). A spread traps (usually) a lighter colour object to a surrounding dark one by expanding its edges slightly until the two colours overlap. It is always preferable to expand a lighter colour to a darker one as it is the darker colour that defines the edge. Originally spreads were created by overexposing the film slightly when creating the separations but contemporary processes provide automatic trapping, including spread. → 5.105 TRAPPING

5.070 *knockout (printing)*

5.100 *spread*

5.101 tone compression The inevitable result of printing an image, causing a reduction of the range of tones from light to dark.

5.102 toner The very fine plastic powder used in laser (and equivalent LED page printers and photocopiers) to produce an image. Standard machines use black toner but colour printers use yellow, cyan and magenta toners also. The fine nature gives toner good electrostatic properties that ensure the image is transferred to the electrically charged drum prior to being fused onto the paper substrate.

5.103 total area coverage A measure of the amount of ink applied by a printing press. The total area coverage (**TAC**) ranges from 0% (when no ink is applied) through to 400% with nominal 100% coverage with each of the four inks. In practice the maximum TAC is 300%.

5.104 total ink limit The maximum ink density achievable by a printer (or printing press). The nominal maxima are black 100% and a total ink limit of 300%.

5.105 trapping The slight and deliberate overlap of two adjacent colours designed to prevent any gaps that might otherwise appear between the two due to slight misregistration between printing plates. Choke is a particular form of trapping; a choke traps a light background to a darker (and enclosed) foreground object by expanding the boundary of the inner object. Compare this with spread, where a dark background extends over its normal boundary to trap a lighter subject. The term '**wet trapping**' describes the process of printing where each colour is applied before the previous has dried. → 5.100 SPREAD

5.106 ultraviolet (UV) light (2) Light waves beyond the visible violet part of the spectrum. As they can be absorbed by certain photosensitive materials, they are used for platemaking, printing inks, etc. Note that UV light also has a detrimental effect on inks used in many printing processes, especially those of ink jets, which should be protected from exposure both before and after printing.

5.107 Undercolour Removal (UCR) Alternate method of generating black in a printed image (the other is Greyscale Component Removal). UCR uses black ink to replace cyan, magenta and yellow in areas

determined to be 'neutral' (i.e. comprising equal components of all three colours). This method tends to be used in undemanding situations, as the lower ink usage means more rapid drying times with little compromise in image quality. → 5.064 GREYSCALE COMPONENT REPLACEMENT (GCR)

Pre-press terms

5.108 Color-Key A proprietary dry proofing system, which was developed by **3M**. → 5.112 DRY PROOF

5.109 contact film Special 'continuous tone' film used to produce contact negatives from a film positive original (or vice versa). Sometimes known as colour-blind film.

5.110 Cromalin A proprietary dry-proofing system from DuPont which uses toners on light-sensitive paper. Also known as 'offpress proofs' or 'prepress proofs'. Though the term is still widely used to describe the **DuPont** process it is often misused when applied to any dry-proofing process.

5.111 direct digital colour proof (DDCP) Any colour proof made directly from digital data without resorting to the intermediate step of using separation films. Typical examples would be proofs produced directly on an inkjet or laser printer. → 2.260 INKJET PRINTER

5.112 dry proof Any colour proof made without printing ink, such as a Cromalin or Matchprint, but particularly proofs produced digitally – from a laser, wax transfer or other 'dry' process. → 5.108 COLOR-KEY; 5.110 CROMALIN

5.113 etch The process of dissolving away parts of a printing plate to leave either a relief image or intaglio image (where the image to be printed is below the surface of the plate) or, on film, to reduce the size of halftone dots. The term can also be used to describe the process of desensitizing the non-image areas (which are protected by a 'ground') of a litho plate to make them receptive to water instead of ink. → 5.006 INTAGLIO; 5.050 DESENSITIZE

5.114 film positive A record of an image on clear film, emulating the original. Used for film assembly and for making printing plates.

5.115 finished art(work) Any illustrative material prepared for reproduction and with no further modifications or alterations required. Despite the term 'art' such material can be largely text (such as a page from a newspaper or magazine) and can be provided digitally. Artwork which includes – or is composed entirely of – text is usually called 'camera-ready artwork'.

5.**116 halftone screen** Originally an overlay screen of glass etched with a grid and used to convert a continuous tone image into halftone dots in order that it can be printed. Computer applications now generate a halftone image digitally without the need for a physical halftone screen, by generating each halftone dot as an individual 'cell'. Sometimes called a '**crossline screen**' or '**contact screen**'.
→ 5.004 HALFTONE (1)

5.**117 imagesetter** A high-resolution output device that is used to generate reproduction-quality copy for printing, either as film negatives or positives, or on photographic bromide paper for use as camera-ready artwork.

5.**118 markup** A set of instructions and specifications prepared for any material to be submitted for typesetting, reproduction or printing. A rough pasteup, for example, will be marked up prior to the creation of a final version. → 5.120 PASTEUP

5.**119 page proofs** Proof copies of pages that have been ordered into the correct sequence (**imposition**). Traditionally, this stage followed approval of the **galley proofs** (the first proofs), printed as a continuous strip of text. However, DTP has effectively dispensed with galley proofs, so the first page proofs are normally run into the page template with formatted stylesheets.

5.**120 pasteup** Traditionally a copy of a page onto which the prepared images and text were pasted to assess the appearance and mark up any alterations (a **rough pasteup**),

or a final copy for photographing and output as film for printing (a camera-ready pasteup). Digital (onscreen) pasteups can now be created on DTP systems and have replaced mechanical pasteup.
→ 5.118 MARKUP

5.**121 photomechanical transfer** A photographic print from a process camera used in the production of camera-ready artwork.
→ 1.127 PROCESS CAMERA

5.**122 prepress** Descriptive term for any one (or all) of the reproduction processes that occur between the design stage and printing. The term is used for the more specific description of colour separations and planning. Sometimes called '**origination**'.

5.**123 progressive proofs** Proofs used in colour printing that show each colour printed separately, and also combined (in different combinations but in the order that they will be finally printed), in order that any deficiencies not seen hitherto can be identified and corrected.

5.**124 proof** A prototype of a printing project that can be (and usually is) taken at each stage of the production. The proof is used to identify shortcomings in the layout or the colour regime at the earliest stage in order that changes can be effected in the most cost-effective way. Proofs can (at appropriate stages) come from inkjet printers, laser printers, colour lasers or from a dry-proofing process (such as Cromalin).

5.**125 trap** An overlap of colour boundaries introduced to a CMYK image, usually at the creation stage, to compensate for misregistration between colour plates when that image is printed. This avoids unsightly 'gaps' between areas of colour.
→ 5.105 TRAPPING

5.105 *trapping (spread)*

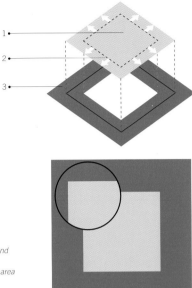

1 = label
2 = label
3 = label

1 Lighter
foreground
colour
2 Spread area
3 Darker
background
colour

5.105 *trapping (choke)*

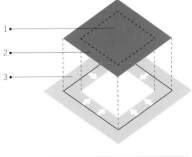

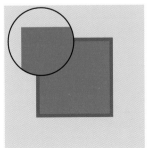

1 Darker
foreground
colour
2 Choke area
3 Lighter
background
colour

6 WEB TERMS

Web

6.**001 absolute URL** A complete address, or 'uniform resource locator' (URL), which takes you to a specific location within a website rather than to the home page of the site. An absolute URL contains the full file path to the page document location on the host server. For example, the URL 'http://www.yourcamera.com' will take you to the 'Your Camera' website, but the absolute URL 'http://www.yourcamera.com/extrainfo/aboutexposure/index.htm' will direct you to the index page for the exposure information section.

6.**002 active hyperlink** The currently selected link in a web browser, often differentiated from other links on the same page by displaying in another colour. Hyperlinks often change colour when selected so that when a page is revisited, the user can see those links visited previously.

6.**003 ActiveX Controls** A proprietary technology from Microsoft designed for enhancing web pages. Like Java 'applets', ActiveX Controls can be downloaded from the Internet. Unlike Java applets, however, ActiveX Controls are not platform-independent and are mainly supported only in Microsoft Windows environments. Web pages featuring ActiveX components may have difficulty running on certain browsers and platforms and hence they should be avoided when cross-platform and cross-browser applications are likely. → 2.124 JAVA

6.**004 address (2)** The string of alphanumeric characters used by Internet users when communicating with each other via email; hence 'email address'. The term is also used informally to describe a website URL.

6.**005 Asymmetric Digital Subscriber Line (ADSL)** A high-speed communications link capable of transmitting large amounts of

data (such as a TV picture) in one direction, and a small amount (such as a telephone call) in the other. Speeds of around 2 mbps (megabits per second) can be achieved – 16 times faster than ISDN. ADSL is useful for downloading information from the web (such as large files and streaming media) but less effective at uploading data.

6.**006 attachment** Any file (such as an image or text document) appended to an email message for electronic transmission. When the email is sent, the attached file, or files, are also sent. Sometimes the files are automatically compressed together for sending. → 6.021 EMAIL/E-MAIL

6.**007 banner** An image on a web page, often animated, and designed to attract attention; usually an advertisement. Most commonly these are stripped across the top of the web page.

6.**008 baud** The unit of transmission of data. The **baud rate** describes the speed of data transmission and is usually equivalent to the number of bits per second transmitted. → 6.009 BIT RATE

6.**009 bit rate** The speed at which data is transmitted across communications channels, measured in bits per second (bps). Modem speeds typically range from 2,400 bps to 56,000 bps, but higher speeds are measured in kilobits (kbps) or even megabits (mbps) per second – ISDN connections, for example, are usually either 65 kbps or 128 kbps. 'Bit rate' is sometimes erroneously referred to as 'baud rate'. → 2.429 BIT; 6.008 BAUD

6.**010 Bookmark** A feature of Netscape's web browsers that can remember the address of frequently visited websites when instructed by the user. Internet Explorer has a similar feature called 'Favorites'. → 6.011 BROWSER

6.**011 browser/web browser** Program that enables the viewing or 'browsing' of World Wide

Web pages across the Internet. Most used browsers are Netscape's 'Navigator' and Microsoft's 'Internet Explorer'. Version numbers are important, as these indicate the level of HTML that the browser supports. The alternate browser 'Opera' is competitive because of its compact size and efficient performance. → 6.041 INTERNET; 6.096 WORLD WIDE WEB (WWW)

6.**012 bulletin board service (BBS)** A facility, usually noncommercial and run by educational and special interest groups, for the exchange of files and information relating (usually) to specialist subjects. BBS can be accessed via the web and an Internet Service Provider (ISP), but (as many BBSs predate the contemporary Internet) they can also be directly accessed via a modem and the BBS's telephone number. (Many of the URLs mentioned at the back of the book have useful forums and discussion rooms on their websites.) → 6.046 INTERNET SERVICE PROVIDER (ISP)

6.**013 channel** A feature of web technology whereby information is automatically transmitted to your web browser, as distinct from having to request it yourself. Channels typically include news, weather and stock market reports, as well as special interest information.

6.**014 Common Gateway Interface (CGI)** A programming technique for transferring data between web server software and other applications (particularly databases).

6.**015 cookie** A small piece of information deposited in the web browser on your hard disk by a WWW site, storing such things as custom page settings or even personal information (e.g. your address or your password for that site). When you revisit a site, the cookie helps bypass selected login features and can bring up a personal front page without any further input. → 6.096 WORLD WIDE WEB (WWW)

6.**016 cyberspace** A colloquialism for the virtual environment (as opposed to 'real' space) in which communication and activities take place, particularly the Internet but also general telecommunication links, computer networks and computers themselves. → 7.079 VIRTUAL REALITY

6.**017 dial-up** A connection to the Internet or to a network which is made by dialling a telephone number for access. Dialling is normally performed automatically by the originating computer or attached external modem.

6.**018 document (2)** The entire contents of a single HTML file. HTML documents are generally referred to as 'web pages', since this is how they are rendered for display by browsers. → 6.011 BROWSER; 6.096 WORLD WIDE WEB (WWW)

6.**019 dynamic HTML/DHTML** Dynamic hypertext markup language. A development of the basic HTML code used to create web pages and web documentation that enables users to add enhanced features such as basic animations and highlighted buttons to web pages without relying on browser plug-ins. DHTML compatibility is built into later versions (version 4.0 or later) of web browsers. → 6.011 BROWSER

6.**020 e-commerce** Contraction of electronic commerce. Commercial transactions conducted electronically over a network or the Internet. Business to business (B2B) transactions have used e-commerce for some time but business to consumer (B2C) transactions are now also commonplace. → 6.021 EMAIL/E-MAIL

6.**021 email/e-mail** Contraction of **electronic mail**. Messages sent from your computer to someone else with a computer, either locally through a network or transmitted over telephone lines using a modem. Email is rarely sent direct from one user to another; instead it is sent to a mailbox (normally on the computer of the addressee's ISP where it remains until collected by that person). → 2.389 CLIENT/SERVER; 6.041 INTERNET; 6.076 SPAM/SPAMMING

6.**022 error correction (code)** The transmission of a data code using an encoding method that enables errors that occur en-route to be detected and (usually) corrected. Error correction techniques are used in conventional modems that are prone to electronic interference, which can corrupt data.

6.**023 Extensible Markup Language (XML)** An evolution (and probable successor) of HTML (the underlying language used on web pages), offering more sophisticated control and formatting. XML allows the creation of user-defined tags, which expands the amount of information that can be provided about the data held in documents. → 6.036 HYPERTEXT MARKUP LANGUAGE (HTML); 6.080 TAG

6.**024 extranet** The part of an organization's internal computer network or intranet which is available to outside users; for example, information services for customers. Extranet hosting is a service provided by third parties to deliver resources via the Internet (or sometimes extranet) and managed either by that third party or by the organization.
→ 6.047 INTRANET

6.**025 Favorites** A feature of Microsoft's Internet Explorer web browser which enables users to bookmark frequently visited websites to speed up future access. The equivalent in Netscape's Navigator is called 'Bookmarks'. → 6.011 BROWSER

6.**026 File Transfer Protocol (FTP)** A standard system for transmitting files between computers across the Internet or a network. Although web browsers incorporate FTP capabilities, dedicated FTP applications provide greater flexibility. Typically, when creating a web page, an FTP application will be used to upload this to the web.

6.**027 forum** An online service that enables users to post messages which other users may respond or add to. These message 'threads' are usually organized around special interests, such as software user groups or popular cultural themes.
→ 6.059 NEWSGROUP; 6.087 USENET

6.**028 global area network (GAN)** A worldwide network of computers, similar to the Internet but linking 'wide area networks' (WANs). → 2.415 WIDE AREA NETWORK (WAN)

6.**029 history (list)** A list of visited web pages logged by your browser during a session on the web. The history provides a means of speedy access to pages already visited during that session. The length of your history list (in terms of time – lists will expire after a predetermined number of days, or entries) can be configured in the browser preferences. → 6.096 WORLD WIDE WEB (WWW)

6.**030 home page** A World Wide Web term used to describe the main page or contents page on a particular site, which provides links to all the other pages on that site. It sometimes has the alternate meaning of the page that your own browser automatically links to when you launch it.

6.**031 host** A networked computer that provides services to anyone who can access it, such as for email, file transfer and access to the web. When you connect to the Internet, and select a website, information will be transferred to you from the host's computer.

6.**032 hostname** The name that identifies the computer hosting a website.

6.**033 hotlist, hot list** A list of links found on a website that provides links to others on a similar theme or considered to be appropriate to the visitor.

6.**034 hyperlink** Short for **hypertext link**. A link embedded in a document which provides

6.030 *home page*

1 Home page address

a direct link to other documents. Conventionally, such links are identified by being underlined or highlighted in a different colour. Clicking on or selecting a hyperlink takes you to another document, part of a document or website. → 6.002 ACTIVE HYPERLINK; 6.035 HYPERTEXT

6.**035 hypertext** A programming concept that links any single word or group of words to an unlimited number of others, typically text on a web page that has an embedded link to other documents or websites. Hypertext links are usually underlined and/or in a different colour to the rest of the text, and are activated by clicking on them. Web browsers are normally configured so that the hypertext link changes colour after a visit to indicate that the visit has occurred. → 6.034 HYPERLINK

6.**036 Hypertext Markup Language (HTML)** A text-based 'page description language' (PDL) used to format documents published on the World Wide Web, and which can be viewed with web browsers. Many web page creation tools help create pages by using WYSIWYG displays in which page elements are positioned by the user and text added appropriately. Such creations are converted to HTML before the website is pasted to its ultimate location.

6.**037 Hypertext Transfer Protocol (http)** A text-based set of rules by which files on the World Wide Web are transferred, defining the commands that web browsers use to communicate with web servers. The vast majority of World Wide Web addresses, or 'URLs', are prefixed with 'http://'. The prefix https:// is normally used to denote a secure server is in use and is normally used by banks and some shopping sites for their online operations. → 6.011 BROWSER

6.**038 image map** An image that features a set of embedded links to other documents or websites. These are activated when the mouse is clicked on the appropriate area. Often the 'front page' of a website contains such a map. → 4.162 SLICE TOOL

6.**039 index page** The first page of any website which is selected automatically by the browser if it is named 'default.htm', 'default.html', 'index.htm' or 'index.html'

6.**040 Integrated Services Digital Network (ISDN)** A telecommunication technology which transmits data on special digital lines

rather than standard analogue lines and is thus much faster. Normal ISDN transmits and receives at 64 kbs, but lines are normally 'paired' to offer 128 kbs. Modifications of basic ISDN can achieve better transfer rates but not all ISPs will be able to communicate via these. Note that ADSL (Asymmetric Digital Subscriber Line) links and Cable Modems (which connect via Cable TV (CATV) systems) are even faster than ISDN lines.

6.**041 Internet** The worldwide network of computers linked by phone (or other connections), providing individual and corporate users with access to information, companies, newsgroups, discussion areas and much more. → 6.096 WORLD WIDE WEB (WWW)

6.**042 Internet Explorer/Explorer** A cross-platform web browser produced by Microsoft. → 6.011 BROWSER; 6.056 NAVIGATOR

6.**043 Internet Protocol (IP)** The networking rules which tie computers together across the Internet. → 6.041 INTERNET; 6.044 INTERNET PROTOCOL (IP) ADDRESS

6.**044 Internet Protocol (IP) address** The unique numeric address of a particular computer or server on the Internet (or any TCP/IP network). Each one is unique and consists of a dotted decimal notation, for example 194.152.64.68. Such addresses can be either permanently assigned to a computer or (in the case of dial-up connections) temporarily assigned. → 6.043 INTERNET PROTOCOL (IP); 6.083 TRANSMISSION CONTROL PROTOCOL (TCP)

6.**045 Internet Relay Chat (IRC)** An Internet facility provided by some ISPs which allows multiple users to type messages to each other and exchange files in real-time on different 'channels' sometimes referred to as 'rooms'. → 6.046 INTERNET SERVICE PROVIDER (ISP)

6.**046 Internet service provider (ISP)** Any organization that provides access to the Internet. Often this is a gateway to the Internet (giving users access to both web pages and email) but many ISPs also provide additional services (such as information and shopping pages) and space for the user to create their own web pages. ISPs are sometimes known as Internet Access Providers (particularly when few or no value-added services are

provided) and as Online Service Providers.
→ 6.012 BULLETIN BOARD SERVICE (BBS)

6.**047 Intranet** A network of computers similar to the Internet but closed to access from the general user. Intranets tend to be used mainly by large corporations, governments and educational institutions in order to share resources and distribute information that is normally classified or to which the organization in question does not want widespread access. → 6.041 INTERNET

6.**048 link** A pointer, such as a highlighted piece of text in an HTML document (a web page, for example) or multimedia presentation, or an area on an image map, which takes the user to another location, page or screen just by clicking on it.
→ 6.034 HYPERLINK; 6.038 IMAGE MAP

6.**049 MacTCP** Acronym for **Macintosh transmission control protocol**, the Mac OS version of TCP. → 6.083 TRANSMISSION CONTROL PROTOCOL (TCP)

6.**050 map file** A file used to contain data relating to an image map → 6.038 IMAGE MAP

6.**051 markup language** A defined set of rules describing the way files are displayed by any particular method. In conventional Internet applications, HTML (and its extensions such as DHTML) is the principal language used for creating web pages. → 5.118 MARKUP

6.**052 Mozilla** Version of the Netscape Communicator source code released in 1998 for development by any interested bodies. As well as providing the

underpinning of **Netscape 6** (through the **Gecko** evolution) it has been employed in creating custom browsers and even control systems for television set-top boxes. → 6.057 NETSCAPE

6.**053 multipurpose Internet mail extensions (MIME)** A format for conveying web documents and related files across the Internet, typically via email.

6.**054 navigation bar** A feature of a web browser, web page or multimedia presentation which helps you to 'navigate' your way through pages by clicking on buttons or text.

6.**055 navigation button** A button in a web browser, web page or multimedia presentation which links you to a particular location or page. → 6.054 NAVIGATION BAR

6.**056 Navigator** A cross-platform web browser produced by Netscape. → 6.011 BROWSER; 6.042 INTERNET EXPLORER; 6.057 NETSCAPE

6.**057 Netscape** Company responsible for pioneering the web browser with its Navigator and Communicator products. Now part of AOL.

6.**058 Network News Transfer Protocol (NNTP)** An Internet standard for the retrieval and posting of news articles. Also known as a '**news server**'. → 6.059 NEWSGROUP; 6.087 USENET

6.**059 newsgroup** A group of users with a shared interest who post and share articles, news and information on the Internet. Such groups can be closed (that is, open only to subscribers or members of a group) or open, where anyone can post information. → 6.087 USENET

6.042 *Internet Explorer*

1 *Menu bar*
2 *Navigation buttons*
3 *Address space*
4 *Page display*

6.**060 online service provider** Alternate (and little used) term for an Internet Service Provider. → 6.046 INTERNET SERVICE PROVIDER (ISP)

6.**061 Opera** Browser from the Norway-based Opera Software A/S offered in Mac, Windows, OS/2, BeOS and Linux variations. Opera's unique selling point is its speed of operation compared with the established browsers.

6.**062 Point-to-Point Protocol (PPP)** The most common means of establishing dial-up connections to the Internet. It provides a method for transmitting packets over serial point-to-point links. It also allows you to use other standard protocols (such as **IPX** and TCP/IP) over a standard telephone connection and can be used for local area network (LAN) connections.

6.**063 portal** An Internet 'front page' that provides controlled access to users. Users accessing the Internet from a portal are given quick links to relevant sites, useful news items and even extracts from other web pages (giving live weather information, for example). Some portals also act as **limiters**, restricting users only to specified sites (and preventing unrestrained Internet access), or used to gather resources in one place: perhaps for educational purposes or to limit children's web access to preferred sites. → 1.520 PICTURE PORTAL

6.**064 Post Office Protocol (POP)** An email protocol for retrieval and storage – a '**POP** account' is what you tell your email software to use to send and retrieve mail.

6.**065 RealAudio** A helper application which enables audio playback in web browsers. **Real Player** (which replays video and audio) is a free download as a browser plug-in.

6.**066 relative URL** A link that is connected to the current web page's URL so that a browser looks for the link in the same location – i.e., website – as the web page currently being displayed. → 6.001 ABSOLUTE URL

6.**067 request** The act of clicking on a button or link in a web browser. In doing so a request is being made of a remote server for an HTML document to be sent.

6.**068 search engine** Used generically to describe both crawler-based engines like **AltaVista**, **Google** or **HotBot** and human-powered directories like **Yahoo**. On the web, search engines provide sophisticated criteria for searching, and provide summaries of each result as well as the website addresses for retrieving more information. Web search engines constantly search and index information on the web to keep it up to date and relevant to the users. → 6.069 SEARCH TOOL

6.**069 search tool** A program that enables specific web pages to be searched. → 6.068 SEARCH ENGINE

6.**070 secure area** The area of a website in which personal or sensitive information can be entered by users. Secure areas are usually identified by the prefix 'https://' in

6.061 *Opera*

1 *Navigation buttons*
2 *Address*
3 *Displayed page*

the URL and are particularly important for commercial transactions made via the web. → 6.037 HYPERTEXT TRANSFER PROTOCOL (HTTP)

6.**071 Shockwave** A proprietary technology developed by Macromedia for creating Director presentations which can be delivered across the Internet and viewed with a web browser. The Shockwave plug-in (which contains Flash plug-in capability), which enables Shockwave material to be viewed on a computer, must be loaded on the viewing machine. → 4.383 FLASH (MACROMEDIA)

6.**072 Simple Mail Transfer Protocol (SMTP)** A text-based TCP/IP protocol used to transfer mail messages over the Internet. → 6.043 INTERNET PROTOCOL (IP); 6.083 TRANSMISSION CONTROL PROTOCOL (TCP)

6.**073 sitemap** An outline view, usually diagrammatic, of all the pages on a particular website and usually showing the interconnections. Site maps are more detailed and complete than index pages when seeking out a particular section. → 6.096 WORLD WIDE WEB (WWW)

6.**074 snail mail** Term for the standard postal system, compared with email.

6.**075 source code** In the context of the Internet, an alternative name for HTML.

6.**076 spam/spamming** A colloquial term for an unsolicited email or newsgroup posting, usually advertising material. The term derives from the television comedy show *Monty Python's Flying Circus* where, in one sketch, a restaurant menu lists food items which can only be ordered if accompanied by 'spam', e.g. sausage and spam, egg and spam, spam and spam, etc. → 6.021 EMAIL/E-MAIL; 6.059 NEWSGROUP

6.**077 spider** The first element of a crawler-based search engine that automatically roams the World Wide Web, gathering and cataloguing information in order that searches can be accurately performed. → 6.068 SEARCH ENGINE

6.**078 Standard Generalized Markup Language (SGML)** An ISO markup standard for defining and tagging documents which can be used by any computer, regardless of platform. → 1.344 INTERNATIONAL STANDARDS ORGANIZATION (ISO)

6.**079 streaming media** Audio and/or video files that are delivered via the Internet (or other

online connection) and replayed on the recipient's computer in real time. The sent files are usually buffered (to compensate for background or other operations on the computer that might otherwise interrupt the data stream). Media is usually encoded (using, say, QuickTime or RealAudio). Live television/video broadcasts can be streamed across the Internet. The **BBC World TV** channel is an example of live and continuous streaming (and is available via QuickTime).

6.**080 tag** The formal name for a markup language formatting command. A tag is switched on by placing a command inside angle brackets and switched off again by repeating the same command but inserting a forward slash before the command. For example, <bold> makes text that follows appear in bold and </bold> switches bold text off.

6.**081 thread** Postings to an online newsgroup or email distribution list on a theme or subject in which a group of subscribers have a particular interest. The messages are usually followed by any replies, and the replies to those replies. Threaded emails are usually indicated by an icon in the Inbox window.

6.**082 title** Text which appears in the title bar of a web page. If you aim to have search engines pick up your site, it is sometimes useful for this title to include other terms by which some users may search.

6.**083 Transmission Control Protocol/Internet Protocol (TCP/IP)** The industry standard for the provision of data communications between computers and particularly over the Internet. Originally devised as an alternative to the US Department of Defense protocols which did not include a check for successful transmission of data, it ensures reliability by retransmitting lost and corrupted data packets, and ensures that an application on the receiving end of a connection will receive bits and bytes in the same order in which they were sent.

6.**084 Uniform Resource Locator (URL)** The unique address of every web page on the WWW. Every resource on the Internet has a unique URL which begins with letters that identify the resource type, such as 'http' or 'ftp' (determining the communication protocol to be used), followed by a colon and two forward slashes. After this comes the '**domain name**' ('host'), which can have several parts to it, then, after a slash, the directory name followed by path names to any particular file; for example, http://www.digiwis.com/home.htm. Usually if a file name is not stated, the browser will default to the file name 'default.html', 'default.htm', 'index.html' or 'index.htm', which is usually the location of the home page. → 6.037 HYPERTEXT TRANSFER PROTOCOL (HTTP)

6.**085 Uniform Resource Name (URN)** A permanent name for a web resource.

6.**086 URL-encoded text** A method of encoding text for passing requests from your web browser to a server. → 6.067 REQUEST

6.**087 Usenet** Acronym for **user's network**, in which a vast number of articles, categorized into newsgroups, are posted by individuals on every conceivable subject. These articles are hosted on servers throughout the world on which you can post your own articles to people who subscribe to those newsgroups. Special **'newsreader' software** is required to view the articles. → 6.027 FORUM; 6.059 NEWSGROUP

6.**088 user group** A group of people who share their experiences, knowledge, problems, etc., either generally or in relation to a specific software application or type of computer. Many application vendors offer user groups for users to share information (and to have that information analysed by the host!), but many independent user groups also operate under the auspices of enthusiasts and subject-matter experts. → 6.059 NEWSGROUP

6.**089 VRML** Virtual Reality Modelling Language, an HTML-type programming language designed to create 3D scenes called 'virtual worlds' and generally usable with any web browser.

6.**090 watermarking** The technique of applying a tiled graphic to the background of a web page, which remains fixed no matter what foreground materials scroll across it.

6.**091 web authoring** The process of writing (in HTML or XML format) documents for publishing on the World Wide Web. → 6.096 WORLD WIDE WEB (WWW)

6.**092 web master** The person responsible for managing a website. On small personal websites this is usually the site's creator, but on larger sites it is often the responsibility of a nominee in the IT support division.

6.**093 web page** A published HTML document on the World Wide Web. → 6.095 WEBSITE; 6.096 WORLD WIDE WEB (WWW)

6.**094 web server** A computer ('host') that is dedicated to web services. This could be held by an ISP, a hosting company or by the organization whose pages are hosted.

6.**095 website** The address, location (on a server), and collection of documents and resources for any particular interlinked set of web pages.

6.**096 World Wide Web (WWW)** The term used to describe the entire collection of web servers all over the world which are connected to the Internet. The term also describes the particular type of Internet access architecture which uses a combination of HTML and various graphic formats, such as GIF and JPEG, to publish formatted text which can be read by web browsers. Colloquially termed simply 'the **web**' or, sometimes by the shorthand '**W3**'. → 6.011 BROWSER; 6.041 INTERNET

6.**097 WWW** Prefix for website addresses accessible via the World Wide Web. Also the acronym for that term. → 6.096 WORLD WIDE WEB (WWW)

6.**098 XMODEM** A standard communications protocol that transfers data in blocks of 128 K. → 6.099 YMODEM; 6.100 ZMODEM

6.**099 YMODEM** A standard communications protocol that provides error-checking while transferring data. → 6.098 XMODEM; 6.100 ZMODEM

6.**100 ZMODEM** A standard communications protocol that can provide continuous data transfer despite interruptions or pauses. → 6.098 XMODEM; 6.099 YMODEM

7 GENERAL TERMS

General

7.001 8-bit The allocation of 8 bits (or 1 byte) to each pixel, giving a picture a screen display of 256 greys or colours, and 256 text characters. → 2.429 BIT

7.002 alphanumeric Any character that is either alphabetic or numeric (0 to 9). Alphabetic characters are normally those between and including A to Z, but, depending on the application, special alphabetic characters (e.g., those with accents) or even different alphabets (such as the Greek or Cyrillic) are permitted.

7.003 ANSI (American National Standards Institute) A US organization devoted to defining standards such as those used for programming languages and represents the US at the ISO → 1.319 AMERICAN STANDARDS ASSOCIATION (ASA); 1.344 INTERNATIONAL STANDARDS ORGANIZATION (ISO)

7.004 archive quality Media (including data recording media, but more commonly printing papers and inks) designed to last (almost) indefinitely. Archive quality printing paper and mounting boards are those that do not give off gases or seep chemicals that might affect the printing inks used on the printing surface. Archive quality inks are those resilient to strong incident light (particularly UV) and inert with regard to the printing paper. Often archive quality is expressed with caveats such as 'when exposed to indirect lighting' or 'when stored in a fume-free environment'.

7.005 binary Literally, having two outcomes or two components. The binary number system has the base 2 and so all values are expressed as combinations of 1 and 0, including logical states (true/false). These states can be represented in computers as on/off or circuit closed/circuit open, hence the binary system underpins digital computing, developed by **Claude Shannon** in the 1940s.

7.006 bleed Term used in graphics, printing and photography to describe an image that extends beyond the edge of the paper upon which it is printed and outside the trim marks, leaving no borders. → 5.023 CORNER MARKS

7.007 bleeding The spread of ink or dyes beyond their intended position resulting in a loss of definition and precision. The use of multiple wet inks or inappropriate ink–paper combinations can contribute to bleeding.

7.008 collage An image assembled from elements drawn from different sources. Originally used to describe those pieces produced by pasting together images culled from magazines (say) or fabric swatches. Now also describes images built by image editing but with the disparate nature of the separate components still obvious. Also known as a montage or (for photographic subjects) a photomontage.

7.009 comb filter Electronic filter used to split a video signal into brightness (luminance) and colour (chrominance) components.

7.010 consumer In this context, the term is used to describe the user of products whose demands are less than those of the professional, semi pro, or even keen amateur. Image-editing products for consumers make no presumptions about knowledge levels and are designed for casual and 'leisure' use. → 7.063 PROSUMER

7.011 copyright The right of a person who creates an original work to protect that work by controlling how and where it may be reproduced. This does not necessarily mean that ownership of the work itself automatically signifies ownership of copyright (or vice versa). Ownership of copyright is only transferred if the creator of the work assigns it in writing. While certain aspects of copyright are broadly controlled by international agreement, as defined by the **Universal Copyright**

Convention (**UCC**), there are some differences from country to country, particularly when it comes to the period, or 'term', for which a work is protected (in most countries this is seventy years after its creator's death). In the United States, the Pan-American agreement decrees that ownership of an '**intellectual property**' (the legal description of copyright ownership) be established by registration, whereas in the United Kingdom it exists automatically by virtue of the creation of the work. There is often confusion between copyright in a work and the 'right' to publish it – ownership of the right to publish a work in one country may not extend to other countries, and it does not necessarily signify ownership of copyright. Equally, ownership of copyright may be shared – the author of a book, for example, may own copyright of the text, whereas copyright in the design of the book may be owned by its designer or publisher. → 7.012 COPYRIGHT NOTICE/LINE

7.**012 copyright notice/line** The indication of ownership of copyright in a work ('form of notice'), particularly one that is reproduced, as required by the Universal Copyright Convention. This states that all the first and subsequent editions of a work bear the word 'Copyright' or the symbol '©' (most publishers include both), the year of publication (or of first publication if it is a straight reprint), and the name of the owner of the copyright in the work. Thus a notice would appear: 'Copyright © 2001 A. N. Author'. → 7.011 COPYRIGHT

7.**013 cursor** The name for the blinking marker that indicates the current working position in a document; for example, the point in a line of text at which the next character will appear when you strike a key on the keyboard. The cursor may be represented by a small vertical line or block and is not to be confused with the 'pointer' – the marker indicating the current position of the mouse.

7.**014 dark current** Noise that builds up on a CCD (charge-coupled device) when it is not exposed to light and which is due to small background charges. All CCDs suffer from this effect to a degree but it is not normally significant until very dim subjects are imaged. Then the signal-to-noise ratio (the ratio of the image charge levels to the dark current) will become small and poor. and usually grainy or blotchy results will ensue. → 1.011 CHARGE-COUPLED DEVICE (CCD)

7.**015 data warehouse** A large repository of data (usually corporate) which is stored either at a company's location or by a third party so it is accessible but away from data that is used day to day.

7.**016 digital audio tape (DAT)** 4 mm-wide magnetic tape used to record audio digitally with minimal compression (compared with the now discontinued digital compact cassette format, DCC, which used digital compression). DAT tapes are robust and have been used as the media in some tape backup systems.

7.**017 digital compact cassette (DCC)** A digital audio recording method that is partially 'slot compatible' with conventional cassettes (analogue compact cassettes can be played in DCC machines). DCC uses a data compression technique that removes redundant data. DAT and MiniDisc have effectively killed this format. → 2.346 MiniDisc (MD); 7.016 DIGITAL AUDIO TAPE (DAT)

7.**018 digital domain** General descriptive term to denote information handling or activity that takes place digitally. Image editing occurs in the digital domain, even if the original image was not created digitally.

7.**019 dynamic range** In electronic imaging, the range of light levels recordable by a CCD or other electronic imaging device. → 1.011 CHARGE-COUPLED DEVICE (CCD)

7.**020 electronic media** General term to describe media that uses electronic means for dissemination and delivery of information. Hence, although CD-ROMs and the Internet would qualify, magazines would not, even though electronic means are used to gather and produce them.

7.**021 electronic publishing (EP)** General term that describes information distributed by electronic media. → 7.020 ELECTRONIC MEDIA

7.**022 flicker** Rapid variations in brightness ('**strobing**') due to a light source flashing at high speed (usually a computer monitor or a fluorescent tube). Persistence of vision tends to even out variations, though some change can be detected at lower frequencies, particularly when the source is viewed close up or in peripheral vision.

7.**023 font** Set of characters sharing the same type characteristics and size.

7.**024 fractal** Infinitely variable shapes, often characterized by extreme irregularity and defined by complex but precisely defined mathematical expressions. A principal characteristic is self-similarity, wherein a magnified part of a fractal appears identical to the 'parent' shape and has identical visual and mathematical properties. Fractals are categorized into sets, including Mandelbrot and Julia sets. Some Photoshop filters (notably Kai's Power Tools, versions 5 and 6) make extensive use of fractal mathematics and patterning, allowing users to make bold graphics from scratch and to use image elements as the basic element. Fractal routines are being used in proprietary image compression routines (such as those from Genuine Fractals) in order to enable dramatic reductions in size but with limited effect on image quality. → 4.360 GENUINE FRACTALS; 4.361 GENUINE FRACTALS PRINT PRO; 4.366 KAI'S POWER TOOLS (KPT)

7.**025 frame (2)** A single still picture from a movie or animation sequence. Also a single complete image from a TV picture (which normally comprises two interlaced fields, each of which carries alternate line information).

7.**026 frames per second (FPS)** The number of individual still images that are required to make each second of an animation or movie sequence. Movie films and PAL/SECAM television use a frame rate of 25 FPS, NTSC television uses a rate of 30 FPS.

7.**027 frequently asked question (FAQ)** FAQ is a shorthand term used to denote frequently asked questions among a help or support suite. FAQs are designed to address (and pre-empt) some obvious questions, avoiding the need for technical support personnel to deal with these.

7.**028 generation** Successive copies of data. Although digital data is often applauded for the ability for multiple generations to be created with no loss in quality, this presumes no digital compression regimes are being invoked. Using a lossy compression method such as JPEG can cause severe artefacts that compromise image quality cumulatively over very few generations.

7.**029 graduation** The smooth transition of one colour to another.

7.**030 graphic** A generic term for any illustration or drawn design, but often reserved for bold iconic designs such as those featured in logos and signs.

7.**031 graphic arts** An all-encompassing term to describe all or any of the crafts involved in reproduction by means of any of the many printing processes. It should be distinguished from '**graphic design**', which involves providing a graphic solution to a specific problem and the implementation of that solution by any suitable means.

7.**032 Hertz (Hz)** Oscillations, or vibrations, per second. The UK's mains electricity

7.025 *frame (interlaced image from TV screen)*

7.029 *graduation*

frequency is 50 Hz, that in the US is 60 Hz; the clock speed of a computer CPU could be 500 MHz (500 million Hertz).

7.033 highlight To mark an item, such as a section of text, icon or menu command, to indicate that it is selected or active.

7.034 horizontal format Term for a page printed with the upright dimension less than the horizontal. In photography the corresponding term is landscape format. → 5.071 LANDSCAPE FORMAT

7.035 image library A source of original images in any format that can be used for any specific purpose on the payment of an appropriate fee. That fee usually varies according to usage – a picture to be used in an advertisement will invariably cost a great deal more than the same picture for use in a school textbook. Some image libraries, or **picture libraries**, specialize in specific subjects such as reportage, architecture or fine art. → 4.412 IMAGE RESOURCE; 7.011 COPYRIGHT

7.036 Image Magic Proprietary name for many of Kodak's 'consumer-level' imaging products including PictureCD and some services delivered via the Internet.

7.037 image size A description of the dimensions of an image. The parameters used will depend upon the application. For paste-ups and printing use, linear dimensions are often the most important; in digital imaging both the resolution and digital file size can be the most important.

7.038 insertion point The point in a document or dialogue box at which the next character

or action typed on the keyboard will appear. It is indicated by a blinking vertical line (**'text insertion bar'**) which can be positioned by using the pointer and clicking.

7.039 interactive A description of any activity that involves an immediate and reciprocal action between a person and a machine, typically a computer or a computer-based device (such as **Interactive Television**). → 7.040 INTERACTIVE MODE

7.040 interactive mode A mode offered by an application that permits data to be handled 'live' as it is input, rather than being processed in batches (batch mode). Sometimes called real-time processing, spelling and grammar checks are normally conducted in interactive mode, with the errors being highlighted with suggestions for changes which can be implemented or ignored. → 7.039 INTERACTIVE; 7.067 REAL-TIME

7.041 International Press Telecommunications Council (IPTC) A body responsible for defining the standards for image and image text transmission. Importantly, the standard describes the inclusion and embedding of information such as captions, credits and keywords.

7.042 Julia set Fractal set. Along with the Mandelbrot set, a feature of certain fractal pattern generators in later versions of Kai's Power Tools. → 7.024 FRACTAL

7.043 Kelvin temperature scale (K) A unit of measurement that describes the colour of a light source, based on absolute darkness rising to incandescence. → 1.373 COLOUR TEMPERATURE

7.024 *fractal*

7.042 *Julia set*

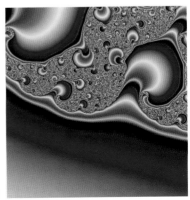

7.044 **kilo** A unit of metric measurement representing 1,000 (from the Greek 'khilioi' for 'thousand'). However, although the term is widely used as a measure of computer data ('kilobyte', for example), computers use a binary system (pairs of numbers) in which each number is doubled: 2; 4; 8; 16; 32; 64; 128; 256; 512; 1,024, etc. Thus 'kilobyte' in a data context does not mean 1,000, but 1,024 (2^{10}). → 7.051 MEGA

7.045 **laser** Acronym for **light amplified by stimulated emission of radiation**. A light source of almost pure wavelength, lasers are used as the data reading mechanism in optical discs (e.g., CD-ROM) and as the read and write mechanism in rewritable CD-ROMs.

7.046 **light sensitive** Any material or device that responds either chemically or digitally to light striking it, such as a photographic emulsion, a litho plate, or a photosite (the light sensor of a CCD). → 1.011 CHARGE-COUPLED DEVICE (CCD); 1.331 EMULSION

7.047 **light table/box** A table or box with a translucent glass top lit from below, giving a colour-balanced light suitable for viewing colour transparencies and for colour-matching them to proofs.

7.048 **lightfast** The permanence of a photo (or other image) under specified lighting conditions. → 7.004 ARCHIVE QUALITY

7.049 **line art** Diagrams and graphics comprising (normally) black lines on a white background and featuring no intermediate tones.

7.050 **Mandelbrot set** A fractal set that, along with the Julia set, is a feature of certain fractal pattern generators in later versions of Kai's Power Tools. → 7.024 FRACTAL

7.051 **mega** A unit of metric measurement representing 1,000,000. Although the term is used widely as a measure of computer data ('megabyte', for example), computers use a binary system (pairs of numbers) in which each number is doubled: 2; 4; 8; 16; 32; 64; 128; 256; 512; 1,024, etc., thus 'megabyte' in a data context does not mean 1,000,000 but 1,048,576 (2^{30}). → 7.044 KILO

7.052 **mottling** An image artefact that can appear when an image containing large areas of flat colour or gentle gradients is sharpened. Small elements of noise in these areas tend to be regarded as valid data by the sharpening algorithm and increase their prominence. JPEG images are particularly prone to mottling.

7.053 **multimedia** A generic and somewhat loose term for any combination of digital media (such as sound, video, animation, graphics and text) used together in various combinations in a software product or presentation.

7.054 **object-oriented** A software technology which uses mathematical points, based on 'vectors' (information giving both magnitude and direction), to define lines and shapes; these points being the 'objects' referred to. Distinct from a graphic shape as an object (an 'object' in computer programming is a database of

7.049 *line art*

7.052 *mottling (800%)*

mathematical formulae). The data for each shape is stored in these points, which in turn pass information from one to another on how the paths between them should be described – as straight lines, arcs or Bézier curves. The quality of the line between each point is determined entirely by the resolution of the output device – a line produced by an imagesetter at 2,400 dpi will be very much smoother than the same line output on a laser printer at 300 dpi or viewed on a monitor. The alternative technology for rendering computer images is that of 'bitmapped' graphics, which are edited by modifying individual pixels or by turning them on or off.

7.**055 online help** A file that gives help and advice, always available while that application is being used. Also describes help available via Internet connections.

7.**056 optical character recognition (OCR)**
The process of having text read directly by a computer (or rather, a computer application) rather than having that text input by typing. Typically, this is achieved using OCR applications, via a scanner, that interpret the scan as text that can then be treated as editable text. Advanced OCR software can read pages from newsprint or magazines, for example, where text is divided between columns.

7.**057 perspective** A technique of rendering 3D objects on a 2D plane, duplicating the 'real world' view by giving the same impression of the object's relative position and size when viewed from a particular point: the shorter the distance, the wider the perspective; the greater the distance, the narrower the perspective.

7.**058 pictogram/pictograph** A simplified, pictorial symbol distilled to its salient features to represent an object or concept. Used in graphic design and signage.

7.**059 pit** A tiny cavity burned by a laser in the surface of an optical disc (CD, CD-ROM, DVD or **LaserDisc**). It equates to one bit of digital information.

7.**060 pixel** Acronym for **picture element**. The smallest component of a digitally generated image, such as a single dot of light on a computer monitor. In its simplest form, one pixel corresponds to a single bit: 0 = off, or white, and 1 = on, or black. In colour or greyscale images or monitors,

one pixel may correspond to several bits: an 8-bit pixel, for example, can be displayed in any of 256 colours (the total number of different configurations that can be achieved by eight 0s and 1s). To display colour onscreen, each pixel has 24 bits, i.e., 8 bits each for R, G and B. This allows for 256 x 256 x 256 colour combinations or 16.7 million colours.
→ 1.525 RESOLUTION

7.**061 primitives** A set of basic forms (such as cubes, cylinders, spheres and polygons) that can be used in combination as the basis of complex 2- or 3-dimensional shapes. Landscape rendering application Bryce uses a range of primitives to build its landscape forms. → 4.002 BRYCE; 4.379 CANOMA

7.**062 property** The attributes of a digital object, such as size, position, colour, orientation, etc.

7.**063 prosumer** Marketing term used to describe the intermediate market segment between the consumer (who buys digital camera equipment nominally for recreational and leisure use) and professionals. Broadly speaking, an enthusiast with a relatively large budget.

7.**064 public domain (PD)** Media that is available for use by anyone free of all copyrights, because such copyright has either lapsed or been renounced by the copyright holder. Public domain material can comprise literary works, images or even computer software. In the latter case it has often become public domain purely because the author has declared it so. Not to be confused with 'shareware', for which a fee is usually required.

7.**065 raster image** An image defined as rows of pixels or dots.

7.**066 raster(ization)** Deriving from the Latin word **rastrum**, meaning 'rake', the method of displaying (and creating) images employed by video screens, and thus computer monitors, in which the screen image is made up of a pattern of several hundred parallel lines created by an electron beam 'raking' the screen from top to bottom at a speed of about one-sixtieth of a second. An image is created by varying the intensity of the beam at successive points along the raster. The speed at which a complete screen image, or frame, is created is called the 'frame' or 'refresh' rate. → 2.476 RASTER IMAGE PROCESSOR (RIP)

7.067 real-time Events that happen on a computer at the same time they were actioned. For example, a character appearing onscreen when a key is pressed or an image edit whose effect is applied to the image as the tool is moved over it. Virtually all image-editing actions happen in real-time (although on some systems where the memory provided is less than ideal there may be a slight lag between the cursor movement and the application of the effect). → 7.040 INTERACTIVE MODE

7.068 reflective art Artwork (painting, graphic or image) with opaque backing, viewed only from reflected light (rather than from transmitted light in the case of a transparency).

7.069 sensitize To make something, such as a piece of paper, sensitive to something else, such as light. In printing, this includes making the image areas of a printing plate ink-receptive by applying a special coating to an aluminium printing plate.

7.070 smearing Image artefact of some early CCDs and early TV picture tubes. Overexposure of a group of pixels results in halation and solarization effects to the source and a bright line (following the pixel columns of the overexposed pixels) above and below the source.

7.071 string A sequence of alphanumeric characters (and some other special characters and spaces).

7.072 tear sheet A page that has been removed from a publication and used or filed for future reference. Often used by published photographers as part of a portfolio of their work or as a collection of inspirational imagery gleaned from magazines.

7.073 transmissive art Artwork produced on a transparent or translucent backing, such as photographic transparencies or display artwork designed to be viewed with a light source behind the image. Such a light

source needs to be matched to the colour balance of the transparency for colour accuracy.

7.074 upright format Format in which the longest edge of the page is vertical. Equivalent to portrait format in photographic printing and printing terminology. → 5.085 PORTRAIT FORMAT

7.075 USM Abbreviation for both Unsharp Masking (a sharpening technique) and ultrasonic motor (a silent lens focusing mechanism devised by Canon). → 1.251 ULTRASONIC MOTOR (USM); 1.486 UNSHARP MASKING (USM)

7.076 value A particular tint of colour. Also a quantity assigned to a parameter, variable or symbol that will change with application and circumstance.

7.077 vector A mathematical description of a line that is defined in terms of physical dimensions and direction. Vectors are used in drawing packages (and some image editors such as Photoshop 6) in order to define shapes (**vector graphics**) that are both position- and size-independent.

7.078 virtual Something that does not exist physically in the 'real' world but appears as if it does. Virtual memory is memory (usually on the hard disk) that is perceived to the user and the current application to be an extension of the computer's RAM. → 2.322 VIRTUAL MEMORY

7.079 virtual reality A simulated 3D environment that the user can explore onscreen or using special virtual reality peripherals. Users can sometimes interact with the virtual environment by using these peripherals to point, hold or 'move around' the environment.

7.080 wireframe A three-dimensional shape with no 'surface' or texture applied. Because computers achieve such rendering, particularly over curved surfaces by using many small polygons, the form (at a crude rendering resolution) can look as if it is created with chicken wire. → 4.425 RENDER

7.077 *vector (vector graphics)*

Vector lines comprising the illustration elements (such as the lips) can be pushed, pulled and even rescaled.

Vector components (unlike bitmaps) retain quality when resized.

7.080 *wireframe*

BOOKS

Digital imaging and photography

The Complete Guide to Digital Imaging Joël Lacey *Thames & Hudson* London 2002

The Complete Guide to Digital Photography Michael Freeman *Thames & Hudson* London 2001

The Digital Imaging A to Z Adrian Davies *Focal Press* Oxford 1999

Digital Photography Handbook Tim Daly *Argentum* London 1999

The Digital Photography Handbook Simon Joinson *Metro Books* London 1998

Electronic Imaging for Photographers Adrian Davies, Phil Fennessy *Focal Press* Oxford 1994

Silver Pixels Tom Ang *Argentum* London 1999

Application-specific titles

Adobe Illustrator 9: Advanced Digital Illustration *Prentice Hall* December 2000

Adobe Photoshop 6 and Illustrator 9.0: Advanced Classroom in a Book Adobe Creative Team *Adobe Press* San Jose June 2001

Adobe Photoshop 6.0 for Photographers Martin Evening *Focal Press* Oxford 2001

Adobe Photoshop 6.0 Web Design Michael Baumgardt *Adobe Press* San Jose 2001

CorelDRAW 10: The Official Guide Steve Bain *Osborne McGraw-Hill* Berkeley December 2000

Easy Adobe Photoshop 6 Kate Binder *Que* Indianapolis 2001

Paintshop Pro 7 in Easy Steps Stephen Copestake *Computer Step*, Southam (Warwickshire, UK) May 2001

Paintshop Pro 7 Explained N. Kantaris *Bernard Babani (Publishing)* London June 2001

Photo-Paint 10 Dave Huss *Osborne McGraw-Hill* Berkeley December 2000

The Photoshop User's A–Z Peter Cope *Thames & Hudson* London 2001

Software

Canvas
www.deneba.com

Fireworks, Freehand, Flash
www.macromedia.com

Paintshop Pro
www.jasc.com

PhotoImpact, PhotoExpress
www.ulead.com

Photo-Paint, CorelDRAW!
www.corel.com

Photoshop, ImageReady, Illustrator
www.adobe.com

Photosuite
www.mgisoft.com

Picture Publisher
www.micrografx.co

WEBSITES

Note that website addresses can change, and sites can appear and disappear almost daily. Use a search engine to help you find new arrivals or check addresses.

Digital imaging and photography sites

The Complete Guide to Digital Photography
www.completeguidetodigitalphotography.com

creativepro.com: news and resources for creative professionals
www.creativepro.com

The Digital Camera Resource Page: consumer-oriented resource site
www.dcresource.com

Digital Photography: news, reviews, etc.
www.digital-photography.org

Digital Photography Review: products, reviews
www.dpreview.com

ePHOTOzine
www.ephotozine.com

The Imaging Resource: news, reviews, etc.
www.imaging-resource.com

Listing of photographic sites
www.uk250.co.uk/photography

panoguide.com: panoramic photography
www.panoguide.com

pcphotoreview.com: resource site with online store for the US market
www.pcphotoreview.com

PhotoBox: digital photography and imaging services for the UK and EU, plus public galleries
www.photobox.co.uk

Photolink International: education in photography and other related fields
www.photoeducation.net

photo.net: photography resource site – community, advice, gallery, tutorials, etc.
www.photo.net

Royal Photographic Society (information, links)
www.rps.org

ShortCourses: digital photography: theory and practice
www.shortcourses.com

Digital cameras by manufacturer

Canon
http://www.canon.com/products/

Fuji Photo Film Co.
http://home.fujifilm.com/products/digital/digital camera/

Kodak
http://www.kodak.com/

Minolta Co.
http://www.dimage.minolta.com/

Nikon Corporation
http://www.nikon-image.com/eng/Lineup/

Olympus
http://www.olympus.com/

Sony Corporation
http://www.sonystyle.com/digitalimaging/